Shadow Banking

Roy J. Girasa

Shadow Banking

The Rise, Risks, and Rewards of Non-Bank Financial Services

palgrave
macmillan

Roy J. Girasa
Lubin School of Business
Pace University
Pleasantville, New York, USA

ISBN 978-3-319-33025-9 ISBN 978-3-319-33026-6 (eBook)
DOI 10.1007/978-3-319-33026-6

Library of Congress Control Number: 2016946986

Printed on acid-free paper

This Palgrave Macmillan imprint is published by Springer Nature
The registered company is Springer International Publishing AG
The registered company address is: Gewerbestrasse 11, 6330 Cham, Switzerland

Richard J. Kraus
Gary Tidwell

Also by Roy Girasa

Cyberlaw: National and International Perspectives
Corporate Governance and Finance Law
Laws and Regulations in Global Financial Markets

Preface

The origin of this text was suggested by a representative of Palgrave Macmillan at the Eastern Economic Association in 2015, when it was noted that I was to deliver a paper on shadow banking. Although two of my books had already been published by Palgrave Macmillan on the law of finance, I had not included any discussion of shadow banking and the legal ramifications of this most important aspect of the financial world. The paper that was delivered served as an outline for the expanded text, which I hope will be of use to practitioners in the field and to academics.

It is always difficult to name and thank the persons responsible not only for this volume but also for encouragement and assistance, including colleagues and representatives of Palgrave Macmillan. The book is dedicated to Richard J. Kraus, who was not only the chairperson who initially caused my employment as a university professor 35 years ago at the Lubin School of Business of Pace University in New York but has also served as a great friend and spiritual adviser. The book is also dedicated to Gary Tidwell who retained me on behalf of the National Association of Securities Dealers (now FINRA) to instruct representatives of the Saudi Arabia Capital Markets Authority and its Banking Authority concerning the explanation of rules and regulations governing the expansion of its stock market. He continues to be an inspiration and a good friend.

Many thanks to my colleagues, particularly Richard J. Kraus, Philip Cohen, Joseph DiBenedetto, and Jessica Magaldi, as well as my adviser Susanne Marolda. Similarly, so many thanks for the extraordinary efforts of Sarah Lawrence, Allison Neuburger of Palgrave Macmillan, and my editor, Soundarrajan Sudha. Lastly, my profound thanks to my muse, Camille D'Agostino Angrisano.

Contents

Acronyms and Abbreviations

ABCP	Asset-backed commercial paper
ABS	Asset-backed securities
AEI	American Enterprise Institute
AIFM	(EU) Alternative Investment Fund Managers
AIFMD	(EU) Directive on Alternative Investment Fund Managers
AIG	American International Group Inc.
AIGFP	AIG (American International Group) Financial Products Corp.
AIMA	Alternative Investment Management Association.
AMLF	(FED) Asset-Backed Commercial Paper Money Market Mutual Fund Liquidity Facility
ATM	Automated teller machines
AUM	Assets under management
BCBS	Banking Committee on Banking Supervision
BHC	Bank holding company
BIS	Bank for International Settlements
BRRD	(EU) Directive for Bank Recovery and Resolution
CalPERS	California Public Employees' Retirement
CBRC	China Banking Regulatory Commission
CCAR	(FED) Comprehensive Capital Analysis and Review
CCP	Central counterparties
CDO	Collateralized debt obligation
CDS	Credit default swaps
CFTC	Commodity Futures Trading Commission
CHIPS	Clearing House Payments Company, LLC
CIC	China Investment Corporation
CIRC	China Insurance Regulatory Commission
CIVs	Collective investment vehicles

CMBS	Commercial mortgage-backed securities
CMG	Crisis Management Groups
CMOs	Collateralized mortgage obligations
COMI	Center of main interest
COUNCIL	Financial Stability Oversight Council
CORA	Community Reinvestment Act of 1977
CP	Commercial paper
CPFF	(FED) Commercial Paper Funding Facility
CPI	Consumer Price Index
CPO	Commodity Pool Operators
CRA	Credit rating agencies
CRD	IV (EU) Capital Requirements Regulation and Directive
CSDR	Central Securities Depositories Directive
CTA	Commodity Trading Advisers
DBDs	Diversified broker-dealers
DGP	(FDIC) Debt Guarantee Program
Dodd-Frank	Dodd-Frank Wall Street Reform and Consumer Protection Act of 1977
DTC	Depository Trust Company
ECSC	European Coal and Steel Community
EDTF	Enhanced Disclosure Task Force
EIOPA	European Insurance and Occupational Pensions Authority
EMIR	European Market Infrastructure Directive
ESFS	European System of Financial Supervisors
ESMA	European Securities and Markets Authority
ESRB	European Systemic Risk Board
EU	European Union
EURIBOR	European Interbank Offered Rate
EURATOM	European Atomic Energy Community
FANNIE MAE	Federal National Mortgage Association
FBO	Foreign Banking Organizations
FDIC	Federal Deposit Insurance Corporation
FED	Federal Reserve System
FFIEC	Federal Financial Institutions Examination Council
FHC	Financial holding company
FICC	Fixed Income Clearing Corporation
FINRA	Financial Industry Regulatory Authority
FMU	Financial market utility
FOMC	Federal Open Markets Committee
FRBNY	Federal Reserve Bank of New York
FREDDIE MAC	Federal Home Loan Association Corporation
FSB	Financial Stability Board

GAAP	Generally accepted accounting principles
GDP	Gross domestic product
GECC	General Electric Capital Corporation
GINNIE MAE	Government National Mortgage Association
GNE	Gross Notional Exposure
G-SIB	Global systemically important bank
G-SIFI	Global systemically important financial institution
G20	Group of 20 largest economies
IAIS	International Association of Insurance Supervisors
ICC	ICE Clear Credit LLC
IFRS	International Financial Reporting Standards
IMF	International Monetary Fund
IFRS	International Financial Reporting Standards
IOLTAs	Interest on Lawyers Trust Accounts
IOSCO	International Organization of Securities Dealers
KA	Key Attributes of Effective Resolution for Financial Institutions
LIBOR	London Interbank Offered Rate
LLC	Limited Liability Company
MAR/CSMAD	Market Abuse Regulation and Directive on Criminal Sanctions for Market Abuse
MBS	Mortgage-backed securities
MiFID	Markets in Financial Instruments Directive
MiFIR	Market In Financial Instruments Directive
MMF	Money market fund
MMIFF	(FED) Money Market Investor Funding Facility
NAIC	National Association of Insurance Commissioners
NASD	National Association of Securities Dealers
NAV	Net asset value
NBNI	Non-bank non-insurer financial entities
NOW	Negotiable order of withdrawal account
NRSRO	Nationally recognized statistical ratings organization
NSCC	National Securities Clearing Corporation
NYSE	New York Stock Exchange
OCC	Office of the Comptroller of the Currency
OFAC	Office of Foreign Assets Control
OFI	Other financial intermediaries
OFR	Office of Financial Research
OLA	Orderly Liquidation Authority
OPCC	Options Clearing Corporation
OTC	Over the counter
PDCF	(FED) Primary Dealer Credit Facility
RAA	Credit Ratings Agency Reform Act of 2006

REITS	Real estate investment finds and trusts
REPOS	Repurchase agreements
RMBS	Residential mortgage-backed securities
SFTs	Securities financing transactions
SIFI	Systemically important financial institution
SIPC	Securities Investor Protection Corporation
SIV	Structured investment vehicle
SPV	Special purpose vehicle
SSM	(EU) Single Supervisory Mechanism
STRIPS	Separate trading of registered interest and principal securities
TAGP	(FDIC) Transaction Account Guarantee Program
TALF	(FED) Term Asset-Backed Securities Loan Facility
TARP	Troubled Assets Relief Program
TIPS	Treasury Inflation-Protected Securities
TLGP	(FDIC) Temporary Liquidity Guarantee Program
UCITS	Management companies of undertakings for collective investment in transferable securities
UNCITRAL	United Nations Commission on International Trade Law
WAL	Weighted average life
WAM	Weighted average maturity
XML	eXtensible mark-up language

List of Figures

List of Tables

List of Appendices

Introduction

The term "shadow banking" appears to imply a sinister development in the financial services environment. Rather, it simply refers to the broad range of financial services that in many ways are duplicative of traditional banking services but are exempt from both the onerous regulatory environment and from its mainly consumer protective reimbursements in the event of losses. In this text we first examine the traditional banking sector of the economy, its history, which in the past several decades has substantially altered the landscape, and the laws and regulations placed upon it that led to alternative financial mechanisms in order to escape its costly oversight.

Definitions of "Shadow Banking"

There are many definitions of shadow banking, none of which is all-inclusive and all of which are dependent upon the approaches that scholars and organizations opine in examining the term. "Shadow banking" was originally coined by Paul A. McCulley in 2007 when he attended the Kansas City Federal Reserve Bank annual symposium in Jackson Hole, Wyoming. The meeting was organized to discuss the financial crisis then occurring nationally and globally. It focused on systemic risk and, in particular, what the author dubbed the "shadow banking system," which he noted was "the whole alphabet soup of levered up non-bank investment conduits, vehicles, and structures."[1]

In a series of Staff Reports issued by the Federal Reserve Bank of New York (FRB), the authors defined "shadow banks" as "financial intermediaries that conduct maturity, credit, and liquidity transformation without explicit access to central bank liquidity or public service credit guarantees."[2] Similarly, two of the authors in a later FRB report defined the term as "a web of specialized financial institutions that channel funding from savers to investors through a range of securitization and secured funding techniques."[3] Other definitions are comparable: "The system of non-deposit taking financial intermediaries including investment banks, hedge funds, monoline insurance firms and other securities operators";[4] "all financial activities, except traditional banking, which require a private or public backstop to operate";[5] and "The financial intermediaries involved in facilitating the creation of credit across the global financial system, but whose members are not subject to regulatory oversight. The shadow banking system also refers to unregulated activities by regulated institutions."[6]

The essence of the stated and other comparable definitions is the conduct of financial transactions that earlier were almost the exclusive province of the banking sector but have become allegedly devoid of regulation by entities such as the Federal Reserve Board (FED), the Federal Deposit and Insurance Corporation (FDIC), and other major governmental regulatory organizations. As we shall later note, it would be misleading to characterize the shadow banking system as being devoid of regulation; rather, many federal and state statutes and regulations continue to apply to these entities, differing from those imposed on the traditional banking sector.

Division of Text

The approach taken herein is a comparative one, in which we will discuss traditional banking and then how shadow banking differs from it. Included in the discussion are the origins, history, purposes, risks, regulatory constraints, and projected future evolution of both financial sectors of the economy. The text is divided into three areas. The traditional banking sector examines non-bank or shadow banking financial segments of the economy and explores the international regulatory environment.

In Part One, Chap. 1, we discuss traditional banking; its history; the evolution of statutory enactments that initially forbade the intertwining of commercial and investment banking; the repeal of the separation; the banking crisis commencing in 2007; and the statutory enactment that sought to prevent the alleged excesses of the industry. In Chap. 2, we review the Dodd-Frank Act and its impact upon the traditional banking industry. The statute was thereafter elaborated in a series of regulations issued by the FED, the FDIC, and, in particular, the Financial Stability Oversight Council (Council).

In Part Two, Chap. 3, we focus on the main subject of the text, that of shadow banking. We review many segments of the financial community that have performed those services that for the most part were initially offered by the traditional banking sector and also the many innovative and often almost incomprehensible products and services offered as alternative financial mechanisms. We continue in Chap. 4 to examine the risks of the alternative offerings, and the seemingly but misleading lack of regulatory oversight. Included is a major attempt by an alleged systematically important shadow bank to avoid such designation, so as to avoid the regulatory oversight not allegedly intended by statutory enactments.

Chapters 5 and 6 discuss types and processes of shadow banking. Chapter 7 is a discussion of insurance as a focus for regulation. Finally, we look at international institutions, their recommendations, and attempts to protect against irresponsible and aberrant behavior of the financial services and products offered. In particular, we review the output of the Basel Accords, the International Monetary Fund (IMF), the European Union (EU), the People's Republic of China, and other important global players. We conclude with a discussion of possible future developments that appear to sharply curtail the freewheeling financial developments of non-bank entities.

Notes

1. Paul A. McCulley, *Teton Reflections*, PIMCO GLOBAL BANK FOCUS, (September, 2007), http://www.pimco.com/en/insights/pages/gcbf%20august-%20september%202007.aspx.
2. Zoltan Pozsar, Tobias Adrian, Adam Ashcraft, and Hayley Boesky, *Shadow Banking*, p. 2, FEDERAL RESERVE BANK OF NEW YORK STAFF REPORTS, No. 458 (July 2010, rev. Feb. 2012), http://www.scribd.com/doc/237269076/Pozsar-Adrian-Ashcraft-Boetsky-Shadow-Banking-Federal-Reserve-Bank-of-New-York-Staff-Reports-N-458-July-2010#scribd.

3. Tobias Adrian, and Adam B. Ashcraft, *Shadow Banking Regulation*, FEDERAL RESERVE BANK OF NEW YORK STAFF REPORTS No. 559 (April 2012), p. 2, http://www.newyorkfed.org/research/staff_reports/sr559.html.
4. *Definition of shadow banking*, FINANCIAL TIMES, http://lexicon.ft.com/Term?term=shadow-banking.
5. Stijn Claessens, and Lev Ratnovski, *What is Shadow Banking?* IMF WORKING PAPER (Feb. 2014), www.imf.org/external/pubs/ft/wp/2014/wp1425.pdf.
6. *Shadow Banking System* INVESTOPEDIA www.investopedia.com/terms/s/shadow-banking-system.asp.

CHAPTER 1

Traditional Banking in the United States and Its Evolution as Bank Holding Companies

1.1 Traditional Banking

There are essentially three methods by which individuals, businesses, other entities, and even governments who require financial support for household goods, mortgage loans, business loans, and innumerable other purposes may secure funds: (1) direct lending from one person to another, (2) "traditional banking," and (3) "non-bank" or "shadow bank" financing. The simplest method of lending is by a *direct loan* of money given by one person to another, which typically occurs between individuals who are related to one another without the use of a third party (Fig. 1.1). The second method, whereby money is lent to borrowers, is traditional banking. By *traditional banking* we refer to the process known as *financial intermediation* whereby depositors place their money into a checking or savings account in a bank, which then acts as an intermediary between the depositors and borrowers to whom the bank lends the money deposited at a predetermined interest rate. The money deposited generally does not earn interest for the depositors if placed in a checking account, but may receive interest if placed in other accounts such as a savings account, certificate of deposit, or other interest-bearing accounts (Fig. 1.2). The third method is shadow bank financing (non-bank financing), which is the focus of this text.

Traditional banking depositors are legal persons who may be individuals living in households, partnerships, corporations, or other legally recognizable entities. Borrowers may consist of similar persons, ranging

Roy J. Girasa, *Shadow Banking*, DOI 10.1007/978-3-319-33026-6_1

Fig. 1.1 Simplest form of financing

Fig. 1.2 Traditional banking

from individuals requiring automobile loans or mortgage loans for the purchase of homes to businesses needing money to further their interests. Of course, borrowing and lending may be accomplished under the first method without the third party intermediary by direct lending from the lender to the borrower; this often takes place between relatives or friends and even between anxious sellers of homes and buyers who are unable to obtain mortgage financing from mortgage lenders, usually in times of financial distress.

Traditional banking, as stated in the historical evolution discussed hereafter, has evolved well beyond ordinary lending to households and businesses to a third method of financing, whereby banks act as financial intermediaries accomplishing maturity and credit transformation, often using the vehicle of bank holding companies. The rise of shadow banking was due to a number of circumstances, the most important of which was to avoid significant governmental regulation (*regulatory arbitrage*). Through subsidiary entities, banks may engage in diverse investments from insurance to securities, repurchasing agreements, and other financial transformations.

Banks were once divided into commercial banks, which accomplished what was discussed above, and investment banks, which were engaged in providing financial capital for business entities by acting as underwriters, as agents in the securities market, and in other related activities. The larger banks later expanded to interstate banking and, thereafter, became international in scope, providing means for global payments and credits and engaging in a complex relationship with other local, national, and international banks. Central banks, such as the US FED, play a major role in monetary policy, keeping inflation and deflation under control, adding liquidity to the banking system when needed, and fostering well-being in the overall economy in a number of other ways.

1.2 Role and Types of Transformation of the Financial System

1.2.1 Role

The role of the financial system is to serve the economic well-being of business entities and their consumers. It does so by the performance of a variety of functions, namely *financial intermediation* whereby lenders, such as individual, corporate, or government investors, provide the funds that are ultimately utilized by businesses and individuals in the form of business loans to operate or expand enterprises and consumer loans, including home mortgages and automobile loans; *risk transformation* and *insurance* to protect against devastating losses; *organization of the payment system*; *provision for payment and transaction services* that permit consumers to make purchases through a variety of means such as automated teller machines (ATMs), checks, credit cards, and other such means; and the *creation of markets* that permits trade and pricing of financial instruments and their risks.[1]

1.2.2 Transformations

The banking system is not perfect, as witnessed by the many bank failures and panics that have gripped the USA and other nations. The problem is that banks and other financial intermediaries, such as savings and loan associations and credit unions, engage in activities that inherently encompass potential risks over an extended time frame, namely a *qualitative asset transformation* or *maturity transformation* whereby banks take short-term deposits and then convert them into long-term loans, an example being mortgage loans; *liquidity transformation*, where a bank's assets are less liquid than its liabilities; and *credit transformation*, wherein banks spread their risk by providing loans to a variety of persons, individuals, and businesses, each having a varying degree of quality. It can readily be understood that banks and other mortgage or other long-term loan lenders may become subject to financial distress if depositors, for a variety of reasons, decide to withdraw their deposits suddenly, as in a so-called "run" on a bank. The long-term lender may be unable to immediately satisfy the lenders' demand for immediate withdrawals.[2]

As a result of negligence, malfeasance, and incompetence, it became necessary that banks be regulated by governmental entities, such as the requirements that they maintain minimum capital reserves, have diligent loan policies, and maintain customer confidence to prevent a sudden run on bank deposits. Fortunately, at least in the USA and the European Union (EU), there are supportive systems such as the US FDIC (Federal Deposit Insurance Corporation), which insures all deposit accounts up to $250,000 per depositor per insured bank, including checking and savings accounts, money market deposit accounts, negotiable order of withdrawal (NOW) accounts, cashier's checks, money orders, and certificates of deposit; and in the EU a Directive that provides €100,000 comparable coverage.[3] Not insured in the USA, even if purchased through a bank, are mutual funds, stocks, bonds, life insurance policies, annuities, or municipal securities.[4] Depositors in the USA have no legitimate reason to fear that their deposits will not be honored up to the insured sums.

1.3 Historical Development of the US Banking System

Traditional banking has had a checkered history, having commenced at the inception of the new Republic with the creation of the First Bank of the United States (1791–1811) under the leadership of Alexander Hamilton, named the first US Secretary of the Treasury under President George Washington. The bank expanded with branches in a number of cities which, along with state banks, flourished in competition with each other. The Second US Bank was created in 1816 following the end of the War of 1812 with Great Britain. The issuance of bank notes was performed by state banks because of the lack of a national currency, which led to problems of redemption because of the varieties of state currencies, which often could not be redeemed at face value, particularly in other states.

The War of 1812 illustrated the weakness of the system, and events culminated in the Panic of 1819. In the seminal case of *McCulloch v. Maryland*,[5] the State of Maryland sought to impose a tax on the federal bank. The US Supreme Court, in a decision by the famed Chief Justice John Marshall, determined that Congress had the right to create a bank under its delegated power under Article I of the US Constitution to make "all laws which shall be necessary and proper, for carrying into execution." Thus, the Maryland tax was declared by the Court to be contrary to the US Constitution.[6] There were continual debates concerning the powers of the federal bank vis-à-vis state banks primarily led by President Andrew Jackson (term of 1829–1837) who believed that the expansion of the US Bank was destructive of states' rights. His actions in attempting to negate the federal bank's jurisdiction and power led to another of the many financial panics that occurred in US history. In the midst of the Civil War of 1861–1865, however, Congress enacted the National Banking Act,[7] which established standards for banks including minimum capital requirements and issuance of loans, as well as the imposition of a 10 % tax on state banknotes, which effectively removed them from circulation.[8]

1.3.1 The Federal Reserve System

The Federal Reserve Act of 1913,[9] whose statutory objectives for monetary policy were to maximize employment, stabilize prices, and moderate long-term interest rates, created the national system of banks known as the FED that has existed to the present day. Its structure consists of a seven-member Board of Governors of the Federal Reserve System (Board) who serve 14-year terms and whose duties include overseeing and supervising the 12 Federal Reserve Banks; the US payments system; the financial services industry; the guidance of monetary action; the setting of reserve requirements for depository institutions; the conduct of studies of current financial issues affecting the nation; and the approval of changes in discount rates recommended by the Federal Reserve Banks. The Board's most important responsibility is participating in the Federal Open Market Committee (FOMC), which determines the direction of the nation's monetary policy.[10]

Additional organizational elements of the FED include the following: (1) 12 Federal Reserve Banks and 24 branches serving their respective regions, storing currency and coin; processing checks and electronic payments; supervising commercial banks in their regions; managing the US Treasury's payments; selling government securities; and assisting with the Treasury's cash management and investment activities; (2) member banks (about one-third of all state banks and all national banks); (3) three statutory advisory councils: the Federal Advisory Council, the Consumer Advisory Council, and the Thrift Institutions Advisory Council, which advise the Board on matters of current interest; and (4) some 17,000 other banks, savings and loan associations, and credit unions that are subject to the FED's regulations.

The Act required all national banks to be members of the Federal Reserve System and to maintain levels of capital reserves with one of the 12 Federal Reserve Banks. The member banks must deposit a percentage of their customers' savings account and checking account deposits in a Federal Reserve Bank. State banks are also eligible to become members of the Federal Reserve System with all the attendant benefits thereto, including federal protection of deposits. The FED conducts monetary policy; supervises and regulates banks; protects consumer rights; provides financial services to the government and financial institutions; and makes loans to commercial banks.

The Great Depression that commenced in 1929 and ended with the entry of the USA into World War II led to a congressional inquiry concerning its causes. It was noted that there were bank panics almost every 20 years (1819, 1836, 1857, 1873, 1893, 1907, and 1929), and discovered that among the major causes were heavy investments in securities by bank affiliates in the 1920s; serious conflicts of interest between banks and their affiliates; speculative investments by banks; and high-risk ventures. Accordingly, the Banking Act of 1933,[11] better known as the Glass-Steagall Act, became the law of the land.

1.3.2 The Glass-Steagall Act of 1933 and Bank Separation

The Glass-Steagall Act, in essence, significantly limited the ability of commercial banks to engage in the business of stock and securities by compelling the separation of banks into commercial banks and investment banks. The principal sections of the Act are §§16, 20, and 21. §16 set forth the functions of a commercial bank, namely (1) discounting and negotiating promissory notes, drafts, bills of exchange, and other evidences of debt; (2) receiving deposits; (3) buying and selling exchange, coin, and bullion; (4) loaning money on personal security; and (5) obtaining, issuing, and circulating notes.

§20 of the Act forbade a member bank from engaging in the issuance, flotation, underwriting, public sale, distribution of, or participation in stocks, bonds, debentures, notes, or other securities. To protect against excessive risk, it further stated that: "The business of dealing in investment securities by the association shall be limited to purchasing and selling such securities without recourse, solely upon the order, and for the account of, customers, and in no case for its own account, and the association shall not underwrite any issue of securities." §21 forbade firms that engaged in the business of the issuance, underwriting, selling, or distributing of stocks, bonds, debentures, notes, or other securities, from receiving, at the same time, deposits, certificates of deposits, or other evidences of debt. The payment of interest on accounts was restricted by the Act and under Regulation Q to prevent ruinous competition.[12] Other restrictions, particularly as set forth in the Bank Holding Act of 1956,[13] included the grant of power to the FED to regulate bank holding companies, prohibit multi-state banking, and restrict banks from possessing non-bank entities.

1.3.3 *The Riegel-Neal Interstate and Branching Efficiency Act of 1994*

As a result of FED jurisdiction and the commercial/investment bank separation, bank panics that occurred virtually every other decade did not transpire after 1933 until many decades later in 1987 and, most recently, in 2008. It has been alleged by many bank experts that these later occurrences were due to the expansion and enlargement of banks to other states and by the removal of the separation of commercial and investment banks. The Riegel-Neal Banking and Branching Efficiency Act of 1994 repealed the prohibition of interstate banking by permitting banks to purchase banks in other states or to establish branches therein.[14] Under the Act, the FDIC was given jurisdiction over state non-member banks; the Office of the Comptroller of Currency received jurisdiction over state non-member banks; and the FED was given supervision over state member banks. Applicants for expansion were judged by their compliance with the Community Reinvestment Act of 1977 (CORA),[15] which mandated reinvestment by out-of-state banks in the local communities where they were located.

The Act, as amended by CORA, later became contentious, with different attitudes held by the major political parties. In general, Democrats attributed the financial and banking crisis of 2007–2009 to the repeal of the Glass-Steagall separation of banks, while Republicans attributed the downfall in large part to the efforts of "liberal" political figures, who caused banks under the CORA to grant loans to mainly minority persons who could ill-afford the mortgage loans. CORA §109(b) provides that regulations promulgated under the Riegle-Neal Act concerning permission to open out-of-state branches are to ensure that the branches reasonably assist in meeting the needs of the communities in which the branches are located.

CORA §109(c) states that if the appropriate banking agency determines, among other considerations, that less than one-half of the deposits received from depositors in the host state results in loans to the host state, then the agency shall review the portfolio of the bank to determine whether the bank is reasonably helping to meet the credit needs of the communities served by the bank in the host state. If the agency makes such a determination, then the out-of-state bank may not be permitted to open a new interstate branch in the host state unless it provides reasonable assurances to the satisfaction of the appropriate federal banking agency that it will substantially help to meet the credit needs of the community that the new branch will serve.

1.3.4 Gramm-Leach-Bliley Act of 1999

Internationally, foreign banks offered a multitude of services. For example, the Hong Kong and Shanghai Bank, which was established in Hong Kong when it was a British colony, in 1865, and later became HSBC, offered a multitude of services that combined commercial and investment activities. Japanese banks, which also offered services on a broad scale, dominated the top ten of banks worldwide by the 1970s. In the 1990s, US banks complained that they could not compete with foreign multi-service banks that offered both commercial and investment banking services. The share of total private financial assets held by these US banks declined from 60 % to 35 % for the period of 1970–1995. After intensive lobbying and sympathy from members of Congress fearful of Japanese expansion, in 1999 the Financial Services Modernization Act, popularly known as the Gramm-Leach-Bliley Act, was enacted.[16]

The first section of the Act, §101(a), explicitly repealed §20 of the Glass-Steagall Act that separated commercial from investment banks. §103 permits a financial holding company to engage in any financial activity, and to acquire and retain the shares of any company engaged in any activity that is *financial* in nature or incidental thereto, provided it does not pose a substantial risk to the safety and soundness of depository institutions or to the financial system generally. *Financial activities* include:

- Lending, exchanging, transferring, investing for others, or safeguarding money or securities;
- Insuring, guaranteeing, or indemnifying against loss, harm, damage, illness, disability, or death, or providing and issuing annuities, and acting as principal, agent, or broker for purposes of the foregoing, in any state;
- Providing financial, investment, or economic advisory services, including advising an investment company;
- Issuing or selling instruments representing interests in pools of assets permissible for a bank to hold directly;
- Underwriting, dealing in, or making a market in securities.

Thus, banks were now able to pursue any financial activity subject to the FED's determination to be financial in nature or incidental to such activity. Banks could offer services that included insurance and securities underwriting and merchant banking. Whereas banks had avoided panics for twice the time period that had historically been the case, the banking crisis of 2007–2009 raised issues of the soundness of the Glass-Steagall repeal and "too-big-to-fail" bank holdings.

1.4 Dodd-Frank Act Bank Requirements

The financial crisis of 2007–2009 led to the passage of the Dodd-Frank Wall Street Reform and Consumer Protection Act of 2010 (Dodd-Frank).[17] Although one of the sponsors of the Act, Senator Chris Dodd, stated that many sections of the Act were bipartisan in nature, with senators of the Democrat and Republican parties having participated in the written sections, passage took place without gaining the votes of any Republicans in the House of Representatives and the Senate. The 1000 page Act contains numerous subtitles that sought to alleviate many of the problems that allegedly caused the financial crisis. Banking regulation is contained in Title VI, known as the Bank and Savings Association Holding Company and Depository Institution Regulatory Improvements Act of 2010.

Title VI includes sections explicitly dealing with bank holding companies created under Gramm-Leach-Bliley to permit expansion of permissible financial activities, but, rather than restoring the Glass-Steagall separation of commercial banks from investment banks, its major emphasis is that a bank holding company be "well-capitalized and well-managed."[18] §38(b) of the Federal Deposit Insurance Act[19] defines "well-capitalized" as follows: "An insured depository institution is 'well-capitalized' if it exceeds the required minimum level for each relevant capital measure." Dodd-Frank raised the standard of well-capitalized to where its total risk-based capital ratio is 10 % or greater, a Tier I risk-based capital ratio of 6 % or greater, and a leveraged capital ratio of 5 % or greater.

1.4.1 The Volcker Rule

The financial crisis of 2007–2009 led to the closures of hundreds of banks, which was somewhat reminiscent of the closures that occurred in the Great Depression. Initially, there was governmental reluctance to come to the rescue of certain banks and financial institutions, such as Lehman Brothers, but it became clear to the then Secretary of the Treasury, Henry Paulson, that a failure to intervene might lead to the collapse of the entire global financial system. A debate ensued concerning the cause of the financial collapse, with some proponents, mainly Democrats, believing that the major cause for the crisis was the repeal of Glass-Steagall. They later pointed to the $6.2 billion London Whale trader investment banking loss by JP Morgan Chase in 2012 with respect to speculative trading in the United Kingdom (UK) as illustrative of their viewpoint.

The "Volcker Rule," named after the former chairman of the Federal Reserve Board (Board), Paul Volcker, acting as an adviser to President Barack Obama, was promulgated pursuant to Title VI, §619 of Dodd-Frank, which added a new §13 to the Bank Holding Company Act. It prohibits an insured depository institution and holding company controlling an insured depository institution from engaging in proprietary trading and further prohibits the sponsoring and investing in hedge funds and private equity funds. The term *proprietary trading* was given a broad definition, to include acting as a principal or custodian for an affiliated third party; a trading account used by the entity to acquire or be financially involved in short-term resale; the prohibition of purchasing, selling, or otherwise acquiring or disposing of stocks, bonds, and other financial instruments for the bank's own account; or acquiring or retaining ownership interests in, sponsoring, or having certain relationships with a hedge fund or private equity fund.

The Rule became effective on July 21, 2012 but banks were allowed two years in which to comply. The date was later extended to July 16, 2016 and will be extended again to one year thereafter with respect to "legacy covered funds owned prior to December 31, 2013."[20] Banks are to comply with the prohibition of proprietary trading activities by July 21, 2015. A number of Federal agencies are responsible for the implementation of the Rule, including the Office of the Comptroller of the Currency (OCC), the FDIC, the US Securities and Exchange Commission (SEC), and the Commodity Futures Trading Commission (CFTC).

1.4.2 *Additional Prohibitions: Credit Rating Agencies*

A problem that existed below the regulatory radar screen was the inherent conflict of interest that affected credit rating agencies (CRAs) such as Standard & Poor's, Fitch Group, and Moody's Investor Services. CRAs are paid for their services by the corporate entities that are being rated thanks to prior statutory and regulatory requirements that new issues of securities and a multitude of other financial instruments, such as government and corporate bonds, mortgage-backed securities, and collateralized debt obligations, have to undergo ratings by an accredited ratings agency. Whereas initially the model for the agencies in the early twentieth century was one in which the investor paid for the service, it was transformed to one in which the issuer pays. There was no prohibition that disallowed a company that was issuing a security from asking more than one agency how it would rate its security and then select the one that gave it the highest ratings. These agencies, reliant upon income from corporate entities, faced possible conflict of interest in seeking to obtain corporate business.

CRAs benefited from SEC rules that created the category of a "nationally recognized statistical rating organization" (NRSRO) and gave recognition to the three ratings agencies mentioned above, which allegedly met the requirements of the organization. Under Rule 15c3-1 of the Securities Exchange Act of 1934, broker-dealers were required, when computing net capital, to deduct from their net worth certain percentages of the market value of their proprietary securities positions. Inasmuch as the SEC was concerned with the level of risk assumed by these firms, it took the position that securities held by a broker-dealer, which were rated instrument grade by a NRSRO, permitted it to deduct a smaller percentage in determining its net capital. The SEC expanded its use of the NRSRO to money market funds and other financial instruments. When later defaults took place, for example, that of Orange County, California, and the Washington Public Power Supply System bonds, the SEC took note of the criticisms of its position by the US Department of Justice and other commentators.

As a result, Congress enacted the Credit Rating Agency Reform Act of 2006 (RAA), which was aimed to improve ratings quality from the agencies to protect investors and the public by fostering accountability, transparency, and competition among them. Nevertheless, CRAs continued to issue ratings that at times were highly erroneous. An additional problem arose owing to a multitude of newly created financial instruments which often appeared to be beyond the expertise of the agencies. Inasmuch as ratings were "opinions" and not statements of fact, investors relying on the ratings were not able to commence litigation against the CRAs for the erroneous and misleading ratings that occurred with respect to particular new issues.

IOSCO Principles
The International Organization of Securities Commissions (IOSCO) was also concerned with credit ratings that affected not only US but also global investors. Accordingly, it issued a Code of Conduct for Credit Rating Agencies,[21] based on the principles of (1) quality and integrity in the rating process; (2) independence and conflicts of interest; (3) transparency and timeliness of ratings disclosure; and (4) confidential information. The IOSCO Code of Conduct is set forth in Appendix 1 of this chapter.

1.4.3 Dodd-Frank Act and CRAs

The Dodd-Frank Act sought to remedy the problem of conflicts of interest and other issues affecting CRAs by the addition of a new title that was devoted to credit rating agencies. Thus, Title IX, §939A of the Act, mandated that each federal agency shall, to the extent applicable, review any regulation issued by such agency that requires the use of an assessment of the creditworthiness of a security or money market instrument and any references to or requirements in such regulations regarding credit ratings. Each such agency is required to remove any reference to or requirement of reliance on credit ratings and to substitute in such regulations such standard of creditworthiness as each respective agency shall determine to be appropriate for such regulations. In making their determination, the agencies are to establish, to the extent feasible, uniform standards of creditworthiness for use by each such agency, taking into account the entities regulated by each such agency and the purposes for which such entities would rely on such standards of creditworthiness.

An issue arose concerning the potential civil and also criminal liability of CRAs for misstatements and omissions from their analyses in issuing credit ratings. Previously, Rule 436(g) of the Securities Act of 1933 had insulated CRAs from civil liability by providing that the security rating given by an NRSRO to debt securities, convertible debt securities, or preferred stock was not to be considered a part of the registration statement prepared or certified by an expert. The effect of the 436(g) exemption was to insulate NRSROs from possible liability for material misstatements or omissions in the registration statement. The Dodd-Frank Act repealed Rule 436(g), and by doing so appeared to expose NRSROs to possible liability for alleged misstatements or omissions. As a result, NRSROs complained that the repeal of the Rule would lead to far fewer credit ratings and subsequently less disclosure, and would also add substantially to the cost of the procurement and reporting of ratings because of the need of NRSROs to effect due diligence.[22]

On July 22, 2010, the SEC issued interpretive guidance, *Compliance and Disclosure Interpretations*, which clarified its position with regard to its mandates concerning NRSRO reports.[23] The SEC appeared to relieve NRSROs in part of their fears of substantial litigation relating to the contents of their reports and their use by issuers. The SEC stated, in its *Issuer Disclosure-Related Ratings Information*, that the repeal of Rule 436(g) would not require consent from a NRSRO if its credit ratings were provided in registration statements or prospectuses concerning changes to a credit rating, the issuer's liquidity, the cost of funds for the registrant issuer, or the terms of agreement referring to credit ratings. New oversight for credit rating agencies began with the SEC Office of Credit Ratings examining the rating agencies annually. The rating agencies are subject to new disclosures about their methods and are open to investor lawsuits. In addition, to include a rating in a registration statement, the registrant must include the rating agency's consent in the filing.

The Dodd-Frank Act mandates that each NRSRO should establish, maintain, enforce, and document the creation of an effective internal control structure implementing and adhering to the policies, procedures, and methodologies for determining credit ratings. CRAs are to consider the factors that may be established by the SEC and submit an annual internal controls report to the agency, which is to include:

1. A description of the responsibility of the NRSRO's management in establishing and maintaining an effective internal control structure;
2. An assessment of the effectiveness of the internal control structure of the NRSRO; and
3. The attestation of the chief executive officer or equivalent person concerning the above.[24]

The Act further provides for the suspension or revocation of the registration of a NRSRO or persons employed by it or with respect to a particular class of securities for misconduct, or for failure of accurate ratings over a sustained period of time.[25]

IOSCO's fourth principle under the "independence and conflicts of interest" heading is reflected in the Dodd-Frank Act in its provision that the SEC is mandated to provide rules for the separation of ratings from the NRSRO's sales and marketing sections. Each NRSRO must report to the SEC any person employed by it within the last five years who secured employment with any obligor, issuer, underwriter, or sponsor of a security during the 12-month period prior to employment by the NRSRO, if such employee was a senior officer of NRSRO, participated in any capacity in determining the credit rating of the employing firm, or supervised an employee who performed such a rating.[26]

The Dodd-Frank Act mandated that the SEC establish an Office of Credit Ratings to administer rules respecting NRSROs for the protection of users of their services, to promote accuracy in rating ratings issued by them, and to ensure that the ratings were not unduly influenced by conflicts of interest. The Office was to be staffed by its own director and staff, who were obliged to conduct annual examinations of each NRSRO. Among the requirements of the annual examination are ascertaining that the NRSRO is in compliance with policies, methodologies, and rating methodologies of NRSROs; that conflicts of interest be avoided; that implementation of ethical policies and supervisory controls takes place; and complaints are processed. Reports of the examination are to be made available to the public in the Office's annual report.[27]

Transparency of Ratings Performance

IOSCO's third principle under "transparency and timeliness of ratings disclosure" has its comparable provision in the Dodd-Frank Act "(q) Transparency of Ratings Performance". The SEC requires each NRSRO to publicly disclose information concerning its initial rating of each type of obligor, security, and money market instruments as well as any changes to those ratings so as to permit users to evaluate their accuracy and compare the performance of the different NRSROs. Performance standards have to be made clear and informative to investors and include information over a period of years for a variety of ratings types. Rules are promulgated whereby NRSROs set forth their procedures and methodologies, including qualitative and quantitative data and models, assumptions underlying the credit rating procedures and methodologies, the potential limitations and types of risks excluded from the credit ratings, and whether and to what extent third party due diligence services have been used by the NRSRO.

Corporate Governance, Organization, and Management of Conflicts of Interest

CRA members are independent of the NRSRO. The determination as to whether the directors are independent includes the requirement that they may not accept any consulting, advisory, or other forms of compensation from the NRSRO or otherwise be associated with the rating organization. A director's compensation is not linked to the business performance of the NRSRO. The term of office is not to exceed five years but the actual period of tenure is a pre-agreed set period. The board of directors has the responsibility to assure the establishment, maintenance, and enforcement of policies and procedures for the determination of credit ratings, assure an effective internal control system, have in place policies and procedures to avoid conflicts of interest, and provide for compensation and promotion policies and practices for the NRSRO.[28]

1.4.4 Prohibition of Certain Mergers

§622 of Dodd-Frank, "Concentration Limits on Large Financial Institutions," amended the Bank Holding Act of 1956 to forbid the merger, consolidation, or acquisition of virtually all assets or control by financial institutions by any other means if the total consolidated liabilities of the acquiring *financial company* exceeded 10 % of the aggregated consolidated liabilities of all financial companies at the end of the prior calendar year. Exceptions which led to even greater enlargement of banks included acquisition of banks in danger of default. Relevant here is the applicability of this section to shadow banking. The definition of *financial company*, in addition to traditional banking institutions, also includes "a non-bank financial company supervised by the Board under Title I of the Dodd-Frank Wall Street Reform and Consumer Protection Act."[29]

§622(C) also states that "with respect to an insurance company or other non-bank financial company supervised by the Board, such assets of the company as the FED's Board shall specify by rule, in order to provide for consistent and equitable treatment of such companies." The rule is subject to the recommendations of the Financial Stability Oversight Council

(Council). In accordance with the stated provision, the FRB issued a Final Rule,[30] which measures a financial company's *liabilities* as its risk-weighted assets, plus the amount of assets deducted from the financial company's regulatory capital multiplied by an institution's specific risk-weight, minus the financial company's total regulatory capital. The proposed definition is equal to the inverse of the institution's total capital ratio minus one, a definition that was designed to add back a risk-weighted amount for assets that had been deducted from capital (considered to be risky) without penalizing a firm for having a high amount of capital.[31]

§623 of Dodd-Frank amended the Federal Deposit Insurance Act to require the responsible agency to disapprove an application for an interstate merger transaction if the result of the merger was to permit the insured depository institution to control more than 10 % of the total amount of deposits of the insured depository institutions. There are exceptions for the acquisition or control of institutions in danger of default. Among the practices that caused a threat to the US banking sector were loans based on derivative transactions and other high-risk loans. The total non-secured loans and extensions of credit made by national banks are restricted by statute not to exceed 15 % of their unimpaired capital and unimpaired surplus. The total loans and extensions of credit by a national bank fully secured by readily marketable collateral with a market value at least equal to the amount of funds outstanding are not to exceed 10 % of the unimpaired capital and unimpaired surplus of the association.

§610 of Dodd-Frank includes in its definition of "loans and extensions of credit" credit exposure on derivative transactions; repurchase agreements; reverse repurchase agreements; and securities lending and borrowing transactions. State banks are also made subject to the credit exposure limits with respect to derivative transactions. The Act places limitations on lending to insiders as well as to purchases of assets from them unless the transaction is on market terms, represents more than 10 % of the capital stock and surplus of the covered bank, and has been approved by a majority of the board of directors of the institution.

Thus, in summary, the comments above illustrate the significant degree to which bank institutions are subject to statutory and regulatory provisions, many of which were enacted and promulgated after the financial crisis of 2007–2009. As a result of these restrictions, there has been a decided endeavor to avoid and bypass the onerous provisions through the creation of bank holding companies.

1.5 Bank Holding Companies

A large majority of US banks, and approximately 80 % of commercial banks, are owned by bank holding companies (BHCs) under the supervision of the FED. About 73 % of small banks with assets of under $100 million are owned by BHCs, and this rises to 95 % for banks with assets of over $10 billion.[32] The legislation permitting BHCs is the Bank Holding Act of 1956,[33] which originally was intended to limit banks from entering into non-bank activities. By a later amendment under the Gramm-Leach-Bliley Act, BHCs were permitted to register with the FED as financial holding companies (FHCs), which allowed banks to expand operations into many traditionally non-bank services, such as insurance underwriting, securities investments, and other permissible financial endeavors, subject to regulations by the FED. To the extent that the FHC engages in non-bank activities, for example those of broker-dealers, other governmental agencies, such as the SEC, may exercise jurisdiction.

Under Regulation Y, §225.81, an FHC is a BHC that complies with the requirements of the statute and regulations, include that it be capitalized, well managed, and has elected to become an FHC. Almost all BHCs are FHCs. The top tier of BHCs, as of September 18, 2014, are: JP Morgan Chase with $2,520 billion in assets (14 % of total BHCs); Bank of America, $2,172 billion (11 %); Citigroup Inc., $1,910 billion (11 %); Wells Fargo & Co., $1,599 billion (9 %); the Goldman Sachs Group Inc., $860 billion (5 %); and all other BHCs, $8,358 billion (48 %).[34]

1.5.1 Definition

The Bank Holding Act of 1956 defines a *bank holding company* as any company which has *control* over any bank or any company that is or becomes a bank holding company. By control is meant ownership, control, or power to vote 25 % or more of any class of voting securities of the bank or company, or where the FED determines, after notice and opportunity to hear, that the company directly exercises a controlling influence over the management or policies of the bank or company. Having 5 % or less of the voting shares is presumed to indicate a lack of control. Also excluded from the definition of control is where the bank is acting in a fiduciary capacity (lack of sole discretionary authority to exercise voting rights); as an underwriter; participating solely in a proxy solicitation; receipt of the shares in collection of a debt; and other related exceptions for limited time frames as determined by the FED.[35] The Board is responsible for regulating and supervising bank holding companies even if the bank owned by the holding company is under the primary supervision of a different federal agency (OCC or the FDIC).

1.5.2 Dodd-Frank Changes to the Bank Holding Act

As a result of the difficulties BHCs faced during the last financial crisis, the Dodd-Frank Act caused significant changes in the regulatory environment governing their operations. §165 of the Act requires the FED to establish prudential standards for BHCs with total consolidated assets of $50 billion or more as well as non-banks (shadow banks) in order to prevent or mitigate risks to the financial stability of the USA (see Chap. 4). The Act mandates enhanced prudential standards as set forth by the FED to be more stringent than the standards of BHCs that do not meet the monetary threshold.

1.5.3 FED's Final Rule of Enhanced Prudential Standards for BHCs

Accordingly, the FED issued a Final Rule, "Enhanced Prudential Standards for Bank Holding Companies and Foreign Banking Organizations," that is applicable to BHCs and foreign banking organizations, but deferred to a later date a Final Rule governing non-bank organizations; albeit the BHC Final Rule will operate as a baseline for the later non-bank Final Rule. In essence, a BHC meeting the $50 billion threshold in the USA is required to continue to meet the capital planning and stress testing requirements previously imposed with enhanced liquidity requirements, risk-management requirements, and the debt-to-equity limit with respect to those companies which the Council determines pose a grave threat to the financial stability of the USA. In addition, a publicly traded BHC with total consolidated assets of $10 billion or more is subject to risk-committee requirements.[36]

1.5.4 Requirements for BHCs with Total Consolidated Assets of $10 Billion but Less Than $50 Billion

The Final Rule distinguishes between publicly traded BHCs of more than $10 billion and under $50 billion from those that are not publicly traded. For BHCs that are not publicly traded, the Rule mandates that the company run annual stress tests. This affects a BHC with average total consolidated assets for the previous four quarters of more than $10 billion and less than $50 billion; a savings and loan association with total consolidated assets of more than $10 billion; and a state member bank with total consolidated assets of over $10 billion, each of the above being designated a "covered entity." The objective of the annual company-run stress test is to ensure that large, complex banking institutions have robust, forward-looking capital planning processes that account for their unique risks, and to help ensure that institutions have sufficient capital to continue operations during times of economic and financial stress.[37]

In conducting the annual stress test, covered companies are to use data as of September 30 and report their stress test results to the FED or other applicable agency. In addition, covered companies must conduct a "mid-cycle" test and report the results to the FED. Dodd-Frank stress test rules align the timing of annual company-run stress tests with the annual supervisory stress tests of covered companies. Covered companies in the USA use at least three scenarios provided by the FED by no later than November 15 of each calendar year, namely, baseline, adverse, and severely adverse scenarios, to determine their potential impact upon the company should it be compelled to confront any of them. The FED may also require a covered company with significant trading activity, as it determines this, to include a trading and counterparty component in its adverse and severely adverse scenarios in the stress test required by the Rule. The FED may also require the covered company to include one or more additional components that the FED may determine in the company's adverse and severely adverse operations or activities, or where it is based on the company's financial condition, size, complexity, risk profile, scope of operations or activities, or risks to the US economy.

In addition to the stress test, a covered company must conduct a stress test by July 5 during each stress test cycle based on data as of March 31 that calendar year, unless the date of the test and the date for collected data is extended by the FED in writing. In conducting a stress test a covered company must estimate for each scenario: (1) losses, pre-provision net revenue, provision for loan and lease losses, and net income; and (2) the potential impact on pro forma regulatory capital levels and pro forma capital ratios (including regulatory capital ratios, the Tier 1 common ratio, and any other capital ratios specified by the FED), incorporating the effects of any capital actions over the planning horizon and maintenance of an allowance for loan losses appropriate for credit exposures throughout the planning horizon.[38]

Management Oversight

The senior management of a covered company must establish and maintain a system of controls, oversight, and documentation, including policies and procedures that are designed to ensure that its stress testing processes are effective in meeting the requirements of the Final Rule. The policies and procedures must, at a minimum, describe the covered company's stress testing practices and methodologies and processes for validating and updating the company's stress test practices and methodologies pursuant to law, regulations, and supervisory guidance. There are similar requirements for the mid-cycle stress test. The board of directors of the covered company, or a committee thereof, must approve and review the policies and procedures of the stress testing processes at least annually or when economic conditions or the condition of the covered company may warrant it. The company's board and senior management must consider the results of the analysis it conducts: when making changes to the company's capital structure; when assessing the covered company's exposures, concentrations, and risk positions; and in the development or implementation of any plans that the covered company has for recovery or resolution.

The covered company must report the results of the stress test to the FED by January 5 and July 5 of each calendar year unless the time frame has been extended, and a summary thereof on March and September of each calendar year. With respect to the severely adverse scenario, the company is to disclose:

- A description of the types of risks included in the stress test;
- A general description of the methodologies used in the stress test, including those employed to estimate losses, revenues, provision for loan and lease losses, and changes in capital positions over the planning horizon;
- Estimates of the company's pre-provision net revenue and other revenue; provision for loan and lease losses, realized losses or gains on available for sale and held-to-maturity securities, trading and counterparty losses, and other losses or gains; net income before taxes; loan losses (dollar amount and as a percentage of average portfolio balance) in the aggregate and by sub-portfolio, including domestic closed-end first-lien mortgages; domestic junior lien mortgages and home equity lines of credit; commercial and industrial loans; commercial real estate loans; credit card exposures; other consumer loans; and all other loans; and pro forma regulatory capital ratios and the Tier 1 common ratio, as well as any other capital ratios specified by the FED;

- An explanation of the most significant causes for the changes in regulatory capital ratios and the Tier 1 common ratio; and
- With respect to a stress test conducted pursuant to section 165(i)(2) of the Dodd-Frank Act by an insured depository institution that is a subsidiary of the covered company and that is required to disclose a summary of its stress test results under applicable regulations, changes in regulatory capital ratios, and any other capital ratios specified by the FED for the depository institution subsidiary over the planning horizon, including an explanation of the most significant causes for the changes in regulatory capital ratios.[39]

Baseline, Adverse, and Severely Adverse Hypothetical Scenarios

Each covered company must publicly disclose a summary of the results of its company-run stress test under the severely adverse scenario provided by the FED through the company's primary supervisor. The adverse and severely adverse scenarios are not forecasts but rather hypothetical scenarios designed to assess the strength and resilience of financial institutions and their ability to continue to meet the credit needs of households and businesses in stressful economic and financial environments. The baseline scenario represents expectations of private sector forecasters.[40]

The *baseline scenario* is very similar to the average projections from surveys of economic forecasters. Thus, the baseline scenario for the USA used by the FED for 2015 is for a sustained, moderate expansion in economic activity. Real gross domestic product (GDP) grows at an average rate of just under 3 % per year over the scenario; the unemployment rate declines modestly, reaching 5¼ % by the end of the scenario in the fourth quarter of 2017; and the consumer price index (CPI) inflation averages just over 2 % per year. Companies estimate their losses, pre-provision net revenue, provision for loan and lease losses, net income, and the potential impact on pro forma regulatory capital levels and pro forma capital ratios.[41]

The *adverse scenario* refers to a set of conditions that affects the US economy or the financial condition of a company that is more adverse than in the baseline scenario and may include trading or other additional components. For 2015, the FED's scenario was characterized by the USA experiencing a mild recession beginning in the fourth quarter of 2014 and lasting through the second quarter of 2015. There is a global weakening in economic activity and an increase in US inflationary pressures that, overall, results in a rapid increase in both short- and long-term US Treasury rates. In the scenario, bank funding costs react strongly to rising short-term rates. It is a hypothetical scenario designed to assess the strength of banking organizations and their resilience to an unfavorable economic environment.

The *severely adverse scenario* includes trajectories for 26 variables. These include 14 variables that capture economic activity, asset prices, and interest rates in the US economy and financial markets and three variables (real GDP growth, inflation, and the US/foreign currency exchange rate) in each of four countries or country blocks (the euro area, the UK, developing Asian countries, and Japan). The severely adverse scenario features a substantial weakening in global economic activity, accompanied by large reductions in asset prices. In the scenario, the US corporate sector experiences increases in financial distress that are even larger than would be expected in a severe recession.

The market shock component for the severely adverse scenario is built around a sudden sharp increase in general risk premiums and credit risk, combined with significant market illiquidity, associated, in part, with the distress of one or more large leveraged entities that rapidly sell a variety of assets into an already fragile market. In addition, there is a significant rise in the unemployment rate, its total increase of a similar magnitude to those experienced in severe US contractions during the past half-century. By the end of 2015, the level of real GDP is approximately 4½ % lower than its level in the third quarter of 2014, and it begins to recover thereafter. This hypothetical scenario to assess the strength of the BHCs and their reliance in a severely adverse economic environment includes a rise in oil prices (Brent crude) to approximately $110 per barrel and other shock events.

1.5.5 *Requirements for* **Publicly Traded** *BHCs with Total Consolidated Assets of $10 Billion and Less Than $50 Billion*[42]

The Final Rule requires that the BHC maintain a risk committee that approves and periodically reviews the risk-management policies of its global operations and oversees the operation of its global risk-management framework.

Risk-Management Framework

The risk-management framework is to be determined in accordance with the company's structure, risk profile, complexity, activities, and size. It must include the following:

- Policies and procedures establishing risk-management governance, risk-management procedures, and risk-control infrastructure for its global operations; and
- Processes and systems for implementing and monitoring compliance with such policies and procedures, including:
  - Identifying and reporting risks, risk-management deficiencies, emerging risks, and ensuring effective and timely implementation of actions to address emerging risks;
  - Establishing managerial and employee responsibility for risk management;
  - Ensuring the independence of the risk-management function; and
  - Integrating risk management and associated controls with management goals and its compensation structure for its global operations.

Corporate Governance Requirements

The risk committee must:

- Have a formal, written charter that is approved by the BHC's board of directors;
- Meet at least quarterly and otherwise as needed, and fully document and maintain records of its proceedings, including risk-management decisions;
- The risk committee must include at least one member with experience in identifying, assessing, and managing risk exposures of large, complex firms; be chaired by a director who has not been an officer or employee of the BHC during the past three years; is not a member of the immediate family; who is, or has been within the last three years, an executive officer of the BHC; and is an independent director of the BHC.

1.5.6 Enhanced Prudential Standards for BHCs with Total Consolidated Assets of $50 Billion or More

Risk Factors

The Board noted the following risk factors as well as other factors, including the following:

- Equity indices of all developed market and of developing and emerging market nations to which companies with significant trading activity may have exposure, along with term structures of implied volatilities;
- Cross-currency foreign exchange rates or all major and many minor currencies, along term structures of implied volatilities;
- Term structures of government rates (e.g., US Treasuries, interbank rates (e.g., swap rates), and other key rates (e.g., commercial paper) for all developed markets and for developing and emerging market nations to which companies may have exposure;
- Term structures of implied volatilities that are key inputs to the pricing of interest rate derivatives;
- Term structures of futures prices for energy products, including crude oil (differentiated) by country of origin), natural gas and power;
- Term structures of futures prices for metals and agricultural commodities;
- *Value-drivers* (credit spreads or instrument prices themselves) for credit-sensitive product segments including corporate bonds, credit default swaps, and collateralized debt obligations by risk; non-agency residential mortgage-backed securities and commercial mortgage-backed securities by risk and vintage; sovereign debt; and municipal bonds; and
- Shocks to the values of private equity positions.

Risk-Management and Risk Committee Requirements

For BHCs with total consolidated assets for the past four quarters of $50 billion or more, the Final Rule imposes much stricter standards. They include requirements for risk management and risk committee, liquidity risk management, and stress testing and buffer requirements. The risk-management framework requirements are essentially the same as for BHCs with $10 billion and less than $50 billion of consolidated assets as described above. The corporate governance requirements, however, are more detailed. They provide, in addition to the requirement for a formal, written charter approved by the BHC's board of directors, as follows:

- An independent committee of the board of directors that has, as its sole and exclusive function, responsibility for the risk-management policies of the BHC's global operations and oversight of the operation of the BHC's company's global risk-management framework;
- Report directly to the BHC's board of directors;
- Receive and review regular reports at least quarterly from the BHC's chief risk officer; and
- Meet at least quarterly, or more frequently as needed, and fully document and maintain records of proceedings, including risk-management decisions.

In addition, however, there is the requirement that the BHC appoints a chief risk officer with experience in identifying, assessing, and managing risk exposures of large, complex financial firms. The chief risk officer's responsibilities include overseeing the establishment of enterprise-wide risk limits and monitoring compliance thereof; implementing and monitoring the above policies and procedures; management risks and risk control framework and the company's testing of them; and reporting risk-management deficiencies and emerging risks to the risk committee as well as resolving them in a timely manner. The BHC must also ensure that the compensation and other incentives provided to the chief risk officer are consistent with providing an objective assessment of the risks taken by the BHC. Reports by the chief executive officer are to be made to both the risk committee and to the company's chief executive officer.

Liquidity Risk-Management Requirements

The BHC's board of directors is responsible to:

- Approve, at least annually, the acceptable level of liquidity risk that the BHC may assume in connection with its operating strategies, taking into account the BHC's capital structure, risk profile, complexity, activities, and size;
- Receive, at least twice a year, information provided by senior management to determine whether the BHC is operating in accordance with its established liquidity risk tolerance; and
- Approve and periodically review the liquidity risk-management strategies, policies, and procedures established by senior management. The risk committee must approve the contingency funding plan at least annually as well as any material revisions to the plan prior to the plan's implementation.

Senior Management Responsibilities

The senior management of a BHC is responsible for the establishment and implementation of strategies, policies, and procedures to manage potential risk to its financial condition or safety that the company may face by the market's perception that the company is unable to meet its cash and collateral obligations. It must oversee the development and implementation of liquidity risk measurement and reporting systems; determine at least quarterly whether the BHC is operating in accordance with such policies and procedures; and whether the BHC is in compliance with the Final Rule's mandates and establish procedures regarding the preparation of such information.

Senior management must also report to the board of directors or the risk committee concerning the liquidity risk profile and tolerance of the BHC at least quarterly, It must approve, before implementation, new products and business lines and evaluate the liquidity costs, benefits, and risks of each new business line and each new product that could have a significant effect on the company's liquidity risk profile. In doing so, it must consider whether the new business line or product comes within the company's established liquidity risk tolerance and whether it may create any unanticipated liquidity risk which is within the company's established liquidity risk tolerance. It must review the cash-flow projections at least quarterly to ensure that the liquidity risk is within the established liquidity risk tolerance, and establish and review with compliance the BHC's liquidity risk limits.

Senior management is responsible for approving liquidity stress testing practices, methodologies, assumptions, and results thereof at least quarterly; approve the size and composition of the liquidity buffer; and establish and maintain a review function that is independent of management functions that execute funding to evaluate its liquidity risk management. The independent review function must meet regularly to review and evaluate the adequacy and effectiveness of the company's liquidity risk-management processes, including its liquidity stress test processes and assumptions; assess whether the company's liquidity risk-management function complies with applicable laws, regulations, supervisory guidance, and sound business practices; and report material liquidity risk-management issues to the board or the risk committee in writing to allow for corrective action.

Cash-Flow Projections

The BHC must produce and establish a methodology for making comprehensive cash-flow projections that project cash flows that arise from assets, liabilities, and off-balance-sheet exposures over short- and long-term time horizons and update them at least monthly. The projections are to include cash flows arising from contractual maturities, intercompany transactions, new business, funding renewals, customer options, and other potential events that may impact liquidity. Additional requirements include making reasonable assumptions of future behavior; identification and quantification of discrete and cumulative cash flow mismatches; details concerning the company's capital structure, risk profile, complexity, currency exposure, activities, and size of the BHC; and establish a contingency funding plan to address liquidity needs during liquidity stress events which the Final Rule sets forth.

There are requirements concerning the liquidity management process in the event of liquidity stress events; a contingency funding plan for monitoring emerging liquidity stress events; testing periodically the components of the plan; monitoring liquidity risk limits and controlling liquidity risk exposures and funding needs; intra-day liquidity risk exposure; and how all these are to be addressed.

Liquidity Stress Testing Requirements

The BHC must conduct stress tests to assess the potential impact of the liquidity stress scenarios on its cash flows, liquidity position, profitability, and solvency, taking into account its current liquidity condition, risks, exposures, strategies, and activities. It must consider its balance-sheet exposures, off-balance-sheet exposures, size, risk profile, complexity, business lines, organizational structure, and other characteristics that affect its liquidity risk profile in conducting its stress test. With respect to stress scenarios that are to be addressed, the Final Rule specifies the method, frequency, and reflection of adverse market events, all based on the company's financial condition, size, complexity, risk profile, scope of operations, or activities. For assets used as a cash-flow source, the fair market value of the asset must be discounted to reflect any credit risk and market volatility of the asset.

There are requirements concerning the policies and procedures of governance around the company's liquidity stress testing practices, methodologies, and assumptions that provide for the incorporation of the results of liquidity stress tests in future stress testing and for the enhancement of stress testing practices over time; .the establishment of and maintenance of a system of controls and oversight that is designed to ensure that its liquidity stress testing processes are effective and approved by the chief risk officer; and the maintenance of management information systems and data processes sufficient to enable it to effectively and reliably collect, sort, and aggregate data and other information related to liquidity stress testing.

Liquidity Buffer Requirements
The BHC must maintain a liquidity buffer that is sufficient to meet the projected net stressed cash-flow need over the 30-day planning horizon of the required liquidity stress test. The liquidity buffer must consist of highly liquid assets that are unencumbered, including cash and securities issued or guaranteed by the USA, a US government agency, or a US government-sponsored enterprise. It may also include any other asset that the BHC demonstrates to the satisfaction of the FED has low credit risk and low market risk, is readily traded in a secondary market at a price reasonably related to the last sales price, and is a type of asset that investors historically have purchased in periods of financial market distress during which market liquidity has been impaired. The liquidity buffer must not contain significant concentrations of highly liquid assets related to the BHC's risk, except cash and government securities.

The Final Rules respecting global systemically important BHCs and foreign banking organizations are discussed in Chap. 4. Readers should be aware that the Dodd-Frank Act remains controversial inasmuch as its final passage was made without one vote from either a Republican Senator or a Republican member of the House of Representatives. Some Republican candidates for the Presidency, for the election that will take place in 2016, have called for its total repeal, while other candidates have indicated that some amendments to the Act should be enacted. As late as July 2015, there were Republican attempts to alter the asset threshold of banks deemed "too big to fail" from $50 billion to $500 billion and permitting regulators flexibility to exempt banks from enhanced prudential requirements, with the measure having cleared the US Senate Banking Committee on a party-line vote. The basis for the measure is to ease requirements for banks that do not meet the enhanced threshold and to permit more flexibility in the granting of mortgages. Passage of the measure will not be successful because of the need for a super majority of 60 votes from 100 members in the Senate for passage. If a Democrat remains as President, the passage there of would nevertheless be vetoed if it were to occur (Table 1.1).[43]

1.6 International Banking Requirements

1.6.1 *Basel III Requirements and Implementation*

The Basel Committee, based in Basel, Switzerland, is composed of the governors from the central banks or related institutions from 26 countries and the Hong Kong special administrative region (SAR). Its mission is to act as the primary global standard-setter for the prudential regulation of

Table 1.1 Requirements for US Bank Holding Companies[a]

Size	*Requirements*
Total consolidated assets of more than $10 billion but less than $50 billion	Company-run stress tests
Total consolidated assets equal to or greater than $10 billion but less than $50 billion (if publicly traded)	Risk committee
Total consolidated assets of $50 billion or more	Risk-based and leverage capital Risk management Risk committee Liquidity risk-management, stress testing, and buffers Supervisory stress tests Company-run stress tests Debt to equity limits (upon grave threat determination)

[a]*Id.* at 17245

banks in order to strengthen the regulation, supervision, and practices of banks worldwide. It is also a forum for cooperation among the members on banking supervisory matters. It began in 1973 after the collapse of the Bretton Woods system of managed exchange rates.[44]

Global Regulatory Framework for Banks and Banking Systems

The Basel Committee on Banking Supervision of the Bank for International Settlements, in an endeavor following the 2007–2009 financial crisis to strengthen the global capital framework, sought to raise the resilience of the banking sector based upon the Committee's three pillars set forth in Basel II. The three pillars are minimum capital requirements, supervisory review, and disclosure. Basel III proposed a number of reforms for adoption by central banks to help contain systemic risks that occurred because of procyclicality and the interconnectedness of financial institutions. Among the reforms were:

- Raising the quality, consistency, and transparency of the capital base. The recommendations include that Tier 1 capital base be of common shares and retained earnings or comparable levels of high quality Tier 1 capital for non-joint stock companies. Other Tier 1 capital base must consist of subordinated instruments with fully discretionary non-cumulative dividends, or coupons, and have neither a maturity date nor an incentive to redeem. Deductions from capital and prudential filters are harmonized internationally.

- Enhancing risk coverage. Reforms introduced under Basel III are:
  - Banks must determine their capital requirement for counterparty credit risk using stress inputs;
  - Banks will be subject to a capital charge for potential mark-to-market losses associated with a deterioration of the creditworthiness of a counterparty;
  - In order to strengthen standards for collateral management and initial margining, banks with large and illiquid derivative exposures to a counterparty will have to apply longer margining periods as a basis for determining the regulatory capital requirement;
  - To address systemic risk arising from banks' interconnectedness through the derivatives markets in coordination with IOSCO and the Committee on Payments and Settlement Systems, the Committee states that the capitalization of bank exposures to central counterparties (CCP) will be based in part on the compliance of the CCP with the said standards. Moreover, a bank's collateral and mark-to-market exposures to CCPs meeting the standards will be subject to a low-risk weight of 2 % and default exposures to CCPs will be subject to risk-sensitive capital requirements.
  - Counterparty credit risk-management standards are to be enhanced in a number of areas, including treatment of *wrong-way* risk (where the exposure increases when the credit quality of the counterparty deteriorates) and guidance for the sound backtesting of counterparty credit exposures.[45]
- Supplementing the risk-based capital requirement with a leverage ratio. To address the build-up of excessive on- and off-balance-sheet leverage in the banking system that contributed to the financial crisis and is adjustable for the differences in accounting systems, the Committee introduced a leverage ratio requirement: to constrain leverage in the banking sector, to aid in mitigating the risk of destabilizing deleveraging processes that can damage the financial system and the economy; and introduce additional safeguards against model risk and measurement error by supplementing the risk-based measure with a simple, transparent, independent measure of risk.
- Reducing procyclicality and promoting countercyclicality buffers. The measures taken had the following objectives:

- Dampen any excess cyclicality of the minimum capital requirement;
- Promote more forward-looking provisions;
- Conserve capital to build buffers at individual banks and in the banking sector that can be used in stress; and
- Achieve the broader macro-prudential goal of protecting the banking sector from periods of excess credit growth.

Accordingly, the Committee (1) advocated a change in the accounting standards towards an expect loss approach; (2) updated its supervisory guidance to be consistent with the expected loss approach, and addressed initiatives to stronger provisioning in the regulatory capital framework. It also introduced a framework to promote the conservation of capital and the build-up of adequate buffers above the minimum that can be drawn down in periods of stress; give supervisors stronger tools to promote capital conservation in the banking sector; and introduce a regime which will adjust the capital buffer established previously through the capital conservation mechanism.

The Committee also addressed systemic risk and interconnectedness. To mitigate risks arising from firm-level exposures among global financial institutions, it introduced:

- Capital incentives for banks to use central counterparties for over-the-counter derivatives;
- Higher capital requirements for trading and derivatives activities and complex securitizations and off-balance-sheet exposures (e.g., structure investment vehicles);
- Higher capital requirements for interfinancial sector exposures; and
- Introduction of liquidity requirements that penalize excessive reliance on short-term. Interbank funding to support longer dated assets.[46]

The Committee also developed two minimum standards for funding liquidity: a liquidity coverage ratio so that high-quality liquid assets held in the stock should be unencumbered, liquid in markets in time of stress, and, ideally, be central bank eligible; and a net stable funding ratio that required a minimum number of stable sources of funding at a bank relative to the liquidity profiles of the assets and the potential for contingent liquidity needs arising from off-balance-sheet commitments over a one-year time frame.[47]

Large Exposure to a Single Counterparty

The Basel Committee on Banking Supervision set forth standards for measuring and controlling large exposures, that is, large losses resulting from the sudden default of a single counterparty, in addition and complementary to its risk-based capital standard.[48] The Committee noted that investors withdrew funds from other banks when an announcement was made of material losses related to asset-back securities and collateralized debt obligations were incurred by unrelated large banks. It ascertained from the financial crisis that material losses by one systemically important financial institution (SIFI) could trigger catastrophic consequences for global financial stability. Thus, an internationally active bank was to consider its exposure to any counterparty, with the exception of exposure to sovereigns and their central banks and any exposure guaranteed by or secured by financial instruments issued by the sovereign.

A *large exposure* is defined as equal to or above 10 % of the bank's eligible capital base. Where such exposure exists, the bank is to report to the supervisor not only large exposures to a single counterparty but also all other large exposures, exempted exposures that meet the 10 % capital standard, and a bank's 20 largest counterparties. Under no circumstances is the exposure to be higher than 25 % of the bank's eligible capital base to a single counterparty. A *single counterparty* includes a group of connected counterparties wherein one counterparty has control over the others. Banks are required to assess the interconnectedness between counterparties, as exemplified by voting agreements among them and significant influence over appointments of administrative personnel and senior management. Economic interdependence is illustrated where 50 % or more of the counterparty's gross receipts or expenditures is derived from transactions with the other counterparty; where there are guarantees of exposure; or where the financial problems or insolvency of one counterparty would cause difficulties to the other counterparties.

Banks are to consider their on- and off-balance-sheet exposure to counterparties as well as the credit risk of securities financing transactions. Off-balance-sheet items are to be converted into credit exposure equivalents through the use of credit conversion factors for large exposure frameworks. The framework details eligible credit risk mitigation techniques, treatment of maturity mismatches, recognition of the techniques in reduction of original exposure, and recognition of exposures to credit risk mitigation providers. A bank must add any exposures to a single counterparty arising in the trading book to any other exposures to the said counterparty.

Banks may offset long and short positions in the same issue if the issuer, coupon, currency, and maturity are identical. Positions in different issues from the same counterparty may be offset only when the short position is junior to the long position or if the positions are of the same seniority.

The standards also set forth treatment of specific exposure types. Included are sovereign exposures and entities connected with sovereigns and interbank exposures which are essentially exempt from the standards framework. Covered bonds are subject to legal requirements for special public supervision to protect bond holders. Banks are also to consider exposures to collective investment undertakings, securitization vehicles, and other structures. Banks are also required to identify third parties that may constitute additional risks, as exemplified by third parties such as originator, fund manager, and liquidity and credit protection providers. There are special rules for global systemically important banks (G-SIBs) wherein the large exposure limit applied to a G-SIB's exposure to another G-SIB is set at 15 % of the eligible capital base (Tier 1). When a bank becomes a G-SIB, it and other G-SIBs must apply the 15 % limit within 12 months of this event. Member countries may apply more stringent standards affecting G-SIBs. Implementation of this standard was to be accomplished by January 1, 2015.[49] The US G-SIBs and implementing regulations are discussed in Chap. 4. The Basel III core principles for effective banking supervision are set forth in Appendix 2 to this chapter.

1.6.2 Basel Committee Guidelines for Identifying and Dealing with Weak Banks

The Basel Committee on Banking Supervision issued a report concerning how the supervisory community, the resolution committee, and the international financial institutions advising supervisors are to deal with weak banks. A *weak bank* is defined by the Basel Committee as "one whose liquidity or solvency is unimpaired or will soon be impaired unless there is a major improvement in its financial resources, risk profile, business model, risk management systems and controls, and/or quality of governance and management in a timely manner." Where a bank is unable to be viable, then it should be resolved without severe systemic disruption and at no cost to taxpayers.[50]

The guiding principles for a supervisor, according to the report, are as follows:

- *Early identification of risk.* Supervisors have the responsibility to incorporate forward-looking tools such as an early warning system; reviews of governance and management; and stress tests.
- *Early intervention.* Supervisors should be prepared to act promptly and intervene at an early stage. The problem to date is that supervisory authorities failed to intervene with weak banks and even permitted their expansion and ultimate collapse.
- *Effectiveness.* Consistent with the core principles for effective banking supervision and other Basel Committee guidance, the supervisor is to use its best efforts, including all costs in the case of a G-SIB costs such as instability of the financial system.
- *Flexibility.* Supervisors should be flexible when applying recovery measures and react decisively when a bank is beyond assistance.
- *Clear internal governance processes.* Supervisors should design their own governance processes to ensure that their discretionary decisions are taken at a level within the organizational hierarchy that is appropriate to the situation at hand.
- *Consistency.* Supervisory actions should be consistent and well understood, so as not to distort the competitive environment and to minimize confusion and uncertainty in times of crisis.
- *Transparency and cooperation.* Banks and the relevant authorities should dispense a high degree of information-sharing and transparency about their intended actions.
- *Avoiding potential systemic problems.* All banks should be subject to the same supervisory and regulatory framework. Although larger banks may pose systemic risk because of their interconnectedness with other parts of the financial community, small banks also pose critical issues for the financial community.
- *Early preparation.* Supervisors should take early preparatory steps to ensure that banks are able to respond to critical situations. Systemic banks, in particular, should be obliged to have a recovery plan in place in the event of a financial crisis.[51]

The Basel Committee noted the symptoms and causes of bank problems. Symptoms include poor asset quality, lack of profitability, loss of capital, excessive leverage, excessive risk exposure, reputation problems, and liquidity concerns. These symptoms generally arise from causes that include an inappropriate business model in the particular environment in which the bank operates, inappropriate governance, poor decision-making by senior management, and/or a misalignment of internal incentive structures with external shareholder/stakeholder interests.

Other risk factors contributing to a bank's difficulties are credit and liquidity risk, market risk, operational risk, and interest rate or strategic risk. These difficulties arise from poor corporate governance such as weak oversight by the board of directors, compensation policies, and the absence of an effective internal controls. Other factors include poor lending policies, excessive concentrations across the business mode, structural imbalances in a bank's liquidity position, excessive risk taking such as by speculative trading, overrides of constraints in existing policies and procedures, excessive balance-sheet growth, and fraud and criminal activities (e.g., money laundering).

Supervisors should conduct on- and off-site examinations and reviews, forward-looking supervision, regulatory reporting, early warning indicators, business model assessment, appropriate governance risk management and controls, stress testing, review of recovery plans, and resolvability assessment.[52] The balance of guidelines is extensively presented; these concern macro-prudential surveillance and responses that deal with weak banks and resolutions.

The general principles for corrective action in the report are:

- The fulfillment of supervisory objectives, including financial stability and depositor protection;
- Immediate corrective action, whereby the bank and supervisor should promptly prevent the problems from growing and exacerbating the bank's weaknesses;
- Senior management commitments for corrective action or, as an alternative, replacement of senior management;
- Proportionality, whereby corrective action should be appropriate to the circumstances and scale of the problem; and
- Comprehensiveness, whereby both causes and weaknesses must be addressed by the corrective program.[53]

As illustrated by the rules, regulations, and principles discussed above, banking institutions are subject to extensive oversight by regulators. Thus, officers and directors of such institutions have endeavored to find alternate methodologies to avoid and escape what are perceived to be regulatory strangleholds. This explains the rise of shadow or non-bank alternative systems that have until now lacked regulatory oversight. In Chap. 2, we will examine the nature of shadow banking through a review of the economic mechanisms that motivated and brought it about, its systemic risks, backstops for the system, and the recommendations of international organizations.

Notes

1. European Commission, *Economic Review of the Financial Regulation Agenda*, Commission Staff Working Document (May 15, 2014), at 23–24, https://www.google.com/search?q=European+Commission,+Economic+Review+of+the+Financial+Regulation+Agenda,+Commission+Staff+Working+Document+(May+15,+2014),+SWD+(2014)+158+final.&rls=com.microsoft:en-US&ie=UTF-8&oe=UTF-8&startIndex=&startPage=1&gws_rd=ssl.
2. For a more detailed discussion, see David Luttress, Harvey Rosenblum, and Jackson Thies, *Understanding the Risks Inherent in Shadow Banking: A Primer and Practical Lessons Learned*, Federal Reserve Bank of Dallas Staff Papers, No. 18 (Nov. 2012), https://www.google.com/?gws_rd=ssl#q=David+Luttress%2C+Harvey+Rosenblum%2C+and+Jackson+Thies%2C+Unserstanding+the+Risks+Inherent+in+Shadow+Banking:+A+Primer+and+Practical+Lessons+Learned%2C+Federal+Reserve+Bank+of+Dallas+Staff+Papers%2C+No.+18+(Nov.+2012).
3. Directive 2009/14/EC of the European Parliament and of the Council of 11 March 2009 amending Directive 94/19/EC on deposit-guarantee schemes as regards the coverage level and the payout delay, http://eur-lex.europa.eu/legal-content/EN/TXT/?uri=CELEX:32009L0014.
4. Federal Deposit Insurance Corporation, *Understanding Deposit Insurance* and *What's Covered*, https://www.fdic.gov/deposit/deposits/.
5. 17 U.S. (4 Wheat.) 36 (1819).
6. The power to declare laws as being contrary to the US Constitution was previously decided in the case of *Marbury v. Madison*, 5 U.S. 137 (1803).
7. National Banking Act of 1864, Ch. 106, 13 Stat. 99, June 3, 1864.
8. For a detailed discussion of the history of traditional banking and banking regulation in general, see Roy J. Girasa, *Laws and Regulation in Global Financial Markets*, Ch. 5, Palgrave Macmillan (2013).
9. Ch. 6, 38 Stat. 251, 12 U.S.C. Ch. 3 (1913).
10. Federal Reserve, *The Structure of the Federal Reserve System*, https://www.federalreserveeducation.org/about-the-fed/structure-and-functions.
11. Pub.L. 73-66, 48 Stat. 162 (1933).

12. 12 U.S.C. Part 217.
13. 12 U.S.C. §§1841 et seq.
14. Pub.L. 103-328, 108 Stat. 2338, 12 U.S.C. 1811 (1994).
15. 12 U.S.C. 2901 et. seq.
16. Pub.L. 106-102, 113 Stat. 1338 (1999).
17. Pub.L. 111-203, H.R. 4173 (2010).
18. Dodd-Frank Act, §606.
19. Pub.L. 81-797, 64 Stat. 873(1950).
20. http://fdic.gov/news/board/2011Octno6.pdf.
21. International Organization of Securities Commissions, *Code of Conduct for Credit Rating Agencies* (rev). https://search.yahoo.com/yhs/search?p=International+Organization+of+Securities+Commissions%2C+Code+of+Conduct+for+Credit+Rating+Agencies&ei=UTF-8&hspart=mozilla&hsimp=yhs-002.
22. Scott Hirst, *Including Credit Ratings in Registration Statements*, http://blogs.law.harvard.edu/corpgov/2010/08/19/9ncluding-credit-ratings-in-registration-stat.
23. http://sec.gov/divisions/corpfin/guidance/securitiesactrules-interps.htm#233.04.
24. *Id.*, Sec. 932A(3).
25. *Supra*, Note 15, Sec. 932(a) amending Sec. 15E of the *Securities Exchange Act* of 1934.
26. *Id.*
27. Title IX, *Investor Protections and Improvements to the Regulation of Securities*, Subtitle C of the Dodd-Frank Act, *Improvements to the Regulation of Credit Rating Agencies.*
28. *Id.*
29. 12 U.S.C. 1467a(e)(2)(E).
30. 12 CFR Part 251, *Concentration Limits on Large Financial Institutions* (Nov. 4, 2014).
31. *Id.* III(A)(1).
32. Partnership for Progress, *Bank Holding Companies*, https://www.FEDpartnership.gov/bank-life-cycle/manage-transition/bank-holding-companies.
33. 12 U.S.C. §1841.
34. Federal Bank of Chicago, *Top Banks and Holding Companies*, https://www.chicagoFED.org/banking/financial-institution-reports/top-banks-bhcs.
35. *12 U.S.C. §1841 et seq.*
36. Federal Reserve System, Enhanced Prudential Standards for Bank Holding Companies and Foreign Banking Organizations and Register, Final Rule, 79 Fed. Reg. 59 (March 27, 2014), 12 CFR Part 252 at 17242.

37. Office of the Comptroller of the Currency, *Dodd-Frank Stress Test* (*Company-Run*), http://www.occ.gov/tools-forms/forms/bank-operations/stress-test-reporting.htm. The website also provides a template for the mandated stress test.
38. Stress test Final Rule may be found in Federal Register, Vol. 77, No. 198 (Oct. 12, 2012) 12 CFR Part 252 at §252.141 Company-Run Stress Test Requirements; Final Rules, at 62393,§252.141.
39. *Id.* at §252.145.
40. Board of Governors of the Federal Reserve System, *Press Release* (Nov. 15, 2012), http://www.federalreserve.gov/newsevents/press/bcreg/20121115a.htm.
41. Board of Governors of the Federal Reserve System, *2015 Supervisory Scenarios for Annual Stress Tests Required under the Dodd-Frank Act Stress Testing Rules and the Capital Plan Rule* (Oct. 23, 2014), http://www.federalreserve.gov/newsevents/press/bcreg/bcreg20141023a1.pdf.
42. Federal Reserve, *supra*, note 24 at 17317.
43. Andrew Taylor, *Senate GOP Adds Dodd-Frank Rewrite to $21B Funding Bill* (July 22, 2015), ABC NEWS, *http://abcnews.go.com/US/wireStory/senate-gop-adds-dodd-frank-rewrite-21b-funding-32618885.*
44. Bank for International Settlements, *About the Basel Committee*, http://www.bis.org/bcbs/about.htm?m=3%7C14%7C573.
45. Basel Committee on Bank Supervision, *Basel III: A global regulatory framework for more resilient banks and banking systems*, (Dec. 2010), http://www.bis.org/publ/bcbs189_dec2010.htm.
46. *Id*, at 2–6.
47. *Id.* at 8–9.
48. Basel Committee on Banking Supervision, *Standards: Supervising framework for measuring and controlling large exposures* (April 2014), Bank for International Settlements, http://www.bis.org/publ/bcbs283.htm.
    The comments made are from the Standards.
49. *Id.*
50. Basel Committee on Banking Supervision, *Guidelines for Identifying and Dealing with Weak Banks* (July 2015), Executive summary, Bank for International Settlements, https://www.google.com/?gws_rd=ssl#q=Basel+Committee+on+Banking+Supervision%2C+Guidelines+for+Identifying+ad+Dealing+with+Weak+Banks+(July+2015)+Bank+for+International+Settlements%2C+.
51. *Id*, at 6–7.
52. *Id.*at 8.
53. *Id* at 28–29.

Appendix 1: Iosco Code of Conduct for Credit Rating Agencies

Quality and Integrity. Among the indicia of quality and integrity are the following:

- The adoption, implementation, and enforcement of written procedures to ensure opinions are based on all known information;
- Rating methodologies that are rigorous, systematic, and be subjected to objective validation;
- Individuals performing the ratings are to be qualified with knowledge and experience in the particular financial instrument being rated;
- Avoidance of misrepresentations and maintenance of records for a reasonable period of time;
- Assessment whether it has adequate and qualified personnel to perform the ratings which are to be objectively conducted without bias and utilizing methodologies in a consistent manner; and
- Monitor and update opinions by regularly reviewing the issuer's creditworthiness.

Independence and Avoidance of Conflicts of Interest. Among the recommendations are:

- A CRA should not forbear or refrain from taking a rating action based on the potential effect of the action on the CRA, an issuer, an investor, or other market participant;
- A CRA and its analysts should use care and professional judgment to maintain both the substance and appearance of independence and objectivity and be influenced only by factors relevant to the credit assessment;
- The credit rating a CRA assigns to an issuer or security should not be affected by the existence of or potential for a business relationship between the CRA and the issuer;
- A CRA should separate, operationally and legally, its credit rating business and CRA analysts from any other businesses of the CRA, including consulting businesses that may present a conflict of interest;
- A CRA and its analysts should use care and professional judgment to maintain both the substance and appearance of independence and objectivity and be influenced only by factors relevant to the credit assessment; and

- A CRA should separate, operationally and legally, its credit rating business and CRA analysts from any other businesses of the CRA, including consulting businesses that may present a conflict of interest.

Transparency and Timeliness of Ratings Disclosure. Among the recommendations are:

- A CRA should distribute in a timely manner its ratings decisions regarding the entities and securities it rates and publicly disclose its policies for distributing ratings, reports and updates;
- A CRA should indicate with each of its ratings when the rating was last updated and the CRA should disclose to the public, on a non-selective basis and free of charge, any rating regarding publicly issued securities, or public issuers themselves, as well as any subsequent decisions to discontinue such a rating, if the rating action is based in whole or in part on material non-public information;
- A CRA should publish sufficient information about its procedures, methodologies and assumptions (including financial statement adjustments that deviate materially from those contained in the issuer's published financial statements and a description of the rating committee process, if applicable) so that outside parties can understand how a rating was arrived at by the CRA; and
- Where a CRA rates a structured finance product, it should provide investors and/or subscribers with sufficient information about its loss and cash-flow analysis so that an investor allowed to invest in the product can understand the basis for the CRA's.

Treatment of Confidential Information. Among the recommendations are:

- A CRA should adopt procedures and mechanisms to protect the confidential nature of information shared with them by issuers under the terms of a confidentiality agreement or otherwise under a mutual understanding that the information is shared confidentially;
- Unless otherwise permitted by the confidentiality agreement and consistent with applicable laws or regulations, the CRA and its employees should not disclose confidential information in press releases, through research conferences, to future employers, or in conversations with investors, other issuers, other persons, or otherwise;

- A CRA should use confidential information only for purposes related to its rating activities or otherwise in accordance with any confidentiality agreements with the issuer;
- CRA employees should take all reasonable measures to protect all property and records belonging to or in possession of the CRA from fraud, theft or misuse. CRA employees should not selectively disclose any non-public information about rating opinions or possible future rating actions of the CRA, except to the issuer or its designated agents;
- CRA employees should not share confidential information entrusted to the CRA with employees of any affiliated entities that are not CRAs. CRA employees should not share confidential information within the CRA except on an "as needed" basis; and
- CRA employees should not use or share confidential information for the purpose of trading securities, or for any other purpose except the conduct of the CRA's business.

Appendix 2: Basel III Core Principles for Effective Banking Supervision

Supervisory Powers, Responsibilities and Functions

- ***Principle 1 – Responsibilities, objectives and powers:*** An effective system of banking supervision has clear responsibilities and objectives for each authority involved in the supervision of banks and banking groups. A suitable legal framework for banking supervision is in place to provide each responsible authority with the necessary legal powers to authorise banks, conduct ongoing supervision, address compliance with laws and undertake timely corrective actions to address safety and soundness concerns.
- ***Principle 2 – Independence, accountability, resourcing and legal protection for supervisors:*** The supervisor possesses operational independence, transparent processes, sound governance, budgetary processes that do not undermine autonomy and adequate resources, and is accountable for the discharge of its duties and use of its resources. The legal framework for banking supervision includes legal protection for the supervisor.
- ***Principle 3 – Cooperation and collaboration:*** Laws, regulations or other arrangements provide a framework for cooperation and

collaboration with relevant domestic authorities and foreign supervisors. These arrangements reflect the need to protect confidential information.

- ***Principle 4 – Permissible activities*:** The permissible activities of institutions that are licensed and subject to supervision as banks are clearly defined and the use of the word "bank" in names is controlled.
- ***Principle 5 – Licensing criteria*:** The licensing authority has the power to set criteria and reject applications for establishments that do not meet the criteria. At a minimum, the licensing process consists of an assessment of the ownership structure and governance (including the fitness and propriety of Board members and senior management) of the bank and its wider group, and its strategic and operating plan, internal controls, risk management and projected financial condition (including capital base). Where the proposed owner or parent organisation is a foreign bank, the prior consent of its home supervisor is obtained.
- ***Principle 6 – Transfer of significant ownership*:** The supervisor has the power to review, reject and impose prudential conditions on any proposals to transfer significant ownership or controlling interests held directly or indirectly in existing banks to other parties.
- ***Principle 7 – Major acquisitions*:** The supervisor has the power to approve or reject (or recommend to the responsible authority the approval or rejection of), and impose prudential conditions on, major acquisitions or investments by a bank, against prescribed criteria, including the establishment of cross-border operations, and to determine that corporate affiliations or structures do not expose the bank to undue risks or hinder effective supervision.
- ***Principle 8 – Supervisory approach*:** An effective system of banking supervision requires the supervisor to develop and maintain a forward-looking assessment of the risk profile of individual banks and banking groups, proportionate to their systemic importance; identify, assess and address risks emanating from banks and the banking system as a whole; have a framework in place for early intervention; and have plans in place, in partnership with other relevant authorities, to take action to resolve banks in an orderly manner if they become non-viable.
- ***Principle 9 – Supervisory techniques and tools*:** The supervisor uses an appropriate range of techniques and tools to implement the supervisory approach under the Core Principles for Effective Banking Supervision 11 and deploys supervisory resources on a proportionate basis, taking into account the risk profile and systemic importance of banks.

- ***Principle 10 – Supervisory reporting*:** The supervisor collects, reviews and analyses prudential reports and statistical returns from banks on both a solo and a consolidated basis, and independently verifies these reports through either on-site examinations or use of external experts.
- ***Principle 11 – Corrective and sanctioning powers of supervisors*:** The supervisor acts at an early stage to address unsafe and unsound practices or activities that could pose risks to banks or to the banking system. The supervisor has at its disposal an adequate range of supervisory tools to bring about timely corrective actions. This includes the ability to revoke the banking license or to recommend its revocation.
- ***Principle 12 – Consolidated supervision*:** An essential element of banking supervision is that the supervisor supervises the banking group on a consolidated basis, adequately monitoring and, as appropriate, applying prudential standards to all aspects of the business conducted by the banking group worldwide.
- ***Principle 13 – Home-host relationships*:** Home and host supervisors of cross-border banking groups share information and cooperate for effective supervision of the group and group entities, and effective handling of crisis situations. Supervisors require the local operations of foreign banks to be conducted to the same standards as those required of domestic banks.

Prudential Regulations and Requirements

- ***Principle 14 – Corporate governance*:** The supervisor determines that banks and banking groups have robust corporate governance policies and processes covering, for example, strategic direction, group and organisational structure, control environment, responsibilities of the banks' Boards and senior management, and compensation. These policies and processes are commensurate with the risk profile and systemic importance of the bank.
- ***Principle 15 – Risk management process*:** The supervisor determines that banks have a comprehensive risk management process (including effective Board and senior management oversight) to identify, measure, evaluate, monitor, report and control or mitigate all material risks on a timely basis and to assess the adequacy of their capital and liquidity in relation to their risk profile and market and macro-

economic conditions. This extends to development and review of contingency arrangements (including robust and credible recovery plans where warranted) that take into account the specific circumstances of the bank. The risk management process is commensurate with the risk profile and systemic importance of the bank.

- ***Principle 16 – Capital adequacy*:** The supervisor sets prudent and appropriate capital adequacy requirements for banks that reflect the risks undertaken by, and presented by, a bank in the context of the markets and macroeconomic conditions in which it operates. The supervisor defines the components of capital, bearing in mind their ability to absorb losses. At least for internationally active banks, capital requirements are not less than the applicable Basel standards.
- ***Principle 17 – Credit risk*:** The supervisor determines that banks have an adequate credit risk management process that takes into account their risk appetite, risk profile and market and macroeconomic conditions. This includes prudent policies and processes to identify, measure, evaluate, monitor, report and control or mitigate credit risk (including counterparty credit risk) on a timely basis. The full credit lifecycle is covered including credit underwriting, credit evaluation, and the ongoing management of the bank's loan and investment portfolios.
- ***Principle 18 – Problem assets, provisions and reserves*:** The supervisor determines that banks have adequate policies and processes for the early identification and management of problem assets, and the maintenance of adequate provisions and reserves.
- ***Principle 19 – Concentration risk and large exposure limits*:** The supervisor determines that banks have adequate policies and processes to identify, measure, evaluate, monitor, report and control or mitigate concentrations of risk on a timely basis. Supervisors set prudential limits to restrict bank exposures to single counterparties or groups of connected counterparties.
- ***Principle 20 – Transactions with related parties*:** In order to prevent abuses arising in transactions with related parties and to address the risk of conflict of interest, the supervisor requires banks to enter into any transactions with related parties on an arm's length basis; to monitor these transactions; to take appropriate steps to control or mitigate the risks; and to write off exposures to related parties in accordance with standard policies and processes.
- ***Principle 21 – Country and transfer risks*:** The supervisor determines that banks have adequate policies and processes to identify, measure, evaluate, monitor, report and control or mitigate country

risk and transfer risk in their international lending and investment activities on a timely basis.

- ***Principle 22 – Market risks***: The supervisor determines that banks have an adequate market risk management process that takes into account their risk appetite, risk profile, and market and macroeconomic conditions and the risk of a significant deterioration in market liquidity. This includes prudent policies and processes to identify, measure, evaluate, monitor, report and control or mitigate market risks on a timely basis.
- ***Principle 23 – Interest rate risk in the banking book***: The supervisor determines that banks have adequate systems to identify, measure, evaluate, monitor, report and control or mitigate interest rate risk in the banking book on a timely basis. These systems take into account the bank's risk appetite, risk profile and market and macroeconomic conditions.
- ***Principle 24 – Liquidity risk***: The supervisor sets prudent and appropriate liquidity requirements (which can include either quantitative or qualitative requirements or both) for banks that reflect the liquidity needs of the bank. The supervisor determines that banks have a strategy that enables prudent management of liquidity risk and compliance with liquidity requirements. The strategy takes into account the bank's risk profile as well as market and macroeconomic conditions and includes prudent policies and processes, consistent with the bank's risk appetite, to identify, measure, evaluate, monitor, report and control or mitigate liquidity risk over an appropriate set of time horizons. At least for internationally active banks, liquidity requirements are not lower than the applicable Basel standards.
- ***Principle 25 – Operational risk***: The supervisor determines that banks have an adequate operational risk management framework that takes into account their risk appetite, risk profile and market and macroeconomic conditions. This includes prudent policies and processes to identify, assess, evaluate, monitor, report and control or mitigate operational risk on a timely basis.
- ***Principle 26 – Internal control and audit***: The supervisor determines that banks have adequate internal control frameworks to establish and maintain a properly controlled operating environment for the conduct of their business taking into account their risk profile. These include clear arrangements for delegating authority and responsibility; separation of the functions that involve committing the bank, paying away its funds, and accounting for its assets and liabilities; reconcili-

ation of these processes; safeguarding the bank's assets; and appropriate independent internal audit and compliance functions to test adherence to these controls as well as applicable laws and regulations.

- ***Principle 27 – Financial reporting and external audit:*** The supervisor determines that banks and banking groups maintain adequate and reliable records, prepare financial statements in accordance with accounting policies and practices that are widely accepted internationally and annually publish information that fairly reflects their financial condition and performance and bears an independent external auditor's opinion. The supervisor also determines that banks and parent companies of banking groups have adequate governance and oversight of the external audit function.
- ***Principle 28 – Disclosure and transparency:*** The supervisor determines that banks and banking groups regularly publish information on a consolidated and, where appropriate, solo basis that is easily accessible and fairly reflects their financial condition, performance, risk exposures, risk management strategies and corporate governance policies and processes.
- ***Principle 29 – Abuse of financial services:*** The supervisor determines that banks have adequate policies and processes, including strict customer due diligence rules to promote high ethical and professional standards in the financial sector and prevent the bank from being used, intentionally or unintentionally, for criminal activities.

CHAPTER 2

Shadow Banking (Non-Bank Financial Intermediation)

Shadow banking, in essence, is composed of non-bank financial intermediation that historically has operated outside the traditional banking system but lacks the protections afforded to traditional or regular banks, and also avoids onerous statutory and regulatory obligations. In traditional banking intermediation, banks receive deposits from depositors which then are used to fund loans to borrowers. Owing to the Federal Deposit Insurance Corporation (FDIC), the FED's discount window, and other governmental guarantees, there is relative safety attributable to the said deposits.

In shadow banking financial intermediation, particularly credit intermediation,[1] these guarantees were wanting, albeit it was believed that such intermediation was safe because of credit lines and tail-risk insurance in the form of wraps and guarantees invested by private lenders that included commercial banks and insurance companies. The forms of funding were by means of securitizations, such as mortgages, loans, and receivables, which were combined into securities and tranches and secured lending backed by mortgages and other assets. The financial downturn of 2007–2009 revealed the fault lines of the shadow banking system, as well as traditional banking, albeit depositors in the latter institutions were protected by enhanced $250,000 per account FDIC guarantees.

Although having a serious downturn during the financial crisis of 2007–2009, it is conservatively estimated that non-bank financial intermediation (other financial intermediaries (OFI)) grew to $75 trillion in 2014, having advanced by some $5 trillion from the prior year. OFI assets constituted 25 % of total global financial assets, half of banking system

Roy J. Girasa, *Shadow Banking*, DOI 10.1007/978-3-319-33026-6_2

assets, and 120 % of gross domestic product (GDP).[2] At the end of 2013, the national jurisdictions which held assets of non-bank financial intermediaries were mainly the USA (33 %); the euro area (34 %); the United Kingdom (UK) (12 %); and China (4 %).[3] The Financial Stability Board (FSB) divided the OFI into sub-sectors as of the end of 2013 as follows:

- Other Investment Funds had assets in excess of $24 trillion, which accounted for 38 % of Non-Bank Financial Intermediation assets in 2013. Equity Funds accounted for more than half of all the reported Other Investment Funds assets in 2013 amounting to $12.4 trillion, while Fixed Income Funds totaled $7.6 trillion (32 %), and $4.1 trillion (17 %) were held in Other Funds;
- Broker-dealers—$9.3 trillion or 12 % of OFI, mainly concentrated in the UK, USA, Japan, Canada, and South Korea;
- Structured finance vehicles—$5 trillion (8 %) held mainly in the USA and the UK;
- Finance companies, $4.1 trillion (6 %) and money market funds (MMFs)—-$3.8 trillion (6 %) mainly in the USA and the euro area; real estate investment funds and trusts (REITs); and trust company assets—$2 trillion (3 %);
- Hedge funds—$0.1 trillion (0.2 %); but the figure appears to be underestimated owing to the omission of off-shore holdings;

The shadow banking industry is extraordinarily complex. Its main components, which will be discussed here, are securitization, hedge funds, repurchase agreements (repos), MMFs, and insurance funds (Fig. 2.1).

2.1 Economic Mechanisms Motivating Shadow Banking

Much of the literature concerning shadow banking emanates from staff reports from the Federal Reserve Bank of New York (FRBNY), particularly those of Tobias Adrian, Adam Ashcraft, Zoltan Pozsar, and Hayley Boesky, the International Monetary Fund (IMF), and reports from other federal reserve banks. Discussion in this segment is based substantially upon these reports.[4] The motivating economic factors for the ascendancy of shadow banking, according to the authors mentioned, are as follows:[5]

- *Creation of safe assets through specialization.* Shadow banking intermediation, through use of chains of non-bank financial intermediaries,

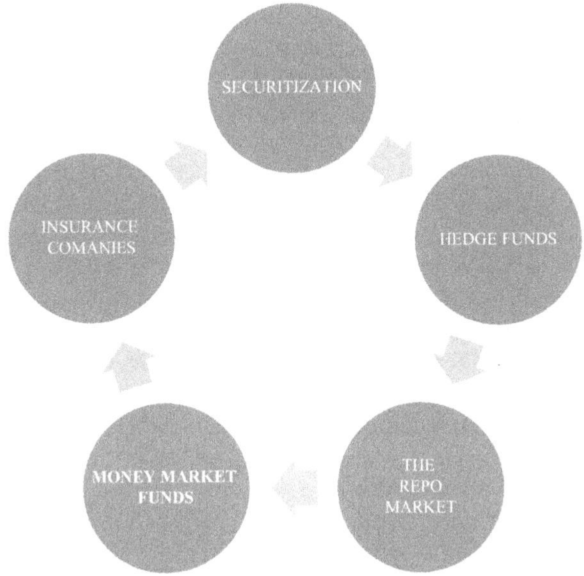

Fig. 2.1 Main components of shadow banking

transforms risky, long-term loans such as subprime mortgages into short-term, less risk, money-like instruments through a series of non-bank financial intermediaries rather than within the one institution as in traditional banking institutions.

- *Accommodation of cash-pools' demand for safe, short-term liquid assets.* Need for safe-short-term liquid assets substantially exceeds the assets provided by short-term government debt, which are often accompanied by higher return.[6]
- *Collateral intermediation.* Intensive reuse of scarce collateral to support a larger volume of financial transactions.[7]
- *Mispriced guarantees from government backstops.* By definition, unlike the traditional banking sector, credit intermediation is without guarantees such as deposit insurance and other, mainly government, intervention programs. Thus, shadow banking is amenable to credit runs by investors, although it does have access to credit lines from commercial banks. There was a distortion of pricing of shadow banking activities owing to government backstops under the auspices of banking holding companies, which indirectly supported shadow banking activities.

- *Regulatory arbitrage.* Defined as restructuring of financial activity aimed at avoiding taxes, disclosure, and/or capital requirement, it increases net cash flows to the sponsor by lessening the costs of regulation. It can be accomplished by conducting business and by providing services outside the statutory and regulatory oversight by national regulators.
- *Agency problems.* There were informational frictions in the securitization of subprime mortgage credit such as the informational problems between lenders and originators; between lenders and investors; between servicers and borrowers; and other such gaps.
- *Transformation of funds through intermediation.* It is accomplished through *maturity transformation*, whereby short-term funds are invested in longer-term assets; *liquidity transformation*, whereby cash-like liabilities are used to buy harder-to-sell assets such as loans; leverage that uses techniques such as borrowing money to buy fixed assets to magnify the potential gains (or losses) on an investment; and *credit risk transfer*, where the risk of a borrower's default is transferred from the originator of the loan to another party.[8]
- *Short-term funding and runs.* The financial frictions that led to excessive risk-taking and significant credit losses occurred during the financial crisis, thereby illustrating the vulnerability to runs.[9]
- *Additional influences.* The rise of information costs; the relative use of credit funded by commercial paper (CP) versus bank-intermediated credit that reflects the advantages of avoiding bank regulations that require reserve and capital requirements; the rise of money market mutual funds (MMMFs) as a result of Regulation Q,[10] which placed ceilings on interest that banks could offer; and the implementation of Basel I in 1990 followed by Basel II and Basel III, which raised the capital requirements on most bank loans from 5 % to 8 %, and encouraged the rise of shadow banking by inducing more securitization.[11]

Staff members at the IMF similarly stated that the key drivers behind the growth of shadow banking are the tightening of regulation of commercial and investment banks, ample liquidity conditions, and demand by institutional investors. The authors noted, in their review of literature on shadow banking, that there was a need and a demand for private money to satisfy the investment needs of institutional cash investors which exceeded the supply of short-term government debt and insured deposits, and that the prevailing legal rules effectively subsidized the use of some derivatives and repo contracts.

Thus, according to one Discussion Note, the two main functions of shadow banking are securitization and collateral intermediation. The securitization function (discussed at length in Chap. 5) seeks to create long-term safe assets for savers by unbundling and repacking risks and tranching their cash flows to transfer credit risks, and also by creating short-term safe assets by using maturity transformation vehicles funded in short-term money markets. Its collateral intermediation function is served by reducing counterparty risk through secured funding, securities lending, and hedging, including over-the-counter derivatives.[12]

The two functions serve two common intermediation roles, namely: (1) in its *liability-side role*, by providing safe claims in securitization or by increasing the safety of claims in collateral transformation for agents in the financial system; and (2) in its *asset-side role*, by providing credit to borrowers that occurs when safe liabilities help to attract savings. There are important linkages with traditional commercial banks which are active in securitization chains, as well as the use of services of dealer banks which act primarily in intermediating collateral. The processes take place through securitization chains which transform risky assets into safe and liquid claims by tranching of claims and the use of puts from the main banking system and through collateral chains which use collateral to reduce counterparty risk between borrowers and lenders. The processes link ultimate savers, including short-term household and corporate savings and long-term household savings, through the asset management complex, and borrowers, who include corporations and households, as well as investors such as hedge funds.[13]

Whereas banks operated via a one-stop process transforming deposits by investors, mainly from households to business and consumer loans, the shadow credit intermediation process involves a series of steps or "vertical slicing," generally as follows:

- Loan origination—e.g., auto and mortgage loans by finance companies funded by CP (unsecured promissory notes with maturity up to 270 days) and by medium-term notes;
- Loan warehousing—by single and multi-seller conduits and funded through asset-backed commercial paper (ABCP);
- Asset-backed securities issuance (ABS)—securities that derive their value and income collateralized by a pool of assets and conducted by broker-dealers;

- ABS warehousing—inventory financing of loans to manufacturers and others backed by goods or commodities held in trust as collateral for the loans, facilitated through trading books and funded through repos, total return swaps, or hybrid and repo conduits;
- ABS CDO issuance—pooling and structuring of ABS into collateralized debt obligations (CDOs) which are structured asset-backed securities conducted by broker-dealers' syndicate desks;
- ABS intermediation—conducted by limited-purpose finance companies, structured investment vehicles (SIVs), securities arbitrage conduits, and credit hedge funds funded by repos, ABCP, bonds, and capital notes;
- Wholesale funding—funding of the above is by money market intermediaries (MMFs, direct money market investors, and others).[14]

Scholars at the FRBNY noted that there are three-subgroups of the shadow banking system, namely (1) the *government-sponsored* shadow banking subsystem; (2) the *internal* shadow banking subsystem; and (3) the *external* shadow banking subsystem. They suggested that the shadow banking system originated in the depths of the Great Depression of the 1930s with the creation of government-sponsored enterprises including the Federal Home Loan Bank (FHLB) system in 1932, the Federal National Mortgage Association (Fannie Mae) in 1938, the Government National Mortgage Association (Ginnie Mae) in 1968, and the Federal Home Loan Mortgage Association (Freddie Mac) in 1970. Acting like shadow banks, albeit backed by taxpayers, they originated the warehousing of loans and created the *originate-to-distribute* model of securitized credit intermediation. Unlike banks which are funded by deposits, these loans were funded through the capital market, which issued short-term and long-term agency debt securities. The securities were purchased by money market investors and fixed-income mutual funds.

The *internal* shadow banking subsystem emulated the government-sponsored shadow banking system, with banks expanding their horizons from funding and holding loans until maturity to shadow banking activities through holding companies sanctioned by the legal developments outlined previously. Through the vertical and horizontal slicing of credit intermediation, coupled with off-balance-sheet securitization and asset management techniques, the large banks were now able to increase profitability, this being permitted by greater use of capital which no longer had to be retained until maturity. The bank holding companies (BHCs) generally originated loans through the bank's subsidiaries; warehoused and accumulated loans managed through their broker-dealer subsidiaries with funding from wholesale funding markets and liquidity enhancements by the subsidiaries; securitized the loans and transferred them to special-purpose vehicles; and funded the safest tranches in off-balance ABS intermediaries managed through their asset-management subsidiaries.

The *external* shadow banking subsystem also involves origination, warehousing, and securitization, but much of the funding is from offshore financial centers. Thus, the authors suggested that the external system has the following elements: (1) the credit intermediation process consists of diversified broker-dealers; (2) the process also includes independent, non-bank specialist intermediaries; and (3) the credit puts are provided for by private credit-risk repositories.

Unlike banks with multiple BHCs, broker-dealers generally operate by outsourcing warehousing functions to BHCs or to independent multiseller conduits. Dealers run internal credit hedge funds, fund trading books, and fund repo conduits. The independent specialists-based credit intermediation process includes stand-alone and captive finance companies that engage in loan origination; independent multiseller conduits that are concerned with loan warehousing; limited-purpose finance companies; SIVs; and credit hedge funds that involve ABS intermediation. The model is based on an *originate-to-fund* model rather than an *originate-to-distribute* model of the government-sponsored shadow banking system and credit intermediation processes of BHCs and diversified broker-dealers (DBDs). The third category of private credit-risk repositories includes mortgage insurers, monoline insurers, diversified insurance companies, and credit hedge funds which provide tail-risk insurance (risk of asset or portfolio moving more than three standard deviations from the mean from its current price) for structure credit products.[15]

Shadow banking intermediation may take place utilizing all or some of the steps stated above, which is typical of the process that clearly is more complex than traditional and more "shadowy" of the intermediation process. It is anticipated that shadow banking will continue to grow as corporate lending migrates from traditional banking to the non-bank sector. Nevertheless, the IMF warns that shadow banking in the USA will pose greater risks to domestic financial stability than comparable banking in the euro area and the UK.[16]

2.2 Systemic Risks of Shadow Banking

Systemic risk, in this context, is a risk that in the event of distress potentially has the effect of causing serious financial consequences to other parts of the financial system. Other definitions include the following:

- Risk that originates within, or spreads through, the financial sector (e.g., owing to insufficient solvency or liquidity buffers in financial institutions), with the potential for severe adverse effects on financial intermediation and real output.[17]
- The potential that an event, action, or series of events or actions will have a widespread adverse effect on the financial system and, in consequence, on the economy.[18]

A central purpose of the Dodd-Frank Act is to prevent systemic risk to the entire financial system by entities that are "too big to fail." The designation was clearly aimed at the several banks which controlled a vast percentage of deposits, any of which could bring about the financial collapse of the global financial system without governmental intervention. The question arises whether and to what extent shadow banking poses systemic risks to the financial community both within the USA and abroad? One of the alleged problems generated by the collapse of Lehman Brothers was the tightening of credit standards and the tendency of banks to become much more risk averse. Risks were simply transformed from traditional banks to shadow banks, which found it profitable to assume the risks that traditional banks were no longer able or felt it desirable to pursue.

Regulators had paid little attention to shadow banks and, as a result, ***payday loans*** (generally, unsecured loans to individuals in advance of receipt of funds from employment repayable with interest), ***crowdfunding*** (financing of new projects by numerous individuals, usually accomplished through proposals from the Internet), securitized products, money market funds, and repurchase agreements became the province of shadow banking. Firms such as Blackstone, Cerberus Capital Management, and Avenue Capital stepped in to provide the capital for smaller companies.[19]

The alleged problem with shadow banking is that, while some commentators such as Bill Winters, formerly of JP Morgan Chase and head of Renshaw Bay, a shadow banking company, believe that the rise of shadow banking is healthy for the economy, other commentators, for instance Professor Steven Schwarcz of Duke University, bemoaned the fact that

Dodd-Frank focused on traditional banks and essentially ignored shadow banking. Schwarcz recommends the removal of protection of the limited liability of managers of shadow banking firms, which creates moral hazard. According to this view, managers who do not have "skin in the game" are more likely to take risks that expose their firms to market failure. Most shadow banking firms are owned and operated by investor-managers who may profit extraordinarily from high-risk exposure but have little to lose because of limited liability exemptions.[20] Similarly, Professor Richard Carnell of Fordham University believes that any confidence in shadow banking is misplaced.[21]

Federal Reserve Bank Governor Daniel K. Tarullo, in testimony before the Senate Committee on Banking, Housing, and Urban Affairs, noted that although much attention was devoted to strengthening the regulation of banks after the crisis of 2007–2009, a major element of the financial crisis was the precipitous unwinding of large sums of short-term wholesale funding to financial firms outside the traditional banking sector. The risks concern not just a few small non-bank financial firms but also systemic classes of such firms and vulnerabilities intrinsic to short-term funding markets.[22]

2.2.1 Recommendations to Lessen Systemic Risk

The FSB suggested that systemic risk can arise from the interconnectedness between the banking sector and the shadow banking entities, both directly and indirectly. Shadow banking entities may be directly owned by banks or benefit directly or indirectly from them as part of the bank's intermediation chain. There may be funding interdependence, for example, through the holding of assets, such as debt securities of each other's assets. There may be indirect interdependence and risk exposure as a result of investments in similar assets or exposure to common counterparties.[23] Among the FSB recommendations to lessen risks of the shadow banking sector are the following:

- Establish a system-wide monitoring framework—assess global trends and risks;
- Strengthen the oversight and regulation of shadow banking as follows:
  - Mitigate risks in banks' interactions with shadow banking entities—reduce risks from shadow banking to core banking system;

- The Basel Committee on Banking Supervision has made a series of policy recommendations to strengthen the reliance of banks by providing guidance for prudential regulatory purposes to limit regulatory arbitrage opportunities;[24] proposed a supervisory framework for measuring and controlling large exposures; and introduced a more internationally consistent and risk-sensitive capital treatment for banks' investment in equity of funds.

  - Reduce susceptibility of MMFs to "runs";

- IOSCO developed recommendations of common standards to the regulation and management of MMFs among the global jurisdictions.[25] They include requirements such as that the funds be converted into floating net asset value (NAV) where feasible.

  - Improve transparency and align incentives in securitization;

- FSB is in accord with IOSCO's recommendations that reforms be implemented, especially those relating to retention requirements and measures that enhance transparency and standardization of securitization products.

  - Dampen procyclicality and other financial stability risks in securities financing transactions;

- Reduce risks associated with shadow banking's heavy dependence on short-term wholesale funding that entails risks from maturity and liquidity transformation; and

  - Assess and mitigate systemic risks posed by other shadow banking entities and activities as follows:

- Assessment based on economic functions or activities;
- Adoption of policy tools; and
- Information-sharing process.[26]

Federal Reserve Governor Daniel K. Tarullo suggested to the Senate Committee mentioned above the following recommendations of needed reforms:

- The need to increase the transparency of shadow banking markets to enable regulators to monitor signs of excessive leverage and unstable maturity transformation outside regulated banks, especially transactions organized around an exchange of cash and securities, where gaps still exist;
- The need to reduce further the risk of runs on MMMFs;
- The need to be sure that initiatives to enhance the resilience of the tri-party repo market are successfully completed.[27]

Scholars at the IMF suggested that there were three pressing needs for regulating risks of shadow banking:

- Develop a comprehensive regulatory approach to dealer banks. The authors noted that the dealer banks' business model is inherently fragile because it combines high leverage, procyclical businesses, and unstable, uninsured wholesale funding. While all 14 major banks are systemically important financial institutions (SIFIs), nevertheless they had access to central bank liquidity facilities because of their relationship with commercial banks, even though the depository portion of the banks was as low as 5 %. While offering stability, moral hazard is created because dealers can shift risky assets to the bank's subsidiary. Dealer banks have greater incentives to increase risks than commercial banks because of their lesser regulatory and supervision. The authors suggest a comprehensive framework for regulating broker-dealers comparable to that of banks;
- Progress on MMFs. MMFs are systemic and fragile, as evidenced by the latest financial crisis, which demonstrated that in times of stress asset values drop, thereby requiring governmental intervention. Among possible courses of action to lessen systemic risk are the introduction of capital requirements; requiring a floating NAV (already accomplished in the USA); and using two-class claims on assets, one redeemable at par and the other contingent on the NAV;
- Progress on the tri-party repo market. Heavy reliance on the two private clearing banks (Bank of New York and JP Morgan) creates systemic risks which are not solved by limited the duration of intraday exposures and improving collateral management. The authors suggested that more study is needed.[28]

In addition, the IMF authors noted that a major reason for the rise of shadow banking was due to the demand for safe, short-term liquid assets larger than those provided by short-term government debt. The mismatch created incentives to generate private safe securities which could become unstable and pose systemic risk. Other scholars suggested that the mismatch be addressed by having the government periodically expand the money supply of safe, short-term liquid instruments to lessen the reliance on the shadow banking system. The authors, however, believed that while governmental intervention does address systemic risk, there may nevertheless be problems with and limitations to such action because of the need for government to depart from widely accepted minimal cost rules in debt management. In doing so, it may create moral hazard by reason of the private sector's expectations that government will accommodate its demand for specific types of assets and demand-side policies, and may implicitly subsidize banks' investments in market-based debt instruments.[29]

Thomas M. Hoenig, the Vice-Chairman of the FDIC, in a paper written together with Charles S. Morris, Vice President and Chief Economist of the Federal Reserve Bank of Kansas City, noted that shadow banking activities are engaged in by both commercial and investment banks, thereby blurring the formerly sharp distinction between both forms of banking. Through financial holding companies, banks have engaged in trading and ABS underwriting; that is, securities backed by loans, leases, auto loans, receivables, credit card debt but not mortgages. The added activities have exposed banks to market risk from trading and from having to roll over uninsured wholesale money market fund (MMF) risks.

It is hypothesized that large investment banks, by changing their business model from partnerships to corporate entities, have also expanded risk by adding leverage and by direct investments and loans that are now on their balance sheets. The largest financial companies, through shadow banking activities, are lending long term using short-term funds, thereby exposing them to the same type of risk that traditional banking possesses but without government backstops. According to the authors, bank subsidiaries are now exposed to MMF runs because banks provide credit lines for the ABCP backed by other financial assets that fund ABS through their subsidiaries such as off-balance-sheet conduits and SIVs; that is, a pool of investments earning a credit spread of moneys by taking on the risk between long-term structured products and short-term liabilities.[30]

The combination of traditional banking and non-bank activities have made bank governance less manageable because of their complexity, which necessitates understanding all the business lines and their interactions; the allocation and pricing of capital across the activities; reduction of transparency which reduces market discipline; supervision of a bank's operations and risk-management policies, including monitoring its financial condition, lending, operations, and overseeing high-frequency transactions such the thousands of daily trades necessitating continuous supervision; difficulty in pricing deposit insurance; and resolution of large, complex banks that becomes more difficult, thereby requiring more complex regulations.

The authors noted that there are six major activities of commercial, investment, and shadow banks, namely: (1) deposit taking and lending to individuals and businesses by commercial banks; (2) underwriting securities (stocks and bonds) and providing advisory services by investment banks; (3) asset and wealth management services for individuals and businesses; (4) dealing and market making in securities, repos, and over-the-counter derivatives; (5) brokerage services for retail, professional, and institutional investors as well as hedge funds; and (6) proprietary trading for the firms' own account and by owning hedge and private equity funds.

The authors then postulated that the first three categories are core banking services which have little in common with the remaining three categories and are difficult to assess, monitor, and control. Thus, they propose restricting the activities of banking organizations to their primary core services because: (1) they lack the ability to do trading; (2) securities inventory used to facilitate trading is difficult to distinguish from proprietary assets; and (3) hedge fund services often finance their services with so-called "free balances," which are highly instable. Additional restrictions that should be in place include limits on bank investments to loans and investment in investment-grade securities because of the complexity of other financial instruments and off balance sheets that ultimately put a bank's capital at risk.[31]

Moreover, the authors stated that merely reforming commercial and investment bank activities would increase the shift to shadow banking and its attendant risks. Therefore, shadow banking should also be reformed by MMMFs having floating net asset values rather than the fixed $1 NAV which the FED later adopted. The second recommended reform concerned the potential disruptions from repo financing of shadow banks. They suggested that the bankruptcy laws for repurchase agreement collateral revert to the pre-2005 rules which did not exempt mortgage-related assets for the law's automatic stay when a repo borrower defaulted on the repurchase agreement, except with respect to US government and agency securities, bank certificates of deposits, and bankers' acceptances.

The 2005 amendments to the Bankruptcy Code expanded the definition of repos to include mortgage loans, mortgage-related securities, and interest from them. As a result, repos, collateralized by mortgage-backed securities (MBSs);[32] collateralized mortgage obligations (CMOs);[33] commercial mortgage-backed securities ((CMBS)—mortgage-backed security based on commercial rather than residential mortgages); and CDOs backed by mortgage-related assets were exempt from the automatic stay that would have made them subject to the further orders of the bankruptcy court. The net result was the sharp increase in price volatility of subprime MBS when subprime defaults began reducing MBS income flows.[34]

Scholars at the American Enterprise Institute (AEI) dispute whether the Federal Reserve or the Council has the authority to regulate shadow banks. According to Peter J. Wallison of the AEI and former counsel to President Ronald Reagan, the Dodd-Frank Act does not give either entity explicit power to regulate shadow banking. Congress was concerned with large financial institutions that could pose prudential risk to the financial system and not with control of transactions with each other. They are carrying out the recommendations of the FSB particularly as they relate to MMMFs, which are the major source of short-term funding in the capital markets. The Council designated the same three US insurance firms (AIG, Prudential, and MetLife) that the FSB labeled as SIFIs. The FSB source of authority is contrary to statutory authority. Moreover, Title I of Dodd-Frank limits the Council's authority to firms if it determines that their material distress or activities could cause instability to the US financial system, but Title VIII of Dodd-Frank gives the Council authority to designate firms as systematically important. Such power may introduce moral hazards into the relationship between clearing houses and firms using their services. Title VIII does not set forth standards to be applied in making this designation.[35]

Scholars at the IMF warn that parts of the shadow banking system are fragile and can pose systemic risks, and presently commonly lack appropriate supervisions and regulation and procedures for safety net access and resolution. Among the pressing needs are the development of a comprehensive regulatory approach to dealer banks which combine high leverage, procyclical businesses, and unstable, uninsured wholesale funding. It urges progress on MMFs which remains systemic and fragile by offering on par guarantees that cannot be accomplished without government support in times of stress when asset values drop as well as progress on the tri-party market, particularly the heavy reliance by US major banks which creates systemic risk. It was noted that the complexity of shadow banking makes it more difficult to resolve problems in times of stress, as, for example, in contracts between multiple agents and restructuring household mortgages. Other problems include the mismatch between the supply and demand for safe assets, which then drives incentives to create private safe securities which can become unstable and pose systemic risk.[36] Thus, the IMF warned that the size of shadow banking poses potential financial stability risks especially as additional lending and expansive areas of growth occur.[37]

2.2.2 *Backstops for Shadow Banking*

Although shadow banking is defined as financial intermediation without backstops, the issue arises whether the definition is an accurate reflection of the true state of the alternative to traditional banking. It appears that irrespective of the Dodd-Frank Act, whose provisions state that no funds are to be awarded to non-banking facilities, nevertheless, because of the interconnectedness of traditional banking and shadow banking, governmental intervention and intermediation may be unavoidable. As noted by scholars at the NYFED, particularly after the demise of Lehman Brothers, the FED had to utilize its emergency lending facilities as a backstop to each of the functional steps in the shadow banking credit intermediation facilities. Thus, the FED's Commercial Paper Funding Facility (CPFF) was sourced as a backstop for the issuance of CP and ABCP to provide liquidity for business firms in the short-term funding markets.[38]

Other FED facilities tapped included the Term Asset-Backed Securities Loan Facility (TALF) for ABS issuance, which is a funding facility to assist market participants to meet the credit needs of households and small businesses by supporting the issuance of ABS collateralized by loans of various types to consumers and businesses of all sizes. Under TALF, the FRBNY lent up to $200 billion on a non-recourse basis to holders of certain AAA-rated ABS, backed by newly originated consumer and small business loans. The amount loaned was the market value of the ABS less a haircut,[39] and secured by the ABS. The US Treasury Department, under the Troubled Assets Relief Program (TARP) of the Emergency Economic Stabilization Act of 2008 also provided $20 billion of credit protection to the FRBNY in connection with the TALF.[40]

Additional facilities of the FRBNY used during the financial crisis were: Maiden Lane LLC, which used money loaned by it to facilitate the merger of JP Morgan Chase & Co. and Bear Stearns Companies Inc. by purchasing approximately $30 billion in assets from the mortgage desk at Bear Stearns; Maiden Lane II LLC by which ML II LLC was created to alleviate capital and liquidity pressures on American International Group Inc. (AIG) stemming from its securities lending program by purchasing $20.5 billion in residential mortgage-backed securities (RMBS) from several of AIG's US insurance subsidiaries; Maiden Lane III LLC was created to alleviate capital and liquidity pressures on AIG stemming from credit default swap (CDS) contracts written by AIG Financial Products Corp. (AIGFP); and Maiden Lane III LLC was created to alleviate capital and liquidity pressures on AIG stemming from CDS contracts written by AIGFP by purchasing $29.3 billion in multi-sector CDOs from certain AIGFP counterparties, enabling it to terminate the associated CDS. ML III LLC was CDOs from certain AIGFP counterparties, enabling AIGFP to terminate the associated CDS.[41]

There were additional facilities, mainly at the FRBNY, that sprang from the 2007–2009 crisis. The Primary Dealer Credit Facility (PDCF) was created in March 2008 to aid the functioning of financial markets as an overnight loan facility that provided funding to primary dealers in exchange for a specified range of eligible collateral.[42] The Money Market Investor Funding Facility (MMIFF) was instituted to provide liquidity to US money market investors. Under the MMIFF, the FRBNY provided senior secured funding to a series of special purpose vehicles to facilitate an industry-supported private-sector initiative to finance the purchase of eligible assets from eligible investors.[43]

The Asset-Backed Commercial Paper Money Market Mutual Fund Liquidity Facility (AMLF), administered by the Federal Reserve Bank of Boston, was instituted in response to the significant withdrawal of funds by investors from MMMFs during the financial crisis. It assisted MMMFs that held asset-backed CP to meet withdrawal demands by investors and to foster liquidity in the ABCP market. It was decided that, without the introduction of the Liquidity Facility, there would have been forced sales of ABCP which would have depressed the price of the ABCP and other short-term instruments, thereby leading to greater investor withdrawals and losses to MMMFs generally. Under the program, the FED provided non-recourse loans to US depository institutions, BHCs, broker-dealer subsidiaries of the BHCs, and related firms that were used to purchase eligible ABCP from MMMFs. Borrowers under the AMLF, therefore, served as conduits in providing liquidity to MMMFs, and the MMMFs were the primary beneficiaries of the AMLF.[44]

The FDIC's Temporary Liquidity Guarantee Program (TLGP) was also instituted in response to the financial crisis, seeking to alleviate market fears and to encourage lending. It did so by through two main components, namely: (1) the Transaction Account Guarantee Program (TAGP), an FDIC guarantee in full of non-interest-bearing transaction accounts; and (2) the Debt Guarantee Program (DGP), an FDIC guarantee of certain newly issued senior unsecured debt. The TAGP guaranteed in full all domestic non-interest-bearing transaction deposits, low-interest negotiable order of withdrawal accounts, and interest on lawyers trust accounts (IOLTAs) held at participating banks and thrifts through December 31, 2009. This brought stability and confidence to banks and their business customers by removing the risk of loss from deposit accounts commonly used to meet payroll and other business transaction purposes. The temporary coverage allowed institutions to retain these accounts and maintain the ability to make loans within their communities. It did so by guaranteeing through maturity the senior unsecured debt issued by a participating entity.[45] All of the above programs accomplished successively in whole or in large part their intentions, and have been terminated at an overall profit to the FED.

2.3 International Regulation: IOSCO

2.3.1 Nature of Risk and Regulation

IOSCO explored the nature of risk by stating the definitions, identification, and an analytical framework for assessing systemic risks.[46] It defined "systemic risk" as follows: "Risks, including potential emerging and systemic risks, in financial markets entities, infrastructures, products and activities, which may impact the ability of the securities regulator to meet its regulatory objectives as set out in relevant rules and regulations, regulatory objectives." It noted that the definition differed slightly from that of other governmental and non-governmental organizations in that its definition is not limited to sudden catastrophic events but may take the form of a more gradual erosion of market trust. The IMF/BIS/FSB (International Monetary Fund/Bank for International Settlements/Financial Stability Board) defined systemic risk as "the risk of disruption to financial services that is (i) caused by an impairment of all or parts of the financial system and (ii) has the potential to have serious negative consequences for the real economy."[47]

The complexities and factors identified by IOSCO that may contribute to the convergence of new risks are contractual complexity, proliferation, and exploitation of accounting "opportunities" affecting governance and bonus. Incentives, behavioral overconfidence, and governance inadequacies that lead to excessive risking; which, in turn, may lead to asset price bubbles, then to other macro/micro-distortions, followed by asset price collapse, the destruction of capital liquidity, and finally financial crisis.[48]

To determine whether risks are systemic, IOSCO first divided indicators of risk into macro- and micro-level indicators.

2.3.2 *Macro-Level Indicators of Systemic Risk*

- Financial stress as illustrated by financial stress indexes and deviations from long-term value of assets;
- Market imbalances as exemplified by market significantly above long-term average, strong inflows into an asset class, and levels of leverage at historical highs;

  Macro-economic data as shown by interest rate fluctuation; negative real interest rates connected to size of country liquidity abundant, risk-pricing will be blurred, credit-bubble indicator; price/earnings indicator of global markets; inflation; economic growth rates; flows of funds; changes to the money supply and credit growth; interbank lending; and asset purchase programs by central banks;

- Fiscal debt sustainability as demonstrated by sovereign debt; overall indebtedness of market participants, issuers or individuals in aggregate;
- Asset prices and spreads as illustrated by asset prices and spreads (credit, equity, and commodity markets; and
- Other indicators such as international capital flow and geopolitical environment.[49]

2.3.3 *Micro-Level Indicators of Systemic Risk*

- Size: relative size of the market impacted by the risk in terms of monetary value or transaction value; assets and flow indicators;
- Liquidity: liquidity in market indicators and dependence on specific liquidity on global/market liquidity indicators; credit market/bond market stability indicator; securitization and collateral indicators, for example, level on collateralization;

- Cross jurisdictional: claims and liabilities across other jurisdictional entities;
- Transparency: correlation between markets, products, and institutions correlator; counterparty concentration, exposure, and collateralization indicators; intra-financial system assets and liabilities indicators
- Substitutability and institution structure: scale of exposure to individual assets, markets, and institutions indicators; risk-neutral probability of default for each institution indicator; qualitative assessments of availability of alternatives/substitutes;
- Market integrity and efficiency: market manipulation indicator; broker/client indicators; insider trading indicator;
- Concentration: scale of exposure to individual assets, markets, and institutions indicators; risk-neutral probability of default for each institution indicator;
- Behavior: herding/flow of funds especially among the top five biggest products invested into or top five most aggressive firms and their most beneficial activities;
- Incentive structure: margining schedule/haircuts; trends of remuneration practices;
- Leverage: leverage and spread of moneys indicator;
- Regulation: proportion of unregulated transactions indicator; dark trading, non-listed exchange traded funds; existence and nature of under-regulated areas of markets; and
- Complexity: complexity indicator; portfolio penetration indicator; qualitative assessment of investor/market participant understanding of products in markets.[50]

IOSCO identified the factors to assess whether the risk identified is systemic. Many of the factors are identified as indicators above, with the first three stated being necessary for there to be systemic risk, while those remaining may exacerbate any of the first three. They are, in summary: size; interconnectedness; lack of substitutes/concentration; leverage; typology and structure of assets and liabilities; contagion; liquidity; transparency (or opacity); behavior; quality (level, gaps); and complexity.[51]

2.4 Conclusion

Shadow banking is designed to provide services comparable to those of traditional banking as well as engagement in a multitude of other functions, without extensive regulation by governmental entities such as the FED. Nevertheless, it is highly questionable, irrespective of Dodd-Frank prohibitions against the rescue of systemically important financial institutions by taxpayers, whether the government has any realistic alternative to provide monetary funding should a financial crisis occur that would seriously endanger the well-being of these institutions. It appears that the compromise alternative is to make certain that these institutions have systems in place that would negate the need for such funding should distress occur. Thus, regulatory arbitrage, which is a hallmark of shadow banking, is substantially limited by governmental intrusion into shadow banking, particularly by systemic-type institutions that meet the $50 billion threshold. The remaining chapters will contain a review of governmental intrusion that has and continues to occur in shadow banking.

Notes

1. According to Zoltan Pozsar, Tobias Adrian, Adam Ashcraft, and Hayley Boesky, *Shadow Banking*, FEDERAL RESERVE BANK OF NEW YORK STAFF REPORTS, No. 458 (July 2010, rev. Feb. 2012) at 4–5, http://www.scribd.com/doc/237269076/Pozsar-Adrian-Ashcraft-Boetsky-Shadow-Banking-Federal-Reserve-Bank-of-New-York-Staff-Reports-N-458-July-2010#scribd "Credit intermediation provides savers with information and risk economies of scale by reducing the costs involved in screening and monitoring borrowers and by facilitating investments in a more diverse loan portfolio. Credit intermediation involves credit, maturity, and liquidity transformation. Credit transformation refers to the enhancement of the credit quality of debt issued by the intermediary through the use of priority of claims.... Maturity transformation refers to the use of short-term deposits to fund long-term loans, which creates liquidity for the saver but exposes the intermediary to rollover and duration risks. Liquidity transformation refers to the use of liquid instruments to fund illiquid assets."
2. *Global Shadow Banking Monitoring Report 2014*, FINANCIAL STABILITY BOARD (Oct. 30, 2014) at 2–10, www.fsb.org/wp-content/uploads/r_141030.pdf?page_moved=1. The updated sum of $75 trillion is also noted by Simon Richards, *Bringing shadow banking out of the dark*, (Dec. 10, 2014), http://www.bobsguide.com/guide/news/2014/Dec/10/bringing-shadow-banking-out-of-the-....
3. *Id.* at 12.
4. Among the staff reports emanating from the Federal Reserve Bank of New York are the following: Zoltan Pozsar et al., *supra*, at note 1, Adrian, Tobias, *Dodd-Frank One Year On: Implications for Shadow Banking*, FEDERAL RESERVE BANK OF NEW YORK STAFF REPORT, no. 533 (Dec. 2011), https://www.google.com/?gws_rd=ssl#q=Adrian%2C+Tobias%2C+Dodd-Frank+One+Year+On:+Implications+for+Shadow+Banking%2C+Staff+Report%2C+Federal+Reserve+Bank+of+New+York%2C+No.+533+%28Dec.+2011%29%2C+.

Tobias Adrian, and Adam B. Ashcraft, *Shadow Banking Regulation*, FEDERAL RESERVE BANK OF NEW YORK STAFF REPORT, no. 559 (April 2012), https://search.yahoo.com/yhs/search?p=Adrian%2C+Tobias+and+Adam+B.+Ashcraft%2C+Shadow+Banking+Regulation%2C+Staff+Report%2C+Federal+Reserve+Bank+of+New+York%2C+No.+559+%28April+2012%29%2C&ei=UTF-8&hspart=mozilla&hsimp=yhs-001.

Tobias Adrian, and Adam B. Ashcraft, *Shadow Banking: A Review of the Literature*, FEDERAL RESERVE BANK OF NEW YORK STAFF REPORT, no. 580 (Oct. 2012), https://www.google.com/?gws_rd=ssl#q=Adrian%2C+Tobias+and+Ashcraft%2C+Shadow+Banking:+A+Review+of+the+Literature%2C+Staff+Report%2C+Federal+Reserve+Bank+of+New+York%2C+No.+580+%28Oct.+2012%29%2C+.

Tobias Adrian, Adam B. Ashcraft, and Nicola Corelli, *Shadow Banking Monitoring*, FEDERAL RESERVE BANK OF NEW YORK STAFF REPORT, no. 638 (Sept. 2013), http://www.newyorkfed.org/research/staff_reports/sr638.pdf.

Tobias Adrian, *Financial Stability Policies for Shadow Banking*, FEDERAL RESERVE BANK OF NEW YORK STAFF REPORT, no. 664 (Feb. 2014), https://www.google.com/?gws_rd=ssl#q=Adrian%2C+Tobias%2C+Financial+Stability+Policies+for+Shadow+Banking%2C+Staff+Report%2C+Federal+Reserve+Bank+of+New+York%2C+No.+664i, 28Feb.+2014%29%2C+.

5. Tobias Adrian, *Financial Stability Policies for Shadow Banking*, *id.*, citing Adrian and Adam B. Ashcraft, *id.*, and Tobias Adrian, Adam B. Ashcraft, and Nicola Cetorelli, *Shadow Banking Monitoring*, *id.*
6. Stijn Claessens, Zoltan Pozsar, Lev Ratnovski, and Mnmohan Singh, *Shadow Banking: Economics and Policy*, IMF STAFF DISCUSSION NOTE (Dec. 4, 2012), 25, https://search.yahoo.com/yhs/search?p=Stijn+Claessens%2C+Zoltan+Pozsar%2C+Lev+Ratnovski+and+Mnmohan+Singh%2C+Shadow+Banking%3A+Economics+and+Policy%2C+IMF+Staff+DiscU.S.sion+Note+%28Dec.+4%2C+2012%29%2C&ei=UTF-8&hspart=mozilla&hsimp=yhs-002.
7. *Id.* at 14.
8. Laura E. Kodres, *What is Shadow Banking?*, 50 INTERNATIONAL MONETARY FUND FINANCE AND DEVELOPMENT, No. 2 (June, 2013), http://www.imf.org/external/pubs/ft/fandd/2013/06/basics.htm.
9. *See* supra note 7 at 2–7.
10. U.S.C. Title 12, Part 217, which prohibited the payment of interest on demand deposits, was removed by the FED's Final Rule, Federal Register Vol.76, No. 137 (July 18, 2011), http://www.gpo.gov/fdsys/pkg/FR-2011-07-18/pdf/2011-17886.pdf.
11. John V. Duca, *What Drives the Shadow Banking System in the Short and Long Run?*, DALLASFED WORKING PAPER No. 1401 (Feb. 2014), https://search.yahoo.com/yhs/search?p=John+V.+Duca%2C+What+Drives+the+Shadow+Banking+System+in+the+Short+and+Long+Run%3F%2C+DallasFed+

Working+Paper+No.+1401+%28Feb.+2014%29%2C&ei=UTF-8&hspart=mozilla&hsimp=yhs-002.

12. Stijn Claessens, Zoltan Pozsar, Lev Ratnovski, and Manmohan Singh, *Shadow Banking: Economics and Policy*, IMF STAFF DISCU.S.SION NOTE, SDN/12/12 (Dec. 4, 2012), https://www.google.com/search?q=Stijn+Claessens,+Zoltan+Pozsar,+Lev+Ratnovski,+and+Manmohan+Singh,+Shadow+Banking%3A+Economics+and+Policy,+IMF+Staff+DiscU.S.sion+Note,+SDN%2F12%2F12+(Dec.+4,+2012),&rls=com.microsoft:en-U.S.&ie=UTF-8&oe=UTF-8&startIndex=&startPage=1&gws_rd=ssl.
13. *Id.* at 5–6, 19.
14. Zoltan Pozsar, Tobias Adrian, Adam Ashcraft, and Hayley Boesky, *Shadow Banking*, FEDERAL RESERVE BANK OF NEW YORK, ECONOMIC POLICY REVIEW (Dec. 2013), at 6–7, https://search.yahoo.com/yhs/search?p=Zoltan+Pozsar%2C+Tobias+Adrian%2C+Adam+Ashcraft%2C+and+Hayley+Boesky%2C+Shadow+Banking%2C+Federal+Reserve+Bank+of+New+York%2C+Economic+Policy+Review+%28Dec.+2013%29%2C+at+6-7.&ei=UTF-8&hspart=mozilla&hsimp=yhs-002.
15. *Id.* at 7–13.
16. *Risk Taking, Liquidity, and Shadow Banking: Curbing Excess While Promoting Growth*, (Oct. 2014), IMF GLOBAL FINANCIAL STABILITY REPORT (Oct. 2014), www.imf.org/external/pubs/ft/gfsr/2014/02/. It should be noted that staff reports from the FED, IMF, and other governmental and non-governmental agencies are the views of the authors and not necessarily those of the agencies themselves, albeit it appears that they also substantially reflect the views of the agencies.
17. Nicholas Blancher, Srobona Mitra, Hanan Morsy, Akira Otani, Tiago Severo, and Laura Valderrama, *Systemic Risk Monitoring* ("SysMo") Toolkit – A User Guide, IMF WORKING PAPER, WP/13/168 at 6, www.**imf**.org/external/pubs/ft/wp/2013/wp13168.pdf.
18. OICU-IOSCO, *Risk Identification and Assessment Methodologies for Securities Regulation*, at 7, IOSCOPD443.pdf.
19. www.federalreserve.gov/.../bcreg20121115a4.pd=.
20. Steven L. Schwarcz, The Governance Structure of Shadow Banking: Rethinking Assumptions About Limited Liability, 90 NOTRE DAME LAW REVIEW (forthcoming), http://scholarship.law.duke.edu/faculty_scholarship/3155. A summary of the article discussed at the HARVARD LAW SCHOOL FORUM ON CORPORATE GIVERNANCE AND FINANCIAL REGULATION may be found at http://blogs.law.harvard.edu/corpgov/2014/02/06/the-governance-structure-of-shadow-banking/.
21. Lauren LaCapra, and David Henry, *Analysis: Five years after Lehman, risk moves into the shadows*, REUTERS, (Sept. 12, 2013), *available at* www.reuters.com/article/2013/09/12/U.S.-lehman-fiveyear-analysis-idU.S.BRE98B0562....

22. Governor Daniel K. Tarullo, *Dodd-Frank Implementation*, Testimony before the Committee on Banking, Housing and Urban Affairs, U.S Senate, July 11, 2013, http://www.federalreserve.gov/newsevents/testimony/tarullo20130711a.htm.
23. Financial Stability Oversight Council, *Basis for the Financial Stability Oversight Council's Final Determination Regarding Metlife, Inc.*, at 21–23 (Dec. 18, 2014), http://www.treasury.gov/initiatives/Council/designations/Documents/MetLife%20Public%20Basis.pdf.
24. The Basel Committee on Banking Supervision is the global standard-setter for the prudential regulation of banks. It provides a forum for cooperation on banking supervisory matters and seeks to strengthen the regulation, supervision, and practices of banks worldwide. It is located at the Bank for International Settlements in Basel, Switzerland, and is staffed by experts from member countries, http://www.bis.org/bcbs/about.htm?m=3%7C14%7+C573.
25. The International Organization of Securities Commissions (IOSCO) is an international organization that is the international body that brings together the world's securities regulators. It develops, implements, and promotes adherence to internationally recognized standards for securities regulation. It works intensively with the G20 and the Financial Stability Board (FSB) on the global regulatory reform agenda, http://www.iosco.org/about/?subsection=about_iosco.
26. Financial Stability Board, *Strengthening Oversight and Regulation of Shadow Banking: An Overview of Policy Recommendations*, (Aug. 29, 2013), http://www.financialstabilityboard.org/wp-content/uploads/r_111027a.pdf?page_moved=1.
27. *See supra* note 20.
28. Claessens et al., IMF Note *supra*, note 6, at 24–25.
29. *Id.* at 26–27.
30. Thomas M. Hoenig and Charles S. Morris, *Restructuring the Banking System to Improve Safety and Soundness* (Dec. 2012), https://ideas.repec.org/h/wsi/wschap/9789814520294_0021.html.
31. *Id.* at 21–22.
32. Mortgage-backed securities (MBSs) are debt obligations that represent claims to the cash flows from pools of mortgage loans, most commonly on residential property. Mortgage loans are purchased from banks, mortgage companies, and other originators and then assembled into pools by a governmental, quasi-governmental, or private entity. The entity then issues securities that represent claims on the principal and interest payments made by borrowers on the loans in the pool, a process known as securitization. Most MBSs are issued by Ginnie Mae, Fannie Mae, and the Federal Home Loan Mortgage Corporation (Freddie Mac). Securities and Exchange Commissions, *Mortgage-Backed Securities*, http://www.sec.gov/answers/mortgagesecurities.htm.

33. Collateralized mortgage obligations (CMOs) are a type of mortgage-backed security that are bonds that represent claims to specific cash flows from large pools of home mortgages. The streams of principal and interest payments on the mortgages are distributed to the different classes of CMO interests, known as tranches, according to a complicated deal structure. Each tranche may have different principal balances, coupon rates, prepayment risks, and maturity dates (ranging from a few months to 20 years. Securities and Exchange Commission, *Collateralized Mortgage Obligations (CMOs)*, http://www.sec.gov/answers/tcmos.htm.
34. *Id.* at 26–29.
35. Peter J. Wallison, *The regulators' war on shadow banking*, (Jan.2015), AMERICAN ENTERPRISE INSTITUTE RESEARCH, www.aei.org/+publication/regulators-war-shadow-banking/.
36. Stijn Claessens, *supra*, note 13, at 23–25.
37. ABA Dodd-Frank Tracker, *IMF Calls for Greater Regulation of 'Shadow banking*, (Oct. 2, 2014), http://regreformtracker.aba.com/2014/10/imf-calls-for-greater-regulation-of.htm.
38. Pozsar, *supra*, at note 14, at 13.
39. A "haircut" reflects credit risk and, for traded assets, the historical volatility of the asset's price and the liquidity or illiquidity of the market in which the asset is traded; it is the difference between the market value of an asset that is used as collateral for a loan and amount of the loan. The Federal Reserve applies larger haircuts, and thus assigns lower lendable values, to assets for which no market price is available than to comparable assets for which a market price is available. Borrowers may be required to pledge additional collateral if their financial condition weakens. Collateral is pledged under the terms and conditions specified in the Federal Reserve Banks' standard lending agreement. Board of Governors of the Federal Reserve System, *Credit and Liquidity Programs and the Balance Sheet*, http://www.federalreserve.gov/monetarypolicy/bst_riskmanagement.htm.
40. *Id.*, and Board of Governors of the Federal Reserve System, *Term Asset-Backed Securities Loan Facility*, http://www.federalreserve.gov/monetarypolicy/talf.htm.
41. Federal Reserve Bank of New York, *Maiden Lane Transactions*, http://newyorkfed.org/markets/maidenlane.html#.
42. New York Federal Reserve System, *Primary Dealer Credit Facility*, http://www.newyorkfed.org/markets/pdcf.html.
43. Federal Reserve Bank of New York, *Money Market Investor Funding Facility*, http://www.federalreserve.gov/monetarypolicy/mmiff.htm.
44. New York Federal Reserve System, *Money Market Mutual Fund Liquidity Facility*, http://www.federalreserve.gov/newsevents/reform_amlf.htm.

45. Federal Deposit Insurance Corporation, *Temporary Liquidity Guarantee Program*, https://www.fdic.gov/regulations/resources/TLGP/index.html.
46. The comments hereinafter are from OICU-IOSCO, *Risk Identification and Assessment Methodologies for Securities Regulation* (June, 2014), http://hb.betterregulation.com/external/IOSCO%20Issues%20Report%20on%20Risk%20Identification%20and%20Assessment%20Methodologies%20-%2026%20Jun%2014.pdf.
47. BIS is the acronym for the Bank for International Settlements located in Basel, Switzerland, which was established on May 17, 1930 and, according to its website, is the world's oldest international financial organization. It is composed of 60 member central banks, representing countries that collectively constitutes 95 % of world GDP. The mission of the BIS is to serve central banks in their pursuit of monetary and financial stability, to foster international cooperation in those areas, and to act as a bank for central banks. Bank for International Settlements, *About BIS*, https://www.bis.org/about/index.htm.
48. *Id.*
49. *Id* at 27.
50. *Id. at* 28, citing Werner Bijerk, Rohni Tendulkar, Samad Uddin and Shane Werner, *Systemic Risk Identification in Securities Markets*, STAFF WORK PAPER (July 2012), https://search.yahoo.com/yhs/search?p=Werner+Bijerk%2C+Rohni+Tendulkar%2C+Samad+Uddin+and+Shane+Werner%2C+Systemic+Risk+Identification+in+Securities+Markets%2C+Staff+Working+Paper+%28July+2012%29.&ei=UTF-8&hspart=mozilla&hsimp=yhs-002.
51. *Id.* at 29–30.

Appendix 1: IOSCO Principles of Securities Regulation[52]

The 30 principles of securities regulation are based upon three objectives of securities regulation. These are:

- The protection of investors;
- Ensuring that markets are fair, efficient and transparent;
- The reduction of systemic risk.

The 30 principles need to be practically implemented under the relevant legal framework to achieve the objectives of regulation described above. The principles are grouped into Nine categories.

A. *Principles Relating to the Regulator*

1. The responsibilities of the Regulator should be clear and objectively stated.
2. The Regulator should be operationally independent and accountable in the exercise of its functions and powers.
3. The Regulator should have adequate powers, proper resources, and the capacity to perform its functions and exercise its powers.
4. The Regulator should adopt clear and consistent regulatory processes.
5. The staff of the Regulator should observe the highest professional standards, including appropriate standards of confidentiality.
6. The Regulator should have or contribute to a process to monitor, mitigate, and manage systemic risk, appropriate to its mandate.
7. The Regulator should have or contribute to a process to review the perimeter of regulation regularly.
8. The Regulator should seek to ensure that conflicts of interest and misalignment of incentives are avoided, eliminated, disclosed, or otherwise managed.

B. *Principles for Self-Regulation*

9. Where the regulatory system makes use of Self-Regulatory Organizations (SROs) that exercise some direct oversight responsibility for their respective areas of competence, such SROs should be subject to the oversight of the Regulator and should observe standards of fairness and confidentiality when exercising powers and delegated responsibilities.

C. *Principles for the Enforcement of Securities Regulation*

10. The Regulator should have comprehensive inspection, investigation, and surveillance powers.
11. The Regulator should have comprehensive enforcement powers.
12. The regulatory system should ensure an effective and credible use of inspection, investigation, surveillance, and enforcement powers, and implementation of an effective compliance program.

D. *Principles for Cooperation in Regulation*

13. The Regulator should have authority to share both public and non-public information with domestic and foreign counterparts.

14. Regulators should establish information-sharing mechanisms that set out when and how they will share both public and non-public information with their domestic and foreign counterparts.
15. The regulatory system should allow for assistance to be provided to foreign Regulators who need to make inquiries in the discharge of their functions and exercise of their powers.

E. *Principles for Issuers*

16. There should be full, accurate, and timely disclosure of financial results, risk, and other information which is material to investors' decisions.
17. Holders of securities in a company should be treated in a fair and equitable manner.
18. Accounting standards used by issuers to prepare financial statements should be of a high and internationally acceptable quality.

F. *Principles for Auditors, Credit Ratings Agencies, and other information service providers*

19. Auditors should be subject to adequate levels of oversight.
20. Auditors should be independent of the issuing entity that they audit.
21. Audit standards should be of a high and internationally acceptable quality.
22. Credit rating agencies should be subject to adequate levels of oversight. The regulatory system should ensure that credit rating agencies whose ratings are used for regulatory purposes are subject to registration and ongoing supervision.
23. Other entities that offer investors analytical or evaluative services should be subject to oversight and regulation appropriate to the impact their activities have on the market or the degree to which the regulatory system relies on them.

G. *Principles for Collective Investment Schemes*

24. The regulatory system should set standards for the eligibility, governance, organization, and operational conduct of those who wish to market or operate a collective investment scheme.
25. The regulatory system should provide for rules governing the legal form and structure of collective investment schemes and the segregation and protection of client assets.

26. Regulation should require disclosure, as set forth under the principles for issuers, which is necessary to evaluate the suitability of a collective investment scheme for a particular investor and the value of the investor's interest in the scheme.
27. Regulation should ensure that there is a proper and disclosed basis for asset valuation and the pricing and the redemption of units in a collective investment scheme.
28. Regulation should ensure that hedge funds and/or hedge funds' managers/advisers are subject to appropriate oversight.

H. *Principles for Market Intermediaries*

29. Regulation should provide for minimum entry standards for market intermediaries.
30. There should be initial and ongoing capital and other prudential requirements for market intermediaries that reflect the risks that the intermediaries undertake.
31. Market intermediaries should be required to establish an internal function that delivers compliance with standards for internal organization and operational conduct, with the aim of protecting the interests of clients and their assets and ensuring proper management of risk, through which management of the intermediary accepts primary responsibility for these matters.
32. There should be procedures for dealing with the failure of a market intermediary in order to minimize damage and loss to investors and to contain systemic risk.

I. *Principles for Secondary Markets*

33. The establishment of trading systems including securities exchanges should be subject to regulatory authorization and oversight.
34. There should be ongoing regulatory supervision of exchanges and trading systems, which should aim to ensure that the integrity of trading is maintained through fair and equitable rules that strike an appropriate balance between the demands of different market participants.
35. Regulation should promote transparency of trading.
36. Regulation should be designed to detect and deter manipulation and other unfair trading practices.

37. Regulation should aim to ensure the proper management of large exposures, default risk, and market disruption.
38. Securities settlement systems and central counterparties should be subject to regulatory and supervisory requirements that are designed to ensure that they are fair, effective, and efficient, and that they reduce systemic risk.

Notes

52. International Organization of Securities Commissions, *Objectives and Principles of Securities Regulation* (June, 2010).
53. IOSCO, supra, note 25.

Appendix 2: IOSCO Recommendations Concerning Risk Management[53]

Structure

1. *Integration into Existing Risk-Management Framework*

The identification, monitoring, mitigation, and appropriate management of systemic risk emerging from securities markets or affecting securities markets and the review of the regulatory perimeter should be integrated into securities regulators' risk-management frameworks through formalization of processes and arrangements including support by formal committee structures.

2. *Clear Responsibilities in relation to Systemic Risk*

Securities regulators should have a clear understanding of their responsibilities in:

- Identifying, monitoring, mitigating, and appropriately managing systemic risks related to securities markets; and
- Contributing to processes in relation to other financial markets.

This understanding should be based on a clear definition of systemic risk. It should also entail an understanding of securities regulators' responsibilities in relation to macro-prudential risks which may require consideration of and contributing to the identification and management of those risks.

3. *Clear Responsibilities in Relation to Reviewing the Regulatory Perimeter*

The responsibilities of the securities regulator in jurisdictional arrangements to review the regulatory perimeter should be clear. These arrangements should allow for identification of risks posed by unregulated products, markets, market participants, and activities.

Arrangements should consider the potential for regulatory arbitrage, which might emerge outside the securities regulators' mandate but may affect the discharge of its statutory functions (even where the securities regulator does not have the explicit power to intervene). In such instances, securities regulators should be able to raise awareness of issues or to pass them on to other relevant authorities within its jurisdiction to act. This action may include seeking to introduce requirements under its rule-making powers or seeking changes in legislation.

Systems/Processes

1. *General Arrangements*

Arrangements to identify, monitor, mitigate, and manage systemic risk and review the perimeter of regulation should:

(i) Entail a holistic and systematic analysis of entities, products, markets, market infrastructures, and activities across securities markets that could be the source of systemic risk or that could raise concerns about the regulatory perimeter. The analysis should use a combination of quantitative and qualitative tools;
(ii) Involve the systematic and robust analysis of accessible, reliable, and good-quality data (including micro- and macro-economic data and market intelligence) either collected by the securities regulator or sourced from other agencies or parties (including prudential supervisors);
(iii) Include mechanisms to assist in understanding the evolving functioning of securities markets;
(iv) Involve engagement with market participants to better understand emerging risks, systemic and otherwise. This engagement may take

the form of surveys, formal consultations, informal round tables, individual meetings, and other forms;

(v) Include documentation about the work performed in assessing potential systemic risks at each stage of the assessment process, and documentation about the status of steps taken to mitigate identified risks;

(vi) Allow for periodic reassessment of procedures and outcomes; and

(vii) Provide for policy and/or regulatory actions, where appropriate in the context of the regulatory mandate, based on the assessments conducted.

2. *Systemic Risk Arrangements*

These arrangements should, in addition to the general arrangements set out above:

(i) Provide a broad understanding of the financial markets environment in which securities regulators operate and on which assessments of systemic risk can be made. The understanding should have a global focus. It should also take into account the interconnections between different products, markets, market infrastructures, and activities across securities markets;

(ii) Complement reviews undertaken by prudential regulators, where appropriate, by incorporating analysis of the operation of securities markets and the interplay between various markets and participants; and

(iii) Include the development and use of indicators to calibrate systemic risk emerging from (or affecting) securities markets. The indicators should contain specific qualitative and quantitative criteria.

3. *Regulatory Perimeter Arrangements*

These arrangements should, in addition to the general arrangements set out above:

(i) Involve securities regulators systematically identifying, prioritizing, and determining the scale and scope of emerging risks from different entities, activities, markets, and products in financial markets that could serve as the basis for deciding whether and what type of regulatory action or intervention is warranted;

(ii) Build on existing risk identification frameworks by requiring securities regulators to proactively go beyond existing regulatory boundaries to identify potential risks; and
(iii) Recognize that different approaches may be required to discern and assess different types of risks; just as having a single perspective may not prove effective, having only one risk approach similarly may not suffice. For example, a different approach may be warranted for known risks that are being re-evaluated, as opposed to emerging risks being considered for the first time, particularly if they are emerging outside the regulatory perimeter.

Cooperation and Coordination

- *Intra-Jurisdictional Cooperation.* Systemic risk is a relevant concern to all financial regulators in a given jurisdiction. A strong information sharing framework should be in place between relevant regulators and supervisors. This information-sharing framework should cover the identification, monitoring, mitigating, and appropriate management of systemic risks. The framework should be supported by formal co-operation or institutional arrangements. Regulators should ensure they understand the specific mandate, role, and powers of other regulators in their jurisdiction to facilitate the effectiveness of the framework.
- *Cross Border Cooperation and Coordination.* Securities regulators should communicate information and data about identified systemic risk(s) with regulators in other jurisdictions, under established procedures or arrangements and/or supported by bilateral and/or multilateral agreements. IOSCO should consider developing multilateral arrangements on how such information and data could be shared. IOSCO should also explore how the identification, mitigation, monitoring, and appropriate management of systemic risk and reviews of the regulatory perimeter could be coordinated among its members.

Culture and Resourcing

- *Culture.* Securities regulators should seek to build an organizational culture that supports and serves as a foundation to processes in relation to systemic risk and reviewing of the regulatory perimeter. Securities regulators should seek to ensure awareness of their systemic risk and regulatory perimeter review arrangements and commitment to the effective and meaningful operation of such arrangements (including promotion of *professional skepticism*) as key elements of their organizational culture.

- *Resourcing.* To support the effectiveness of the risk arrangements outlined in these recommendations, the securities regulator should have appropriately skilled and adequate human and technical resources.

CHAPTER 3

Governance of Shadow (Non-Bank) Financial Institutions

The financial crisis that commenced in 2007, particularly in the banking sector, caused the US Congress to commence inquiries concerning the causes as well as the possible remedies, to lessen its impact upon the national economy and its inevitable impact upon the global economy. The crisis was brought about when banks and other home finance lenders granted mortgage loans to unqualified borrowers, which often totaled the entire cost of the home to be purchased and also the substantial closing costs. The security was the home, the price of which kept escalating significantly.

The mortgage note executed by the borrowers was payable at an adjustable rate of interest that often began at a so-called "teaser" rate, which was a deliberately priced lower rate to attract customers. The borrowers were often unqualified, barely able to pay the loan even if no additional expenses were added to their living expenses; but provided the rate remained constant and the borrowers kept their employment status, the new homeowners were able to make monthly payments. In theory, in the event the borrowers could no longer afford the home, they could simply resell it, often at a higher price from the one they had originally paid. Mortgage lenders were induced to grant such loans because they were able to charge exorbitant sums as closing costs, which included points (a "point" is 1 % of the mortgage sum) and other fees at the time of closing of title.

There was little or no risk to the lenders because they immediately packaged the loans into packages of loans called "tranches." Tranches of varying quality were then sold to unwitting buyers worldwide, including major

Roy J. Girasa, *Shadow Banking*, DOI 10.1007/978-3-319-33026-6_3

banks, who received relatively high rates of interest on money paid for the loans, believing they were among the safest secured investments. When the adjustable rates of interest rose, however, many borrowers could no longer pay their loans. When the borrowers defaulted, a downward financial death spiral commenced, leading to a total of 3.1 million mortgage foreclosure filings and 861,664 home foreclosures in 2008 alone.[1] The consequences of the loss of homes led to the collapse of banks engaged in mortgage financing, losses of jobs, whereby unemployment doubled to over 10 %, a tightening of credit that severely harmed businesses, and other financial consequences leading to US and global recession.

There were other causes of the recession that were uncovered, such as the credit rating agencies' gross carelessness or negligent rating of financial products as discussed in Chap. 2, and hedge funds and swap-related abuses that had to be addressed by legislation. The US Congress, through its respective finance committees in the Senate and the House of Representatives, commenced a series of hearings that brought about the Dodd-Frank Act over the unanimous political opposition of the Republican Party, even though many of its members contributed significantly to the almost 1000-page enactment. The focus herein is on its application to non-bank financial institutions.

3.1 The Dodd-Frank Act and Its Application

The Dodd-Frank Act is composed of 16 titles, most of which initially were to be separate enactments but for political expediency came under the umbrella of one Act, legally entitled:

> An Act to promote the financial stability of the United States by improving accountability and transparency in the financial system, to end "too big to fail," to protect the American taxpayer by ending bailouts, to protect consumers from abusive financial services practices, and for other purposes.

Its short title, according to the legislation, is the Dodd-Frank Wall Street Reform and Consumer Protection Act; it is better known as the Dodd-Frank Act, named after its US Senate and House of Representatives sponsors, Senator Christopher Dodd of Connecticut and Representative Barney Frank of Massachusetts, both of whom have now retired from their elected offices. The title divisions encompass a vast array of financial services and governmental supervision, including regulation of hedge funds, insurance, swap markets, securities investors' protection, consumer financial protection, and mortgage reform.

The discussion that follows is applicable to shadow banks, known as "non-bank financial companies," and derives from Title I, "Financial Stability," which is at the core of the Act, inspired by the significant downturn of the economy that commenced in 2007. An ostensible need for regulation arose in the sectors of the economy that were previously unregulated or minimally regulated except for criminal penalties for outright fraudulent activity. The financial crisis was due in part by the lack of regulatory authority or enforcement of existing regulations, particularly in the securities sector of the economy. As a result, the economy suffered grievously in a manner that was reminiscent of the Great Depression of the 1930s, and it also affected the global economy.

Lessons learned from the prior major financial crisis brought about major governmental financial intervention. Through the Troubled Asset Relief Program (TARP) initiated under the Presidency of George W. Bush in October 2008, and other governmental intervention in the Obama administration, the crisis abated. It was natural for Congress to inquire, as it did during the Great Depression, as to the causes of the financial crisis. After months of inquiry, both in the House of Representatives under the leadership of Congressman Barney Frank, who headed the House Financial Services Committee, and Senator Christopher Dodd, who led the Senate Committee on Banking, Housing, and Urban Affairs, the Dodd-Frank Act was enacted over the unanimous opposition of the Republican members of the Senate and House of Representatives, even though, as stated previously, many Republican members had contributed significantly to the provisions of the Act.

Among the promoters of the legislation was the vice-chairman of the Federal Reserve, Stanley Fischer, who noted that while there had been significant progress in financial stability since the last financial crisis (2007–2009), as evidenced by increasing bank capital and liquidity and the requirement that most derivative transactions go through organized exchange, nevertheless problems remained with the shadow banking system. He stated that 20 % of the financial system as measured by the size of assets was held by the banking system but 80 % was in non-banking. While some of the non-banking institutions were regulated, such as insurance companies, other firms were unregulated. He noted that the non-banking sector was a system that interacts with the banking system, which could cause significant harm if there was failure therein.[2]

3.1.1 Title I. Financial Stability and Application to Shadow Banks (Non-Bank Financial Companies)

The authority for the regulation of shadow banks (non-banks) is derived from §113 of the Dodd-Frank Act, "Authority to Require Supervision and Regulation of Certain Non-bank Financial Companies".[3] It states that US non-bank financial companies and certain foreign non-bank financial companies designated affirmatively by a two-thirds vote of voting members by the Board of Governors of the Federal Reserve System (Board) should be subject to prudential standards if the newly created Financial Stability Oversight Council (Council) determines that (1) material distress at the US non-bank financial company, or (2) based upon the nature, scope, size, scale, concentration, interconnectedness, or mix thereof of a non-bank financial company, could pose a threat to the financial stability of the USA.[4] In accordance with this authority, the Council issued a Final Rule and Interpretive Guidance which elaborated upon the statutory provisions and offers guidance to the affected companies.[5]

The word *company* is not defined in Title I; however, the Council, in its Final Rule, gives a broad interpretation "to include any corporation, limited liability company, partnership, business trust, association, or similar organization."[6] The Dodd-Frank Act defines a "non-bank financial company" as a:

- Company (other than a bank holding company, a Farm Credit System institution ... or a national securities exchange (or parent thereof);
- Clearing agency (or parent thereof unless the parent is a bank holding company);
- Security-based swap execution facility, or security-based swap data repository registered with the Commission; or a
- Board of trade designated as a contract market (or parent thereof); or a
- Derivatives clearing organization (or parent thereof unless the parent is a bank holding company), swap execution facility, or a swap data repository register with the Commodity Futures Trading Commission); that is
  - *Predominantly engaged* in financial activities [emphasis added]; and
  - Incorporated or organized under U.S. laws or any state thereof.[7]

A *significant non-bank financial company* is one that is any non-bank financial company supervised by the Federal Reserve Board (FRB) and any other non-bank financial company that had $50 billion or more in total consolidated assets at the end of its most recent fiscal year. A "foreign non-bank financial company" is one that is incorporated in a country other than the USA and is predominantly engaged in, including a branch in the USA, in financial activities.[8]

Predominantly engaged. A company is predominantly engaged in financial activities if:

1. The annual gross revenues derived by the company and all of its subsidiaries from activities that are financial in nature ... and, if applicable, from the ownership or control of one or more insured depository institutions, represents *85 percent* or more of the consolidated annual gross revenues of the company [emphasis added]; or
2. The consolidated assets of the company and all of its subsidiaries related to activities that are financial in nature and, if applicable, related to the ownership or control of one or more insured depository institutions, represents *85 percent* or more of the consolidated assets of the company [emphasis added].[9]

The 85 % threshold is a statutory requirement and cannot be modified by the Board. The regulations define "consolidated annual gross financial revenues" and "consolidated total financial assets" as that portion of the of the consolidated annual gross revenues or assets of the company using applicable accounting standards (US generally accepted accounting principles (GAAP), International Financial Reporting Standards (IFRS), or Council-designated accounting standards) that are derived by the company or subsidiaries from *financial activities* in the USA or by virtue of its ownership, control, or activities of an insured depositary institution.[10] "Financial activities" is extensively defined in the Regulations to include virtually any and all conceivable activities financial in scope. The major categories of financial activities with numerous subdivisions within each category are as follows:

- Lending, exchanging, transferring, investing for others, and safeguarding money or securities;
- Insurance activities;

- Issuing or selling instruments representing interests in pools of bank-permissible assets;
- Underwriting, dealing, and market making;
- Merchant banking;
- Insurance company portfolio investments;
- Lending, exchanging, transferring, investing for others, safeguarding financial assets other than money or securities, and other activities;
- Extending credit and servicing loans;
- Activities related to extending credit;
- Leasing;
- Operating non-bank depository institutions;
- Trust company functions;
- Financial and investment advisory activities;
- Agency transactional services for customer investments;
- Investment transactions as principal;
- Management consulting and counseling activities;
- Courier services and printing and selling Magnetic Ink Character Recognition encoded items;
- Owning shares of a securities exchange;
- Mutual fund administrative services;
- Insurance agency and underwriting;
- Community development activities;
- Money orders, savings bonds, and traveler's checks;
- Data processing;
- Certification services;
- Providing employments histories;
- Check-cashing and wire-transmissions services;
- Postage, vehicle registration, public transportation services;
- Real estate title abstracting;
- Management consulting services;
- Travel agency;
- Mutual funds activities; and
- Commercial banking activities.[11]

Many of the listings above have numerous subcategories that provide extensive elaboration. Thus. as illustrated, the definition of "financial activities" is all-encompassing, omitting a few categories such as goodwill and cash but not cash equivalents.

3.2 The Financial Stability Oversight Council

The Council was established pursuant to §111 of the Dodd-Frank Act. It is located within the US Department of the Treasury in the Office of Financial Stability within the Office of Domestic Finance. It is composed of ten voting members, who serve six-year terms, and five non-voting members, who serve two-year terms. The voting members are:

The Secretary of the Treasury, who serves as Chairperson of the Council;
The Chairperson of the Board of Governors;
The Comptroller of the Currency;
The Director of the Bureau;
The Chairman of the Securities and Exchange Commission;
The Chairperson of the Corporation;
The Chairperson of the Commodity Futures Trading Commission;
The Director of the Federal Housing Finance Agency;
The Chairman of the National Credit Union Administration Board; and
An independent member appointed by the President, by and with the advice and consent of the Senate, having insurance expertise.

The members who serve in an advisory capacity as non-voting members of the Council, are:

The Director of the Office of Financial Research;
The Director of the Federal Insurance Office;
A State insurance commissioner, to be designated by a selection process determined by the State insurance commissioners;
A State banking supervisor, to be designated by a selection process determined by the State banking supervisors; and
A State securities commissioner (or an officer performing like functions), to be designated by a selection process determined by such State securities commissioners.[12]

3.2.1 Voting by Council Members

Decisions generally require a majority affirmative vote by voting members, although most important determinations require a two-thirds vote with the affirmative vote of the Chairperson. Non-voting members participate in Council meetings, proceedings, discussions, and deliberations unless the Chairperson together with the affirmative vote by the voting members exclude the non-voting members when necessary to protect the free exchange and confidential supervisory information.[13]

3.2.2 *Purposes and Duties of the Council*

The Board of Governors is responsible for the supervision of the Council, to identify risks to US financial stability, promote market discipline, and to respond to threats to the stability of the US financial system.[14] With respect to non-bank financial institutions, the Act requires supervision "for non-bank companies that may post risks to the financial stability of the United States in the event of their material financial distress or failure…."[15] The Council is responsible for making recommendations concerning which non-bank financial companies are to be supervised by the Board of Governors and become subject to heightened prudential standards for risk-based capital and other financial instruments. If the Council is unable to make a recommendation, it may request the Board of Governors to conduct an examination of the US non-bank financial company and its subsidiaries to determine whether the company should come under its supervision.

The Dodd-Frank Act explicitly states that the purposes and duties of the Council are as follows:

Purposes

The purposes of the Council are:

- To identify risks to the financial stability of the U.S. that could arise from the material financial distress or failure, or ongoing activities, of large, interconnected bank holding companies or non-bank financial companies, or that could arise outside the financial services marketplace;
- To promote market discipline, by eliminating expectations on the part of shareholders, creditors, and counterparties of such companies that the Government will shield them from losses in the vent of failure; and
- To respond to emerging threats to the stability of the U.S. financial system.[16]

Duties
The duties of the Council are:

- Collect information from member agencies, other Federal and State financial regulatory agencies, the Federal Insurance Office and, if necessary to assess risks to the United States financial system, direct the Office of Financial Research to collect information from bank holding companies and non-bank financial companies;
- Provide direction to, and request data and analyses from, the Office of Financial Research to support the work of the Council;
- Monitor the financial services marketplace in order to identify potential threats to the financial stability of the United States;
- To monitor domestic and international financial regulatory proposals and developments, including insurance and accounting issues, and to advise Congress and make recommendations in such areas that will enhance the integrity, efficiency, competitiveness, and stability of the U.S. financial markets;
- Facilitate information sharing and coordination among the member agencies and other Federal and State agencies regarding domestic financial services policy development, rulemaking, examinations, reporting requirements, and enforcement actions;
- Recommend to the member agencies general supervisory priorities and principles reflecting the outcome of discussions among the member agencies;
- Identify gaps in regulation that could pose risks to the financial stability of the United States;
- Require supervision by the Board of Governors for non-bank financial companies that may pose risks to the financial stability of the United States in the event of their material financial distress or failure, or because of their activities pursuant to section 113;
- Make recommendations to the Board of Governors concerning the establishment of heightened prudential standards for risk-based capital, leverage, liquidity, contingent capital, resolution plans and credit exposure reports, concentration limits, enhanced public disclosures, and overall risk management for non-bank financial companies and large, interconnected bank holding companies supervised by the Board of Governors;

- Identify systemically important financial market utilities and payment, clearing, and settlement activities;
- Make recommendations to primary financial regulatory agencies to apply new or heightened standards and safeguards for financial activities or practices that could create or increase risks of significant liquidity, credit, or other problems spreading among bank holding companies, non-bank financial companies, and United States financial markets;
- Review and, as appropriate, may submit comments to the Commission and any standard-setting body with respect to an existing or proposed accounting principle, standard, or procedure;
- Provide a forum for –
  - Discussion and analysis of emerging market developments and financial regulatory issues; and resolution of jurisdictional disputes among the members of the Council; and
- Annually report to and testify before Congress on –
  - The activities of the Council;
  - Significant financial market and regulatory developments, including insurance and accounting regulations and standards, along with an assessment of those developments on the stability of the financial system;
  - Potential emerging threats to the financial stability of the United States;
  - All determinations made under section 113 (described below) of Title VIII, and the basis for such determinations;
  - All recommendations made under section 119 and the result of such recommendations; and
  - Recommendations – to enhance the integrity, efficiency, competitiveness, and stability of U.S. financial markets; to promote market discipline; and to maintain investor confidence.[17]

3.2.3 *Council Procedures Under Dodd-Frank Act*

Council Committee Structure

The Council has explicit authority to appoint special advisory, technical, or professional committees as needed to carry out its functions.[18] Thus, it acts through use of a committee structure to conduct the non-bank determination process.

- *Deputies Committee.* Composed of a senior official from each of the member committees, the Deputies Committee's major function is to coordinate and oversee the interagency work performed by the staff of the committees.
- *Systemic Risk Committee.* The Systemic Risk Committee and its two subcommittees, the Institutions Subcommittee and the Markets Subcommittee, have the responsibility of providing the structure for an analysis of threats to the financial stability of the USA that may emerge together with leveraging existing expertise and experience. It includes senior staff members whose duties include prioritizing sources of systemic risk and supervising the work of its subcommittees.
  - The *Institutions Subcommittee*'s function is to identify and analyze risk, including the identification of structural issues affecting financial stability, new financial products, and exposures to particular risks. It will also provide a forum for the sharing of information concerning systemic issues and other relevant issues;
  - The *Markets Subcommittee's* major function is similar to that of the Institutions Subcommittee, but concentrates on issues affecting financial stability including trends in volatility or liquidity, market structure, or asset valuations.
- *Designations of Non-bank Financial Companies Committee.* This is the committee most pertinent to our discussion. Its major function is to identify and designate non-bank financial companies that are to be supervised by the Federal Reserve System's Board of Governors. Much of its work is conducted by working groups, which provide forums where outside experts can discuss industry-related topics. Its most active working group has been the Insurance Working Group, which was responsible for analyzing and evaluating the largest insurance companies who were later named as SIFIs, namely AIG, GE Capital, Prudential, and MetLife. The Insurance Working Group performs the grunt work of preparing draft memoranda, periodic briefings, and updates to the Deputies Committee, which then reviews and makes recommendations to the Council. The Council then decides the appropriate action that should be taken.
- *Designations of Financial Market Utilities and Payment, Clearing, and Settlement Activities Committee.* This assists the Council in designating financial market utilities and payment, clearing, and settlement activities.

- *Heightened Prudential Standards Committee*: This aids the Council in making recommendations for heightened prudential standards by designated SIFIs with respect to designated and large, interconnected bank holding companies. Other functions include supporting the Council in its monitoring of current developments, recommending supervisory priorities and principles, and identifying gaps in regulation that could pose risks.
- *Orderly Liquidation Authority, Resolution Plans*: This committee assists the Council in the recommendations regarding resolution plan requirements, resolution plans, and rule-making.
- *Data*: The Data Committee collects and shares data particularly with the Office of Financial Research (OFR) and coordinates with the OFR on data standardization efforts.[19]

3.3 Considerations for Making SIFI Determinations

3.3.1 US Companies

§113(a)(2) of the Dodd-Frank Act states the factors that the Council is to consider in determining whether a US non-bank financial company is to be supervised by the Board of Governors of the Council:

> (A) The extent of the leverage of the company;
> (B) The extent and nature of the off-balance-sheet exposures of the company;
> (C) The extent and nature of the transactions and relationships of the company with other significant non-bank financial companies and significant bank holding companies;
> (D) The importance of the company as a source of credit for households, businesses, and State and local governments and as a source of liquidity for the United States financial system;
> (E) The importance of the company as a source of credit for low-income, minority, or underserved communities, and the impact that the failure of such company would have on the availability of credit in such communities;
> (F) The extent to which assets are managed rather than owned by the company, and the extent to which ownership of assets under management is diffuse;
> (G) The nature, scope, size, scale, concentration, interconnectedness, and mix of the activities of the company;

(H) The degree to which the company is already regulated by one or more primary financial regulatory agencies;
(I) The amount and nature of the financial assets of the company;
(J) The amount and types of the liabilities of the company, including the degree of reliance on short-term funding; and
(K) Any other risk-related factors that the Council deems appropriate.[20]

3.3.2 *Foreign Non-Bank Companies*

Included within the jurisdiction of the Board of Governors on a comparable two-thirds affirmative vote are foreign non-bank financial companies supervised by the Board. The considerations are virtually identical to those of US companies except that they relate to exposures and activities in the USA. Thus, (B) relates to US off-balance exposures; (D) only to US households, businesses, and state and local governments; (E) to underserved communities within the USA; and (J) liabilities used to fund activities and operations in the USA. With respect to (J) above, reference is made to the extent to which the company is subject to prudential standards on a consolidated basis in its home country that are administered and enforced by a comparable foreign supervisory authority.[21]

The extension of jurisdiction based on comparable voting and considerations applies also to any company organized in the USA or abroad that may pose a threat to the financial stability of the USA, including companies seeking to evade the application of the Act.[22]

Anti-Evasion Provisions

In anticipation that some non-bank financial companies may attempt to evade the provisions of the Act, the Council, either on its own initiative or at the request of the Board of Governors, may require that the financial activities of a company shall be supervised by the Board of Governors, subject to the Council's prudential standards, on a two-thirds vote including an affirmative vote of the Chairperson, if it determines that:

- Material financial distress related to, or the nature, scope, size, scale, concentration, interconnectedness, or mix of the financial activities conducted directly or indirectly by a company incorporated or organized in the U.S. or any state therein, or the financial activities in the U.S. of a company incorporated or organized in a country other than the U.S. would pose a threat to the financial stability of the U.S.;

- The company is organized or operates in such a manner as to avoid the application of the Act's provisions; and
- The said financial activities of the company shall be supervised by the Board of Governors and subject to prudential standards under the Act.[23]

"Financial Activities" Covered by the Act

The financial activities governed by the Act are defined in §4(k) of the Bank Holding Act of 1956.[24] They include:

- The ownership or control of one or more insured depository institutions, but excludes purely internal company financial activities;
- Lending, exchanging, transferring, investing for others, or safeguarding money or securities;
- Insuring, guaranteeing, or indemnifying against loss, harm, damage, illness, disability, or death, or providing and issuing annuities, and acting as principal, agent, or broker for purposes of the foregoing, in any State;
- Providing financial, investment, or economic advisory services, including advising an investment company;
- Issuing or selling instruments representing interests in pools of assets permissible for a bank to hold directly;
- Underwriting, dealing in, or making a market in securities;
- Engaging in any activity that the Board has determined, by order or regulation that is in effect on the date of the enactment of the Gramm Leach Bliley Act, to be so closely related to banking or managing or controlling banks as to be a proper incident thereto (subject to the same terms and conditions contained in such order or regulation, unless modified by the Board);
- Engaging, in the USA, in any activity that a bank holding company may engage in outside the USA;

3.3.3 Financial Data Collection

The Council works closely with the OFR for the acquisition of data to be utilized in its determinations. The OFR, other federal and state financial regulatory agencies, and the Federal Insurance Office are authorized to submit information to the Council. The Council may require the submission of periodic reports from any non-bank financial company or bank holding company being considered for a proposed or final determination to be submitted to the OFR, in order to assess whether the company poses a threat to the financial stability of the USA. Before requiring the submission of the reports, the Council is, to the greatest extent possible, to coordinate efforts with the other agencies or foreign authorities with respect to such submissions and rely on the information for its proposed or final determinations. All non-public reports are to remain confidential unless otherwise required by law.[25]

3.3.4 *The Office of Financial Research*

The OFR was a newly created office within the US Treasury Department under the Dodd-Frank Act, whose major function is to assist the Council in making a "systematically important financial institution" SIFI determination. Headed by a Director appointed by the President subject to Senate confirmation for a six-year term, it is composed of a Data Center, a Research and Analysis Center, and a Technology Center (the statute mandated only the first two). The OFR may require submission of periodic and other reports from any financial company to aid it in assessing whether a financial activity or financial market in which the company participates or which the company itself may pose a threat to the financial stability of the USA. If the financial company is regulated by another government agency, then the OFR is to coordinate with that domestic or foreign agency in collection and assessment.

The statutory duties of the Data Center are to collect, validate, maintain, and make available to the Council all data necessary to assist the Council in rendering a SIFI determination. The Research and Analysis Center is to develop and maintain independent analytical capabilities and computer resources in order to develop and maintain metrics and reporting systems for risks to the financial stability of the USA. Other duties include standardizing the types and formats of data reported and collected; developing tools for risk assessment and monitoring; and making available the results of its activities and assisting member agencies in determining the types and formats of data authorized by the Dodd-Frank Act to be collected by member agencies (Fig. 3.1).[26]

3.3.5 *Application of Determination Standards*

The Council's mandate is to determine whether a non-bank financial company may experience material distress that could pose a threat to the financial stability of the USA (First Determination Standard),[27]

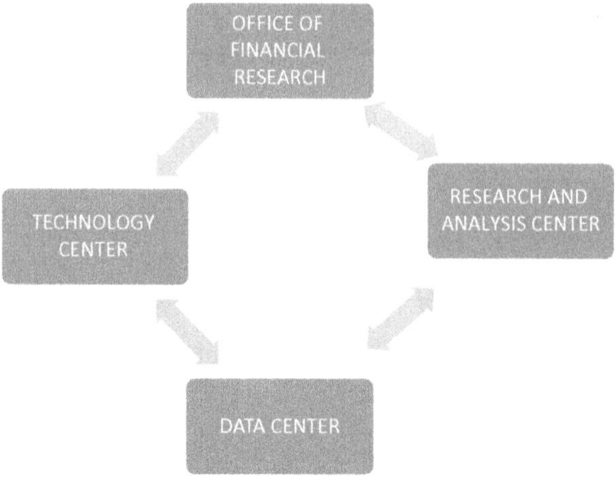

Fig. 3.1 Office of Financial Research

or whether the nature, size, scale, concentration, interconnectedness, or mix of the activities of the non-bank financial company could pose a threat to the financial stability of the USA (Second Determination Standard). The Final Rule defines the Council's meaning and application of these terms.

3.3.6 *Threat to the Financial Stability of the USA*

According to the Determination Standards of the Dodd-Frank Act, the Council was mandated to determine whether a threat to the stability to the financial stability of the USA exists that would be sufficiently severe to inflict significant damage on the broader economy. There are several identifiable channels through which such impairment may take place:

Exposure
The Council considers the extent to which a non-bank financial company's exposure to creditors, counterparties, investors, or other market participants is significant enough to materially impair them and thereby pose a threat to US financial stability. In its initial analysis of non-bank financial companies with respect to this channel, the Council considers the total consolidated assets, credit default swaps outstanding, derivative liabilities, total debt outstanding, and leverage ratio.

Asset Liquidation

The Council also considers whether the company under consideration holds assets that, if liquidated quickly, would cause asset prices to fall and thus significantly disrupt trading or funding in key markets or would cause significant losses or funding problems for other firms with similar holdings. The Council acknowledges that not all non-bank financial companies hold assets that are subject to such market disruption but just those financial companies whose funding and liquid asset profile rely heavily on short-term funding. The Council initially looks at total consolidated assets and short-term debt ratio.

Critical Function or Service

The Council looks into whether a non-bank financial company is no longer able or willing to provide a critical function or service that is relied upon by market participants and for which there are no ready substitutes. It reviews the company's competition for markets in which it participates and for the services it provides. Included among the considerations are the provision of liquidity to the US financial system; the provision of credit to low-income, minority, or underserved communities, or the provision of credit to households, businesses and state and local governments; the non-bank financial company's market share; and the ability of other firms to replace those services.

Other factors that the Council might consider a threat to the US financial system are whether the non-bank financial company is complex or opaque, and whether its bankruptcy would disrupt key markets or have a material adverse impact on other financial firms or markets. The Council can rely on other transmission channels through which the non-bank financial company may adversely affect other firms and pose a threat to the financial stability of the USA.[28]

Material Financial Distress

The First Determination Standard is that of *material financial distress*. The Council has the authority to subject a non-bank financial company to supervision by the Board of Governors and prudential standards if it determines that material financial distress at the non-bank financial company could pose a threat to US financial stability. Material financial distress is defined as when a non-bank financial company is in imminent danger of insolvency or defaulting on its financial obligations. In order to make the assessment, the Council examines how the firm will respond in the context of a period of overall stress in the financial services industry and in a weak macro-economic environment.

Nature, Scope, Size, Scale, Concentration, Interconnectedness, or Mix of Activities

The Second Determination Standard is based on the nature, scope, size, scale, concentration, interconnectedness, or mix of activities which may pose a threat to US financial stability. It does not matter whether the non-bank financial company is actually experiencing financial distress. The Council's determination is based on its judgment that a firm meets one of the statutory Determination Standards. The Dodd-Frank Act requires the Council to consider ten factors in its evaluation of whether a non-bank financial company may potentially pose a threat to US financial stability, as well as any other risk-related factors that the Council deems appropriate. Accordingly, the Council organized the ten factors into six categories: size, interconnectedness, substitutability, leverage, liquidity risk and maturity mismatch, and existing regulatory scrutiny.

3.3.7 Six-Category Analytic Framework

The Council's Final Rule states the Council's determination is to be based on one of the two Determination Standards. In order to make the determination, the Council utilizes a six-category analytic framework. Each of the six categories is applied using quantitative and qualitative data relevant to the six categories being applied to the company under investigation. Each of the six categories reflects the company's potential to pose a threat to US financial stability. The first three categories, size, substitutability, and interconnectedness, concern the Council's assessment of the potential impact of financial distress on the broader economy, in other words its ability to provide either critical financial services for which there are limited substitutes or that are so highly connected with other financial firms or markets that its distress could cause significant impact upon other companies, markets and consumers, thereby posing a threat to the financial stability of the USA. The remaining three categories, leverage, liquidity risk, and maturity mismatch, and existing regulatory scrutiny of the non-bank financial company assess the vulnerability of highly leveraged non-bank financial companies with a high degree of liquidity risk or maturity mismatch, and which without regulatory scrutiny are more likely to be more vulnerable to financial distress.[29]

Interconnectedness

A major concern for the Council is the direct or indirect linkages that a financial company has to other financial companies. This factor is important in determining whether material financial distress or activities of a non-bank financial company will cause adverse direct or indirect exposures to counterparties, including creditors, trading and derivatives counterparties, investors, borrowers, and other participants in the financial markets, so as to pose a threat to the US financial system. Among the considerations are:

- Counterparties' exposure to a non-bank financial company, including derivatives, reinsurance, loans, securities borrowing and lending, and lines of credit that facilitate settlement and clearing activities;
- Number, size, and financial strength of a non-bank financial company's counterparties, including the proportion of its counterparties' exposure to the non-bank financial company, relative to the counterparties' and the proportion of the counterparties' exposure to the non-bank financial company, relative to the counterparties' capital;
- Identity of a non-bank financial company's counterparties, reflecting the concentration of the non-bank financial company's assets financed by particular firms and the importance of the non-bank financial company's counterparties to the market;
- Aggregate amounts of a non-bank financial company's gross or net derivatives exposures and the number of derivatives counterparties;
- The number of gross notional credit default swaps outstanding for which a non-bank financial company or its parent is the reference entity;
- Total debt outstanding, which captures a non-bank financial company's source of funding;
- Reinsurance obligations, which measure the reinsurance risk assumed from non-affiliates net of retrocession.

Substitutability

Substitutability captures the extent to which other firms could provide similar financial services in a timely manner at a similar price and quantity if a non-bank financial company withdraws from a particular market. It also captures situations in which a non-bank financial company is the primary or dominant provider of services in a market that the Council determines to be essential to US financial stability. The evaluation includes the company's market share of the product or service under assessment; and the ability, costs, and timeframe for competitors to expand to meet the market's needs especially in times of distress. Metrics that will be used to assess substitutability include:

- Market share using a quantitative measure, such as loans originated, loans outstanding, and notional transaction volume, of the company and its competitors in the market under competition;
- The stability of market share across the firms in the market over time;
- The market share of the company and its competitors for products or services that serve a similar economic function to the primary market under consideration.

Size

Size refers to the number of financial services or amount of financial intermediation that the non-bank financial company provides. Size may also concern how the effects of the company's financial distress are transmitted to other firms, especially where they are highly interconnected. Although generally measured by the company's assets, liabilities, and capital, the Council also takes into account off-balance-sheet assets and liabilities, numbers of customers and counterparties, and their unique and distinct nature. Metrics that may be used include the firm's:

- Total consolidated assets or liabilities;
- Total risk-weighted assets;
- Off-balance-sheet exposures where a non-bank has a risk of loss, for example, lines of credit;
- Extent to which assets are managed rather than owned by the firm and the extent of their diffusion;
- Direct written premiums of insurance companies under all lines of business;
- Risk in force, in other words the aggregate risk exposure from risk underwritten in insurance related to certain financial risks, such as mortgage insurance;
- Total originations, by loan type, in number and dollar amounts.

Leverage

Leverage is the risk factor that looks at a company's exposure or risk in relation to its equity capital. Risk of financial distress may come about by

(1) increasing a company's exposure relative to capital, making it more likely that its losses will exceed its capital; and (2) by increasing the company's liabilities, when leverage may lead to the company's dependence on its creditors' willingness to fund its balance sheet. The company's distress may cause it to increase the size of its asset liquidation, and its distress may spread to other firms by increasing their exposure to the company. Metrics that can be used to assess leverage include:

- Total assets and total debt measured relative to total equity;
- Gross notional exposure of derivatives and off-balance-sheet obligations relative to total equity or to net assets under management;
- The ratio of risk to statutory capital;
- Changes in leverage ratios.

Liquidity Risk and Maturity Mismatch

Liquidity risk refers to the risk that a company may not have sufficient funding to satisfy its short-term needs, either through its cash flows, maturing assets, or assets saleable at prices equivalent to book value, or through its ability to access funding markets. The Council may examine the company's assets to determine if it possesses in times of distress cash instruments or readily marketable securities such as Treasury securities which may be easily redeemed. It may also examine whether the company has adequate long-term funding or can otherwise mitigate liquidity risk.

Maturity mismatch refers to the difference between maturities of a company's assets and liabilities. This mismatch may affect the company's ability to survive stress, which may be limited by its inability to have readily available funding or to withstand shocks in the yield curve. A company relying on short-term funding to finance long-term positions may find itself compelled to sell assets at low market prices or suffer significant market pressure. With respect to life insurance (relevant to the MetLife case discussed in Chap. 7), liabilities may have maturities of 30 years or more, whereas the market availability of equivalently long-term assets may be limited, exposing the company to interest rate fluctuations and reinvestment risk. Metrics that may be used by the Council to assess these risks include:

- Fraction of assets that are classified as level 2 and 3 under applicable accounting standards as a measure of how much of a non-bank financial company's balance sheet is composed of hard-to-value and potentially illiquid securities;

- Liquid asset rations which indicate the company's ability to repay short-term debt;
- Ratio of unencumbered and highly liquid assets to the net cash outflows that the company would incur in a short-term scenario;
- Callable debt as a fraction of total debt;
- Asset-backed financing versus other funding;
- Asset-liability duration and gap analysis;
- Short-term debt as a percentage of total debt and as a percentage of total assets.

Existing Regulatory Scrutiny

The Council will consider the extent to which non-bank financial companies are already subject to regulation, including the consistency of the regulation across non-bank financial companies within a sector, and providing similar services and the statutory of those regulators. The metrics that may be used by the Council are:

- The extent of state or federal regulatory scrutiny, including the processes or systems for peer review; interregulatory coordination and cooperation; and whether existing regulators have the ability to impose detailed and timely reporting obligations, capital and liquidity requirements and enforcement actions; and to resolve the company;
- Existence and effectiveness of consolidated supervision, and a determination of whether and how non-regulated entities and groups within a non-bank financial company are supervised on a group-wide basis. For entities based outside the USA, the Council will consider the extent to which a non-bank financial company is subject to prudential standards on a consolidated basis that are administered and enforced by a comparable foreign supervisory authority in its home country.

3.3.8 Council's Three Stage Process to Determine SIFI Designation

According to the Council's Final Rule,[30] the Council will follow a three-stage process that becomes increasingly more vigorous to arrive at whether the company is to be designated as a SIFI.

Stage 1

The first stage is based on available public and regulatory quantitative and qualitative data using quantitative metrics, together with qualitative analysis, to arrive at a Proposed Determination. The Stage 1 thresholds applicable to non-bank financial companies are quantitative in nature, to wit, the size, interconnectedness, leverage, liquidity risk, and maturity mismatch. The Council will conduct an additional review in Stage 2 if the company meets both the size threshold and any one of the other stated thresholds. The thresholds are as follows:

- $50 billion in *total* consolidated assets (same threshold sum under Dodd-Frank Act for subjecting bank holding companies to enhanced prudential standards);
- $30 billion in gross notional credit default swaps outstanding for which a non-bank financial company is the reference entity; As defined in the Final Rule, *gross notional value* equals the sum of credit default swaps contracts (CDS) bought or equivalently sold. CDS refers to credit derivative contracts whereby a buyer of the swap makes periodic payments to the seller of the contract up until the maturity of the contract, and if the underlying debt is in default, the seller agrees to be responsible for the payment thereof;
- $3.5 billion of derivatives liabilities; *derivatives liabilities* equal the fair value of derivative contracts in a negative position. According to the Final Rule, for non-bank financial companies that disclose the effects of master netting agreements and cash collateral held with the same counterparty on a net basis, the Council intends to calculate derivative liabilities after taking into account the effects of these arrangements. The threshold is used in connection with the determination of the extent of interconnectedness and higher counterparty exposure throughout the financial system.
- Total debt outstanding of $20 billion. The debt includes secured and unsecured loans; bonds, repurchase agreements; commercial paper; securities lending arrangements; surplus notes (for insurance companies); and other forms of indebtedness. It is also an indication of interconnectedness with the broader financial system which holds a large proportion of the debt. Had this threshold been applied during the financial crisis of 2007–2009, it would have exposed the material financial distress of Bear Stearns, Countrywide, and Lehman Brothers.

- Leverage ratio of 15:1 of total consolidated assets, excluding separate accounts to total equity. The exception of excluded separate accounts was due to the fact that they were not available to general creditors of a non-bank financial company. As for the total debt outstanding, this threshold would also have captured major financial companies experiencing financial distress; and
- Short-term debt ratio of 10 % of total debt outstanding with a maturity of less than 12 months in total consolidated assets, excluding separate accounts. Similarly, the threshold would have captured the material financial distress of financial firms as stated on the prior two thresholds.

The thresholds are subject to revision at least every five years. If a non-bank financial company meets the thresholds, then the Council proceeds to Stage 2 for the company's consideration and evaluation. The Council reserves the right to evaluate a company based on firm-specific qualitative or quantitative factors even where the thresholds are not met, if it believes that the firm may pose a systemic threat to US financial stability. The Council will use GAAP if information is available in determining the thresholds or other standards and principles if the data is not available. Furthermore, it will make the threshold determination, based on the most recent available data, of global assets, liabilities, and operations of the company and its subsidiaries. For foreign non-bank financial companies, the Stage 1 thresholds will be based solely on US assets, liabilities, and operations of the company and its subsidiaries. Based on this analysis, the Council intends to contact those non-bank financial companies that the Council believes merit further evaluation in Stage 3 (the "Stage 3 Pool").

Stage 2

Where one of the Determination Standards has been met for qualification as a SIFI, the Council proceeds to Stage Two wherein it conducts what it terms a "robust analysis" of the potential threat that each of the non-bank financial companies could pose to the US financial system. It evaluates the risk profile and characteristics of each of the companies in the Stage 2 pool based on a wide range of quantitative and qualitative industry-specific and company-specific factors. It uses a six-category analytic framework (discussed below) and prioritize the non-bank financial companies. In addition, the Stage 2 evaluation includes a review, based on available data, of qualitative factors, including whether the resolution of a non-bank financial company could pose a threat to US financial stability, and the extent to which the non-bank financial company is subject to regulation. Thereafter, a consultation process may take place with the appropriate primary financial regulatory agencies or home country supervisor of each subsidiary of the company. After data has been received from sources such as the OFR and from the company's primary financial regulatory agencies, it may then request submission of reports from the company.

Stage 3

In Stage 3, the Council, in consultation with the OFR,[31] makes an evaluation of all of the information received in the first two Stages as well as from public and regulatory sources and from the company under consideration. The review focuses on whether the non-bank financial company could pose a threat to US financial stability because of the company's material financial distress or the nature, scope, size, scale, concentration, interconnectedness, or mix of activities of the company. If the non-bank financial company has been selected for additional review in Stage 3, it is sent a Notice of Consideration, which generally includes a request for more information from the company as well as affording the company to submit such other documents that it deems relevant to the Council's determination (Fig. 3.2).

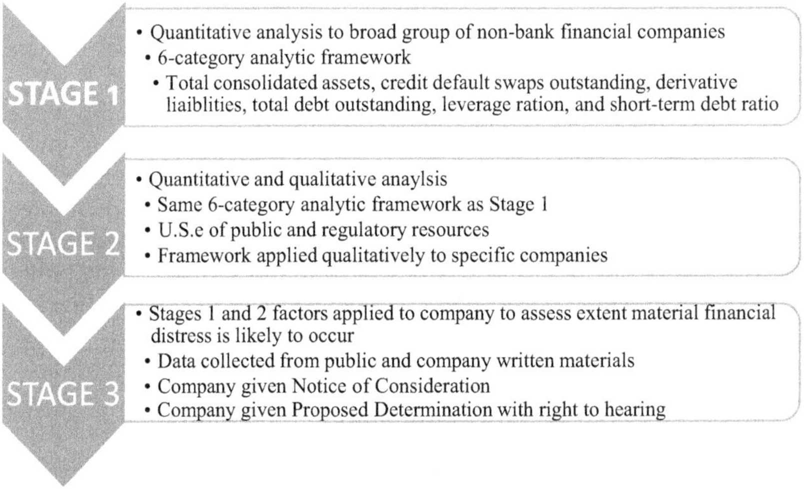

Fig. 3.2 Council three-stage evaluation process

Before requiring the submission of reports from any non-bank financial company that is regulated by a member agency or any primary financial regulatory agency, the Council, acting through the OFR, will coordinate with such agencies (see below). The type of information requested is likely to be quantitative and qualitative and may include confidential business information such as internal assessments, internal risk-management procedures, funding details, counterparty exposure or position data, strategic plans, resolvability, potential acquisitions or dispositions, and other anticipated changes to the company's business or structure that could pose a threat to the financial stability of the USA. All submitted data is kept confidential.

In making its evaluation during Stage 3, the Council examines additional factors that may not be readily quantifiable but yet can pose a danger to US financial stability or mitigate against such danger. They may include whether the company is already subject to significant regulatory scrutiny or whether its operations and complexity are obscure. Stage 3 analysis includes an examination of the firm's resolvability, which may mitigate or aggravate the potential of a non-bank financial company to pose a threat to US financial stability. The analysis entails an assessment of the complexity of the non-bank financial company's legal, funding, and operational structure, and any obstacles to the rapid and orderly resolution of the non-bank financial company in a manner that would mitigate the risk that the non-bank financial company's failure would have a material adverse effect on financial stability.

Other factors for examination are the firm's legal entity and cross-border operations; the ability to separate functions and spin off services or business lines; the likelihood of preserving franchise value in a recovery; maintaining continuity of critical services within the legal entity; the firm's intra-group dependency for liquidity and funding; payment operation, risk-management needs; and the size and nature of the firm's intra-group transactions. The Council understands that the information needed to conduct an in-depth analysis may vary significantly and is dependent on the type of firm and information available from governmental and public sources. For foreign non-bank financial companies, the Council is likely to consult with foreign regulatory authorities.

3.3.9 *Proposed Determination Procedures*

The non-bank financial company will be considered for a Proposed Determination after completion of the three stages stated above. The Council reviews the documentation and, after the review, the Council, by a vote of two-thirds of its members including an affirmative vote of the Council Chairperson, may make a Proposed Determination to designate the company as a SIFI. It then transmits the Proposed Determination to the affected company, including an explanation of the basis for its Proposed Determination. Before providing the company with this, it advises the firm that this is its intention, so as to afford the company an opportunity to submit written materials to the Council to contest the consideration. The materials address the company's view concerning whether material financial distress or the nature, size, scale, concentration, interconnectedness, or mix of its activities could pose a threat to the financial stability of the USA. The notice is to be given at least 30 days before making the consideration.[32]

If the Council determines that the firm is not a SIFI, then it shall notify it either before or after the Proposed Determination, reserving the right to conduct such an examination at a later date. Once a Proposed Determination is made, the company may request a hearing in writing within 30 days of receipt of the Proposed Determination. If the company requests a hearing in accordance with the procedures set forth in §1310.21(c) of the Council's rule, the Council will set a time and place for such a hearing. After this hearing, the Council considers all categories, metrics, thresholds, and channels to make a final assessment .[33] It then determines by a vote of two-thirds of the voting members (including the affirmative vote of the Chairperson) whether to subject the company to supervision by the Board of Governors and prudential standards.

If the non-bank financial company makes a timely request for an evidentiary hearing, then the Council is to provide it with written notice of its final determination a maximum of 60 days after the termination of the hearing, including an explanation of the basis for its decision. If a timely request for a hearing is not given, the Council is to provide the company with a Final Determination and the written basis for its decision a maximum of ten days after the date when the hearing would have taken place and at least one business day before publicly announcing the Final Determination.[34] A non-bank financial company that is subject to a Final Determination may bring an action up to 30 days after receipt of the Final Determination in the US district court in the area where the company's home office is located or in the District of Columbia federal district court, for an order requiring that the Final Determination be rescinded. The standard of review is that the Final Determination was arbitrary and capricious.[35]

The statute provides for an emergency exception whereby the Council may waive or modify the above notice requirements if it determines after a two-thirds vote including the affirmative vote of the Chairperson that such waiver or modification is necessary or appropriate to prevent or mitigate threats posed by the non-bank financial company to the financial stability of the USA.[36] The Council is to provide written notice to the company of the waiver or modification as soon as practicable, but not more than 24 hours later. The company may then transmit a request for an evidentiary hearing. The Council is to consult with the primary financial US regulatory agency, or home country supervisor if a foreign entity is involved, at a time and in a manner it deems appropriate. The affected company has ten days after receipt of the notice to request a hearing in writing, which is to be honored by the Council not more than 15 days thereafter. The Council then has 30 days in which to make a Final Determination, notify the company of the waiver or modification, and then make public its decision.[37]

3.3.10 Re-Evaluation and Rescission

The Council may rescind any determination by a two-thirds vote of the Council and affirmative vote of the Chairperson if it determines that the non-bank financial company no longer comes within the standards that caused it to be named an SIFI. The evaluation is to be made at least annually. The Council provides the appropriate notice to the company of its pending determination, so as to afford the company time to resend written materials, generally within 30 days or such other (increased) time that the Council may determine. The affected company may thus contest the prior or pending determination with written materials concerning whether it continues to pose a threat to the financial stability of the USA. Included in the materials are whether material financial distress or the nature, scope, size, scale, concentration, interconnectedness, or mix thereof could pose such a threat.[38]

3.3.11 Backup Examination of the Board of Governors

The Dodd-Frank Act provides that if the Council is unable to determine whether the financial activities of a US non-bank financial company poses a threat to the financial stability of the USA based on reports of the OFR, member agencies, and the Federal Insurance Office, or based upon reports of any non-bank financial company assessing the extent to which a financial activity or financial market in which the company participates, the

Council may request the Board of Governors to conduct an examination of the company to determine whether it should be supervised by the Board as a SIFI. The Council then reviews the results of the said investigation in connection with any proposed or final determination.[39]

3.3.12 *Additional Regulatory Oversight and Compliance*

Additional compliance-related issues include those dealt with by the Office of Foreign Assets Control of the US Department of the Treasury (OFAC) [40] which administers and enforces economic and trade sanctions based on US foreign policy and national security goals against targeted foreign countries and regimes, terrorists, international narcotics traffickers, those engaged in activities related to the proliferation of weapons of mass destruction, and other threats to the national security, foreign policy or economy of the USA. OFAC acts under Presidential national emergency powers, as well as authority granted by specific legislation to impose controls on transactions and freeze assets under US jurisdiction. Many of the sanctions are based on United Nations and other international mandates, are multilateral in scope, and involve close cooperation with allied governments.

3.4 The GE Capital Corporation SIFI Designation

The application of enhanced prudential standards to General Electric Capital Corporation Inc. (GECC) when the Council determined the company should be designated as a SIFI presents the issue of whether such standards were excessive.. Whether the result will cause other designated firms to arrive at similar conclusions awaits future determination.

3.4.1 *SIFI Determination*

On July 8, 2013, the Council issued a Final Determination that material financial distress at GECC could pose a threat to the financial stability of the USA, and thus should be subject to enhanced prudential standards and supervision by the Board of Governors of the Federal Reserve System. The proposed determination was forwarded to GECC on June 3, 2013, which decided on June 28, 2013 not to contest the determination.[41] The Council noted that GECC is a significant participant in the global economy and is interconnected to financial intermediaries through its financing activities and its funding model. As a wholly owned subsidiary of the General Electric Company, it is a savings and loan holding company and one of the largest holding companies in the USA with total assets of $539 billion at the end of 2012. In that year it had outstanding credit to over 243,000 commercial customers, 201,000 small businesses, and to 57 million consumers in the USA. Its total liabilities were $457 billion, composed of $3 billion of commercial paper; $9 billion of other short-term borrowings; $44 billion of current long-term debt; $225 billion of long-term unsecured debt; $30 billion of non-recourse asset-backed securities and collateralized holdings; and $46 billion of worldwide deposit.

The Council alleged that GECC was interconnected with large financial institutions through its activities in wholesale short-term funding markets and was a significant issuer of commercial paper in the USA. Its global connection with large banks and large non-bank financial companies was due to the latter's purchase of GECC commercial paper and long-term debt and the provision of backup lines of credit. Money market mutual funds and asset managers were also interconnected with GECC through purchases of commercial paper. SIFI determination was warranted, according to the Council, because a material financial distress at GECC could trigger a run on money market funds that could lead to a broader withdrawal of investments from the commercial paper market and other short-term funding markets.

GECC also possessed a large portfolio of on-balance-sheet assets comparable to those of the largest US bank holding companies. A sudden inability to access funding markets could lead to a rapid liquidation of assets which would then drive down asset prices and cause significant balance-sheet losses for other large firms and thereby cause severe stress on the overall economy. Other considerations included GECC's credit to a wide range of middle-market companies that are major components of the economy and that 52 % of GECC's assets and 43 % of its revenues were generated outside the USA, so that material distress at the company could cause adverse effects in domestic and global economies alike.[42]

3.4.2 *Application and Order of Enhanced Prudential Standards and Reporting Requirements*

As a result of the Final Determination, the FED issued a notice in the Federal Register on December 3, 2014 requesting comment on the Application of Enhanced Prudential Standards and Reporting Requirements to GECC together with the proposed Order.[43] This Order set forth eight standards that required compliance. Commencing July 1, 2015, GECC had to comply as follows:

- *Capital Requirements*: The Board's capital framework to be structured as if it were a bank holding company, that is an "advance Approaches Board-regulated institution" and a "covered bank holding company";
- *Capital Planning*: The Board's capital plan rule as a non-bank financial company to be supervised by the Board with submission of the capital plan cycle on January 1, 2016;
- *Stress Testing*: compliance with stress testing requirements beginning on January 1, 2017;
- *Liquidity Requirements*: Commencing July 1, 2015, compliance with liquidity standards as though it were a bank holding company with $50 billion or more in total consolidated assets;
  - Compliance with the liquidity coverage ratio as per regulations; and
  - Compliance with the Board's supervisory guidance on principles of sound liquidity risk management;
- *Risk Management*:
  - Maintain a board of directors that has the greater of 25 % or two directors independent of management;
  - Ensure that the chair of the risk committee is among the independent directors; and
  - Comply with the Board's existing risk-management guidance and supervisory expectations applicable to non-bank financial companies supervised by the Board;
- *Restrictions on Intercompany Transactions*: Commencing July 1, 2015, all transactions between GECC or any of its subsidiaries and GE or any of its subsidiaries were to be subject to requirements of the Federal Reserve Act as if it were a "member bank" and GE as if it were an "affiliate";
- *Future Standards*: The Board reserved the right to impose additional enhanced prudential standards to GECC in the future.[44]

3.4.3 GECC'S Initial Response to SIFI Designation and Order

Initially, two detailed comments were sent by letter to Robert deV. Frierson, secretary of the Board of Governors, opposing the decision to designate GECC as a SIFI, both forwarded on February 2, 2015. The first letter was from the 16 "independent directors" of GE in opposition to the Board's requirement that GECC's Board of Directors be reconstituted to include two new outside directors independent not only of GE's Board but also of its independent directors ("independent/independent"). The Order would undermine their authority as independent directors and disrupt decision-making necessary for the complex governing of GE Capital. They stated that the GE Board was committed to satisfying GECC's heightened obligations as a SIFI, but emphasized that the Board had already established a Risk Committee to foster best-in-class enterprise risk management and corporate governance practices.

This action had been taken in 2011 immediately after the enactment of the Dodd-Frank Act. GECC's Risk Committee was composed of four independent directors with extensive experience in financial services and risk management, including the former chairperson of the Securities and Exchange Commission (SEC), Mary Shapiro. The Risk Committee met formally 20 times and in multiple other informal meetings in 2014 to review GECC's risk-management policies as well as its capital, resolution, and recovery plans. The directors further emphasized that requiring "independent/independent" directors would fragment GECC's board and hinder the management of its enterprise risks. The fragmentation of the Board would, in their opinion, be counterproductive and lead to weak corporate governance, blurring the lines of accountability and collaboration necessary. As an alternative, if the Board adhered to its demand, the letter suggested that a majority of GECC's Board of Directors should be independent of management and chaired by one its independent directors.[45]

The Chairman of the Board and CEO of GE Capital, Keith S. Sherin, made a separate 57-page response to the Proposed Designation dated February 2, 2015. This was coupled with annexes containing opinion letters from a Delaware law firm (GECC and GE are Delaware corporations); a commentary by the former Delaware Chancellor William B. Chandler III; and from Jonathan R. Macey, Professor of Law of the Yale Law School. The comments of the independent directors of GECC regarding "independent/independent" directors were repeated, together with a number of other comments in opposition to the Board's Proposed Designation and Order. The arguments may be summarized as follows:

- The requirement to add "independent/independent" directors to the GECC Board was inconsistent with settled principles of corporate law; exceeded the Federal Reserve's authority under Dodd-Frank §165; and was counterproductive in light of the company's robust governance structure;
  - Delaware corporate law provided for the fiduciary duties owed by directors of a wholly owned subsidiary such as GECC;
  - The independent/independent director requirement unequivocally conflicted with governing state law;
  - By displacing settled principles of state corporate law through federal legislation, without any indication in the statutory text or legislative history of §165 that the Federal Reserve was authorized to do so, the independent/independent director requirement exceeded the Federal Reserve's authority under well-established legal principles;
  - The independent/independent director requirement was inconsistent with the Federal Reserve's own regulatory practices and those of other US financial regulators, and there was no explanation or apparent grounds for the discrepancy;
  - Even if the Federal Reserve had the requisite authority, an independent/independent director requirement would interfere with a strong and continuously improving framework for enterprise risk management under the leadership of the GE Risk Committee while ignoring more effective alternatives;
  - Other measures to which GECC did not object, most notably §23B-like requirement and capital planning and capital distribution requirements, obviated any ostensible need for independent/independent directors and would suffice to ensure appropriate controls on the relationship between GE and GECC;
  - If the Federal Reserve continued to believe that special governance standards should apply to GECC, the Federal Reserve should instead require that a majority of GECC's directors be independent under normal standards of independence and that GECC's board by chaired by an independent director.
- The Federal Reserve should not treat GECC in the same manner as significantly larger, more complex, global systemically important banks (G-SIBs), and should also engage in further analysis and calibration with respect to the application of a BHC-style regulation to GECC;

- GECC was notably smaller, less complex, and less systemically significant than G-SIBs, including US banking organizations (the letter discussed with charts the size, interconnectedness, substitutability, complexity, and cross-jurisdictional activity that ostensibly illustrated its considerably lower involvement than other firms);
- The proposed order should not adopt a default view – implicitly or explicitly – that G-SIB regulations should apply to GECC;
- Beyond the question of G-SIB treatment, the Federal Reserve should consider the calibration of capital, leverage, liquidity, and other rules that will apply to GECC and study the Proposed Order's likely effect on key constituencies such as middle-market borrowers;
- GECC's enhanced prudential standards should also reflect a thorough consideration of GEC's significant improvements in many key metrics viewed as indicators of impact on U.S. financial stability;

• Certain aspects of BHC capital and liquidity rules should be modified to reflect GECC's specific circumstances;

  - The Federal Reserve should provide limited extensions of transition periods for certain enhanced prudential standards – the letter suggested adjustments concerning capital planning and stress testing requirements; daily averaging of on-balance exposures; intraday liquidity monitoring requirements; and liquidity reporting;
  - GECC should be allowed to apply the accumulated other comprehensive income filter to investment securities held by its legacy insurance businesses;
  - GECC's calculation of the liquidity coverage ratio should be tailored to reflect GECC's inability to hold significant Federal Reserve Bank balances;

• The Proposed Order should be further tailored to grandfather historical §23B (restrictions on Transactions with affiliates) transactions; and
• Due process concerns:

  - Failure to provide a sufficient justification for the proposed standards;
  - Failure to examine the propriety of the proposed standards under the tailoring requirements of §165; and
  - Failure to assess the alternatives available to the Federal Reserve.[46]

The Annexes to the Sherin letter to the FRB concern the GECC views as expressed above. The law firm of Sidley Austin LLP., in an opinion letter to GECC dated January 29, 2015, asserted that under Delaware law the directors of a wholly owned subsidiary (as GECC is to GE) that is incorporated in Delaware and is solvent owe no fiduciary duty other than to the subsidiary's sole stockholder parent. The statement was apparently based on the opinion of William B. Chandler III discussed below. Thus, in the author's opinion, it appeared that designating GECC, rather than GE itself, as a SIFI might have been contrary to standard corporate governance principles.[47]

The letter from the noted former Chancellor of the Delaware Chancery Court, William B. Chandler III, to the General Counsel to the Board of Governors of the Federal Reserve System and to the Director of the Division of Banking Supervision and Regulation of the Board, opined that the proposed independent/independent director requirement was "out of step with, and invites serious misapprehensions of the fundamental tenets of Delaware corporate law,..." Chandler discussed at length Delaware law as it pertained to the obligations of GECC directors to the parent corporation. He stated that for independent/independent directors to owe their fiduciary duties otherwise appeared to violate Delaware corporate law that discourages divided loyalties in the boardroom. Moreover, the independent members of the GECC Risk Committee were already well positioned to bring well-informed business judgment to the Board and to exercise their duty of good management to both corporations. Delaware law inherently placed checks on directors, including directors of wholly owned subsidiaries and thus were obligated to act in good faith and to comply with all state laws and regulations which are protective of the corporations and their shareholders.[48]

The remaining annexed document reflected the views of Jonathan R. Macey, the Sam Harris Professor of Law, Corporate Finance, and Securities Law at the Yale Law School. He also stated much of what has been outlined above, particularly concerning the independent/independent director requirement. He wrote that the duty of corporations and their boards was to shareholders and not to creditors and regulators. Parent companies such as GE that own subsidiaries should have the same expectations of the subsidiary's directors as other shareholders have of directors of companies in which they own shares. The Board's restrictions on eligibility of who was to serve on boards and on risk committees reduced shareholder value and expectations of investors. GE shareholders were entitled to undivided loyalty enforced by strict fiduciary duties. The FED's proposed expansion had been considered and rejected by state law, in particular by Delaware state law. In Macey's view, regulatory authorities lacked the authority to establish a federal corporate law. State corporate law, not federal law, was the proper source of regulation of distribution of powers. Having reviewed the requirements of the Sarbanes-Oxley Act and the Dodd-Frank Act, he wrote that the existing membership of the Risk Committee was in full accord with its mandates.[49]

3.4.4 *The GE Conundrum: Disgorge or Comply?*

The result of the GECC's SIFI designation and the proposed enhanced prudential standards was the decision of General Electric to divest itself of most of its non-bank financial holdings so as to lessen regulatory oversight requirements. The sale of its real estate and financial services assets for the sum of $23 billion to Blackstone and to Wells Fargo & Co. included the sale of its mortgage commercial real estate loan portfolio for $9 billion to Wells Fargo; US office properties for $3.3 billion to Blackstone; $2.2 billion sale of GE's private equity financing business to Japan's Sumitomo Mitsui Banking Corp; and other office logistics and retail assets in the USA and abroad. The CEO of General Electric, Jeff Immelt, indicated that, with the sale of the financial assets, he would be working with the Council to de-designate GE's SIFI status by 2016.[50] The government had intended to impose minimum capital and liquidity requirements and thereafter, likely within two years, compel stricter regulatory oversight. The company intended to retain much smaller financial units mainly to support its aircraft leasing and sale of its energy and healthcare equipment. The designation was rescinded by the Council in June 2016. It may be that the purchasers of the financial assets will later become subject to Council review as potential SIFIs.

3.5 Financial Market Utilities as SIFIs

§804 of the Dodd-Frank Act grants the authority to designate a financial market utility as a SIFI to the Council. Accordingly, the Council published a Final Rule on July 27, 2011 with respect to its *Authority to Designate Financial Market Utilities as Systemically Important*.[51] Thus, Congress enacted the Dodd-Frank Act requiring enhanced regulation and supervision of SIFI market utilities to provide consistency; promote robust risk management and safety and soundness; reduce systemic risks; and to support the stability of the broader financial system. The statute thereby granted to the Board and a multiplicity of other supervisory agencies an enhanced role in the supervision of risk-management standards and to strengthen the liquidity for SIFI financial market utilities. In accordance with the statutory authority, the FED adopted a Final Rule for Financial Market Utilities.[52] The term *payment, clearing, or settlement activity* refers to an activity carried out by one or more financial institutions to facilitate the completion of financial transactions, except for the offer or sale of a security that comes under the Securities Act of 1933 or any quotation, order entry, negotiation, or other pre-trade activity or execution activity.

A *financial transaction* includes (1) funds transfers; (2) securities contracts; (3) contracts of sale of a commodity for future delivery; (4) forward contracts; (5) repurchase agreements; (6) swaps; (7) security-based swaps; (8) swap agreements; (9) security-based swap agreements; (10) foreign exchange contracts; (11) financial derivatives contracts; and (12) any similar transaction that the Council determines to be a financial transaction. The activities included within the definition of a financial transaction, payment, clearing, and settlement activities include the calculation and communication of unsettled financial transactions between counterparties; the netting of transactions; provision and maintenance of trade, contract, or instrument information; the management of risks and activities associated with continuing financial transactions; transmittal and storage of payment instructions; the movement of funds; the final settlement of financial transactions; and other activities as the Council may determine.[53]

A *financial market utility* (FMU) is defined as any person that manages or operates a multilateral system for the purpose of transferring, clearing, or settling payments, securities, or other financial transactions among financial institutions or between financial institutions and the person. A *designated financial market utility* is one that the Council has designated as systemically important and thus becomes subject to enhanced prudential supervision as a SIFI. The provisions of Title VIII of the Dodd-Frank Act, Payment, Clearing, and Settlement Supervision Act of 2010, are applicable, whereby Congress found that the proper functioning of the financial markets is dependent upon safe and efficient arrangements for the clearing and settlement of payment, securities, and other financial transactions. These utilities and their activities present important risks to the financial system and are deemed to be systemically important.[54]

3.5.1 Standards for SIFI Designation

Designated financial market utilities are required to meet or exceed risk-management standards with respect to their payment, clearing, and settlement activities. These standards include:

- Effective measurement, monitoring, and management of credit risk;
- A framework for the comprehensive measurement, monitoring, and management of credit risk;
- If required to manage its and its participants' credit exposure, it must be with low credit, liquidity, and market risks with conservative haircuts and concentration limits;
- Effective measurement, monitoring, and management of liquidity risk that arise and are to be borne by the designated market utility;
- Provision for clear and final settlement intra-day and, at a minimum, by the end of the day of the value date;
- Money settlements are to be conducted in central bank money where practical and available;
- When the utility operates as a central counterparty, securities, settlement system, or central securities depository, it shall clearly state its obligations with respect to the delivery of physical instruments of commodities and identifies, monitors, and manages the risks associated with such physical activities;
- If it operates as a central securities depository, it must have rules and procedures to help insure the integrity of securities issues and minimizes the risks associated with the safekeeping and transfer of securities;
- If it settles transactions that involves the settlement of two linked obligations, such as a transfer of securities against payment or the exchange of one currency for another, the utility eliminates risk by conditioning the final settlement of one obligation upon the settlement of the other;
- The utility has effective and clearly defined rules and procedures to manage a participant default that are designed to ensure that the utility can take timely action to contain losses and liquidity pressures so that it can continue to meet its obligations;
- A utility that operates as a central counterparty has rules and procedures that enable the segregation and portability of positions of a participant's customers and the collateral provided to the utility with respect to these positions;

- The utility identifies, monitors, and manages its general business risk, which is the risk of losses that may arise from its administration and operation as a business enterprise;
- The utility must safeguard its own and its participants' assets and minimizes the risk of loss on and delay in access to those assets;
- The utility manages its operational risks by establishing a robust operational risk-management framework that is approved by the Board;
- The utility has objective, risk-based, and publicly disclosed criteria for participation, which permits fair and open access;
- The utility identifies, monitors, and manages the material risks arising from arrangements in which firms that are not direct participants in the utility rely on the services provided by direct participants to access the utility's payment, clearing, or settlement facilities, whether the risks are borne by the utility or by its participants as a result of their participation;
- The designated financial market utility identifies, monitors, and manages the material risks arising from arrangements in which firms that are not direct participants in the designated financial market utility rely on the services provided by direct participants to access the designated financial market utility's payment, clearing, or settlement facilities, whether the risks are borne by the utility or by its participants as a result of their participation;
- If it operates as a central counterparty, securities settlement system, or central securities depository and establishes a link with one or more of these types of financial market utilities or trade repositories, the designated utility identifies, monitors, and manages risks related to this link; the utility is efficient and effective in meeting the requirements of its participants and the markets it serves, and has clearly defined goals and objectives that are measurable and achievable, such as minimum service levels, risk-management expectations, and business priorities; the regular review of its efficiency and effectiveness;
- The utility uses, or at a minimum accommodates, relevant internationally accepted communication procedures and standards in order to facilitate efficient payment, clearing, and settlement; and
- The utility has clear and comprehensive rules and procedures; publicly discloses all rules and key procedures, including key aspects of its default rules and procedures; provides sufficient information to enable participants to have an accurate understanding of the risks,

fees, and other material costs they incur by participating in the utility; and provides a comprehensive public disclosure of its legal, governance, risk management, and operating framework.[55]

The process utilized by the Council is similar to the one earlier in this chapter, and is reviewed in stages. In the first stage, the key considerations are:

- Aggregate monetary value of transactions processed by an FMU:

    1. Number of transactions processed, cleared or settled by an FMU;
    2. Value of transactions processed, cleared, or settled by an FMU;
    3. Value of other financial flows that may flow through an FMU.

- Aggregate exposure of an FMU to its counterparties:

    1. Credit exposures to counterparties;
    2. Liquidity exposures to counterparties.

- Relationship, interdependencies, or other interactions of an FMU with other FMUs. or payment, clearing, or settlement activities:

    1. Metrics that measure the relationship and interdependencies of an FMU.

- Effect that the failure of or disruption to an FMU would have on critical markets, financial institutions, or the broader financial system:

    1. Role of an FMU in the market served;
    2. Availability of substitutes.

- Any other factors that the Council deems appropriate.

In Stage Two, the Council conducts a more-in-depth review and analysis of a specific FMU from a quantitative and qualitative viewpoint, with a greater focus on elements that may be particular to a specific FMU or a market. It will use its assessments described above to decide whether a particular FMU meets the SIFI criteria. It will decide: (1) Whether the failure of or a disruption to the functioning of the FMU now or in the future could create, or increase, the risk of significant liquidity or credit problems spreading among financial institutions or markets (the First Determination); and (2) Whether the spread of such liquidity or credit problems among financial institutions or markets could threaten the stability of the financial system of the USA (the Second Determination).[56]

The following financial market utilities have been designated by the Council as SIFIs together with their Supervisory Agencies, thus subjecting them to enhanced prudential standards:

- The Clearing House Payments Company LLC, (CHIPS)—FRB. CHIPS is a real-time, multilateral payment system typically used for large dollar payments, supervised by the Board, and is also under the supervision of and examination by other Federal bank supervisory agencies, under the auspices of the Federal Financial Institutions Examination Council (FFIEC);
- CLS Bank International—FRB. The CLS Bank International is a special purpose bank that settles simultaneously both payment obligations arising from a single foreign exchange (FX) transaction. It also settles the bilateral net payment obligations arising in multiple currencies from over-the-counter (OTC) credit derivatives contracts housed in Depository Trust and Clearing Corporation's Trade Information Warehouse;
- Chicago Mercantile Exchange, Inc.—The Commodity Futures Trading Commission (CFTC). The Exchange, through its US clearing division, provides central counterparty clearing services for futures, options, and swaps contracts;
- The Depository Trust Company (DTC)—SEC; The DTC is a central securities depository and securities settlement system for eligible securities including equities, corporate bonds, and municipal bonds, as well as money market instruments such as commercial paper;
- Fixed Income Clearing Corporation (FICC)—SEC. The FICC is composed of the Government Securities Division (GSD) and the Mortgage-Backed Securities Division (MBSD). GSD is a central counterparty for US Treasury and agency debt securities. MBSD is a central counterparty for US Agency pass-through mortgage-backed securities. FICC is a clearing agency registered with the SEC;
- ICE Clear Credit LLC (ICC)—CFTC. ICC provides central counterparty clearing services for standardized credit-default swap contracts; clears CDS on indices, single-name corporates, and single-name sovereigns. It is a derivatives clearing organization registered with the CFTC and a securities clearing agency registered with the SEC;

- National Securities Clearing Corporation (NSCC)—SEC; The NSCC is a central counterparty that provides clearing and settlement services for US equities, corporate and municipal bonds, exchange-traded funds, and unit investment trusts; and
- The Options Clearing Corporation (OPCC)—SEC. The OCC provides central counterparty clearing services for US options, futures, and options on futures contracts.[57]

The reader will have noted that the designation as a SIFI entails a panoply of enhanced prudential standards that are applicable to that status. In Chap. 4, we will discuss additional obligations faced by shadow banking entities upon receiving the SIFI designation.

Notes

1. Les Christie, *Foreclosures Up a Record 81 % in 2008*, CNN MONEY (Jan. 15, 2009), http://money.cnn.com/2009/01/15/real_estate/millions_in_foreclosure/.
2. Council on Foreign Relations, *The Federal Reserve's Stanley Fischer on Inflation and Financial Stability*,(Dec. 1, 2014), http://www.cfr.org/united-states/federal-reserves-stanley-fischer-inflation-financial-stability/p33884.
3. Title I of the Dodd-Frank Act, *Financial Stability* and its subsection A *Financial Stability Oversight Council.*
4. Dodd-Frank Act, §113(a)(1).
5. Financial Stability Oversight Council, *Authority to Require Supervision and Regulation of Certain Non-bank Financial Companies,* 12 CFR Part 1310.
6. *Id.* at 77.
7. Dodd-Frank Act, §102(a)(4)(B).
8. *Id.*, §102(a)(4)(A).
9. *Id.*, §102(a)(6)(A)(B).
10. Federal Reserve System, Definitions of "Predominantly Engaged in Financial Activities" and "Significant" Non-bank Financial Company and Bank Holding Company, Final Rule, §242.3, 12 C.F.R. Pt 242 (April 5, 2013).
11. *Id.*, Appendix A to Part 242.
12. Dodd-Frank Act §111(b)(1), (c).
13. Dodd-Frank Act, §111(*b*)(3).
14. Financial Stability Oversight Council, *supra* note 5 at 2.
15. Dodd-Frank Act §112(a)(2). The Board of Governors is responsible for making recommendations for the establishment of heightened prudential standards for risk-based capital, leverage, liquidity, contingent capital, resolution

plans and credit exposure reports, concentration limits, enhanced public disclosures, and overall risk management for non-bank financial companies and large, interconnected bank holding companies supervised by the Board of Governors; and to identify systemically important financial market utilities and payment, clearing, and settlement activities.

16. Dodd-Frank Act, §112(a)(1).
17. *Id.*, 112(a)(2).
18. Dodd-Frank Act, §111(d).
19. http://www.treasury.gov/initiatives/Documents/X%20-%20Committee%20Structure%20111910.pdf.
20. *Id.* §113(a)(2). Authority to Require Supervision and Regulation of Certain Non-bank Financial Companies.
21. §113(b) of the Dodd-Frank Act.
22. *Id.*, §113(c).
23. Dodd-Frank Act, §113(c).
24. 12 U.S.C. § 1841, et seq.
25. Dodd-Frank Act §112(d)(3), 12 U.S.C. §1395).
26. *Id.*, §152, 12 U.S.C. §1320.20.
27. Dodd-Frank Act, §113(a)(1).
28. Financial Stability Oversight Council, 12 C.F.R. Pt. 1310 at 77–78.
29. *Id.* at 79–80.
30. Financial Stability Oversight Council, Authority to Require Supervision and Regulation of Certain Non-bank Financial Companies, 77 Fed. Reg. 21637 (Apr. 11, 2012).
31. The Office of Financial Research, according to its website, helps to promote financial stability by looking across the financial system to measure and analyze risks, perform essential research, and collect and standardize financial data. It issues annual reports such as that of 2014 in which it highlighted three specific areas of concern: (1) excessive risk-taking during an extended period of low interest rates and low volatility; (2) an increase in market fragility, resulting in declining market liquidity and persistent risks of asset fire sales and runs, and (3) the migration of financial activity away from banks toward less regulated parts of the financial system. It also issues financial markets monitor, briefs, working papers, and other financial reports and data. http://financialresearch.gov/about/.
32. Council Regulation, *supra*, note 31 at 68–69.
33. *Id.* at 86–87.
34. Dodd-Frank Act §113(e)(4).
35. *Id.*, §113(h).
36. *Id.*, §113(f).
37. Council Regulation, *supra* note 31 at 72–74.
38. Dodd-Frank Act §113(d) and Regulations *supra* note 31 at 74–75.

39. Dodd-Frank Act §112(d)(4).
40. http://www.treasury.gov/about/organizational-structure/offices/Pages/Office-of-Foreign-Assets-Control.aspx.
41. Financial Stability Oversight Council, Basis of the Financial Stability Oversight COUNCIL's Final Determination Regarding General Electric Capital Corporation, Inc. (July 8, 2013). http://www.treasury.gov/initiatives/fsoc/designations/Documents/Basis%20of%20Final%20Determination%20Regarding%20General%20Electric%20Capital%20Corporation,%20Inc.pdf.
42. *Id.*
43. 79FR71768,https://www.federalregister.gov/articles/2014/12/03/2014-28414/application-of-enhanced-prudential-standards-and-reporting-requirements-to-general-electric-capital.
44. *Id.*
45. http://www.federalreserve.gov/SECRS/2015/February/20150203/R-1503/R-1503_020215_129879_536678377188_1.pdf.
46. http://www.federalreserve.gov/SECRS/2015/February/20150224/R-1503/R-1503_020215_129873_536678064720_1.pdf.
47. *Id.*
48. *Id.*
49. *Id.*
50. Ronald Orol, *GE's $23 billion financial asset sale to Blackstone, Wells Fargo, will help it exit Fed oversight*, THE DEAL, N.Y. TIMES (April 10, 2015), (http://www.thedeal.com/content/real-estate/ges-23-billion-financial-asset-sale-to-blackstone-wells-fargo-will-help-it-exit-fed-oversight.php#ixzz3Z5ej8pnO.
51. Financial Stability Oversight Council, Authority to Designate Financial Market Utilities as Systemically Important (July 27, 211), Fed. Reg., 12 C.F.R. Ch. XIII and Pt 1320.
52. Federal Reserve System, Final Rule for Financial Market Utilities (Nov. 5, 2014), 12 C.F.R. Part 234.
53. Dodd-Frank Act §803(5–7).
54. Dodd-Frank Act §802(a).
55. Federal Reserve System, *Financial Market Utilities*, 12 C.F.R. Pt 234.3.
56. *Id.* at 44766.
57. Board of Governors of the Federal Reserve System, Designated Financial Market Utilities, http://www.federalreserve.gov/paymentsystems/designated_fmu_about.htm.

CHAPTER 4

Enhanced Prudential Standards

The consequence of being designated a systemically important financial institution (SIFI) is the imposition of enhanced prudential standards that will ostensibly prevent or mitigate risks to US stability that may arise as a result of material financial distress or failure, or ongoing activities, of large, interconnected financial institutions. In this chapter, we will discuss the statutory and regulatory requirements that alleviate such dangers, their intended application to a formerly major financial company and the result, and a commentary on director independence on corporate boards.

4.1 Statutory Requirements

§165 of the Dodd-Frank Act requires the Board of Governors to establish enhanced prudential standards for non-bank financial companies supervised by the Board and bank holding companies (BHCs) with total assets of $50 billion or more that are more stringent than standards and requirements for companies that do not present risks to the financial stability of the USA. The Board on its own, or pursuant to recommendations of the Council, is to differentiate these companies on an individual basis or by category, taking into account the capital structure, riskiness, complexity, financial activities, whether the company owns an insured depository institution, non-financial activities and affiliations, and any other appropriate risk factors.[1]

Roy J. Girasa, *Shadow Banking*, DOI 10.1007/978-3-319-33026-6_4

The required standards to be established by the Board are risk-based capital requirements and leverage limits; liquidity requirements; overall risk-management requirements; resolution plan and credit exposure report requirements; and concentration limits. In addition, the Board may establish a contingent capital requirement; enhanced public disclosures; short-term debt limits; and other prudential requirements on its own or pursuant to recommendations of the Council. Foreign non-bank financial companies or foreign-based BHCs supervised by the Board are also subject to the said standards but the Board is to take into account whether they are subject to comparable standards within their home countries.[2]

Once a non-bank financial company and certain BHCs receive a SIFI determination, they become subject to enhanced supervision and prudential standards as set forth in the Dodd-Frank Act §165. The Act provides that the Board of Governors is to establish prudential standards for non-bank financial companies as well as BHCs with total assets of $50 billion or more that are more stringent than requirements for companies not meeting the threshold, albeit the Board may raise the threshold above the said sum. The Board, acting on recommendation from the Council or on its own, may differentiate among the companies on an individual basis, taking into consideration their capital structure, riskiness, complexity, financial activities, size, and other related risk factors that the Board deems appropriate.[3]

4.1.1 Required Prudential Standards

The required prudential standards under §165 of the Dodd-Frank Act are to include:

- Risk-based capital requirements and leverage limits unless the Board, in consultation with the Council, deems the requirements to be inappropriate for a company already subject to more stringent requirements under other statutory and regulatory provisions, such as investment company activities or assets under management or structure, in which case the Board shall apply other similarly stringent risk controls;
- Liquidity requirements;
- Overall risk-management and credit exposure report requirements; and
- Concentration limits.[4]

Additional Standards

The Board is also authorized to establish a contingent capital requirement; enhanced public disclosure; short-term debt limits; and other requirements it and the Council deem appropriate.[5] The Board, in prescribing the risk factors, is to take into account the differences among the non-bank financial companies that it supervises and adapt the required standards that are appropriate for the predominant line of business of the company, including assets under management and other activities. Prior to the imposition of prudential standards, other requirements, notices of deficiencies or divestiture orders that under §165 are likely to have a significant impact on the company's regulated subsidiary, the Board is to consult with each Council member who supervises any of the subsidiaries.[6]

Contingent Capital

The enhanced prudential standards also provide that the Board of Governors may issue regulations that require each non-bank financial company that it supervises to maintain a minimum amount of contingent capital that is convertible to equity in times of distress. The factors that the Board are to consider include the results of a study undertaken by the Council and any of its recommendations; an appropriate transition period for the implementation of the capital requirements; and the risk factors referred to above.[7]

Resolution Plan

The Dodd-Frank Act requires a non-bank financial company subject to its supervision to report the plan of the company for rapid and orderly resolution in the event of material financial distress or failure (often described as a "living will") periodically to the Board, the Council, and to the Federal Deposit Insurance Corporation (FDIC). The plan is to include (1) information regarding the manner and extent to which any insured depository institution affiliated with the company is adequately protected from risks arising from its activities; (2) full descriptions of its ownership, structure, assets, liabilities, and contractual obligations; (3) identification of the cross guarantees tied to different securities, identification of major counterparties, and a process for determining to whom the collateral of the company is pledged; and (4) any other information that the Board and the FDIC may require.[8]

In addition, SIFIs and BHCs are to report periodically (1) the nature and extent to which the company has credit exposure to other significant non-bank financial companies and significant BHCs; and (2) the nature and extent to which other significant non-bank financial companies and significant BHCs have credit exposure to that company. The Board of Governors and the FDIC are to review the information provided and advise the entity if the plan is not credible and/or whether there are any deficiencies in the resolution plan that need to be addressed in its resubmission. In the event of a failure to resubmit the resolution plan with such revisions as required in a timely fashion, then the Board and the FDIC may jointly impose more stringent capital, leverage, or liquidity requirements or restrictions on the growth, activities, or operations of the company or any subsidiary thereof, until such time as the company resubmits a plan that remedies the deficiencies.[9]

The Board and the FDIC, after consultation with the Council, may order the SIFI, any company engaged in significant financial activities, BHC, or subsidiaries thereof (covered financial companies) to divest certain assets or operations that have been identified as necessary for the orderly resolution of the company under Title 11 of the Bankruptcy Code (reorganization) if it is failing, as well as imposing more stringent requirements. The plan, however, is not binding upon the bankruptcy court, the receiver, or any other official in connection with the reorganization or dissolution of the company.[10]

In order to assist the SIFI or BHC in formulating the resolution plan, the Board provided a model template under §165(d) of the Dodd-Frank Act.[11] The plan is divided into a public section and a confidential section. The public section is an executive summary of the resolution plan that provides basic information including the names of the entities; a description of core business lines; financial information regarding assets, liabilities, capital, and major funding sources; a description of derivative and hedging activities; list of memberships in material payment, clearing, and settlement systems; the identities of supervising authorities and principal officers; a description of foreign operations; its corporate governance structures and processes for resolution planning; material management information systems; and the company's resolution strategy. The confidentiality section contains the specific resolution plans and related materials.

Credit Exposure Report

The Board shall additionally require these companies to report periodically to the Board on (1) the nature and extent to which the company has credit exposure to other significant non-bank financial companies and significant BHCs; and (2) the nature and extent to which other significant non-bank financial companies and significant BHCs have credit exposure to that company.[12]

Deficiencies of Resolution Plan and Credit Exposure Report

If the Board and the FDIC jointly determine that the resolution plan of the non-bank financial company is not credible or would not result in an orderly resolution of material distress or failure, it shall notify the company of the discrepancies and the company is mandated to resubmit the resolution plan with the appropriate time frame for an orderly resolution. Failure to do so may lead to more stringent capital, leverage, or liquidity requirements or restrictions on the company's growth, activities, or operations. The Board and the FDIC, in consultation with the Council, may order the divestiture of assets or operations. The resolution plan is not binding on a bankruptcy court. The statute does not afford private relief based on a resolution plan under this section. Final Rules were to be issued implementing the statute but at the time of writing have yet to be issued.[13]

Concentration Limits

The Dodd-Frank Act requires the Board of Governors to prescribe standards to limit the risks that an individual company could pose to a non-bank financial company or BHC. Among the statutory requirements are that the regulations prohibit the said companies from having *credit exposure* to any unaffiliated company that exceeds 25 % of the capital stock and surplus, or a lower percentage if the Board determines it necessary in order to mitigate risks to the company and to the financial stability of the USA. *Credit exposure* is defined as: (1) all extensions of credit to the company, including loans, deposits, and lines of credit; (2) all repurchase agreements and all reverse repurchase agreements with the company, and all securities borrowing to the extent that they create credit exposure to the company; (3) all guarantees, acceptances, or letters of credit issued on behalf of the company; (4) all proceeds of or investment in securities issued by the company; (5) counterparty credit exposure to the company in connection with derivative transactions; and (6) other similar transactions as determined by the Board.[14]

Short-Term Debt Limits

The Dodd-Frank Act gives discretionary authority to the Board to issue regulations governing short-term debt limits that could jeopardize the financial stability of the USA. A *short-term debt* is defined by the Act as "such liabilities with short-term maturity that the Board of Governors identifies, by regulation, except that such term does not include insured deposits." Any limit imposed by the Board is to be based on the short-term debt of the company as a percentage of capital stock.[15]

Risk Committee

The Act requires the Board to require non-bank financial companies under its jurisdiction to establish a risk committee within one year from receipt of a final determination as a SIFI. The risk committee is to be responsible for the oversight of the enterprise-wide risk-management practices of the said company. It is to consist of the Board-mandated number of independent directors based on the nature of operations, size of assets, and other appropriate criteria related to the supervised company, and include at least one risk-management expert who has experience in identifying, assessing, and managing risk exposures of large, complex firms.[16]

Leverage Limitation

For non-bank financial companies under the Board's jurisdiction as well as BHCs with total consolidated assets of $50 billion or more, the Board is mandated to require the maintenance of debt to equity ratio of not more than 15:1 if it is determined by the Council that the company poses a grave threat to the financial stability of the USA and that the imposition of the requirement is necessary to mitigate risks. The Council is to consider the risk factors stated earlier in this chapter.[17]

Inclusion of Off-Balance-Sheet Activities in Computing Capital Requirements

The ENRON scandal, which occurred mainly because of the ostensible concealment of off-balance-sheet losses occurring offshore, is likely what Congress had in mind when it required in the Dodd-Frank Act that the Board, subject to exemptions it may determine, take into consideration the inclusion of off-balance-sheet activities in the Board's computation of capital for purposes of meeting capital requirements. An *off-balance-sheet activity* is defined as "an existing liability of a company that is not currently a balance sheet liability, but may become on upon the happening of some future event including the following transactions, to the extent that they may create a liability":

- Direct credit substitutes in which a bank substitutes its own credit for a third party, including standby letters of credit;
- Irrevocable letters of credit that guarantee repayment of commercial paper or tax-exempt securities;
- Risk participation in bankers' acceptances;
- Sale and repurchase agreements;
- Assets sales with recourse against the seller;
- Interest rate swaps;
- Credit swaps;
- Commodities contracts;
- Forward contracts;
- Securities contracts; and
- Such other activities or transactions as the Board of Governors may, by rule, define.[18]

Stress Tests

The Board of Governors, in cooperation with the appropriate governmental financial regulatory agencies, including the Federal Insurance Office, is required to conduct annual analyses of non-bank financial companies under its jurisdiction to evaluate whether the companies have the capital, on a consolidated basis, necessary to absorb losses in the face of adverse economic conditions. The stress testing is to be conducted by providing at least three different sets of conditions including baseline, adverse, and severely adverse conditions. Additional analytic techniques may be developed and required by the Board to identify, measure, and monitor risks to the financial stability of the USA. Companies are to update their resolution plans as the Board may require based on the results of the stress testing.

For the macro-economic scenarios ,the financial and economic variables to be used are:

- Five measures of economic activity and prices: real and nominal gross domestic product (GDP) growth, the unemployment rate of the civilian non-institutional population aged 16 and over, nominal disposable personal income growth, and the Consumer Price Index (CPI) inflation rate;
- Four measures of developments in equity and property markets: the Core Logic National House Price Index, the National Council for Real Estate Investment Fiduciaries, Commercial Real Estate Price Index, and the Chicago Board Options Exchange Market Volatility Index;

- Commercial Real Estate Price Index, the Dow Jones Total Stock Market Index, and the Chicago Board Options Exchange Market Volatility Index; and
- Four measures of interest rates: the rate on the three-month Treasury bill, the yield on the ten-year Treasury bond, the yield on a ten-year BBB investment grade corporate security, and the interest rate associated with a conforming, conventional, fixed-rate, 30-year mortgage.[19]

The international variables provided for in the 2012 Comprehensive Capital Analysis and Review (CCAR) is an annual exercise by the FED to ensure that institutions have robust, forward-looking capital planning processes that account for their unique risks and sufficient capital to continue operations throughout times of economic and financial stress, including in the euro area, and that reflect the consensus views of the economic and financial outlook.

The *baseline* scenario is described as a set of conditions that affect the US economy or the financial condition of a banking organization. Projections under the scenario are used to evaluate how companies would perform in more likely economic and financial conditions. It serves as a point of reference to the severely adverse and adverse scenarios by giving a sense of how much of the company's capital decline could be ascribed to the scenario as opposed to the company's capital adequacy under expected conditions.[20]

Each of the companies with total consolidated assets of $50 billion or more supervised by the Board is required to conduct stress tests twice a year, while those of assets of over $10 billion and which are regulated by a primary Federal financial authority are to do so annually. A report of the companies' findings is to be submitted to the Board as directed. The Board and each federal primary financial regulatory agency are to coordinate with each other as well as with the Federal Insurance Office concerning the methodologies to be used in stress testing, as well as the form and content of the report to be furnished by the affected companies.[21]

4.1.2 SIFIs in Default or in Danger of Default

The Dodd-Frank Act §203(c)(4) states that a covered company in danger of default is a financial company whereby: (1) a case has been, or is likely to be, commenced with respect to the financial company under the Bankruptcy Code; (2) the financial company has incurred, or is likely to incur, losses that will deplete all or substantially all of its capital, and there is no reasonable prospect for the company to avoid such depletion; (3) the assets of the financial company are, or are likely to be, less than its obligations to creditors and others; or (4) the financial company is, or is likely to be, unable to pay its obligations (other than those subject to a bona fide dispute) in the normal course of business.[22]

FDIC Proposed Resolution Authority

The FDIC and the Bank of England together with regulators in the respective countries have developed contingency plans in the event of the failure of a US- or UK-based SIFI that has significant operations within their jurisdictions. The FDIC published for comment a proposed *Resolution of Systemically Important Financial Institutions: The Single Point of Entry Strategy*,[23] whose purpose it is to develop its capabilities for the implementation of the Orderly Liquidation Authority (OLA) established under Title II of the Dodd-Frank Act with respect to SIFIs that are bankrupt. The problem to be addressed was the absence of adequate and credible resolution plans with respect to global SIFIs (G-SIFIs) that was exposed during the last financial crisis. The Financial Stability Board (FSB) identified 28 G-SIFIs in the G20 countries, four of which were in the United Kingdom (UK) and eight in the USA. Approximately 80 % of the reported foreign activities of the eight US G-SIFIs emanate from the UK. The FDIC's receivership authority was limited to federally insured banks and thrift institutions. Because of the lack of authority to place a holding company or affiliates of an insured depositary into FDIC receivership to avoid systemic consequences, its choices were limited to either a bail-out or disorderly bankruptcy.

In the event that a SIFI should fail, Title I and Title II of the Dodd-Frank Act empower the FDIC, the FED and other regulatory authorities with significant new authorities to address the impending bankruptcy. As stated above, financial companies have to devise a "living will" that sets forth how an impending material financial distress or default is to be resolved in a rapid and orderly manner under the Bankruptcy Code. If a SIFI cannot be otherwise liquidated by merger or other comparable resolution with a financially solvent firm that is able to take over the SIFI, then Title II grants the authority to the FDIC to place the SIFI under FDIC receivership. The FDIC, by virtue of its OLA, is enabled to ensure the rapid and orderly resolution of a covered financial company. Title II leaves the mechanism for the exercise of its OLA but states certain policy goals that have to be addressed.

§206 of the Dodd-Frank Act requires the FDIC and the Securities Investor Protection Corporation (SIPC) for broker-dealers to resolve the liquidation in a manner that holds owners and managers responsible for the company's failure and minimizes moral hazard and promotes market discipline while maintaining the stability of the US financial system at no cost to taxpayers. Accordingly, the section requires the FDIC to assure that the main purpose of its liquidation authority is to (1) preserve the financial stability of the USA rather than to preserve the failing financial company; (2) ensure that the shareholders of the covered financial company do not receive payment until after all other claims are fully paid; (3) ensure that unsecured creditors bear losses in accordance with the priority of their claims; (4) ensure that management responsible for the failed condition of the covered financial company is removed; (5) ensure that the members of the board of directors or comparable persons responsible for the failed condition of the covered financial company be removed; and (6) not take an equity interest in or become a shareholder of any covered financial company or any covered subsidiary. The Act leaves it to the FDIC to prescribe such rules or regulations as it deems necessary or appropriate to implement the Act.

The FDIC noted that it had to consider and resolve a number of obstacles that had to be addressed in any resolution. The major impediments it determined were:

- The multiple competing insolvencies among multiple jurisdictions with differing insolvency frameworks, which may cause the risk of discontinuity of critical operations and uncertain outcomes;
- The risk that other foreign jurisdictions may not cooperate with the USA and may seek to protect assets of the defaulting financial company within its borders, thereby raising the specter of US financial stability and/or loss of franchise value, as well as uncertainty in the markets;
- The risk that services provided by an affiliate or third party might be interrupted, or access to payment and clearing capabilities might be lost;
- The risk that counterparty actions might create operational challenges for the company, leading to systemic market disruption or financial instability in the USA; and
- The risk of insufficient liquidity to maintain critical operations, which may arise from increased margin requirements, termination or inability to roll over short-term borrowings, or loss of access to alternative sources of credit.

Accordingly, the FDIC has proposed the "single point of entry strategy." The reason for the designation of one point of entry is the reality that US SIFIs have a holding company corporate structure with a top-tier parent and numerous operating subsidiaries that interconnect with additional entities across multiple jurisdictions globally, each having its own legal and regulatory requirements that make resolution extraordinarily difficult. Operations and funding often take place as needed across multiple borders. Thus, the FDIC proposes that, inasmuch as it is the top-tier company which raises the equity capital of the institution and subsequently downstream equity and some debt funding to its subsidiaries, the losses should be imposed upon the shareholders and creditors of the top-tier holding as well as culpable senior management being removed without imposing cost on taxpayers. The end result, as anticipated by the FDIC, is to create a more stable financial system over the longer term and to preserve financial stability by maintaining the critical services, operations, and funding mechanisms conducted throughout the company's operating subsidiaries.

4.2 Regulatory Prudential Requirements

The difficulty as of this writing is that the Board has yet to promulgate rules and regulations for non-bank financial companies, even though the Final Rule under §165 has been promulgated with respect to BHCs and foreign banking organizations.[24] It appears that this Final Rule will become the baseline for enhanced prudential standards as they apply to non-bank financial companies. The perceived difficulty in not making the Final Rule applicable to non-bank companies is that the types of businesses, structures, and degrees of risk vary widely among these companies, whereas the Rules are more easily formulated with the more homogenized US and foreign BHCs.[25]

The long-anticipated Final Rule for non-bank financial companies is likely to be similar to the Final Rule that was issued by the Board of Governors of the Federal Reserve System on February 18, 2014 that implemented enhanced prudential standards applicable to BHCs and foreign banking organizations with total consolidated assets of $50 billion or more pursuant to §165 of the Dodd-Frank Act.[26] Less enhanced provisions are also made for large sums not meeting the $50 billion threshold. Thus, for publicly traded BHCs with total consolidated assets of $10 billion or more, the firm must establish a risk committee that approves and periodically reviews risk-management policies that is commensurate with its structure, risk profile, complexity, activities, and size.

The risk-management framework is to include policies and procedures establishing risk-management governance, risk-management procedures, and risk-control infrastructure for global operations. It is also to include processes and systems for implementing and monitoring compliance with policies for identifying current and emerging risks; risk-management deficiencies; allocation of risk-managerial responsibilities independent of senior management personnel; maintenance of records of proceedings; having at least one member with experience in identifying, assessing, and managing risk exposures; and assurance of independence in the performance of the said functions.[27] The Final Rule for large non-bank financial companies with comparable total assets is likely to contain similar provisions.

4.2.1 *Enhanced Prudential Requirements*

For BHCs with total consolidated assets of $50 billion or more, enhanced prudential standards are mandated. In addition to the risk-management and risk-committee requirements stated above, there are liquidity risk-management and liquidity stress test requirements. In addition to the less onerous risk-management and risk committee requirements, the larger entities of $50 billion or more must appoint an experienced chief risk officer who is responsible for overseeing the establishment of risk limits on an enterprise-wide basis; implementing ongoing compliance; managing risks and risk controls within the parameters of the company's risk control framework; and monitoring and testing the company's risk controls. He or she is to be responsible for reporting risk-management deficiencies and to resolve them in a timely manner. For liquidity risk-management requirements, the board of directors of the company must approve an acceptable level of liquidity risk in connection with its operating strategies, taking into account its capital structure, risk profile, complexity, activities, and size. The board of directors must approve and periodically approve and periodically review its liquidity risk-management policies and procedures and strategies established by senior management. The risk committee must approve a contingency funding plan and any material revisions thereof.[28]

Senior management must establish and implement strategies, policies, and procedures to effectively manage the company's risk that may impact adversely the market's perception of its inability to meet collateral obligations. It must oversee and implement its liquidity risk management and reporting systems and report to the board at least quarterly the company's liquidity risk profile and liquidity risk tolerance. Senior management must approve new products and business lines that could have a significant effect on the company's liquidity risk profile and review at least annually whether any line or product creates an unanticipated liquidity risk. Further, it must review the cash-flow projections at least quarterly to ensure that the liquidity risk is within the established liquidity risk tolerance and establish liquidity risk limits. It must also engage in stress testing by approval of stress-testing practices, methodologies, and assumptions at least quarterly.

The company must establish and maintain a review function that is independent of management functions that execute funding to evaluate its liquidity risk management. The function must regularly evaluate the adequacy and effectiveness of the company's liquidity risk-management processes and assess whether it is in compliance with applicable laws and regulations. Issues arising from this must be reported to the board or to the risk committee for corrective action. The company must update its cash flow projections, establishing a methodology for making the projections, and include any assumptions and details as to its capital structure, risk profile, complexity, currency exposure, activities, and size of the company.[29] The Final Rule contains a lengthy methodology that is to be utilized in liquidity stress testing and buffer requirements.[30]

Top-tier non-bank financial companies will most likely have similar compliance mandates but dependent on the variant nature of the enterprise.

The FED indicated in its Final Rule that it intends, after a SIFI designation, to assess the business model, capital structure, and risk profile of the SIFI-designated company to determine how the proposed enhanced prudential standards should apply. It would also, where applicable, tailor the application of the standards to that non-bank financial company or to a category of comparable non-bank financial companies. The FED intends to take into account the differences among the SIFIs and BHCs supervised by the Board with total consolidated assets of \$50 billion or more. The FED intends to apply similar enhanced prudential standards to companies that are similar in activities and risk profiles. For BHCs that differ from other BHCs in their activities, balance-sheet structure, risk profile, and functional regulation, it expects to apply more tailored standards.

Governor Daniel Tarullo of the Board of Governors of the Federal Reserve, while noting that many commentators believed the Final Rule was not appropriate for non-bank financial institutions, nevertheless stated that companies similar in activities and profile to BHCs will likely be made subject to the Rule. Companies that differ in their activities, balance-sheet structure, risk profile, and financial regulation will be subject to more tailored standards. In either of the alternatives, the non-bank financial companies will be provided with notice and opportunity to comment prior to determination of their enhanced prudential standards.[31]

4.2.2 *Capital Planning*

A BHC with total consolidated assets of $50 billion or more is mandated to develop and maintain a capital plan. The Board's view is that capital planning at large, complex BHCs is crucial in ascertaining the company's ability to absorb unexpected losses and continue to lend to creditworthy businesses and consumers. In so doing, both the public and the FDIC's insurance program are safeguarded and are critical to the stability and effective functioning of the US financial system. The Federal Reserve's Capital Plan Rule and the associated annual CCAR focus on the amount of capital that a BHC has; the internal practices and policies a firm uses to determine the amount and composition of capital that would be adequate given the firm's risk exposures and corporate strategies; and supervisory expectations and regulatory standards. Adequate capital planning will ensure that BHCs have sufficient capital in a broad range of future macroeconomic and financial market environments by governing the capital actions, including dividend payments, share repurchases, and share issuance and conversion.[32]

The company's board of directors is required to review the robustness of BHC's process for assessing its capital adequacy, ensure that any deficiencies are addressed and remedied, and approve the BHC's capital plan. The plan is to contain the following elements:

- An assessment of the expected uses and sources of capital in its planning that reflects the BHC's size, complexity, risk profile, and scope of operations, assuming both expected and stressful conditions, including estimates of projected revenues, losses, pro forma capital levels, and other relevant capital measures under a range of stressful conditions;
- A calculation of the pro forma Tier 1 common ratio over the planning horizon under expected conditions and under a range of stressed scenarios, and discussion of how the company will maintain

a pro forma Tier 1 common ratio above 5 % under these conditions; a discussion of the results of any stress test required by law or regulation, and an explanation of how the capital plan takes these results into account;

- A detailed description of the BHC's process for assessing capital adequacy, including a discussion of how the BHC will, under expected and stressful conditions, maintain capital commensurate with its risks, maintain capital above the minimum regulatory capital ratios and above a Tier 1 common ratio of 5 %, and serve as a source of strength to its subsidiary depository institutions;
- A discussion of how the BHC will, under expected and stressful conditions, maintain sufficient capital to continue its operations by maintaining ready access to funding, meeting its obligations to creditors and other counterparties, and continuing to serve as a credit intermediary; the BHC's capital policy; and
- A discussion of any expected changes to the BHC's business plan that are likely to have a material impact on the firm's capital adequacy or liquidity.

There are provisions for review of the capital plan by both the Board and the Federal Reserve Bank (FRB) which may include resubmission to cure the plan's inadequacy, if any; restrictions on distribution of capital unless approved by the board of directors of the BHC and/or the FRB with exceptions for well-capitalized BHCs; and provisions for disapproval of the plan and hearing on the merits thereof.[33]

4.2.3 Resolution Plans

Financial Stability Board (FSB)

The FSB adopted guidance for national regimes entitled *Key Attributes of Effective Resolution for Financial Institutions* (KA),[34] pursuant to a mandate from the G20 which approved the document at the Cannes Summit in November 2011. The document addressed the problem of cross-border resolution (bankruptcy reorganization) of financial institutions, permitting financial companies to continue operation at no cost to taxpayers and rendering an effective resolution to claims of creditors. The KA listed 12 essential features that should be made a part of the reorganization, taking into account the varying national legal systems and market environments.

Before addressing each of the features, the FSB stated that an effective resolution regime should accomplish the following:

- Ensure continuity of systemically important financial services and payment, clearing and settlement functions;
- Protect, where applicable and in coordination with the relevant insurance schemes and arrangements, such depositors, insurance policyholders, and investors as are covered by such schemes and arrangements, and ensure the rapid return of segregated client assets;
- Allocate losses to firm owners (shareholders) and unsecured and uninsured creditors in a manner that respects the hierarchy of claims;
- Not rely on public solvency support and not create an expectation that such support will be available;
- Avoid unnecessary destruction of value, and therefore seek to minimize the overall costs of resolution in home and host jurisdictions and, where consistent with the other objectives, losses for creditors;
- Provide for speed and transparency and as much predictability as possible through legal and procedural clarity and advanced planning for orderly resolution;
- Provide a mandate in law for cooperation, information exchange, and coordination domestically and with relevant foreign resolution authorities before and during a resolution;
- Ensure that non-viable firms can exit the market in an orderly way; and
- Be credible, and thereby enhance market discipline and provide incentives for market-based solutions. Jurisdictions should have in place a resolution regime.[35]

The 12 attributes are as follows:

- *Scope.* The scope of the guidance includes any systemically important financial institution, its holding companies, branches, and other entities within its purview, particularly all domestically important G-SIFIs.
- *Resolution authority.* Every national jurisdiction should have a regime devoted to exercising powers of resolution. The resolution authority should be independent; have unimpeded access to the firms requiring resolution; be free of liability for actions or omissions; be able to pursue financial stability, protect investors, policy

holders, and depositors; avoid lessening of value and excessive costs; and consider the impact of its actions on the financial stability of other jurisdictions.

- *Resolution powers.* Resolution should take place before the firm is totally insolvent and before all equity is erased. The resolution authority should be given a wide range of powers, including the following: the power to transfer selected assets and liabilities to a third party; establish bridge institutions to take over and continue operations of the failed firm; be able to remove and replace senior management officials; appoint an administrator to take control of the firm; operate the firm in its entirety; continue essential services of the firm; override rights of shareholders; transfer or sell assets and liabilities and other aspects of the firm; establish a separate asset management vehicle; temporarily stay the exercise of termination rights; impose a moratorium on payments to unsecured creditors and customers; and effect the closure and orderly wind-down of the failed firm. With respect to insurance firms, the resolution authorities should be enabled to undertake a portfolio transfer of all or part of the insurance business to another insurer and discontinue the writing of new business.
- *Set-off, netting, collateralization, segregation of client assets.* The legal framework governing each of the said areas should be clear and transparent. If any of the said rights entitle the holders to exercise acceleration or early termination, the resolution authorities should have the power to stay such rights temporarily not exceeding two business days pending resolution of the claims.
- *Safeguards.* Resolution powers are to be exercised fairly with equality of treatment to creditors of the same class; equity holders are to absorb losses first and there is to be no loss to senior debt-holders unless the subordinated debt has been written off entirely; and creditors are to receive at least the same compensation they would receive in liquidation.
- *Funding of firms in resolution.* Resolution authorities should not be reliant on public or bail-out funds. If such funds are necessary, then provisions should be made to recover the moneys expended from shareholders and unsecured creditors and these should be subject to strict conditions to minimize risk of moral hazard. As a last resort, the firm may be taken over by the public authorities on a temporary basis to continue critical operation while seeking a permanent solution.

- *Legal framework conditions for cross-border cooperation.* The resolution authorities are to cooperate with other national authorities for cross-border insolvencies and not exercise jurisdiction with respect to resolution or insolvency proceedings in another jurisdiction. It may exercise jurisdiction with respect to local branches of foreign firms and cooperate with the other jurisdiction in the orderly transfer of property. National laws should not discriminate against creditors on the basis of their nationality and should provide for transparent and expedited processes to give effect to foreign resolution measures.
- *Crisis Management Groups (CMGs).* Both the home and key host authorities of all G-SIFIs should maintain CMGs for the resolution of all cross-border issues pertaining to the financial crisis of the firm and should include the supervisory authorities, central banks, resolution authorities, finance ministries, and public authorities responsible for the guarantee schemes of jurisdictions that are home or host to entities of the group that are material to its resolution, and should cooperate closely with authorities in other jurisdictions where firms have a systemic presence.
- *Institution-specific cross-border cooperation agreements.* For all G-SIFIs, the home and host countries should have agreements that establish the objectives and processes for cooperation through the CMGs; define the role and responsibilities of each of the national authorities; set out the process for sharing of information; coordinate in the conduct of resolvability assessments; have agreements concerning consultation, information, and implementation measures; and have the agreements made public.
- *Resolvability assessments.* At least for G-SIFIs, resolution authorities are to regularly undertake resolvability assessments concerning the feasibility of resolution strategies, the extent of critical services performed, intra-group exposures, robustness of cross-border cooperation, and information sharing.
- *Recovery and resolution planning.* Jurisdictions should have in place an ongoing process for recovery and resolution planning including a requirement for the firm's senior management to be responsible for providing authorities with an assessment of recovery plans. These plans should include financial and economic functions for which continuity is critical; suitable resolution options to preserve those functions during the wind-down of the firm; data requirements on the firm's business operations, structures, and systemically impor-

tant functions; potential barriers to effective resolution and actions to mitigate those barriers; actions to protect insured depositors and insurance policyholders; and ensure the rapid return of segregated client assets and clear options or principles for the exit from the resolution process.
- *Access to information and information sharing.* There should be no impediment to information-sharing among supervisory authorities, central banks, resolution authorities, finance ministries, and public authorities.[36]

§165(d)(8) of the Dodd-Frank Act states that the Board and the FDIC jointly issue rules and requirements with respect to the submission and content of a resolution plan for *covered companies*, defined as any non-bank financial company supervised by the Board, a BHC having $50 billion or more in total consolidated assets, and any foreign bank of BHC with $50 billion or more in assets connected to and having a functionally regulated subsidiary in the USA that is significant to the critical operations or core business of the foreign entity.[37]

In essence, a covered company is to annually file a resolution plan with the FRB and the FDIC, the substance of which is dependent on its relevant size. Thus, if the covered company has less than $100 billion in total non-bank assets, or if it is a foreign company with the said sum in total US assets, then the filing may be limited to an executive summary of the plan with more limited substance. For all plans, the executive summary should include (1) the key elements of the covered company's strategic plan for rapid and orderly resolution in the event of material financial distress at or failure of the covered company; (2) material changes to the covered company's resolution plan; and;(3) any actions taken by the covered company since filing of the previous resolution plan to improve the effectiveness, mitigate any material weaknesses or impediments of the covered company's resolution plan, or remediate for the effective and timely execution of the resolution plan.[38]

The resolution plan, among other provisions, is to include the following:

- A strategic analysis describing the company's plan for the rapid and orderly resolution of the firm in the event of material financial distress or failure;
- Key assumptions and analyses underlying the plan and assumptions about the economic or financial conditions attendant thereto;

- Range of specific actions to be taken to facilitate a rapid and orderly resolution;
- Funding, liquidity, and capital needs and resources in the event of failure or material distress;
- Strategy and actions to be taken in the event of failure or discontinuation of a material entity, core business line, or critical operation;
- Strategy for protecting any insured depository institutions subsidiary from risks arising from the activities of any non-bank subsidiaries;
- Time needed for successful execution of the plan;
- Identification and description of any potential material weaknesses or impediments for the timely execution of the plan;
- Acts and steps to be taken to remediate or mitigate the weaknesses; and
- Provision of processes for determining the current market values and marketability of the core business lines; and feasibility and assessment of the impact for execution of any sales, divestitures, restructurings, recapitalizations, or similar actions.[39]

The regulation contains detailed requirements concerning corporate governance with respect to resolution planning, including how the plan is integrated into the corporate governance structure; the company's policies, procedures, and internal controls for preparation and approval of the plan; the identity and position of senior management officials responsible for the plan; the nature and extent of reporting to senior executive officers and the board of directors regarding the details of the plan; and a description of contingency planning and relevant risk measures used by the company. The plan is also to contain the company's organizational structure of all material entities in the organization; all legal entities and foreign offices; intellectual property rights; core business lines; balance sheets for all entities; material components of liabilities; collateral pledged; guarantees and contractual obligations including off-balance-sheet exposures; hedging strategies; major counterparties; and other pertinent information.

The company's management information systems are to be set forth in substantial detail. Materials to be added to the plan include a detailed inventory and description of key management information systems and applications; identification and scope of key internal reports; processes for supervisory or regulatory agencies with access to the management information systems; analyses of the systems' capabilities and weaknesses; and its interconnections and interdependencies.[40]

Upon submission of the resolution plan, the Board and the FDIC are to review it within 60 days, and if it is deemed incomplete they are to jointly advise the covered company, which is then to resubmit the plan with the additional data requested. A failure to cure the deficiencies may subject the covered company to more stringent capital, leverage, or liquidity requirements.[41]

4.3 UNCITRAL and US Chapter 15 Bankruptcy Code

The United Nation's Commission on International Trade Law (UNCITRAL) has also given its recommendations with respect to large business enterprises that are multinational and even anational in scope that may become insolvent, thereby affecting a multiplicity of jurisdictions accompanied by often conflicting national rules and regulations. Its Model Law on Cross-Border Insolvency and Guide to Enactment seeks to address the problems that confront investors and other persons affected by the insolvency.[42]

In the USA, a new Chapter 15, "Ancillary and Other Cross Border Cases," was added to the Bankruptcy Code on April 20, 2005 by the Bankruptcy Abuse Prevention and Consumer Protection Act of 2005.[43] It is the US domestic adoption of the Model Law on Cross-Border Insolvency promulgated by UNCITRAL in 1997 and replaced § 304 of the Bankruptcy Code. Similar to a Chapter 11 reorganization proceeding, it seeks to facilitate the rescue of financially troubled businesses in order to protect investments and employees. It applies where assistance is sought by a foreign court or a foreign representative in a foreign proceeding. Thus, a Chapter 15 case is ancillary to the foreign proceeding. Where the primary or complex assets are located in the USA, the proceeding may be one under Chapter 7 (liquidation) or Chapter 11 (reorganization).

The European Union (EU) regulation on cross-border insolvency adopted the provisions of UNCITRAL under Article 15.[44] As amended, the Regulation established a European framework for the member states of the EU. Its emphasis is on the "center of main interests" conveying jurisdiction in the courts of the member state that has primary jurisdiction, while the other member states are to grant recognition in secondary proceedings initiated therein.

4.3.1 UNCITRAL Model Law

The Model Law recognizes that confusion often arises among states (countries) concerning how to resolve issues arising out of insolvencies of companies that are multinational in scope. Accordingly, the Model Law's main objective, while not creating substantive law, is to provide effective mechanisms for states to deal with cross-border insolvencies. Among the countries that have adopted the Model Law in whole or substantial part are the USA, Japan, and the UK.[45]

Purpose of the Model Law

The purpose of the Model Law, as repeated almost verbatim in §1501(a)(1-5) of the US Bankruptcy Code, is to provide effective mechanisms in cross-border insolvency actions to promote the following objectives:

- Cooperation between the courts and other competent authorities of this state and foreign states involved in cross-border insolvency. (§1501(a)(1)(B) repeats the Model Code language and adds "(A) cooperation between courts of the United States, United States trustees, examiners, debtors, and debtors in possession";
- Greater legal certainty for trade and investment;
- Fair and efficient administration of cross-border insolvencies that protects the interests of all creditors and other interested persons, including the debtor;
- Protection and maximization of the value of the debtor's assets; and
- Facilitation of the rescue of financially troubled businesses, thereby protecting investment and preserving employment.[46]

The Model Law recognizes that there are differences in national procedural laws, and does not attempt to promote substantive unification of insolvency laws nor to critique judicial decisions or to instruct judges on how to determine applications for recognition and relief under state law. It modestly seeks to offer a general guidance by pointing out procedural and substantive issues a judge may wish to consider in making a ruling.[47] While recognizing the differences among national laws, it provides *foreign representatives* (persons administering a foreign insolvency proceeding) with access to the courts of states that have enacted the Model Law;[48] determination of whether a foreign insolvency proceeding should be accorded recognition; a transparent regime for foreign creditors to commence or participate in an insolvency proceeding within that state; permits cooperation among courts of the different jurisdictions; and establishes rules for coordination of relief.[49]

4.3.2 *Basic Principles of the Model Law*

Access Principle

The Model Law is based on four basic principles of access, recognition, relief, and compensation and coordination principles as set forth in Articles 25–29.[50] Article 25 of the Model Law provides that the state court shall cooperate to the maximum extent possible with the foreign court or foreign representative. The foreign representative is entitled to commence a proceeding under state law if the conditions of state law are met.[51] It further provides that the court is entitled to communicate directly with, or to request information or assistance directly from, foreign courts or foreign representatives. §1511 of the Bankruptcy Code permits a recognized foreign representative to commence either an involuntary or voluntary proceeding under §§301–303 if the foreign proceeding is a foreign main proceeding. The petition is to be accompanied by a certified order granting recognition and that the court be advised of the foreign representative's intent to commence a case under this section. §1525 states that the US court is to cooperate either directly or through the trustee and communicate with the foreign court or representative subject to the rights of a party in interest to notice and participation.

The question arises whether the foreign representative is entitled to act under state law. It is left to the reviewing court to make the determination based possibly on expert evidence. UNCITRAL's judicial interpretation indicates that a judge may have to be satisfied that there is a foreign proceeding in which recognition is sought, is collective in nature, arose out of a law relating to insolvency, and is under the supervision of a foreign court, and whether the applicant is authorized to administer the reorganization or liquidation of the debtor's assets or affairs.[52]

Recognition Principle

Article 17 of the Model Law states that a foreign proceeding shall be recognized in a state court if it is a *foreign proceeding* as defined under Article 2(a)[53]; the *foreign representative* (defined as person or body authorized in a foreign proceeding to administer the reorganization or the liquidation of the debtor's assets or affairs or to act as a representative of the foreign proceeding) applies for recognition; the application meets Article 15(2) requirements, that is, (1) either a certified copy of the decision commencing the foreign proceeding and appointment of the foreign representative, (2) a certificate affirming such proceedings and appointment of a representative, or (3) other evidence so establishing such proceedings and a representative; and the application is properly submitted. The foreign proceeding may be recognized either as a "foreign main proceeding" (if it takes place in a state where the debtor has the center of its main interests); or a *foreign non-main proceeding* (where the debtor has economic activity operations outside its main center of interests).

Chapter 15, §§1515–1517 of the Bankruptcy Code, sets forth the conditions for recognition of the foreign representative's petition by repeating the above requirements. It also provides that the court may presume recognition when a decision, certificate, or other documents from the foreign proceeding so indicates; and grants an order of recognition after notice and hearing.

Relief Principle

UNCITRAL Model Law Art. 21§ provides for a variety of forms of relief once recognition of a foreign proceeding has been granted: (1) interim (urgent) relief consisting of a stay of the commencement or continuation of individual actions or proceedings or execution concerning the debtor's assets, rights, obligations, or liabilities, as well as suspension of the right to transfer, encumber, or otherwise dispose of the said assets; (2) provide for the examination of witnesses, taking of evidence, or delivery of information concerning the debtor's assets, affairs, rights, obligations, or liabilities; (3) entrust the administration of all or part of the debtor's assets located within the state to the foreign representative or other designated person; and/or (4) grant such other relief available under state law. §§1519 and 1521 of the Bankruptcy Code are in accord.

Cooperation and Coordination Principle

Article 25 of the Model Code obligates the courts of the host and foreign states and foreign representatives to communicate and cooperate with each other to the maximum extent possible so as to ensure that the debtor's insolvency is resolved fairly and efficiently with maximum benefits to creditors. Cooperation consists of the appointment of a person or body to act as the court directs; communication of information by appropriate means; coordination of the administration and supervision of the debtor's assets and affairs; approval or implementation of agreements concerning coordination of proceedings; and the concurrent proceedings of the debtor.[54] The Bankruptcy Code §§1525–1527 repeats these forms of cooperation.

Scope of Application

The Model Law Chapter 1, Article 1, and Bankruptcy Code §1501(b)(1–4) state that cross-border insolvency applies where assistance is sought in the (US) state by a foreign court or a foreign representative in connection with a foreign proceeding; by a foreign country in connection with a cross-border insolvency; a concurrent foreign proceeding and a proceeding in the state where assistance is sought respecting the same debtor; or by creditors or other interested persons in a foreign country who have an interest in commencing a case or proceeding in the country where assistance is sought. The Model Law leaves it to the host country to decide which exclusions apply. Thus, the US Code excludes moneys or other securities required or permitted under state insurance laws for the benefit of US claimholders; an entity subject to proceedings under the Securities Investor Protection Act of 1970;[55] and certain other proceedings.

Public Policy Exception

The Model Law provides that "nothing in this Law prevents the court from refusing to take an action governed by this Law if the action would be manifestly contrary to the public policy of this State."[56] The Bankruptcy Code repeats the provision in §1506 of the Code and further provides that its provisions may not conflict with an obligation of the USA arising out of any treaty or other agreement.[57]

Commencement and Recognition of Foreign Proceedings

The ancillary proceeding commences by the filing of a petition for recognition of a foreign proceeding.[58] The petition may be made by an appointed foreign representative, and is accompanied by a certified copy of the decision of the foreign proceeding appointing the representative, a certificate or other evidence of the foreign court affirming the existence of such foreign proceeding, and the identification of all foreign proceedings respecting the debtor.[59] After notice and hearing, an order recognizing a foreign proceeding is to be entered as a foreign main proceeding if it is taking place where the debtor has the center of its interests or as a foreign non-main proceeding if the debtor has an establishment in the foreign state.[60] Once recognition is given by the US court, there is an automatic stay and the foreign representative may continue to operate the debtor's business in the ordinary course. The US court may authorize preliminary relief as permitted by the Code.[61] If the foreign representative initiates a full bankruptcy proceeding, then relief may be made respecting only the debtor's assets within the USA.[62]

Center of Main Interest (COMI)

Recognition of the foreign proceeding raises the question of whether the foreign proceeding is a "foreign main proceeding" as defined in Article 2(b) of the Model Law, "a foreign proceeding taking place in the State where the debtor has the center of its main interest." It is a crucial issue that underlies the refusal of US courts to give recognition to Russian Federation proceedings in the Yukos actions in the USA where the COM was determined to be in the Russian Federation and not in US courts in the absence of a lack of a substantial interest therein.[63]

Cooperation with Foreign Courts and Representatives

There are extensive provisions concerning cooperation between a domestic court and a foreign court. The provisions include cooperation with the foreign representative or court (in the USA through the appointed trustee) and communication directly with, or requesting of information or assistance from, a foreign court or foreign representative, subject to the rights of a party in interest to notice and participation.[64] The forms of cooperation may be implemented by any appropriate means, including: appointment of a person or body, including an examiner, to act at the direction of the court; communication of information by any means considered appropriate by the court; coordination of the administration and supervision of the debtor's assets and affairs; approval or implementation of agreements concerning the coordination of proceedings; and coordination of concurrent proceedings regarding the debtor.[65]

Relief upon Recognition

Both the Model Code and the Bankruptcy Code provide the following relief upon recognition of a foreign proceeding: staying the commencement or continuation of an individual action or proceeding concerning the debtor's assets, rights, obligations, or liabilities to the extent that they have not been stayed; staying execution against the debtor's assets to the extent they had not been previously stayed; suspending the right to transfer, encumber, or otherwise dispose of any assets of the debtor to the extent that they had not been previously suspended; providing for the examination of witnesses, the taking of evidence or the delivery of information concerning the debtor's assets, affairs, rights, obligations, or liabilities; entrusting the administration or realization of all or part of the debtor's assets within the territorial jurisdiction of the USA to the foreign representative or another person, including an examiner authorized by the court extending relief granted; and granting any additional relief that may be available to a trustee.[66]

The grant of recognition by a domestic court to a foreign main proceeding is binding upon all persons within its jurisdiction. In *In re Tembec Industries*,[67] the US District Court, in its Order Granting Jurisdiction, permanently enjoined all old bondholders taking or continuing any act to obtain possession of, or exercise control over, the debtor or any of its property that is located within the territorial jurisdiction of the USA or any proceeds thereof; to transfer, relinquish, or dispose of any property of the Debtor; and/or commence or continue any action or legal proceeding.[68]

4.4 Final Rule for Global Systemically Important BHCs (G-SIB)[69]

The Board adopted a Final Rule on July 20, 2015 establishing risk-based surcharges requiring the largest, most systemically important US BHCs to further strengthen their capital positions beginning January 1, 2016 and be fully implemented three years thereafter. Under the rule, a BHC that is identified as a G-SIB will have to hold additional capital to increase its resiliency in light of the greater threat it poses to the financial stability of the USA. It follows the Basel III requirements discussed in Chap. 1. The Final Rule establishes the methodology for identifying a US top-tier BHC with total consolidated assets of $50 billion or more as a G-SIB and the methods that those firms will use to calculate a risk-based capital surcharge, which is calibrated to each firm's overall systemic risk. It affects eight US firms identified as G-SIBs, namely the Bank of America Corporation; The Bank of New York Mellon Corporation; Citigroup Inc.; The Goldman Sachs Group Inc.; JP Morgan Chase & Co.; Morgan Stanley; State Street Corporation; and Wells Fargo & Company.

The Final Rule exempts non-bank financial companies supervised by the FRB, which will have to comply with a Final Rule to be issued by the

Board and which will be based on the firm's business model, capital structure, and risk profile to determine whether enhanced prudential standards should apply and tailor the requirements on the multitude of forms that such company may assume. As stated by the Board's Chairperson, Janet L. Yellen:

> The Final Rule before the Board today imposes a risk-based capital surcharge on the most systemically important U.S. bank holding companies. A key purpose of the capital surcharge is to require the firms themselves to bear the costs that their failure would impose on others. In practice, this Final Rule will confront these firms with a choice: they must either hold substantially more capital, reducing the likelihood that they will fail, or else they must shrink their systemic footprint, reducing the harm that their failure would do to our financial system. Either outcome would enhance financial stability. The Final Rule complements other aspects of the Board's enhanced prudential standards for the largest and most systemic U.S. banking firms.[70]

In order to determine whether a BHC is a G-SIB, the Final Rule discusses the methodology for making the determination and two methods to calculate the G-SIB surcharge, the justification for using short-term wholesale funding, and the justification for the G-SIB calibration. The Final Rule also details the role of the surcharge in the capital framework and its implementation and timing. Initially, the Final Rule concerned a BHC with consolidated assets of $50 billion or more, but the Board raised the threshold number to total consolidated assets of $250 billion or more or $10 billion or more on-balance-sheet foreign exposures based on the belief that a BHC with a lower level of consolidated assets is unlikely to pose a systemic risk to the US economy.[71]

In order to determine whether a BHC is a G-SIB, the bank itself (subject to the Board's supervision) would have to annually compute its Method 1 score. The score is based on five broad categories that may indicate systemic risk, each of which is give the same 20 % total weight divided by an equal percentage weight for the subcategories, namely, (1) *size*; (2) *interconnectedness*, which consists of intra-financial system assets, intra-financial system liabilities, and securities outstanding; (3) *substitutability*, which includes assets under custody and underwritten transactions in debt and equity markets; (4) *complexity* with respect to notional amounts of over-the-counter derivatives, trading and available-for-sale securities, and level 3 assets; and (5) *cross-jurisdictional activity* with respect to cross-jurisdictional claims and cross-jurisdictional liabilities. If the BHC exceeds a designated Method 1 score, then it is deemed to be a G-SIB. The surcharge for the particular firm will vary from 0 % to 3.5 % for every 100 basis point increase in score.[72]

The FRB adopted a second method for making the G-SIB determination which would enable a BHC to better predict whether it will be deemed to be a G-SIB and also enable the firm to take steps to reduce its G-SIB surcharge. Method 2 is similar to Method 1 except that in the substitutability category a quantitative measure of the firm's use of short-term wholesale funding is used. The amount of the surcharge also ranges from 0 % for firms not meeting the threshold to gradual increases from 1.0 % with increases to 5.5 % plus a 0.5 percentage point increase for every 100 basis point increase in the score. The table of Coefficients for Method 2 Systemic Indicators shows a greatly enhanced percentage for Level 3 assets that is higher than all of the other systemic indicators combined.

Level 3 assets are short-term wholesale funding which if relied on by a BHC may make it vulnerable in times of stress to runs that undermine financial stability as illustrated during the past financial crisis. When short-term creditors become concerned with a firm's financial outlook, they have strong incentives to withdraw funds before other creditors may become aware, which in turn will lead to a drain of liquid assets. A downward spiral may then take place, whereby the firm may have to engage in a fire sale of its capital assets, which depletes its capital and drives down asset prices in the financial marketplace.[73]

As stated above, the indicators of systemic risk include the following:

- *Size*. A banking organization that possess a large share of total financial activities is more likely to negatively impact the financial markets and the overall financial markets because of its size, the volume of transactions, and the counterparties affected. In the event of distress or failure it would be difficult to other firms to replace it. Size would have been measured by total exposures, which was equal to the BHC's measure of total leverage exposure calculated pursuant to the regulatory capital rule.
- *Interconnectedness*. The greater the interconnectedness of the BHC with other financial institutions and intermediaries, the more likely distress or failure of the institution would impact the overall economy. Interconnectedness is measured by intra-financial system assets, intra-financial system liabilities, and securities outstanding as of December 31 of a given year. The financial institutions referred

to as depository institutions are BHCs, securities dealers, insurance companies, mutual funds, hedge funds, pension funds, investment banks, and central counterparties. Central banks and multilateral development banks are excluded, but state-owned commercial banks are included.

- *Substitutability.* The Final Rule indicated that substitutability is a category of systemic importance. A firm's potential adverse systemic impact depends in part on the degree to which other banking organizations are able to serve as substitutes in the event that the banking organization is unable to perform its role. The rule states three indicators to measure substitutability: (1) assets under custody as of December 31 of a given year: (2) the total value of payments sent over the calendar year; and (3) the total value of transactions in debt and equity markets underwritten during the calendar year. The rule would have a greater impact with respect to a finding of systemic importance for certain banking organizations that are dominant in the provision of asset custody, payment systems, and underwriting services.

The indicator of assets under custody refers to a banking organization that manages or administers the custody or safekeeping of stocks, debt securities, or other assets for institutional and private investors. A collapse of such a G-SIB firm could seriously disrupt financial markets and domestic and global economies. A G-SIB firm that engages in substantial volume of payments will affect many customers in the event of a collapse, because customers would not be able to process payments and could experience liquidity issues. The third factor of systemic importance is the total value of transactions in debt and equity, which in the event of a G-SIB failure could impede new securities issuances and may increase the cost of debt and capital.

- Complexity. Complexity is characterized under the Final Rule as a category of systemic importance. In the event of failure or distress, the more complex a banking organization is, the greater the expense and time necessary to resolve it. Costly resolutions can have negative cascading effects in the markets, including disorderly unwinding of positions, fire sales of assets, disruption of services to customers, and increased uncertainty in the markets. There are three indicators of complexity (1) complexity notional amount of over-the-counter (OTC) derivatives, (2) Level 3 assets, and (3) trading and available-for-sale (AFS) securities as of December 31 of a given year.

OTC Derivatives Activity

According to the Final Rule, a BHC's over-the-counter derivatives activity will be the aggregate notional amount of the company's transactions that are cleared through a central counterparty or settled bilaterally. *Level 3 assets* will be equal to the value of the assets that the BHC measures at fair value as required by regulation. They are generally illiquid assets with fair values that cannot be determined by observable data, such as market price signals or models. The value of the Level 3 assets will be based on internal estimates or risk-adjusted value ranges by the banking organization. With respect to trading and AFS securities, the Final Rule makes note that these can cause a market disturbance through mark-to-market losses and fire sales of assets in times of distress.

Cross-Jurisdictional Activity

The Board stated that the addition of other jurisdictions is a category of systemic importance because of the difficulty and cost of resolution in the event of distress of failure.

Use of Short-Term Wholesale Funding (Maturity of Less Than One Year)

The rule identified five categories of short-term wholesale funding sources: (1) secured funding transactions; (2) unsecured wholesale funding; (3) covered asset exchanges; (4) short positions; and (5) brokered deposits.

- *Secured funding transactions* include repos, securities lending transactions, secured funding from a Federal Reserve Bank or a foreign central bank, Federal Home Loan Bank advances, secured deposits, loans of collateral to effect customer short positions, and other secured wholesale funding arrangements of under one-year maturity. They are characterized as systemic because counterparties are more likely to remove or roll-over the transactions than longer-term funding.
- *Unsecured wholesale funding.* Unsecured wholesale funding includes wholesale deposits; federal funds purchased; unsecured advances from a public sector entity, sovereign entity, or US government-sponsored enterprise; unsecured notes; bonds, or other unsecured debt securities issued by a G-SIB (unless sold exclusively to retail customers or counterparties); brokered deposits from non-retail customers; and any other transaction where an on-balance-sheet unsecured credit obligation has been contracted. It falls under this rubric

because, according to the Rule's commentary, funding from wholesale counterparties presents greater run risk to banking organizations during periods of stress as compared to the same type of funding provided by retail counterparties, because wholesale counterparties facing financial distress are likely to withdraw large amounts of wholesale funding in order to meet financial obligations.

- *Covered asset exchanges.* Covered assets include the fair market value of all assets that a G-SIB must return in connection with transactions where it has provided a non-cash asset of a given liquidity category to a counterparty in exchange for non-cash assets of a higher liquidity category, and the G-SIB and the counterparty agreed to return the assets to each other at a future date. The systemic risk arises from the possibility that the unwinding of such transactions could negatively impact a G-SIB's funding profile in a period of stress because it requires the G-SIB to obtain funding for a less liquid asset or security if the counterparty is unwilling to roll over the transaction.
- *Short positions.* Short positions are transactions where a BHC borrows a security from a counterparty to sell to a second counterparty, and must return the security to the initial counterparty in the future. A short position involving a certain security was assigned the same weight as a secured short-term wholesale funding liability backed by the same asset.
- *Broker deposits and brokered sweep deposits.* Retail brokered deposits and brokered sweep deposits are so characterized because of demonstrable volatility in times of stress, notwithstanding the presence of deposit insurance. The deposits are readily movable from one firm to another during times of stress, as customers and counterparties seek higher interest rates or seek to use those funds for other purposes and on account of the incentives that third-party brokers have to provide the highest possible returns for their clients. Non-brokered deposits or brokered sweep deposits are exempt because of the unlikelihood that they would pose liquidity risks in times of stress.
- *Capital surcharge.* The Final Rule proposes a G-SIB surcharge to the regulatory capital rule's capital conservation buffer.[74] The Rule states that a banking organization must maintain a minimum common equity tier 1 capital requirement of 4.5 %, a minimum tier 1 capital requirement of 6.0 %, and a minimum total capital requirement of 8.0 %. In addition to those minimums, in order to avoid limits on capital distributions and certain discretionary bonus payments,

a banking organization must hold a capital conservation buffer composed of common equity tier 1 capital equal to more than 2.5 % of risk-weighted assets following a phase-in period. The capital conservation buffer is divided into quartiles, each associated with increasingly stringent limitations on capital distributions and certain discretionary bonus payments as the capital conservation buffer approaches zero.

4.4.1 *Enhanced Prudential Standards for Foreign Banking Organizations (FBO)*

The Final Rule, in addition to BHCs, also applied enhanced prudential standards for foreign (non-US) banking organizations that were essentially similar to the regulations applicable to BHCs. An FBO with total consolidated assets of more than $10 billion but less than $50 billion and a foreign savings and loan holding company consolidated assets of more than $10 billion must be subject to capital stress testing regime by its home country that meets US requirements; these include an annual supervisory capital stress test conducted by the home-country supervisor; governance and controls of stress-testing practices by the company's management and board; and, if the company does not meet the said standards, then it must maintain eligible assets in its US branches of not less than 105 % of average value daily of the total liabilities of all branches of the company and conduct an annual stress test of its US subsidiaries annually to verify that it can meet losses as a result of adverse economic conditions. The FBO must certify that it has established a risk committee for its global operations to oversee risk-management policies of the company, and this committee must include at least one member with experience in identifying, assessing, and managing risk exposures of large, complex firms (Table 4.1).

4.4.2 *FBO with $50 Billion or More of Total Consolidated Assets but Under $50 Billion of Combined US Assets*

A FBO meeting the asset requirement must certify to the FED that it meets capital adequacy standards as set forth by its home country in accordance with the Basel Committee Capital Framework, or otherwise meet the Basel standards if the home country does not adhere to the framework. It must also certify to the FED that it maintain a standalone committee on the global board of directors that oversees the risk-management

Table 4.1 Requirements for foreign banking organizations

Size	*Requirements*
Total consolidated assets of more than $10 billion but less than $50 billion	Company-run stress tests
Total consolidated assets equal to or greater than $10 billion but less than $50 billion (if publicly traded)	Risk committee
Total consolidated assets of $50 billion or more, but combined US assets of less than $50 billion	Risk-based and leverage capital Risk management Risk committee Liquidity Capital stress testing Debt to equity limits (upon grave threat determination)
Total consolidated assets of $50 billion or more, and combined US assets of $50 billion or more	Risk-based and leverage capital Risk management Risk committee Liquidity risk management, liquidity stress testing, and buffer Capital stress testing US intermediate holding company requirement (if the foreign banking organization has US non-branch assets of $50 billion or more) Debt-to-equity limits (upon grave threat determination)

policies and has at least one member that has the relevant expertise. The company must also meet liquidity risk-management requirements annually, and report to the FED the results of an internal liquidity stress-testing accordance with the Basel Committee Principles. It must also certify that its home country regime has capital stress-testing requirements that meet Basel standards.

4.4.3 *FBO with Total Consolidated Assets of $50 Billion or More and Combined US Assets of $50 Billion or More*

The regulations impose much more stringent standards than are applicable to a US intermediate holding company. The company must establish a US intermediate holding company or comparable subsidiary organized under US law; be governed by a board of directors pursuant to US law; and report to the FED about the details of the company and certify that it meets the Final Rule's standards. The holding company must meet risk-based and leverage capital standards; risk management and risk committee requirements; liquidity risk management, stress testing and buffers; capital stress testing; and debt-to-equity limits, if it is determined that the company may pose a threat to US financial stability.

In accordance with the said requirements, the FBO is to submit an implementation plan to the FED that includes a list of all US subsidiaries setting forth ownership interest in each subsidiary; a projected timeline for the transfer by the FBO of its ownership interest to the US intermediate holding company; a projected timeline of all planned capital action or strategies of capital accretion; a description of its risk-management practices; a description of the current liquidity stress testing practices of its US operations; and other requirements. The risk-management framework must be commensurate with the structure, size, risk profile, activities, and complexity of the company. There are to be processes in place establishing risk-management governance, procedures, and risk-control infrastructure; systems for implementation and monitoring compliance with the policies and procedures; processes and systems for identifying and reporting risks and risk-management deficiencies of the holding company; and management and employee responsibilities.

Corporate governance requirements include a risk-management committee similar to that stated above but also at least one member who is not an officer or employee of the FBO and not a member of its immediate family. The FBO must certify to the FED that it meets capital adequacy standards of its home country, which are in compliance with Basel capital standards. The risk-management committee, FBO, or holding company must certify at least annually that it has met the acceptable level of liquidity risk given the unique structure, risk profile, size, activities, and capital structure of the firm. The US chief risk officer of the holding company must report to the firm's risk committee on the liquidity risk profile of the FBO's combined US operations and approve new products and business lines after assessing their risks, liquidity costs, and benefits. There are detailed requirements for liquidity and capital stress testing.[75]

4.5 Commentary on Director Independence

The major complaint concerning the imposition of enhanced prudential standards on General Electric Capital Corporation Inc. (GECC) was the requirement of additional independent directors to the Board to the already existing independent directors. The meaning of director independence can be gauged from a number of sources. The ENRON debacle led to the enactment of the Sarbanes-Oxley Act of 2002. §301amended the Securities Exchange Act of 1934 regarding the responsibilities of the audit committee of a publicly traded company with respect to registered public accounting firms. Each member of the audit committee is to be a member of the board of directors and shall be independent. The statute states that in order to be considered independent a member of the audit committee "may not other than in his or her capacity as a member of the audit committee, the board of directors, or any other board committee accept any consulting, advisory, or other compensatory fee from the issuer; or be an affiliated person of the issuer or any subsidiary thereof."[76]

The New York Stock Exchange is much more explicit in defining the meaning of director independence. In its Listed Company Manual defines *independent director* as one where:

- The board of directors affirmatively determines that the director has no material relationship with the listed company (either directly or as a partner, shareholder, or officer of an organization that has a relationship with the company);
- In addition, in affirmatively determining the independence of any director who will serve on the compensation committee of the listed company's board of directors, the board of directors must consider all factors specifically relevant to determining whether a director has a relationship to the listed company which is material to that director's ability to be independent from management in connection with the duties of a compensation committee member, including, but not limited to:

  - The source of compensation of such director, including any consulting, advisory or other compensatory fee paid by the listed company to such director; and
  - Whether such director is affiliated with the listed company, a subsidiary of the listed company or an affiliate of a subsidiary of the listed company.[77]

In a commentary, the Manual states that it is not possible to anticipate or explicitly provide for all circumstances that could signal a lack of independence; albeit ownership of shares in the company, even if significant, is not a bar to independence. With respect to the sources of the directors' compensation, the board should examine whether such compensation would impair the director's independent judgment concerning the company's executive compensation. An "immediate family member" is anyone sharing the person's home, including in-laws. Other factors that may call into question a director's independence are:

- The director is, or has been within the last three years, an employee of the company, or an immediate family member is or within the last three years has been an executive officer of the company;
- The director has received, or has an immediate family member who has received, during any twelve-month period within the last three years, more than $120,000 in direct compensation from the listed company, other than director and committee fees and pension or other forms of deferred compensation for prior service (provided such compensation is not contingent in any way on continued service);
- The director (A) is a current partner or employee of a firm that is the listed company's internal or external auditor; (B) the director has an immediate family member who is a current partner of such a firm; (C) the director has an immediate family member who is a current employee of such a firm and personally works on the listed company's audit; or (D) the director or an immediate family member was within the last three years a partner or employee of such a firm and personally worked on the listed company's audit within that time;
- The director or an immediate family member is, or has been with the last three years, employed as an executive officer of another company where any of the listed company's present executive officers at the same time serves or served on that company's compensation committee;
- The director is a current employee, or an immediate family member is a current executive officer, of a company that has made payments to, or received payments from, the listed company for property or services in an amount which, in any of the last three fiscal years, exceeds the greater of $1 million, or 2% of such other company's consolidated gross revenues.[78]

The National Association of Securities Dealers (NASD), which merged with the regulatory committee of the New York Stock Exchange (NYSE) to form the current Financial Industry Regulatory Authority (FINRA) in 2007, has similar rules defining director independence.

In Chaps. 5 and 6, we will examine four of the critical areas of processes and types of financial intermediation, namely, securitization, repurchase agreements, hedge funds, and mutual funds, particularly money market mutual funds.

Notes

1. Dodd-Frank Act, §165(a), (b)(1).
2. *Id.*, §165(b)(2).
3. Dodd-Frank Act, §165(b).
4. *Id.*, §165(b)(1)(A).
5. *Id.*, §165(b)(1)(B).
6. *Id.*, §165(b)(4).
7. *Id.*, §165(b)(3).
8. *Id.*, §165 (d)(1), www.federalreserve.gov/.../boardmeetings/memo.
9. *Id.*, §165 (d)(2-5).
10. *Id.*, §165(d)(5)(B).
11. http://www.federalreserve.gov/bankinforeg/resolution-plans.htm.
12. *Id.*, §165(d)(2).
13. *Id.*, §165(d)(4-8).
14. Id., §165(e)(1-3).
15. §165(g).
16. §165 (h).
17. *Id.*, §165 (j).
18. *Id.*, §165(k).
19. , Federal Reserve System, *Policy Statement on the Scenario Framework for Stress Testing*, (November 6, 2013), 12 CFR Part 252, http://www.federal-reserve.gov/newsevents/press/bcreg/bcreg20121115a4.pdf.
20. Id at 19.
21. §165(i).
22. §210(a)(1)(E).
23. Federal Deposit Insurance Corporation, *Resolution of Systemically Important Financial Institutions: The Single Point of Entry*, Federal Register, Vol 78, No. 243 (Dec. 18, 2013).
24. *Enhanced Prudential Standards for Bank Holding Companies and for Foreign Banking Organizations*, 12 CFR Part 252, March 27, 2014, eff. June 1, 2014.
25. Noam Noked, *Enhanced Prudential Standards*, THE HARVARD LAW SCHOOL FORUM ON CORPORATE GOVERNANCE AND FINANCIAL REGULAITONS (March 10, 2014), http://blogs.law.harvard.edu/corpgov/2014/03/10/enhanced-prudential-standards/.

26. Federal Reserve System, *Enhanced Prudential Standards for Bank Holding Companies and Foreign Banking Organizations; Final Rule*, 12 CFR 252 (March 27, 2014).
27. *Id.*, §252.22.
28. *Id.*, §152.33.
29. *Id.*, §152.34.
30. *Id.*, §252.35.
31. Governor Daniel Tarullo, *Final rules to implement the enhanced prudential standards of Section 165 of the Dodd-Frank Act*, Feb. 7, 2014, Memorandum to Board of Governors, *www.federalreserve.gov/.../**boardmeetings**/memo....*
32. Federal Reserve Board, *Capital Planning at Large Bank Holding Companies: Supervisory Expectations and Range of Current Practice*, http://www.federalreserve.gov/bankinforeg/stress-tests/ccar/August-2013-Introduction.htm.
33. Federal Reserve System, Part 225 – Bank Holding Companies and Change in Bank Control, (Regulation Y), Subpart A, Capital Planning, 12 CFR §225.8.
34. Financial Stability Board, *Key Attributes of Effective Resolution Regimes for Financial Institutions* (Oct. 15, 2014), *available at* http://www.financialstabilityboard.org/2014/10/r_141015/.
35. *Id.* at 3.
36. *Id.*
37. 12 CFR Part 243.2(f).
38. 12 CFR §243(b).
39. 12 CFR §243.4.
40. *Id.*
41. 12 CFR §§243.5 and 243.6.
42. [17]G.A. Res. 52/158 (Dec. 15, 1997), U.N. UNCITRAL, *UNCITRAL Model Law on Cross-Border Insolvency with Guide to Enactment*, (hereinafter referred to as the "Model Law"), www.uncitral.org/uncitral/en/uncitral_texts/insolvency/1997Model.html.
43. 11 U.S.C. §101 et seq.
44. Council Regulation (EC) No. 1346 (2000) as amended on Dec. 12, 2012, COM (2012) 744 final, 2012/0360 (COD).
45. The countries that have adopted the Model Law and dates of enactment are: Australia (2008); Canada (2005); Chile (2014); Columbia (2006); Eritrea (1998); Greece (1998); Japan (2000); Mauritius (2009); Mexico (2000); Montenegro (2002); New Zealand (2006); Poland (2003); Republic of Korea (2006); Romania (2002); Serbia (2004); Slovenia (2007); South Africa (2000); Uganda (2011); United Kingdom (2000); (British) Virgin Islands (2003); United States (2005). UNCITRAL, *Status*, https://www.uncitral/en/uncitral.texts/insolvency/1997/Model_status.html.
46. Preamble of the Model Law,

47. *op. cit.* No. 2, Guide Part two (I)(1-3) and *UNCITRAL Model Law on Cross-Border Insolvency: The Judicial Perspective*, p. 1, www.uncitral.org/uncitral/en/uncitral_texts/insolvency/2011_Judicial_Perspective.html.
48. Foreign representatives are defined in Model Law, Art. 2(d) as "a person or body, including one appointed on an interim basis, authorized in a foreign proceeding to administer the reorganization or the liquidation of the debtor's assets or affairs or to act as a representative of the foreign proceeding."
49. Model Law Guide, Part Two (I)(3).
50. Model Law, Ch. IV. *Cooperation with foreign courts and foreign representatives.*
51. UNCITRAL. Art. 11.
52. UNCITRAL, *Judicial Perspective*, III(A).
53. UNCITRAL Article 2(a) defines a "foreign proceeding" as a collective judicial or administrative proceeding in a foreign state, including an interim proceeding, relating to insolvency wherein the assets and affairs of the debtor are subject to the control or supervision of the foreign court for the purpose of reorganization or liquidation.
54. Model Code, Article 27.
55. 15 U.S.C. § 78aaa through 15 U.S.C. § 78lll.
56. Article 6 of the Model Code.
57. §1503 of the Bankruptcy Code.
58. Model Code, Article 15 and Bankruptcy Code, §1504.
59. Bankruptcy Code, §1515, and Article 15 of the Model Code.
60. Bankruptcy Code §1517 and Model Code, Article 17.
61. Bankruptcy Code §1520 and Model Code Article 19.
62. Bankruptcy Code §1528.
63. *In re Yukos Oil Co.*, 320 BR 130 (Bankr. Ct., S.D. TX, 2004).
64. *Model Code, Article 26 and Bankruptcy Code §1525.*
65. Model Code, Article 27 and Bankruptcy Code §1527.
66. Model Code, Article 21 and Bankruptcy Code, §1521.
67. Case No. 08-13535 (S.D.N.Y., Oct. 31, 208), http://www.insolvency.ca/en/iicresources/resources/Tembecc.15RecognitionOrder.pdf.
68. For a discussion of the Tembec litigation, see Bruce Nathan and Eric Horn, *Demystifying Chapter 15 of the Bankruptcy Code*, BUSINESS CREDIT (June, 2009).
69. Federal Reserve System, *Regulatory Capital Rules: Implementation of Risk-based Capital surcharges for Global Systemically Important Bank Holding Companies*, 12 CFR Part 217 (July 20, 2015), http://www.federalreserve.gov/newsevents/press/bcreg/bcreg20150720a1.pdf.
70. Janet L. Yellen, *Opening Statement by Chair Janet L. Yellen* (July 20, 2015), Board of Governors of the Federal Reserve System (July 20, 2015), http://www.federalreserve.gov/newsevents/press/bcreg/yellen-statement-20150720a1.htm.

71. Final Rule, *supra* at Note 30, at 6–9.
72. *Id.* at 9–12.
73. *Id.* at 22–29.
74. The FED's Final Rule pertaining to the capital conservation buffer is discussed in 12 CFR 217.11(a) et seq., *available at* http://www.gpo.gov/fdsys/granule/CFR-2014-title12-vol2/CFR-2014-title12-vol2-sec217-11.
75. *Id.* There are excellent reviews and discussions of the Final Rule by Davis Polk, *Foreign Banks: Overview of Dodd-Frank Enhanced Prudential Final Rule* (Feb. 24, 2014); and Covington & Burling LLP, *Federal Reserve Finalizes Enhanced Prudential Standards For Large U.S. Bank holding Companies and Foreign Banking Organizations* (Feb. 24, 2014).
76. Sarbanes-Oxley Act of 2002 ("Public Company Accounting and Reform and Investor Protection Act"), Pub. L. 107-204, 116 Stat. 745, July 30, 2002.
77. NYSE Listed Company Manual, §303A.02 Independent Tests, http://nyse-manual.nyse.com/LCMTools/PlatformViewer.asp?selectednode=chp_1_4_3_3&manual=%2Flcm%2Fsections%2Flcm-sections%2F.
78. *Id.*

CHAPTER 5

Securitization and Repos

Four main areas of non-bank financial institutions or processes for possible inclusion as systemically important financial institutions are securitization, repurchase agreements, hedge funds, and mutual funds, particularly money market mutual funds. In this chapter we will discuss securitization and repossession agreements by stating what each entails, and US and international regulation thereof. In Chap. 6, we continue the discussion, with the focus on hedge funds and money market funds.

5.1 Securitization

Securitization is defined as the structured process whereby illiquid assets, such as mortgages, credit card receivables, auto and other forms of loans and other receivables, are packaged, underwritten, or otherwise transformed into asset-backed securities (ABS) and sold in a more liquid form. The originators of the assets are able to transfer some of the risks associated with the assets, remove them together with the underlying debt from their balance sheets to off balance sheets, add liquidity, and enable them to further engage in expansion or reinvestment activities by gaining broader funding sources by the improvement of their credit ratings at more favorable rates.[1] Investors stand to gain by the attractive yields of principal and interest on the debt offered by the transformed assets as well as by the increased secondary market liquidity, especially when given high

Roy J. Girasa, *Shadow Banking*, DOI 10.1007/978-3-319-33026-6_5

credit ratings. Borrowers from the originators benefit by the increased ability of originators to fund additional requests for loans made available to originators.

There are a variety of forms that securitization may take place dependent on the nature of the ABS. Thus, the security's structure is determined often by the types of collateral backing the security. For example, with respect to mortgage-backed securities (MBS), the underlying mortgage may be for a fixed rate of interest for the entire term of the loan; an adjustable interest rate generally based annually on an index such as the rate of US Treasury securities or the Cost of Funds Index; or a credit line mortgage that most often is also based on an adjustable rate of interest. It may also involve installment loans for automobiles, boats, recreational vehicles, and other consumer products. Theoretically, any type of asset that generates a cash flow may constitute the portfolio supporting the securitized debt, and may include mortgage indebtedness, corporate and sovereign loans, consumer credit, project finance, lease/trade receivables, home equity loans, small business loans, and individualized lending agreements.[2]

The parties to securitization are: the *lender* (originator) which loans money to a borrower who typically executes a promissory note and mortgage on the underlying asset; the *originator*, often a bank or finance company designates the pooled assets to be sold or assigned to a third party, *special purpose vehicle* (*trustee*). The trustee is responsible for administering the trust that holds the underlying asset and which usually disburses the cash flow received from the borrower. The assets are held by the trustee who, acting in a fiduciary capacity,[3] oversees the obligation and performance of the parties and, when appropriate, declares a default if the moneys due and owing are not paid. The servicer of the loan is usually the originator itself, which bills and receives the sums from the borrower and records and transmits them to and for the benefit of the trustee. The trustee, upon receiving the receivables or other assets involved in the securitization, generally issues certificates to the investors, which may be sold in public or private offerings.

The transaction may include:

- *Credit enhancer*, which backs the receipt of the cash flow from the securities as well as aiding in improving the credit rating, pricing, and marketing of the security.
- *Credit enhancement* may be provided by external parties such as a bank by interest-only strips, subordinated securities, by means of a

letter of credit that covers all or a part of the potential losses, or by the internal structure of one or more subordinate security apparatus and a capital account;

- *Rating agencies*, at least in prior years, were critical in evaluating the credit quality of the underlying assets; their role was mandated by certain investors such as insurance companies, pension funds, and commercial banks. They evaluate the quality of the assets, the originator of the assets, the soundness of the transaction, and quality of credit support.
- *Underwriter*, who advises sellers of the security on how to structure, price, and market it. Investors are mainly pension funds, fund managers, insurance companies, and commercial banks up to limited capital requirements, provided the securities meet certain standards.

The credit risk of the underlying assets may be divided into a number of tranches which are rated according to the degree of risk attributed to the particular tranche. The tranches that have the normal expected rate of portfolio losses have priority on the income derived from the underlying assets, while other tranches are divided into increasing risk of losses and lessening of claims on the underlying assets. The tranches with the highest risk ratio also provide the highest potential return on the investment. Other risks that may arise are *reputational risk* from possible negative public opinion of the originator, *strategic risk* to earnings and capital from the exposure to the long-term consequences of securitization, and *credit risk* from the obligors' default as evidenced by the subprime mortgage crisis.

5.1.1 The Subprime Mortgage Fiasco

Perhaps the most significant cause of the financial crisis of 2007–2009 and continuing to a lesser degree in subsequent years, particularly in Europe, was the purchase of subprime mortgages. Mortgages, historically, were among the most valued investments because the underlying security was the homes of individuals who rarely defaulted on loans, particularly when lenders required a minimum of 20 % cash by the borrower toward the purchase thereof (if 10 % or less, lenders required insurance against default). The lenders, often local savings and loan associations, utilized the model of *originate-to-hold* mortgages, which incentivized them to originate and hold mortgages that were highly secure and rarely led to foreclosures. In the event that a foreclosure took place, it was likely that the lender would receive all or most of the sums loaned at the foreclosure sale. The banking sector which issued mortgage loans was subject to relatively strict underwriting standards as set forth by government agencies.

The *originate-to-hold* model was transformed at the turn of the new century to one of *originate-to-secure* model. Originators of mortgage loans became engaged in the practice of persuading borrowers to purchase homes well beyond their financial means. Borrowers often received loans that were not only 100 % of the value of their homes but also included substantial closing costs. Unsophisticated borrowers were often induced to purchase the homes by the initial offer of *teaser rates* (lower than market rates), which, when they later rose substantially, were beyond the ability of the borrowers to pay. A result of the heightened demand for ownership by persons previously unqualified to purchase homes was the escalation of house prices almost daily to an extraordinary degree, which appeared to make the investment a no-lose proposition.

The problem arose when the financial crash of 2007 took place. The value of the homes, which were often substantially and fraudulently over-appraised at the behest of mortgage lenders, descended in value well beyond the amount of the original mortgage loans. Borrowers, even those who could afford the loans, often refused to pay the mortgage indebtedness and evaded their monetary obligations, thereby leading to a massive volume of foreclosures. The mortgage lenders were previously incentivized to approve subprime loans as part of the securitization process by expeditiously packaging the loans into tranches and selling them to ABS investors. These tranches were ranked in accordance with the degree of risks associated with them, so that the lowest returns for investors were for tranches with the lowest degree of risk and returns increased when the degree of risk rose. Owing to the complexity of the relatively new financial instruments, even relatively sophisticated investors were induced to purchase these securities.[4] The Dodd-Frank Act was enacted in part to regulate the gross abuses perpetrated by mortgage lenders and other malfeasants.[5]

5.1.2 Dodd-Frank Act and Securitization

As a result of the crisis brought about by the predatory lending practices of mortgage lenders, the Dodd-Frank Act, particularly Title XIV, Mortgage Reform and Anti-Predatory Lending Act, was the most comprehensive legislative effort to curb the practices. Other Titles under the Act include

Title IX, Investor Protections and Improvements to the Regulation of Securities, and Title X, Bureau of Consumer Financial Protection. In essence, the statute compelled mortgage lenders to have *skin-in-the-game*; that is, they had to be subject to personal losses to the extent of holding at least 5 % of the risk associated with the loan in the event of default by borrowers.[6] The purpose of this provision in the Act was to incentivize mortgage lenders and securitizers to behave more cautiously in their lending practices, whereas previously there was little or no incentive to assure that borrowers were able to meet their obligations of monthly mortgage payments.[7]

Qualified residential mortgages or servicing assets are exempt from the 5 % statutory rule. The requirements for the exemption are if: (1) all of the assets that collateralize the asset-backed securities are qualified residential mortgages or servicing assets; (2) none of the assets that collateralize the asset-backed securities are asset-backed securities; (3) each qualified residential mortgage collateralizing the asset-backed securities is currently performing; and (4) the depositor with respect to the securitization transaction certifies that it has evaluated the effectiveness of its internal supervisory controls with respect to the process for ensuring all assets that collateralize the asset-backed security are qualified residential mortgages or servicing assets, and has concluded that its internal supervisory controls are effective. To the dismay of many observers, the end result was that the decision to impose the 5 % rule was left to government administrators, who succumbed to the threat that few mortgage sums would be available to potential homebuyers if the monetary retention was kept in force.[8]

Dodd-Frank Act Mortgage Requirements

Subtitle A of Title XIV is concerned with Residential Mortgage Loan Origination Standards. A *mortgage originator* is one who for compensation takes a mortgage loan application, assists a customer to apply for a residential mortgage loan, or otherwise holds him/herself out as providing services in connection with such a loan. Recall how mortgage-backed loans were made to unqualified individuals. The Act requires that each mortgage originator be qualified, registered, and licensed as a mortgage originator in accordance with applicable federal and state law and includes their unique identifier on all loan documents. The Act provides exceptions for real estate brokers who are not compensated for the service; or who perform only clerical services; or are a creditor; or under circumstances where there is modification of the mortgage when there is danger of default.[9]

With respect to residential mortgage loans, mortgage originators and other persons are prohibited from receiving or giving financial compensation that varies based on the terms of the loan other than the amount of the principal. They are prohibited from steering any consumer to a residential mortgage loan if he or she lacks a reasonable ability to pay or where there are excessive fees or abusive terms. They may not mischaracterize the credit history of a consumer, the appraised value of the property, or discourage a consumer from applying for a mortgage loan from another less expensive originator. Also prohibited is the receipt of an additional origination fee by the originator who has been or will be paid by the consumer, except for other bona fide expenses or charges.[10] Mortgages with negative amortization are prohibited.

Liability for violations of the Truth-in-Lending Act with respect to a mortgage originator is three times the amount of direct or indirect compensation received plus the costs to the consumer and a reasonable attorney's fee.[11] Moreover, a consumer may raise a violation of the above requirements as a defense and possible setoff in a foreclosure action.[12] A requirement that disputes concerning the residential mortgage loan or the extension of credit under an open ended consumer credit plan be resolved by arbitration is prohibited. Similarly, a statutory cause of action may be not waived under a provision of either type of loan. Other violations of the Truth-in-Lending Act are subject to substantially increased monetary penalties. There is an exemption from liability where the obligor has been convicted of obtaining a residential loan by means of actual fraud.

Minimum Standards for Mortgages

Title XIV, Subtitle B of the Dodd-Frank Act, provides that "no creditor may make a residential mortgage loan unless the creditor makes a reasonable and good faith determination based on verified and documented information that, at the time the loan is consummated, the consumer has a reasonable ability to repay the loan according to its terms, and all applicable taxes, insurance (including mortgage guarantee insurance) and assessments." In order to make such a determination, the creditor is to examine the consumer's credit history, current income, income reasonably assured of receipt, current obligations, and debt-to-income ratio, which are all based on the use of a repayment schedule that fully amortizes the loan over its stated term. Income verification is to be ascertained by a review of the customer's W-2 Form, tax returns, payroll receipts, financial institution records, and other third-party verification. There are additional provisions for calculating the consumer's ability to repay where the loan is with a variable rate or interest-only loans.[13]

There are provisions of required disclosures for variable and fixed rate residential mortgage loans. For variable rate mortgages, where an escrow account is established for the payment of taxes, insurance, and assessments, the initial monthly payment due on the loan shall include the sums held for the said expenses and, thereafter, all amounts due on the loan for principal and interest and the said expenses. For residential mortgage loans, all settlement charges in connection with the loan are to be disclosed, including the aggregate amount of all fees paid to the mortgage originator and the total amount of the interest to be paid over the life of the loan.[14]

The creditor or servicer of the residential mortgage loan shall furnish the obligor, for each billing cycle, a statement that reflects the amount of the principal due on the loan; the current interest rate; the date on which the interest rate may next reset or adjust; the amount of prepayment fee to be charged; a description of any late payment fees; a telephone number and address for any inquiries; the names, addresses, telephone numbers, and Internet addresses of counseling service providers or other programs reasonably available; and other information the Board may prescribe.[15]

Safe Harbor Provisions

Title XIV sought to minimize the approval of residential mortgage loans to unqualified borrowers. It also provides for a "safe harbor" by permitting the creditor a presumption of ability to repay if the loan is a "qualified mortgage." A *qualified mortgage* has the following characteristics:

- Regular periodic payments for the loan may not (1) result in an increase of the principal balance, and (2) allows the consumer to defer repayment of principal;
- It does not result in a *balloon payment* (a scheduled payment more than twice the average of earlier scheduled payments);
- The income and financial resources relied upon to qualify the consumers for the loan are verified and documented;
- For a fixed rate loan the payment schedule fully amortizes the loan over the loan terms and takes into account all applicable taxes, insurance, and assessments;
- For adjustable rate mortgages (ARMs), the maximum rate permitted under the loan for the first five years is stated, coupled with a payment schedule that fully amortizes the loan over the loan term plus taxes, insurance, and assessments;

- Fully complies with rules and regulations relating to total monthly debt to monthly income or other measures of ability to pay regular expenses above the monthly debt;
- Total points and fees do not exceed 3 % of the total loan amount with exclusions for bona fide mortgage rate discount;
- Term of the loan does not exceed 30 years except for high-cost areas; and
- Reverse mortgages meet the standards for a qualified mortgage as set by the Board.[16]

A qualified mortgage is limited with respect to the prepayment penalty it may charge for a consumer for paying all or part of the principal after the loan is consummated. During the first year of the loan, the prepayment penalty may not exceed 3 % of the outstanding balance of the loan; then 2 % if paid in the second year; 1 % for the third year; and no penalty thereafter. If the residential mortgage loan does not meet the above standards, it may not charge a consumer a prepayment penalty.

High-Cost Mortgages

Subtitle C of the Dodd-Frank Act is concerned with *high-cost mortgages*, which are defined as consumer transactions secured by the consumer's principal dwelling, other than a reverse mortgage, if:

1. In the case of a credit transaction secured;

   - By the consumer's principal dwelling, other than a reverse mortgage, by a first mortgage having an annual percentage rate (APR) that exceeds 6.5 % over the prime offer rate for a comparable transaction (8.5 % if the dwelling is personal property for less than $50,000) or
   - By a subordinate or junior mortgage where the APR is more than 8.5 % over prime; or

2. The total points and fees paid in connection with the transaction, other than bona fide charges not retained by the mortgage originator, creditor, or affiliate exceed:

   - Where the transaction is $20,000 or more, 5 % of the total transaction amount; or
   - If less than $20,000, the lesser of 8 % or $1,000; or

3. The credit transaction documents permit the creditor to charge or collect prepayment fees or penalties more than 36 months after the closing of the transaction or where the fees or penalties exceed more than 2 % of the amount prepaid.[17]

There are similar prohibitions on balloon payments; a prohibition on late fees in excess of 4 % with certain qualifications; as well as a prohibition of late fees for the sole failure to pay existing late fees. A high-cost mortgage acceleration of debt may take place only if there is a default in payment or pursuant to a due-on-sale provision, or some other provision of the loan documents. If the same creditor is refinancing the loan, it may not charge a prepayment fee or penalty for the pre-existing note. No charge may be made to modify, renew, extend, or amend a high-cost mortgage or to defer payments thereunder. No fees may be charged for informing or transmitting information concerning the outstanding balance on a high-cost mortgage except for a processing charge if it is done by fax.

Pre-loan counseling is required for a high-cost mortgage from a counselor certified by the Secretary of Housing and Urban Development or by a comparable state authority. The counselor must verify that the consumer has received counseling concerning the advisability of a high-cost mortgage unless he or she can verify that the debtor has received the required statement under the Real Estate Settlement Procedures Act (RESPA).

5.1.3 Asset-Backed Securities (ABS)

§941(a) of Title IX of the Dodd-Frank Act defines an *asset-backed security* as a fixed-income or other security collateralized by any type of self-liquidating financial asset (including a loan, a lease, a mortgage, or a secured or unsecured receivable) that allows the holder of the security to receive payments that depend primarily on cash flow from the asset, including (1) a collateralized mortgage obligation; (2) a collateralized debt obligation; (3) a collateralized bond obligation; (4) a collateralized debt obligation of asset-backed securities; (5) a collateralized debt obligation of collateralized debt obligations; and (6) security that the US Securities and Exchange Commission (SEC) determines by its regulation to be an asset-backed security. In essence, they are bonds or notes other than real estate or mortgage loans (MBS), backed by financial assets such as leases, credit card receivables, student loans, auto loans, and home-equity loans.

The final rule also sets forth underwriting standards for qualifying commercial loans. They include that prior to the origination of the commercial loan, the originator is to have:

- Received a verified and documented financial condition of the borrower:
- Conducted an analysis of the borrower's ability to service its overall debt obligations during the next two years, based on reasonable projections; and
- Determined that, based on the previous two years' actual performance, the borrower had and projected to have a total liabilities ratio of 50 % or less; a leverage ratio of 3.0 or less; and a debt service coverage (DSC) ratio of 1.5 or greater. There were comparable provisions for other asset types.[18]

The SEC's Division of Corporation Finance took note that ABS holders suffered significant losses during the financial crisis, causing a decline in the level of securitization which previously had been a major source of liquidity in the financial sector, particularly in the non-governmental mortgage-backed securities market. Investors were not fully aware of the risks in the underlying mortgages within the pools of securitized assets and, therefore, were unable to properly evaluate and rate the securitization structures. Furthermore, there was a lack of transparency in the securitized pools, failure by senior management of issuers to properly supervise the transactions, insufficient enforcement respecting the representations and warranties in the underlying contracts, and a lack of time for investors to properly evaluate their investment decisions.

§942(b)(1) of the Dodd-Frank Act stated that the SEC is to issue regulation comparable to the mortgage-backed securities, to require any securitizer to retain an economic interest in a portion of the credit risk for any asset that the securitizer, through the issuance of an asset-backed security, transfers, sells, or conveys to a third party, of 5 % or more of standard risk retention.[19] The next subsection requires a multitude of federal agencies to apply similar retention of an economic interest in a portion of the credit risk by securitizers with respect to residential mortgages. Accordingly, pursuant to §942(b) of the Dodd-Frank Act, the SEC issued a final rule to require certain asset classes to provide asset-level information in standardized, tagged data form.

Issuers are required to provide standardized asset-level information for ABS backed by residential mortgages, commercial mortgages, auto loans, auto leases, and debt securities. The asset-level information is to be provided in a standardized, tagged data format called eXtensible Mark-up Language (XML), which allows investors to more easily analyze the data. The disclosure of the information is standardized by defining each data point and delineating the scope of the information required. Although specific data requirements vary by asset class, the new asset-level disclosures generally will include information about the credit quality of obligors; collateral related to each asset; cash flows related to a particular asset, such as the terms and expected payment amounts; and whether and how payment terms change over time. This data is also to be included in the offering prospectus and in required quarterly and annual reports[20]

The Final Rule permits investors additional time to analyze the structure, assets, and contractual rights in ABS transactions by mandating that ABS issuers using a shelf registration statement file a preliminary prospectus with the specific information concerning the ABS at least three business days before the first sale. The requirement of investment grade ratings for ABS shelf offerings was removed as part of the governmental downplaying of the role of credit rating agencies, and it was replaced by the requirement that the chief executive officers of the issuer certify the accuracy of the information contained in the prospectus and the structure of the securitization. In addition, the Final Rule replaced the investment grade requirement with the requirement of a provision in the transaction agreement for the review of the assets for compliance with the representations and warranties upon the occurrence of certain trigger events; a dispute resolution provision in the underlying transaction documents; and the disclosure of investors' requests to communicate with other investors.

Other requirements for ABS include expanded disclosure about transaction parties, including disclosure about a sponsor's retained economic interest in an ABS transaction and financial information about parties obligated to repurchase assets; a description of the provisions in the transaction agreements about modification of the terms of the underlying assets; and a filing of the transaction documents by the date of the final prospectus, which is a clarification of the current rules.[21]

5.1.4 International Regulation

International Monetary Fund

The International Monetary Fund (IMF) recognizes that securitization is essential for economic growth and financial stability by giving issuers and investors the capability of diversification and management of risk by the transformation of illiquid assets into tradable securities and freeing up of capital. The negatives of securitization are the increase of leverage, misalignment of incentives in the financial intermediation chain, and amplification of systemic risk. Accordingly, several staff authors suggested a number of recommendations for ensuring that securitization, which had suffered a precipitous decline from its height in 2006 to 2013, was made available anew. Typically, as with most government papers written by staff members, the views expressed were those of the authors and not officially of the organization but, nevertheless, they were strongly suggestive of the views that officially were disavowed.[22]

The authors noted that the deterioration of loan origination was a major cause of the financial crisis that occurred in the latter part of the first decade. Compensation was dependent on high loan volumes and high commission mortgages rather than suitability of the borrowers or what occurred respecting payment of the loans thereafter. Securitization of the loans evolved through complex and opaque product issuance, resulting in high fees and advanced financial engineering to accomplish the transformation. The loans were rated by credit rating agencies, which often resulted in credit rating agencies' shopping for the best rating, these overstating the ratings for the underlying assets. Investors, taking advantage of monetary policy, sought higher yields, and banks became exposed to structured investment vehicles with high rollover risk. Therefore, the need arose for a comprehensive regulatory and supervisory framework to aid in ensuring robust origination standards. Accordingly, governments, particularly in the USA with the passage of the Dodd-Frank Act, took steps to improve supervision and practices in mortgage origination.[23]

Thus, the policy recommendations of the authors of the study were that broad-based regulatory measures be taken to ensure the high quality of underlying loan origination, such as Dodd-Frank's recommendation that loan officers rather than mortgage officers should select appraisers and maintain records through a property value registry. Prudential policies should include risk-based frameworks defining regulatory provisions and capital requirements; regulations to ensure the collateral that forms the basis of additional borrowing emphasizes cash and income relative to capital gains in asset practices; a focus on borrowers' maximum-to-loan value and debt-to-income ratios, with limits on second liens; and hypothecation of unrealized capital gains.

With respect to securitization intermediaries, the authors noted that the practices by securitization intermediaries from 2000 to 2007 amplified the financial crisis. The problems included ambiguity and lack of enforcement or representations and warranties; conflict of interest affecting quality control; and deficient technological infrastructure. Accordingly, the recommendations included aligning incentives across the entire financial intermediation chain; ensuring originators retain an economic interest in securitization ("skin-in-the-game"); guidance by regulators regarding timely disclosure of relative data underlying loan-level performance; development and standardized *plain vanilla* (basic form) securitizations; and timely information on changes in composition of the collateral pool be provided to investors. Regulators were to ensure that efforts be made to minimize legal ambiguities concerning the rights and obligations of parties to the securitization process; enforce existing contracts and be mindful of conflicts of interests; and provide adequate technical infrastructure and resources by market participants.[24]

Credit agencies' ratings were assumed to be independent and accurate gauges of underlying risks. The problem, however, was the use of the *issuer pays model*, which could lead to bias in favor of the issuer by competing ratings agencies. The USA and the Financial Stability Board (FSB) have removed most references to credit ratings, including for securitizations, and have taken steps to improve corporate governance. Accordingly, the recommendations include the removal of credit ratings for securitizations; finalize rules for the agencies to ensure transparency regarding their relationship with issuers; and embrace standardized definitions underlying securitizations.

Investors, including investment conduits and banks, experienced unexpected losses in securitization during the financial crisis, which regulators are addressing to strengthen the regulatory environment. Incentives for capital arbitrage have been reduced but not eliminated. Thus, the authors recommend that regulators make efforts to improve the consistency of capital charges applied to underlying risk characteristics of tranches and that relevant features of cash flow characteristics and risk mitigation mechanism embedded in securitizations be recognized in the future works of standard setters. Other recommendations are that securitizations be treated comparably to securities with broadly similar risk characteristics; there should be harmonization of industry standards for risk and data disclosure; and development of non-bank institutional investor bases for securitization.[25]

European Union Regulation of Securitization

The European Union (EU) proposed a Regulation on reporting and transparency of securities financing transactions (SFTs).[26] SFTs consist of any transaction that uses assets belonging to the counterparty to generate financing means and are defined as (1) repurchase transactions; (2) securities or commodities lending and securities or commodities borrowing; and (3) any transaction having an equivalent economic effect and posing systemic risks in particular a buy-sell or sell-back transaction.[27] As the title of the Regulation states, its main elements are the provisions for the reporting and transparency of transactions of counterparties to SFTs. On the first business day following the conclusion, modification, or termination of the transaction, the counterparties are required to report the details thereof to a registered trade repository (a legal person that centrally collects and maintains the records of SFTs) or to the European Securities and Markets Authority (ESMA) if a trade repository is not available. Registration of the trade depository is to conform to the requirements of ESMA and is effective throughout the EU when granted. ESMA is to develop technical and uniform standards respecting the application.[28] Trade repositories in non-EU countries may be granted recognition by ESMA provided they make due application to ESMA and the application is approved.

Management companies of undertakings for collective investment in transferable securities (UCITS), UCITS investment companies, and alternated investment fund managers (AIFMs) must inform their investors concerning the use of SFTs and other financing structures. Counterparties have the *right of rehypothecation* (use by a receiving counterparty of financial instruments received as collateral in its own name or for its own account or for the account of another counterparty) when the providing counterparty has been duly informed in writing by the receiving counterparty of the risks involved in granting consent, especially of the potential risks in the event of a default, and the providing counterparty has granted its prior consent as evidenced by the signature of the providing counterparty to a written agreement or equivalent thereof. There must also be transparency with respect to pre-investment documents such as in prospectus and in disclosure documents as directed.[29]

The Directive mandates cooperation between the competent authorities exercising powers granted under the respective directives. There are additional provisions for administrative sanctions, the exercise of supervisory powers and sanctions, reporting of breaches, exchange of information with ESMA by competent authorities, and publication of decisions.[30]

5.2 Repurchase Agreements (Repos)

5.2.1 Repos Defined

The financial crisis of 2007–2009 has been attributed in part to runs of short-term funding with repos as a key player in the crisis. A *repurchase agreement* (repo) is an agreement to sell securities at a particular monetary price with a commitment to repurchase the security at a later date, usually at a higher price. It is a form of a collateralized loan with the difference being that the seller of the security is required to repurchase the asset in which the difference between the sale and purchase price reflects the interest on the loan. An example is where a broker-dealer sells a security, for example a money market mutual fund, and agrees to repurchase the said security the following day in effect with interest. Repos act as a form of short-term funding by financial institutions such as broker-dealers, banks, or mortgage real estate investment trusts.[31] The maturities of repos may be *open* without a specified repurchase date or a *term* with a specified repurchase date. A one-day loan is called an *overnight repo.*

The types of collateral that are generally used are treasuries, agencies, mortgage-back securities, corporate bonds, equity, or other agreed-upon collateral. Cash providers include money market mutual funds, insurance companies, corporations, central and commercial banks, securities lenders, and municipalities. Securities are provided by insurance companies, central and commercial banks, securities firms, and hedge funds. The size of the tri-party form of repurchase agreement was about $1.73 trillion for 2013.

5.2.2 Types of Repos

Repos come in a variety of forms. They include the following:

- *Due Bill Repo.* In a due bill repo, the collateral is not held by the lender but is placed in an internal (bank) account in the name of the borrower for the duration of the trade. The use of a due bill repo is rarely used except by large, low-risk institutions because of the added risk to the lender, which does not have control over the account, and because of the increased use of centralized counterparties.

- *Triparty Repo.* In this popular form of repo, a third party acts as the intermediary between the borrower and the lender. The borrower conveys the collateral to the third party (in the USA the Bank of New York Mellon or JP Morgan Chase is generally used as the third-party), which commonly conveys a substitute collateral to the lender such as an equal amount of stocks or bonds. The agreement among the three parties ordinarily includes a *management service agreement*, which defines the type of collateral the lender is willing to accept such as highly liquid collateral or less liquid collateral. In a typical tri-party repo transaction, the investor, for example a money market fund, sends a cash balance that equals the market value of securities less a haircut to a tri-party securities agent, who then releases the cash to the repo dealer (counterparty) upon receipt of eligible securities. On the settlement date, the dealer returns the cash and interest and receives back the eligible securities from the tri-party securities agent. The agent returns the cash and interest to the money market fund.[32]
- *Whole Loan Repo.* The collateral given by the borrower consists of a loan or other form of obligation in place of a financial security.
- *Equity Repo.* Corporate stocks (equity securities) are used in place of the safer government bonds as the underlying security of the repurchase agreement. There may be more risk and tax implications under these circumstances.
- *Sell/Buy and Buy/Sell Repos.* Rather than a single transaction there are two distinct trades under this repurchase agreement; there is a spot sale and a forward repurchase of the security. The forward price is in relation to the spot price to result in a market rate of return.
- *Reverse Repo.* The borrower takes the collateral security from the lender and immediately sells it on the open and on the settlement date; the borrower then repurchases the said security and delivers it to the lender. The borrower is gambling that the said security will decline in value between the lending and settlement dates. From the lender's viewpoint, the transaction is a repo; from the borrower's viewpoint, it is a reverse repo.
- *Securities Lending.* Securities are lent out usually to go short on the particular security or for use in complex financial structures, and thereafter returns the security to the lender.[33]

Federal Reserve Board

According to the Task-Force on Tri-Party Repo Infrastructure of the FED, the tri-party repo took on major importance during the crisis of 2007–2009, particularly after the failures or near failures of Lehman Brothers, Countrywide Securities, and Bear Stearns. A key concern of policymakers is the impact that the collapse of the triparty repo market would have on securities firms, money market mutual funds, major banks involved in payment and settlements globally, and also the liquidity of Treasury securities. The triparty repo market in 2008 was about $2.8 trillion, and shrank to $1.6 billion shortly thereafter. There are three types of participants in the tri-party repo, namely *securities dealers*, *cash investors*, and *clearing banks*, with the latter acting as intermediaries between the dealers and investors. Securities dealers, the primary ones being banks and securities broker-dealers with the top ten firms accounting for 80 % of the market, sell securities with the promise to repurchase them at a later date. Cash investors, the major ones being money market mutual funds and securities lenders, buy the securities, taking them as collateral. Clearing banks take custody of the securities, value them in their books, and provide services to assist dealers to optimize the use of the collateral.

There are two main types of settlement methods for repos involving the FED according to the Federal Reserve Bank of New York (FRBNY), namely *tri-party* and *delivery versus payment*. In the tri-party repo, the FED and the primary dealers use a tri-party agent to manage the collateral wherein both the Fed and primary dealers have cash and collateral accounts. The tri-party agent ensures that the collateral pledged meets eligibility requirements and is sufficient. The FED trading desk selects winning propositions on a competitive basis from dealers who state the rates they are willing to pay for the agreement versus the various types of collateral. The three types of collateral the FED will accept are: marketable US Treasury securities including STRIPS (separate trading of registered interest and principal securities) and TIPS (Treasury Inflation-Protected Securities); certain US agency obligations; and certain agency "pass-through" for mortgage-backed securities, as well as securities that do not have scarcity value, which in turn creates reserve balances.

The FRBNY makes its payment for the securities by crediting the reserve account of the dealer's tri-party agent, a commercial bank. Upon maturity of the repo, the dealer returns the loan plus interest and the collateral is then returned to the dealer. The credit reserves become extinguished. The collateral posted by the dealer has a *haircut* applied, which refers to its valuation as slightly less than the market value. The haircut reflects the risk to the FED in crediting the reserve account of the dealer, the amount of which is dependent on the nature of the collateral exchanged for the reserve balance credited to the dealer. When the FED uses a *reverse repo*, it is settled on a *delivery versus payment* method, whereby the FED sends the collateral to the dealers' clearing bank which then simultaneously causes the movement of money against the security and the reserve balances are extinguished. Upon maturity, the dealer returns the collateral to the FED, which then triggers a simultaneous return of the dealer's funds.[34]

The agent banks for securities lenders use the repo market to reinvest the cash collateral received when loaning the securities. The two major clearing banks perform the services as described above. Settlement is made daily returning the respective cash and collateral.[35] Issues concerning the FED are: (1) the tri-party repo market's dependence on intra-day credit provided by the clearing banks that extend hundreds of billions of the credit to the dealers until new repos are settled in the evening; (2) risk-management practices that may increase stress in bad times; and (3) the lack of effective and transparent plans to support orderly liquidation of a defaulted dealer's collateral.[36]

The FED also utilizes repos to make collateralized loans to primary dealers or borrows money from primary dealers by use of reverse repos. The term may be overnight, rarely up to 14 days or, theoretically, as long as 65 days. The repo is used by the FED to add balances to the banking system, while the reverse repo has the opposite effect. The use of repos is accomplished through auctions, whereby primary dealers bid on the money to be borrowed using various types of general collateral, while in a reverse repo the FED uses its general collateral (e.g. Treasury bills) to pay the dealer-offered interest rate for money borrowed. The FED's trading desk uses repos to implement monetary policy at the behest of the Federal Open Market Committee, which are useful to offset temporary swings in the level of bank balances caused by volatile factors.[37]

The FED indicated that "[a] stable and well-functioning tri-party repo market is critical to the health and stability of the U.S. financial markets and the U.S. economy" because (1) it creates market liquidity and price transparency for both the US government and corporate securities that foster stable financing costs for US companies and the US government; (2) is interconnected with other payment clearing and settlement services that are vital to financial markets and which are operated by major triparty agent banks; and (3) acts as a critical source of funding for systemically important broker-dealers that are market makers for US government and corporate obligations.

It appears that the FED is experimenting with reverse repos (exchanging Treasury securities owned by the central bank for cash daily) in order to improve central bank control over short-term interest rates. For the first quarter of 2014, $242 billion in cash was exchanged with the FED for Treasuries, making the FED's exchange for bonds for cash the leading lender of them. The presidents of the New York and Boston FED, however, have expressed concern that the exchange on too large a scale may be a destabilizing influence by taking money out of the banking and private markets' sectors and transferring it to the FED.[38]

5.2.3 Regulation of Repos

There is a paucity of regulation governing repos, as with the other major elements of shadow banking. Nevertheless, various governmental agencies have interposed their legal and regulatory requirements, statements of policy, and/or suggestions for financial parties and institutions.[39] The Federal Deposit Insurance Corporation (FDIC), concerned with repos that have incurred significant losses because of default or fraud by counterparties to a repo transaction, inadequate risk management, and the failure to exercise effective control over securities collateralizing the transactions, issued guidelines for depository institutions that enter into repurchase agreements with securities dealers and others. Among the guidelines which the FDIC indicated it would consider in reviewing performances of depository institutions are the following:

- Securities sold under repo agreements collateralized by the US government and agency obligations are to comply with regulations under 17 CFR Parts 403.5 and 450, which include requirements concerning custody of repos; transactions to be transacted pursuant to a written repo agreement which the bank must obtain and confirmation in writing of the specific securities that are the subject of a repo; and disclosure to the customer that they are not insured by the FDIC.
- Antifraud provisions of the Securities Act of 1933 and the Securities Exchange Act of 1934 as they apply to repos;
- Resale transactions of national banks and thrift institutions are subject to the lending limitations of federal law;

- All depository institutions that engage in securities repurchase agreement transactions should establish written credit policies and procedures governing these activities.

In a White Paper prepared by the FRBNY, the following weaknesses were noted by the Bank's task force:

- Operational Arrangements: It was noted that in order to obtain operational efficiencies, the daily unwinding of all transactions required massive amounts of intraday credit to be provided by the two Clearing Banks. It thus recommended that specific actions was needed to fundamentally strengthen the operational arrangements at the heart of the tri-party repo market to reduce the market's reliance on intra-day credit provided by the Clearing Banks and clarify the credit and liquidity risks borne by market participants. In place of the current arrangement there should be ***auto-substitution***, which will allow for the automated substitution of securities collateral supporting a tri-party repo transaction, while that transaction remains in place.
- Dealer Liquidity Risk Management: The Task Force found that some dealers did not properly anticipate the potential for secured financing to be unavailable, even for high quality collateral. There was excessive reliance on short-term repo financing, especially in regard to collateral types that were or became illiquid and subject to valuation uncertainty, contributing to greater leverage in the system. It recommended that dealers reduce and/or eliminate funding as the credit quality of the Dealer deteriorates; account for the loss of secured funding within their liquidity risk management plans and liquidity stress tests; liquidity buffers should be sized accordingly; lengthen and stagger the maturity profile of their financing; seek to combine short-term and long-term financing with the same counterparty; and continue exploring alternative mechanisms that may be able to achieve more durable financing of certain types of securities.
- Margining Practices: The Task Force noted that market participants in many cases did not anticipate the extent to which market conditions could worsen and did not set margins accordingly, leading to procyclical increases in those margins when conditions did worsen during the crisis. Thus, margining practices must be broadly strengthened in the wake of the crisis. Accordingly, it recommended

that market participants should undertake statistical analysis and stress testing of collateral price movements to allow them to assess the potential for losses at different levels of margins and to make decisions based on their appetite and capacity to absorb losses. Cash investors should seek information that allows them to assess the potential concentration of repo counterparties with respect to a particular type of security; where such information is not forthcoming, they should use aggregate market information and/or make conservative inferences.

- Contingency Planning: The Task Force found that often cash investors were unprepared to cope with the consequences of a dealer default, in particular the potential need to manage and liquidate collateral securing a defaulted repo position. It recommended cash investors should develop "liquidation plans" for the management and liquidation of repo collateral in the event of a dealer default. These plans were to cover both practical aspects such as custodial arrangements, stress tests of potential losses due to collateral price movements, and stress tests of possible liquidity needs.
- Transparency: There was insufficient transparency with respect to many aspects of the tri-party market, including its aggregate size and composition, the extent of concentrations, and typical levels of margin. It recommended greater transparency; use of a template for regular publication of key information provided by the clearing banks including the aggregate size of the tri-party market, broken down by asset category, with associated measures of dealer concentration; and margin haircut levels reported by the clearing banks for each asset category.[40]

5.2.4 *Arguments Against Repo Regulation*

Among the claims is that additional regulation discourages repo transactions, "the oil that greases the wheels of the financial system," by decreasing liquidity, which in turn makes it difficult to source particular bonds for delivery and discourages trading. Dealers allegedly are opting to pay the fail charge of 3 % for Treasury bonds rather than pay for the going rate to retrieve the bond needed to deliver back to the lender. In addition, the Dodd-Frank Act makes it more difficult for the FED to backstop the repo market. This, in turn, is causing volatility in the repo markets, raising the costs for short-term financing, which thereby adds to the volatility that lessens bank margins.[41]

Although the FED continues to hold that regulation is needed, it appears that in 2015 there was a shortage of high-quality bonds causing difficulty in the $2.6 trillion US market for repos thereby creating liquidity bottlenecks and stresses in the repo market. The concern is that the scarcity of the high-quality bonds will put pressure on rates and cause less liquidity in the bond and other markets. Factors cited for the shortage include the FED's increase in Treasury holdings after its multiyear stimulus program; the demand for US government bonds due to lower yields on European debt; and additional regulatory requirements forcing big banks to reduce holdings of trading securities in compliance with the Volcker Rule. Examples cited were Goldman Sachs Group Inc.'s repo books which declined by 46 % and Morgan Stanley's which declined by 47 % at the end of 2013. The demand for specific securities caused the rate on overnight repo loans secured by US Treasury notes to minus 3 % in late February 2013 so that financial institutions could have access to specific securities.[42] The FED has been testing overnight reverse repos with a limited set of counterparties to set a floor under short-term interest rates, in order to raise its benchmark interest rate from near zero.[43]

5.2.5 International Regulation

Financial Stability Board

With the Lehman Brothers Holdings Inc. collapse in 2008, the Financial Stability Board issued guidelines "on discounts applied to collateral handed over as part of repurchase-agreement trades and other securities-financing transactions that aren't processed through clearing houses." It also set minimum standards for some types of trades.

A summary of the recommendations by the Financial Stability Board is as follows:

- Authorities should collect more data on securities lending and repo exposures amongst large international financial institutions with high urgency. Such efforts should to the maximum possible extent leverage existing international initiatives such as the FSB Data Gaps Initiative.
- Trade-level (flow) data and regular snapshots of outstanding balances (position/stock data) for repo markets should be collected. Regular snapshots of outstanding balances should also be collected

for securities lending markets and further work should be carried out on the practicality and meaningfulness of collecting trade-level data. Such data should be collected frequently and with a high level of granularity, and should also capitalize on opportunities to leverage existing data collection infrastructure that resides in clearing agents, central securities depositories (CSDs), and/or central counterparties (CCPs).

- The total national and regional data for both repos and securities lending on a monthly basis should be aggregated by the FSB, which will provide global trends of securities financing markets (e.g., market size, collateral composition, haircuts, tenors). The FSB should set standards and processes for data collection and aggregation at the global level to ensure consistent data collection by national and regional authorities and to minimize double-counting at the global level.
- The Enhanced Disclosure Task Force (EDTF) should work to improve public disclosure for financial institutions' securities lending, repo, and wider collateral management activities, taking into consideration the items noted above.
- Authorities should review reporting requirements for fund managers to end-investors against the FSB's proposal, and consider whether any gaps need to be addressed.
- Regulatory authorities for non-bank entities that engage in securities lending (including securities lenders and their agents) should implement regulatory regimes meeting the minimum standards for cash collateral reinvestment in their jurisdictions to limit liquidity risks arising from such activities.
- Authorities should ensure that regulations governing rehypothecation of client assets address the following principles: financial intermediaries should provide sufficient disclosure to clients in relation to rehypothecation of assets so that clients can understand their exposures in the event of a failure of the intermediary; in jurisdictions where client assets may be rehypothecated for the purpose of financing client long positions and covering short positions, they should not be rehypothecated for the purpose of financing the own-account activities of the intermediary; only entities subject to adequate regulation of liquidity risk should be allowed to engage in the rehypothecation of client assets.

- Authorities should adopt minimum regulatory standards for collateral valuation and management for all securities lending and repo market participants.
- Authorities should evaluate, with a view to mitigating systemic risks, the costs and benefits of proposals to introduce CCPs in their interdealer repo markets where CCPs do not exist. Where CCPs exist, authorities should consider the pros and cons of broadening participation, in particular of important funding providers in the repo market.
- Changes to bankruptcy law treatment and development of Repo Resolution Authorities (RRAs) may be viable theoretical options, but should not be prioritized for further work at this stage because of significant difficulties in implementation.
- An appropriate expert group on client asset protection should examine possible harmonization of client asset rules with respect to rehypothecation, taking account of the systemic risk implications of the legal, operational, and economic character of rehypothecation.
- Authorities should adopt minimum regulatory standards for collateral valuation and management for all securities lending and repo market participants.
- Authorities should evaluate, with a view to mitigating systemic risks, the costs and benefits of proposals to introduce CCPs in their interdealer repo markets where CCPs do not exist. Financial intermediaries should provide sufficient disclosure to clients in relation to rehypothecation of assets, so that clients can understand their exposures in the event of a failure of the intermediary.[44]

EU European Market Infrastructure Regulation (EMIR)

To the extent that a repo is a derivative,[45] EMIR substantially impacts the repo market.[46] The Regulation requires counterparties to clear all over-the-counter (OTC) derivative contracts that pertain to a class of these contracts declared by ESMA to be subject to clearing obligations if they have been concluded between two financial counterparties, and by other financial and non-financial counterparties as provided for in the Regulation. ESMA shall establish, maintain, and keep up to date a public register in order to identify the classes of OTC derivatives subject to the clearing obligation taking place correctly and unequivocally. Counterparties and CCPs are to ensure that the details of any derivative contract they have concluded and of any modification or termination of the contract are reported to a trade repository registered by or any other venue recognized by the Regulation.

The details are to be reported no later than the working day following the conclusion, modification, or termination of the contract.

Financial counterparties and non-financial counterparties that enter into an OTC derivative contract not cleared by a CCP are to ensure, exercising due diligence, that appropriate procedures and arrangements are in place; monitor and mitigate operational risk and counterparty risk that includes (1) the timely confirmation, where available, by electronic means, of the terms of the OTC derivative contract, and 2) formalized processes which are robust, resilient and auditable in order to reconcile portfolios; manage the associated risk; identify disputes between parties early and resolve them; and monitor the value of outstanding contracts.

E.U. Directive on Markets in Financial Instruments as Amended (MiFID II)[47]

The 2014 Directive, which repealed the prior 2004 Directive and Regulation, requires member states to promulgate new rules by January 2017, establishing a new framework to make financial markets more efficient, resilient, and transparent. It established uniform requirements with respect to (1) disclosure of trade data to the public; (2) reporting of transactions to relevant competent authorities; (3) trading of derivatives on organized venues; (4) non-discriminatory access to cleaning and to trading in benchmarks; (5) product intervention powers of competent authorities; and (6) provision of investment services by third-country firms following an applicable decision by the EU Commission.

According to the EU, the new framework aims to make financial markets more efficient, resilient, and transparent. It initiates a market structure which closes loopholes and ensures that trading, wherever appropriate, takes place on regulated platforms. It introduces rules on high frequency trading. It improves the transparency and oversight of financial markets—including derivatives markets—and addresses the issue of excessive price volatility in commodity derivatives markets. A new framework will improve conditions for competition in the trading and clearing of financial instruments. Building on the rules already in place, the revised MiFID also strengthens the protection of investors by introducing robust organizational and conduct requirements or by strengthening the role of management bodies. The new framework also increases the role and supervisory powers of regulators and establishes powers to prohibit or restrict the marketing and distribution of certain products in well-defined circumstances. A harmonized regime for granting access to EU professional markets for firms from third countries, based on an equivalence assessment of third country jurisdictions by the Commission, is introduced.[48]

In Chap. 6, we will continue this discussion by talking about hedge funds and money market funds. The systemically important financial institution (SIFI) implications will be reviewed therein.

Notes

1. Much of the discussion is sourced from Comptroller of the Currency, *Asset Securitization: Comptroller's Handbook* (Nov. 1997), https://www.google.com/search?q=Comptroller+of+the+Currency,+asset+Securitizationpercent3A+ComptrollerpercentE2percent80percent99s+Handbook+(Nov.+1997).&rls=com.microsoft:en-US&ie=UTF-8&oe=UTF-8&startIndex=&startPage=1&gws_rd=ssl.
2. Andreas Jobst, *What is Securitization?* (Sept. 2008), https://search.yahoo.com/yhs/search?p=Andreas+Jobstpercent2C+What+is+Securitizationpercent3F+percent28Sept.+2008percent29percent2C+percent2C&ei=UTF-8&hspart=mozilla&hsimp=yhs-002.
3. *Fiduciary capacity* in law implies a special duty of care to act in the best interests of the beneficiary, generally more than ordinary duty of care, and includes acting in the best interests of the beneficiary, avoidance of conflict of interest, self-dealing, loyalty, and prudent care in financial matters.
4. See comments by SEC Commissioner Luis A. Aquilar, *Skin in the Game: Aligning the Interests of Sponsors and Investors*, (Oct. 22, 2014), http://www.sec.gov/News/PublicStmt/Detail/PublicStmt/1370543250034.
5. A detailed explanation of the subprime mortgage credit securitization crisis and the causes of it may be found in Adam B. Ashcraft and Til Schuerman, *Understanding the Securitization of Subprime Mortgage Credit* (March 2008), FEDERAL RESERVE BANK OF NEW YORK SAFF REPORT No. 318, https://www.google.com/search?q=Adam+B.+Ashcraft+and+Til+Schuerman,+Understanding+the+Securitization+of+Subprime+Mortgage+Credit+(March+2008),+Federal+Reserve+Bank+of+New+York+Staff+Report+No.+318,&rls=com.microsoft:en-US&ie=UTF-8&oe=UTF-8&startIndex=&startPage=1&gws_rd=ssl.
6. A copy of the final rule may be found at http://www.gpo.gov/fdsys/pkg/FR-2014-12-24/pdf/2014-29256.pdf.
7. Heath Tarbert and Nancy Lynch, *Dodd-Frank & Securitization: The Basics You Need to Know* (Oct. 4, 2010), https://www.google.com/search?q=Heath+Tarbert+and+Nancy+Lynch,+Dodd-Frank+percent26+Securitizationpercent3A+The+Basics+You+Need+to+Know+(Oct.+4,+2010),&rls=com.microsoft:en-US&ie=UTF-8&oe=UTF-8&startIndex=&startPage=1&gws_rd=ssl.

8. Floyd Norris, *Banks Again Avoid Having Any Skin in the Game*, NEW YORK TIMES (Oct. 23, 2014), http://www.nytimes.com/2014/10/24/business/banks-again-avoid-having-any-skin-in-the-game.html?_r=0.
9. Dodd-Frank Act, § 1401 which amended § 103 of the Truth-in-Lending Act (15 U.S.C. § 1601 et seq.).
10. Dodd-Frank Act § 1403 which amended Chap. 2 of the Truth-on-Lending Act.
11. Dodd-Frank Act, § 1404 which amended § 129B of the Truth-in-Lending Act.
12. Dodd-Frank Act, § 1413 which amended § 130 of the Truth-in-Lending Act.
13. Dodd-Frank Act, § 1411 which amended § 129C of the Truth-in-Lending Act.
14. Dodd-Frank Act, § 1419 which amended § 129(a) of the Truth-in-Lending Act.
15. Dodd-Frank Act § 1420 which amended § 128 of the Truth-in-Lending Act.
16. Dodd-Frank Act, § 1412 which amended § 129C of the Truth-in-Lending Act.
17. Dodd-Frank Act, Subtitle C, § 1431 which amended § 103(aa) of the Truth-in-Lending Act.
18. Credit Risk Retention, Subpart B, §.3 of the particular Department of the Treasury, 12 CFR Part 43; Federal Reserve System, 12 CFR Part 244; Federal Deposit Insurance Corporation, 12 CFR Part 373; Federal Housing Finance Agency, 12 CFR Part 1234; Securities and Exchange Commission, 17 CFR Part 246; and Department of Housing and Urban Development, 24 CFR Part 267.
19. *Id*, Subpart D, §.16.
20. Securities and Exchange Commission, *SEC Adopts Asset-Backed Securities Reform Rules* (Aug. 27, 2014), http://www.sec.gov/News/PressRelease/Detail/PressRelease/1370542776577.
21. *Id.*
22. The recommendations may be found in Miguel Segoviano, Bradley Jones, Peter Lindner, and Johannes Blankenheim, *Securitization: The Road Ahead* (2015), https://www.google.com/search?q=Miguel+Segoviano,+Bradley+Jones,+Peter+Lindner,+and+Johannes+Blankenheim,+Securitizationpercent3A+The+Road+Ahead+(2015),&rls=com.microsoft:en-US&ie=UTF-8&oe=UTF-8&startIndex=&startPage=1&gws_rd=ssl. A prior working paper by the same authors is highly informative of the problems generated by securitization that led to the financial crisis. See Miguel Segoviano, Bradley Jones, Peter Lindner, and Johannes Blankenheim, *Securitization: Lessons Learned and the Road Ahead*, Working Paper (2013), International Monetary Fund, https://www.google.com/search?q=Miguel+Segoviano,+Bradley+Jones,+Peter+Lindner,+and+Johannes+Blankenheim,+Securitizationpercent3A+Lessons+Learned+and+the+Roa

d+Ahead,+Working+Paper+(2013),+International+Monetary+Fund,&rls=com.microsoft:en-US&ie=UTF-8&oe=UTF-8&startIndex=&startPage=1&gws_rd=ssl.
23. *Id.* at 9–10.
24. *Id.* at 11–13.
25. *Id. at 13–25.*
26. European Commission, Directive 2014/0017 (COD).
27. *Id.*, at 3 and Art. 3(6).
28. *Id.* Art. 5.
29. *Id.* Art. 13–14.
30. *Id.*, Articles 20–24.
31. Elizabeth Holmquist and Josh Gallin, *Repurchase Agreements in the Financial Accounts of the United States* (June 30, 2014), FEDS NOTES, http://www.federalreserve.gov/econresdata/notes/feds-notes/2014/repurchase-agreements-in-the-financial-accounts-of-the-united-states-20140630.html.
32. BlackRock, *Understanding Repurchase Agreements, https://www.blackrock.com/cash/institutional/en-us/terms-and-conditions-t3?targetUrl=percent2Fcashpercent2Fliteraturepercent2Fwhitepaperpercent2Funderstanding-repurchase-agreements.pdf.*
33. Financial Web, *The 7 Types of Repurchase Agreements, http://www.finweb.com/loans/the-7-types-of-repurchase-agreements.html#axzz3c35iXIFY.*
34. Federal Reserve Bank of New York, *Repurchase and Reverse Repurchase Transactions* (Aug. 2007), http://www.newyorkfed.org/aboutthefed/fedpoint/fed04.html.
35. Lucinda Brickler, Adam Copeland, and Antoine Martin, E*verything You Wanted to Know about the Tri-Party Repo Market, but Didn't Know to Ask* (April 11, 2011), Liberty Street Economic, Federal Reserve Bank of New York, *http://libertystreeteconomics.newyorkfed.org/2011/04/everything-you-wanted-to-know-about-the-tri-party-repo-market-but-didnt-know-to-ask.html#.VXL9Pc9Viko.*
36. Federal Reserve Bank of New York, *Tri-Party Repo Infrastructure Reform*, (May 17, 2010), at 3.
37. Federal Reserve Board of New York, *Repurchase and Reverse Repurchase Transactions*, http://www.newyorkfed.org/aboutthefed/fedpoint/fed04.html.
38. Michael S. Derby, *Fitch Report: Fed's Reverse Repos Are Reshaping the Securities-Borrowing Market* (June 23, 2014, Real Time Economics, http://blogs.wsj.com/economics/2014/06/23/fitch-report-feds-reverse-repos-are-reshaping-the-securities-borrowing-market/ and *Two Fed Officials Suggest Reverse Repos May Need Borrowing Limits, After All* (June 11, 2014), http://blogs.wsj.com/economics/2014/06/11/two-fed-officials-suggest-reverse-repos-may-need-borrowing-limits-after-all/.

39. Federal Deposit Insurance Corporation, Federal Financial Institutions Examination Council, *Supervisory Policy: Repurchase Agreements of Depository Institutions with Securities Dealers and Others*, https://www.fdic.gov/regulations/laws/rules/5000-2100.html.
40. Federal Reserve Bank of New York, *Tri-Party Repo Infrastructure Reform*, WHITE PAPER (May 17, 2010), http://www.newyorkfed.org/newsevents/news/banking/2010/an100517.html.
41. SNW, *Regulation of Repurchase Agreement (Repo) Market A Long-Term Positive* (Aug. 18, 214), http://snwam.com/blog/2014/8/18/regulation-of-repurchase-agreement-repo-market-a-long-term-positive.
42. Katy Burne, *Pressure in Repo Market Spreads* (April 2, 2015), THE WALL STREET JOURNAL, http://www.wsj.com/articles/pressure-in-repo-market-spreads-1428013415.
43. Matthew Boesler, *Fed Seen Doubling Reverse Repos to Raise Interest Rates* (Sept. 16, 2014) at 6 BloombergBusiness, http://www.bloomberg.com/news/articles/2014-09-16/fed-seen-doubling-reverse-repos-to-raise-interest-rates.
44. Financial Stability Board, *Strengthening Oversight and Regulation of Shadow Banking*, Aug. 29, 2013, at 20–22.
45. Alexander Pierre Faure, *Is the Repo a Derivative*? 2 AFRICAN REVIEW OF ECONOMICS AND FINANCE, No. 2 (June 1 2011), http://papers.ssrn.com/sol3/papers.cfm?abstract_id=2014723.
46. European Union, Regulation No. 648/2012 of the European Parliament and of the Council, *on OTC derivatives, central counterparties and trade repositories*, http://eur-lex.europa.eu/legal-content/EN/TXT/?uri=CELEX:32012R0648.
47. European Union, Regulation No. 648/2012 of the European Parliament and of the Council, *on OTC derivatives, central counterparties and trade repositories*, http://eur-lex.europa.eu/legal-content/EN/TXT/?uri=CELEX:32012R0648.
48. European Commission, *Daily News* (12.06.2014), http://europa.eu/rapid/midday-express-12-06-2014.htm?locale=en.

CHAPTER 6

Hedge Funds and Mutual Funds as SIFIs

6.1 Hedge Funds

Hedge funds began historically in 1949 with the creation of an investment partnership that engaged a number of investment techniques such as leverage, short-selling, and other financial devices which avoided the restrictions of the Investment Company Act of 1940.[1] Until the financial crisis of 2007–2009, the basic theory of governmental regulation was the protection of consumers, unsophisticated investors, and other persons less able to comprehend or defend against the many attempts of those who wished to defraud them or commit other violations. Securities legislation was aimed essentially at compelling disclosure of facts so that average investors could make informed decisions about whether to invest in particular securities. Hedge funds were virtually unregulated because the investors in them were almost always highly sophisticated, either mutual or other investment funds, or persons of substantial wealth. The question arose whether hedge funds might constitute such economic importance that they should be regulated as systemically important financial institutions (SIFIs), especially in the light of the collapse of Long-Term Capital Management LP. Long-Term Capital was a hedge fund management company that collapsed in 1997, requiring a $3.6 billion recapitalization bailout under the auspices of the FED after sustaining a $4.6 billion loss in four months following the 1997 Asian financial crisis.

Roy J. Girasa, *Shadow Banking*, DOI 10.1007/978-3-319-33026-6_6

6.1.1 *Nature and Structure of Hedge Funds*

Hedge funds, in essence, are pools of moneys collected from investors that invoke various investment strategies, often high-risk methods, with the goal of achieving high capital gains. Investors ordinarily pay a small percentage of the invested funds as fees to management which then receives a sizeable percentage, often as much as much as 20 %, of all gains realized but do not share in any shortfalls. Many funds seek to achieve substantial gains by using *leverage* (borrowing to increase investment exposure and risk), investments in derivatives, short-selling, and other speculative investment strategies. Although gains may be substantial (Long-Term Capital had net gains of 21 % in its first year and 43 % and 41 % respectively in the following two years), the potential losses are also magnified.[2]

6.1.2 *Legal Structures of Hedge Funds: USA*

The typical structure of a hedge fund organized in the USA is a limited partnership with a general partner at its apex with full liability and investors as limited partners. As with limited partnerships generally, the general partner is responsible for the daily operations of the fund with unlimited liability, unlike limited partners who have little say except whether or not to invest therein and possibly participate in major decisions of the fund. Their losses, however, are limited to the sums invested. Generally, the said partnership is limited to 99 or fewer investors, to circumvent SEC registration requirements.

To avoid individual personal liability in a limited partnership, the general partner is most often not an individual but usually a limited liability company (LLC) with flow-through tax benefits (all taxable income including distribution of appreciated property and liquidation are paid by the partners and members of the LLC).[3] The hedge fund may be entirely structured as a LLC with managers and controlling members. LLCs are formed in accordance with state law where initiated, and differ from limited partnerships inasmuch as no member has unlimited liability. If an LLC structure is used, it is generally formed in the state of the investment manager; if a limited partnership, then it is generally formed in the US state of Delaware where most large business entities are formed thanks to the pro-business and pro-management environment. The limited partnership gives wide-ranging control to the general partner and defines the control, operation, and fees of the partnership. The corporate form is not used in the USA for hedge funds because of the possibility of double taxation (corporate tax on profits and tax to the investors receiving dividends).

6.1.3 Non US Hedge Funds

For hedge funds formed offshore (almost always in low or no tax jurisdictions) a corporate model is most often used. As with all other corporate models, a board of directors governs the fund. There are three major structures commonly utilized:

- *Single fund (stand-alone) structure.* Non-US- and US-based non-taxable investors, such as pensions and endowments, invest in a single entity whose sponsor and management company is usually an offshore entity but may be US based. It is similar to the LLC general partner with investors as limited partners. Generally, an offshore management company is retained as a separate entity to operate the fund.
- *Side by Side structure.* This is a two-fund structure in which the manager will operate two separate funds, one of which is a US fund and the other an offshore fund. Both funds usually make the same or similar investments based on the requirements of the USA and offshore investors. Administrative issues may arise because of the division of the two funds. Its positive aspect is the separation of tax aspects between the two funds but with added administrative and audit costs.
- *Master-feeder structure.* This structure is most commonly used, also consisting of two funds, a US and offshore fund; but both funds feed into a single portfolio, unlike the side-by-side structure, with the fund manager making the investment decisions and apportioning the results to the two funds. It is a pass-through entity for US tax purposes. Among the positive aspects are efficiency and cost effectiveness, but there is the specter of a conflict of interest.[4]

6.1.4 Risk Management

Hedge funds are inherently risky investments because managers of the fund are under significant pressure to outperform common market and mutual fund investments, thereby compelling high-risk but potentially high-profit investments. Risks that may be incurred are dependent on the nature of the fund and include *liquidity risk*, in times of financial distress; *tail risk*, which are investments made in illiquid securities that occur generally (1) in companies in distress or (2) are newly emerging companies but thereafter become problematical; *tail risk*, which concerns a significant change from the current price of an asset; *event risk*, which is an unanticipated major event such as natural disasters or the sudden shock of oil embargoes that occurred in the late 1970s; *commodity risk*, which entails the sudden lack or overabundance of commodities that may cause major price deviations; *volatility shock*, which is sudden major price fluctuations; and *credit risk*, where hedge funds specializing in distressed securities or fixed-income arbitrage may suddenly face default, especially when there are margin calls in troubled economic periods.[5]

There are no government backstops to guarantee investments or come to rescue hedge fund losses or their demise, unless in rare cases when such funds are systemically important and may cause major financial damage to the entire financial establishment.

Most of the larger hedge funds now have one or more persons whose sole position in the firm is that of risk manager; they often occupy the highest level, together with the chief counsel and chief financial officer. Four-fifths of the firms separate the function of risk manager from fund manager to assure independent oversight. Eighty-four % use off-the-shelf risk *analytics* (information derived from the systematic analysis of meaningful patterns of data or statistics) as part of the portfolio management or trading system.[6] In order to mitigate against sudden withdrawal of investments in times of stress or major crisis, there are hedge fund management tools that may assist in order to help the fund avoid liquidity problems, especially with respect to illiquid investments. They include:

- *Lock-up*, which is the time period in which investors of a hedge fund may not withdraw their initial or later investment, often up to two years and/or twice a year redemption period;
- *Gate*, which is the provision in the hedge fund–investor agreement that limits the aggregate withdrawals during the redemption period by one or even all investors, such as a proviso that withdrawals may take place up to but not more than a given percentage;
- *Key man*, which may either concern a provision in the fund that permits withdrawal from a fund if a key person suddenly departs from the firm or bar asset owners from withdrawal from the fund for a designated time frame owing to the said departure.[7]

The question arises, however, whether the redemption restrictions make investments vulnerable to asset managers' opportunistically using the fund for their own benefit and thus imposing an agency cost on investors. Investors are prevented in the short run from disciplining the manager for, for example, collecting additional management fees. Moreover, redemption restrictions may not be used solely for the benefit of fund managers, for example by gaining additional management fees.[8]

6.1.5 *Regulation of Hedge Funds*

US Hedge Funds

A misconception is that hedge funds are not regulated by the US government. The regulatory landscape in the USA evolved recently with the passage of the Dodd-Frank Act, which set forth new registration and other requirements for hedge fund managers. All financial activities are subject to certain civil and criminal federal and state statutes. The question is not whether there is any regulation but rather whether hedge funds and other financial institutions should be regulated to the same extent as banking institutions. Among the statutory and regulatory provisions that hedge funds are subject to are the following:

- Securities Act of 1933:[9] Rule 506 of Regulation D provides a "safe harbor" from the registration requirements of §4(a)(2) of the 1933 Act which otherwise requires the registration with a self-regulatory organization (FINRA) of an intermediary in a transaction involving the offer or sale of securities. Under the exemption, companies can raise an unlimited amount of money in a private offering, provided that the company does not use general solicitation or advertise to market the securities and provided that the securities are restricted to an unlimited number of accredited investors and up to 35 other purchasers who have sufficient knowledge and experience to make them capable of evaluating the merits and risks of the potential investment. Companies must give non-accredited investors the same type of disclosure documents as those used in registered offerings. Thus, the incentive is to make offerings only to accredited investors;
  - An "accredited investor" includes the following:

- Anyone who earned income that exceeded $200,000 ($300,000 with a spouse) in each of the prior two years and reasonably expects comparable sums for the current year, or an individual person who has a net worth of over $1 million either alone or with a spouse, but excluding the value of the person's private residence (net worth is the person's assets minus liabilities—mortgage is not counted as a deduction from net worth);

- Any organization with assets exceeding $5 million not formed for the purpose of acquiring offered securities;
- Banks, savings and loan associations, partnerships, corporations, brokers, and dealers may be accredited investors;
- Any trust with total assets of $5 million not formed specifically to purchase securities whose purchase is directed by a *sophisticated person* (a person who has sufficient knowledge and experience in finance and business to evaluate the merits and risks of the prospective investment);
- Any entity in which all the equity owners are accredited persons, including officers, directors, and general partners of the issuer of securities.

- Securities Exchange Act of 1934:[10]
- §10(b) is the anti-fraud section of the statute that makes it unlawful for any person, directly or indirectly, in connection with the purchase or sale of any registered security on a national securities exchange or any security not so registered, or any securities-based swap agreement, to use any manipulative or deceptive device forbidden by law or regulation for the protection of investors;
- §10b-5 makes it unlawful to employ any device, scheme, or artifice to defraud, to make any untrue statement of a material fact or to omit to state a material fact necessary in order to make the statements made, in the light of the circumstances under which they were made, not misleading, or to engage in any act, practice, or course of business which operates or would operate as a fraud or deceit upon any person, in connection with the purchase or sale of any security.
- Margin rules which limit use of leverage to purchase and carry publicly traded securities and options;
- FINRA "new issues" Rule 5130 (formerly Rule 2790) places restrictions on the purchase and sale of initial public equity holdings allocations. Under the Rule, a member or associate may not purchase, sell, or continue to hold a new issue to any account in which a restricted person has a beneficial interest. There are a number of exceptions, such as sales or purchases from one member of the selling group to another member of the selling group that are incidental to the distribution of a new issue to a non-restricted person at the public offering price; sales or purchases by a broker-dealer of a new issue at the pub-

lic offering price as part of an accommodation to a non-restricted person who is a customer of the broker-dealer; or purchases by a broker-dealer organized as an investment partnership of a new issue at the public offering price, provided such purchases are credited to the capital accounts of its partners as provided in the Rule;

- Williams Act amendments to the 1934 Act concerning tender offers and proxy contests that provides for mandatory disclosure of information by persons making cash tender offers to shareholders; registration with the US Securities and Exchange Commission (SEC) including source of funds and plans, such as intent to take over the corporation disclosure; and filing with the SEC by any person acquiring more that 5 % of the shares of a publicly traded corporation;
- FINRA Rule 2111 requires, in part, that a broker-dealer or associated person "have a reasonable basis to believe that a recommended transaction or investment strategy involving a security or securities is suitable for the customer, based on the information obtained through the reasonable diligence of the [firm] or associated person to ascertain the customer's investment profile." As stated by FINRA, in general, a customer's investment profile would include the customer's age, other investments, financial situation and needs, tax status, investment objectives, investment experience, investment time horizon, liquidity needs, and risk tolerance;.
- SEC Rule 201 Regulation SHO on short sales. The Rule restricts the price at which short sales may be effected when a stock has experienced significant downward price pressure. Rule 201 is designed to prevent short selling, including potentially manipulative or abusive short selling; from driving down further the price of a security that has already experienced a significant intra-day price decline; and to facilitate the ability of long sellers to sell first upon such a decline.

There are four requirements for the Rule:

- Orders placed with the broker-dealer must be marked "long," "short," or "short exempt."
- Rule 201 requires trading centers to establish, maintain, and enforce written policies and procedures that are reasonably designed to prevent the execution or display of a short sale at an impermissible price when a stock has triggered a circuit breaker by experiencing a price decline of at least 10 % in one day. Once the circuit breaker in Rule 201 has been

triggered, the price test restriction will apply to short sale orders in that security for the remainder of the day and the following day unless an exception applies.

- A broker-dealer is required to have reasonable grounds to believe that the security can be borrowed so that it can be delivered on the date delivery is due before effecting a short sale order in any equity security.
- Rule 204 Brokers and dealers that are participants of a registered clearing agency are required to take action to close out failure to deliver positions.
- The Investment Advisers Act of 1940, as amended,[11] requires most investment advisers to register with the SEC. An investment adviser is defined by §202(a)(11) of the Act as any person or firm that, for compensation, is engaged in the business of providing advice to others or issuing reports or analyses regarding securities. Hedge fund managers would normally be included within the definition of investment advisers, but §203(m) of the Act directs the SEC to exempt from registration any investment adviser solely handling private funds that have less than $150 million in assets under management in the USA.[12]
- The Investment Advisers Act, §205(a)(1) generally restricts an investment adviser from entering into, extending, renewing, or performing any investment advisory contract that provides for compensation, other than a management fee, to the adviser based on a share of capital gains on, or capital appreciation of, the funds of a client (performance compensation or fees) unless the client is a *qualified client* who is described as follows:

  - A natural person who, or a company that, immediately after entering into the contract has at least $1 million under the management of the investment adviser;
  - A natural person who, or a company that, the investment adviser entering into the contract (and any person acting on his behalf) reasonably believes, immediately prior to entering into the contract, either:

- Has a net worth (together, in the case of a natural person, with assets held jointly with a spouse) of more than $2 million. For purposes of calculating a natural person's net worth, the person's primary residence must not be included as an asset;

- Indebtedness secured by the person's primary residence, up to the estimated fair market value of the primary residence at the time the investment advisory contract is entered into, may not be included as a liability (except if the amount of such indebtedness outstanding at the time of calculation exceeds the amount outstanding 60 days before such time, other than as a result of the acquisition of the primary residence, the amount of such excess must be included as a liability); and

  - Indebtedness that is secured by the person's primary residence in excess of the estimated fair market value of the residence must be included as a liability or is a qualified purchaser as defined in section 2(a)(51)(A) of the Investment Company Act of 1940 (15 U.S.C. 80a-2(a)(51)(A)) at the time the contract is entered into;
  - A natural person who immediately prior to entering into the contract is:

- An executive officer, director, trustee, general partner, or person serving in a similar capacity, of the investment adviser; or
- An employee of the investment adviser (other than an employee performing solely clerical, secretarial, or administrative functions with regard to the investment adviser) who, in connection with his or her regular functions or duties, participates in the investment activities of the investment adviser, provided that such employee has been performing such functions and duties for or on behalf of the investment adviser, or substantially similar functions or duties for or on behalf of another company, for at least 12 months.

SEC Enforcement

SEC enforcement has been spotty, but it contains several units within the agency devoted to specific types of unlawful activity by the hedge fund industry as well as other financial entities. The Market Abuse Unit is devoted to investigations involving large-scale market abuses and complex manipulation schemes by institutional traders, market professionals, and other participants particularly on highly sophisticated market structure issues. Its Structured and New Products Unit focuses on complex derivatives and financial products, which include credit default swaps, collateralized debt obligations, and securitized products. The Asset Management Unit, located nationally in some eleven offices, examines unlawful activities of investment advisers, investment companies, hedge funds, mutual funds, and private equity funds. There are specialists within each of the Units, such as hedge fund managers, private equity analysts, and due diligence professionals, who assist in the investigations, train staff, and engage in policymaking.[13]

Unlawful activities by hedge funds are handled by the Asset Management Unit, which examines violations of securities laws by the asset management industry that increasingly encompasses a high percentage of wealth and is more sophisticated and complex than other financial areas. A major focus is on investment advisers, particularly hedge fund advisers, in alternative investments and private finds. With trillions of dollars under management, there is a need for enforcement of violations, even when assisting the sophisticated class of investors who are better able to monitor their investments. Alternative investment vehicles are often complex, illiquid, or opaque instruments, and often lack transparency with respect to their investment strategies. Moreover, less sophisticated investors have entered the hedge fund market as retail orientation of hedge funds has emerged, exposing them directly or indirectly through pensions, endowments, foundations, and other retirement plans. In addition, retailization of hedge funds has made entry by unsophisticated investors possible by invitation through general solicitation and general advertising as a result of the Jumpstart Our Business Startups Act (JOBS Act).[14] Additional problems have emerged because of risks posed by private funds advised by unregistered advisers, who are exempt from registration with respect to funds less than $150 million under management.

Some of the abuses by hedge fund managers identified by the SEC are the following:

- Temptation to overvalue assets to boost compensation, including lax valuation committees and use of side pockets to conceal losing illiquid positions;
- With increasing competition among hedge funds, there is great pressure placed upon managers to demonstrate and market consistently positive performance, causing them to engage in unlawful activities such as insider trading;
- Conflict of interest, whereby managers place their interests above those of the investors;
- The grant of favorable treatment to certain investors through preferential redemptions or side letters; and

- The lack of independent governance that makes the funds susceptible to these abuses and other fraudulent practices.[15]

Non-Governmental Oversight

The essential reason for lessening governmental oversight, according to some commentators, is that investors in hedge funds are almost always sophisticated or wealthy investors with access to knowledgeable financial advisers, attorneys, and accountants. Investors may withdraw their investments at any time subject to the time restrictions stated above. Many major investors are entities controlling money market funds' highly sophisticated pension funds, such as the famed CalPERS (California Public Employees' Retirement), which demands transparency, managerial co-investment, and performance-based compensation in line with results accomplished by the fund. It further requires due diligence by fund managers, including effective internal controls to discourage fraud and the rigorous process of determining which investments to pursue by many other institutional and large investment entities.[16]

Non-US Hedge Funds

A majority of hedge funds are located outside the USA, usually in "offshore" jurisdictions that have favorable tax or no-tax policies, thereby sheltering them from with some exceptions from US tax authorities. Among the best-known foreign jurisdictions are the Cayman Islands, a British Overseas Territory which has no direct tax on income, capital gains, or corporations; the British Virgin Islands; Bermuda; the Bahamas; Luxembourg; Netherlands Antilles; and Ireland; most of which directly or indirectly aid international persons to evade taxation by their home states and even to launder money, albeit in theory most have anti-laundering statutes and allegedly cooperate with tax authorities in their respective jurisdictions.[17]

6.1.6 Hedge Funds as Shadow Banks

Hedge funds are considered to be among the designated non-bank financial institutions that may constitute SIFIs by the International Monetary Fund (IMF), the Financial Stability Board (FSB), and the Federal Reserve Board. Although the European Central Bank includes hedge funds in its description of shadow banking in the European Union (EU), nevertheless it acknowledges that "Whether hedge funds are part of the shadow banking system is debatable." It suggests that more granular data and qualitative information is needed for an in-depth analysis of ascertaining whether hedge funds are part of the shadow banking system.[18]

Opposition to Designation of Hedge Funds as Shadow Banks

There are a number of persons, mainly from the hedge fund sector, who oppose the designation of hedge funds as shadow or non-banks. Among them is the Alternative Investment Management Association (AIMA), which alleges that credit hedge funds are asset managers and not shadow banks in its publication *The Role of Credit Hedge Funds in the Financial System: Asset Managers, Not Shadow Banks.*[19] Initially, AIMA distinguishes shadow banks from non-banks by noting that the word "shadow" conjures up opaque or nefarious activity and implies that their activities are out of the reach of regulators, thereby creating unmonitored risks to the financial system. In addition, the definition of shadow banking as describing a large segment of financial intermediation derived outside the balance sheets of regulated commercial banks and other depository institutions is very broad, and ignores a key distinction between commercial banks and non-banks such as hedge funds, namely multiple deposit creation.

Citing shadow banking scholars,[20] AIMA noted that hedge funds not only are not banks because they are not depository institutions and also do not fulfill shadow banking criteria, but also because they are part of the asset management industry and do not undertake maturity transformation or benefit from implicit or explicit taxpayer guarantees. They play only a subordinated role in the shadow bank 6-chain as being "interconnected along a long vertically integrated, long intermediation chain, which intermediates credit through a range of securitization and secured funding techniques, such as ABCP (asset-backed commercial paper), asset-backed securities, collateralized debt obligations and repos." Credit hedge funds are active only with respect to asset-backed intermediation and are not involved in credit transformation. Moreover, hedge funds are already regulated, as stated above, as well as internationally under the EU's Alternative Investment Fund Managers Directive and the regime promulgated by the International Organization of Securities Commissions (IOSCO).

Other considerations, beside being adequately regulated, are that they are subject to extensive reporting requirements; are small in size in relation to the other components of the financial system; employ low levels of leverage; do not engage significantly in credit, liquidity, or maturity transformation; play only a small role in credit intermediation process; and do not need government support inasmuch as they are safe to fall and not too big to fail.[21] Hedge funds differ substantially from other financial instruments inasmuch as redemption rights tend to be far more restricted; that is, they provide less liquidity owing to restrictions on redemption rights depending on the nature of the investments. If the fund invests heavily in highly liquid instruments, investors are generally able to withdraw their investments monthly or quarterly, but if the major investments are in less liquid assets then withdrawal may be permitted either twice a year or even annually. This permits the fund to avoid forced sales of assets in stress situations, albeit the ultimate outcome may eventually result in the demise of the fund.

Hedge funds are subject to the same trading reporting and record-keeping requirements as other investors in publicly traded securities. They are also subject to a number of additional restrictions and regulations, including a limit on the number and type of investors that each fund may have, as stated above. Many hedge funds operating in the USA are also regulated by the Commodity Futures Trading Commission (CFTC), including advisers registered as Commodity Pool Operators (CPO) and Commodity Trading Advisors (CTA). Hedge funds investing in markets governed by the CFTC would also be regulated by it and be subject to the requirements set forth in the Commodity Exchange Act.

6.2 International Regulation

6.2.1 European Union Regulation

European lawmakers have also undertaken regulatory changes affecting hedge funds in recent years. In 2010 the EU approved the Directive on Alternative Investment Fund Managers (AIFMD), the first EU directive focused specifically on alternative investment fund managers. AIFMD requires hedge funds to register with national regulators and increases disclosure requirements and frequency for fund managers operating in the EU. Furthermore, the Directive increases capital requirements for hedge funds and places further restrictions on leverage utilized by the funds. The AIFMD required EU-based managers to comply with all provisions of the AIFMD once it was adopted at member state level in 2013, while non-EU managers marketing funds in the EU are subject to reporting requirements under an enhanced national private placement regime until they are eligible to or required to market under an EU passport in the future, at which point those non-EU managers will be subject to all of the provisions in the AIFMD. EU member countries were required to adopt the AIFMD into their own national legislation by early 2013. The European Securities and Markets Authority and the European Commission are developing implementing rules and guidance to give effect to the AIFMD.

International regulators have been more aggressive than US regulators in identifying financial institutions that they deem systematically important. Thus, the FSB and IOSCO have suggested that investment funds with more than $100 billion in assets could be labeled as "too-big-to-fail" and thus subject to stricter regulation. Regulation should also be applied to hedge funds that have trading activities of $400 billion to $600 billion. Previously, only banks and insurers were so designated but, according to Mark Carney, Bank of England governor and FSB chairman, "They [hedge funds] are integral to solving the problem of financial institutions that are too big to fail." The recommendations are controversial because, in the view of Dan Walter, managing director of ICI Global, asset managers allegedly do not invest on a principal basis and do not take on balance-sheet risk.[22] Nevertheless, there are deep divisions, just as those in the USA, concerning the sagacity of imposing bank-style regulation on money market funds for the $1.2 trillion EU market; but European lawmakers have blocked action of the EU Commission that sought to increase transparency and stability for the funds.[23]

Fitch Ratings, one of the big three of credit ratings institutions globally, agrees with the FSB and IOSCO assessment. It indicated that the focus of too-big-to-fail should be based on leverage and a fund's dominance of a particular market. The problem is that "If one or more large, heavily regulated funds represent 'the market' this could introduce illiquidity in times of stress." Excessive leverage and a large market footprint could cause systemic risk in such times of stress. It urged regulators to ascertain and understand off-balance-sheet activities of funds that heretofore have been essentially unregulated.[24]

6.2.2 *IOSCO Principles on the Regulation of Hedge Funds*

IOSCO, in conjunction with the FSB, mandates that hedge funds be regulated and, accordingly, proposed for adoption by securities or appropriate regulators six high level principles on the regulation of hedge funds. They are as follows:

- Hedge funds and/or hedge fund managers/advisers should be subject to mandatory registration.
- Hedge fund managers/advisers which are required to register should also be subject to appropriate ongoing regulatory requirements relating to:
  - Organizational and operational standards;
  - Conflicts of interest and other conduct of business rules;
  - Disclosure to investors; and
  - Prudential regulation.
- Prime Brokers and banks which provide funding to hedge funds should be subject to mandatory registration/regulation and supervision. They should have in place appropriate risk-management systems and controls to monitor their counterparty credit risk exposures to hedge funds.
- Hedge fund managers/advisers and prime brokers should provide to the relevant regulator information for systemic risk purposes (including the identification, analysis and mitigation of systemic risks).
- Regulators should encourage and take account of the development, implementation and convergence of industry good practices, where appropriate.
- Regulators should have the authority to co-operate and share information, where appropriate, with each other, in order to facilitate efficient and effective oversight of globally active managers/advisers and/or funds and to help identify systemic risks, market integrity and other risks arising from the activities or exposures of hedge funds with a view to mitigating such risks across borders.[25]

6.3 Mutual Funds

A mutual fund is a type of investment company that pools money from many investors and invests the money in stocks, bonds, money-market instruments, other securities, or even cash.[26] Mutual funds are similar to hedge funds in that both are portfolios of securities managed by professional managers. They differ, however, in that mutual funds are much more regulated by governmental entities to protect mainly unsophisticated investors who directly or indirectly hold their interest through pension funds. Hedge funds attend to the needs of wealthy, sophisticated investors who invest substantial sums in order to qualify as investors unlike mutual fund applicants who need only invest a small sum of money. Hedge funds may increase leverage, engage in speculative positions and leveraging, and short sell stocks.

Initially, mutual funds were created in the 1970s to avoid the restrictions placed on bank deposits concerning the amount of interest to be paid to depositors. Thereafter, they provided additional sources of funding and cash management services. Unlike money market funds, hedge funds need not conform to any standard methodology when calculating performance and are much freer to invest in high-risk investments, including those which are relatively illiquid and difficult to value, and to short sell stocks. Mutual funds come under the jurisdiction of the SEC, which enforces statutory and regulatory provisions dictating how mutual funds can advertise their performance by requiring specific ways to calculate current yield, tax equivalent yield, average total return and after-tax return, and detailed types of disclosure that must be given to investors. The funds are invested in short-term debt and are an important source of funding outside the traditional banking sector with purchases of certificates of deposits and commercial paper and as a source of funding in repo transactions.

Mutual funds also differ substantially from hedge funds with respect to the fees charged to investors, leveraging, pricing, and liquidity practices. Hedge funds generally need not register with the SEC because they are usually limited partnerships deemed to be private offerings that have restrictions concerning the number and type of investors who may purchase them, their resale and withdrawal, and advertising, thus permitting a minimal of disclosure subject only to fraud and fiduciary restrictions. Financial advisers for both funds are required to register with the SEC and conform to rules promulgated by FINRA and state requirements.[27]

Fees are far more extensive for hedge fund managers, which some commentators deride as meaning that if profitable the managers win and if not the investor alone loses, inasmuch as the funds charge a small percentage as management fees but also take a sizeable percentage of any profits as incentive fees, but do not partake in any losses by the fund other than possible withdrawal of funds by the investor. Mutual funds have to be fully disclosed in the offering prospectus in an easy to read format that enables the investor to be fully knowledgeable as to whether the fund is a *load fund*, whereby fees are paid to a broker or investment adviser, or a *no-load fund*, where there are no commission or other sales charges.

6.3.1 Types of Mutual Funds

The basic types of mutual funds are:

- *Money market funds.* A form of mutual funds registered under the Investment Company Act of 1940 and regulated under Rule 2a-7 of the said Act. Developed in the 1970s to give investors the option to purchase a pool of securities that provided higher returns than interest-bearing bank accounts, they are relatively low-risk funds compared to other mutual funds inasmuch as by law they can invest in only certain high-quality, short-term investments issued by the USA. They generally pay dividends reflecting short-term interest rates but usually give lower returns. The risk is that the interest paid on them may be less than that offered by US corporations, and government, state, and local governments, such as by treasury bills, bankers' acceptances, commercial paper, and certificates of deposit. With some $3 trillion in assets, the largest investors are institutional funds.
- *Fixed income funds (bond funds).* Bond funds generally give investors a higher return because they are not restricted to high-quality or short-term investments. The funds generally purchase instruments that give a fixed rate of return such as government bonds and high yield corporate bonds. Risks are dependent on the many different types of bonds in which the fund invests. They include *credit risk*, where the bonds in the fund fail to pay their debts especially when the investment is in high yield but lower rated bonds (unlikely for government bonds such as US Treasury Bonds); *interest rate risk*, which is the risk that the market value of the bonds will go down when interest rates go up; and *prepayment risk*, which is that the bond may be paid early.
- *Equity funds (stock funds).* Stock funds have historically performed much better than investments in corporate bonds, government bonds, and treasury securities. The risk is that of the *market risk* because of the volatility of the stock market. There are a broad variety of equity funds, such as *growth funds*, which focus on stocks that may not pay a regular dividend but have the potential for large capital gains; *income funds*, which invest in stocks that pay regular dividends; *index funds*, which aim to achieve the same return as a particular market index, such as the S&P 500 Composite Stock Price

Index, by investing in all—or perhaps a representative sample—of the companies included in an index; *sector funds*, which may specialize in a particular industry segment, such as technology or consumer products stocks; large-mid-and small cap funds, value stocks; or a combination of the above; and *fund-of-funds*, which is a fund that invests in other funds.[28]

6.3.2 Regulation of Mutual Funds

US Regulation

The mutual fund industry, as stated previously, is heavily regulated and is less susceptible to "runs" than other financial institutions. The major statutory and regulatory enactment and rules stated hereinafter are based on the primary statutory authority, the Investment Company Act of 1940 (Act of 1940) as amended.[29] The regulations applicable to the mutual fund industry include the following:

- *Daily valuation.* Rule 22c-1 requires shares of mutual funds (any registered investment company) issuing any redeemable security to sell, redeem, or repurchase the security at a price based on the current net asset value (NAV) of the security computed daily Monday through Friday as of the close of trading. When market quotations are not readily available, funds must value portfolio securities and all other assets by using their fair value as determined in good faith by the board of directors of the funds. (See below SEC Final Rule.) A fund is not required to calculate its net asset value on days on which changes in value will not materially affect current net asset value, days on which no redemption, purchase, or sell orders for the fund's shares are received, and on holidays.
- *Right of Redemption.* §22(e) of the Act of 1940 states that open-end funds may not suspend the right of redemption, and open-end funds may not postpone the payment of redemption proceeds for more than seven days following receipt of a redemption request.
- *Liquidity.* A mutual fund is required to maintain a high level of liquidity. It is permitted, however, to invest 15 % of its assets in *illiquid assets* (10 % for money market funds), defined as an asset which may not be sold or disposed of in the ordinary course of business within seven days at approximately the value at which the mutual

fund has valued the investment on its books. Nevertheless, the board of directors of the fund is expected to monitor portfolio liquidity on an ongoing basis to determine whether, in light of current circumstances, an adequate level of liquidity is being maintained.

- *Leverage.* §18(f)(1) prohibits a mutual company from issuing any class of senior security, or selling any class of senior security of which it is the issuer, except that the investment company may borrow from a bank provided that immediately after any such borrowing there is asset coverage of at least 300 % for all of its borrowings.
- *Diversification.* Mutual fund companies are required to have their investments diversified, that is, §5(b)(1) of the 1940 Act provides that at least 75 % of the value of its total assets is represented by cash and cash items (including receivables), government securities, securities of other investment companies, and other securities be limited in respect of any one issuer to an amount not greater in value than 5 % of the value of the total assets of such management company and to not more than 10 % of the outstanding voting securities of such issuer.
- *Investment of Securities of Other Investment Companies.* §12(d) (d)(1)(A) makes it unlawful for a mutual fund to (1) purchase or acquire any security issued by a registered investment company that is more than 3 % of the total outstanding voting stock of the acquired company; (2) purchase securities issued by the acquired company having an aggregate value in excess of 5 % of the value of the total assets of the mutual company; or (3) to purchase securities issued by investment companies other than treasury stock with an aggregate value in excess of 10 % of the total value of the mutual company. There are a number of exceptions for exchange traded funds and for shares of money market funds.
- *Transactions with Affiliates.* §17(a) of the 1940 Act prohibits certain transactions, including the purchase of securities and borrowing or loaning money between mutual funds and their affiliated persons (investment advisers; companies the fund controls or 5 % or more of whose securities are held by the fund; persons who control the fund; and persons who are under common control of the fund). The prohibition is also applicable to a company controlled by the mutual fund or is a joint or several participant with such person, principal underwriter, or affiliated person, The fund may apply for exemptions of proposed transactions, which will be granted by the SEC if it is

satisfied that the terms are reasonable and fair, are not overreaching, and are consistent with policy as provided in the statute and regulations.

- *Custody of Securities.* §17(f) of the 1940 Act provides that the fund is obligated to place and maintain its securities and other investments in the custody of a qualified bank which is to act as a trustee for said securities or a company which is a member of a national securities exchange, subject to such rules and regulations as the SEC may from time to time prescribe for the protection of investors. The cash proceeds from the sale of securities and similar investments and other cash assets of the company shall also be kept in the custody of the trustee bank or approved trustee, except that the fund may maintain a checking account in the said institutions.
- *Provisions Concerning Conduct of Officers and Directors.* §17 (g) provides that any officer or employee with access to securities or funds of the fund must be bonded to protect investors from theft or other malfeasance. §17(h) prohibits the fund's charter, certificate of incorporation, articles of association, indenture of trust, or by-laws from containing any provision which protects or purports to protect any director or officer of such company against any liability to the company or to its security holders to which he would otherwise be subject by reason of willful misfeasance, bad faith, gross negligence, or reckless disregard of the duties involved in the conduct of his office. Similarly, §17(i) prohibits contracts or agreements that purport to exempt them from their wrongful conduct.
- Rule 38a-1 requires each investment company and investment adviser registered with the SEC to adopt and implement written policies and procedures reasonably designed to prevent violation of the federal securities laws, review those policies and procedures annually for their adequacy and the effectiveness of their implementation, and designate a chief compliance officer to be responsible for administering the policies and procedures. The chief compliance officer of a fund is to report directly to the fund board to ensure that all funds and advisers have internal programs to enhance compliance with the federal securities laws.
- SEC CFR Part 270 provides that for a fund to rely on exemptive rules under the Act, it must satisfy the fund governance standards as follows: (1) at least 75 % of the directors of the fund must be independent directors or, if the fund board has only three directors,

all but one of the directors must be independent directors; (2) the chairman of the board must be an independent director; (3) the board must perform a self-assessment at least once annually; (4) the independent directors must meet separately at least once a quarter; and (5) the independent directors must be affirmatively authorized to hire their own staff. Moreover, a fund is to retain copies of written materials that the board considers when approving the fund's advisory contract.
- *Dodd-Frank Act Application.* The Dodd-Frank Act, §939A, requires agencies, including the SEC, to ascertain whether their regulations require the use of an assessment of creditworthiness of a security or money market instrument and any references regarding credit ratings, and to remove such references or requirements of reliance on credit ratings. They are to substitute such standard of creditworthiness as they deem appropriate for their regulations and to establish feasible, uniform standards of creditworthiness applicable to their agencies and the purposes for which reliance is made on the said standards.

There are numerous other rules that provide for audit committees and their approval of the retention of independent accounts; requirements that audited statements be sent to shareholders twice a year and within 60 days of the close of the fiscal year; implementation of anti-laundering programs; SEC review of books and records of the fund; ineligibility of certain persons convicted of particular crimes from serving as an employee, officer or director; and other provisions. Thus, it is beyond dispute that mutual funds are given extensive regulation unlike some other shadow banking entities.

Mutual Funds' Use of Derivatives

An unregulated area of concern to the SEC is the use of derivatives by mutual funds. A *derivative* is a contract between two or more parties whose value is determined by fluctuations in the underlying asset.[30] A *derivative transaction* includes any transaction that is a contract, agreement, swap, warrant, note, or option that is based, in whole or in part, on the value of, any interest in, or any quantitative measure or the occurrence of any event relating to, one or more commodities, securities, currencies, interest or other rates, indices, or other assets. It has also been used to refer to instruments that are created by separating other financial instruments into constituent pieces, for example, mortgage derivatives. They may be standard or customized, traded on an exchange or over the counter, liquid or illiquid, novel or familiar, leveraged or unleveraged. Derivatives may increase or reduce portfolio risk. Mutual funds use derivative products for a number of reasons, including hedging interest rate, currency, and other market risks. Their use by mutual funds varies from limited use to significant investments. Long-term municipal bond funds use derivatives to seek increased tax-exempt returns. Funds that invest internationally may use derivative investments to lessen currency risks.[31]

Mutual funds use *currency derivatives* to increase or decrease exposure to specific currencies, to hedge against adverse impacts on their portfolio caused by currency fluctuations, and to seek additional returns; *interest rate derivatives* to modify their exposure to the gains or losses arising from changes in interest rates and to seek enhanced returns; *credit derivatives* to allow a fund to assume an investment position concerning the likelihood that a particular bond, or a group of bonds, will be repaid in full upon maturity; and *equity derivatives* to enhance investment opportunities (e.g., by using foreign index futures to obtain exposure to a foreign equity market). Equity derivatives can also be used by funds as an income-producing strategy by, for example, selling equity call options on a particular security owned by a fund. A fund also may use equity derivatives (usually stock index futures) to "equitize" cash.[32]

For decades the SEC has indicated a desire to impose regulatory authority on the said use of derivatives by mutual funds. On August 31, 2011, in a Concept Release,[33] it sought comments on possible proposals that include: derivatives under the senior securities restrictions of the Investment Company Act; derivatives under the Act's diversification requirements; exposure to securities-related issuers through derivatives; portfolio concentrations; and valuation of derivatives. The SEC is concerned with exploring the benefits, risks, and costs associated with funds' use of derivatives. It has also been exploring issues relating to the use of derivatives by funds such as:

- Whether current market practices involving derivatives are consistent with the leverage, concentration, and diversification provisions of the Investment Company Act;
- Whether funds that rely substantially upon derivatives, particularly those that seek to provide leveraged returns, maintain and implement adequate risk management and other procedures in light of the nature and volume of their derivatives investments;

- Whether funds' boards of directors are providing appropriate oversight of the use of derivatives by the funds;
- Whether existing rules sufficiently address matters such as the proper procedures for a fund's pricing and liquidity determinations regarding its derivatives holdings; and
- Whether existing prospectus disclosures adequately address the particular risks created by derivatives; and whether funds' derivative activities should be subject to any special reporting requirements.

The issues raised by the SEC have been a cause for concern to mutual funds which fear a bank-like regulation regime is in the offering. The then US Senator Carl Levin of Michigan alleged that the use of derivatives by mutual funds diverted investment dollars from stocks and bonds and caused volatility in the financial marketplace. His comments were attacked as a misconception of the use of derivatives, which facilitate the transfer of risks to other parties and thus achieve an efficient allocation of risks. Their proper uses include that of an international equity fund manager who wants to transfer risk of foreign stock holdings particularly with respect to currency volatility, or the use of Treasury futures to adjust duration risk, or credit-default swaps being used to manage credit risk. Derivatives are, according to the naysayers of regulation, a cost efficient way to gain, hedge, or short exposures with respect to certain assets.[34]

Money Market Final Rule

Money market mutual funds (MMFs) arose in 1971 because banks were restricted in the amount they could pay in interest for funds deposited with them. Depositors, seeking higher rates of interest, looked for other sources such as corporate bonds and treasury bills, and mainly settled on the purchase of MMFs which offered higher rates for the pooled funds. These funds began to emulate banking services, such as offering checking accounts and other bank-like services. Moreover, until later changes in the law by virtue of the Riegel-Neal Interstate and Branching Efficiency Act of 1994 (discussed in Chap. 2) that permitted interstate banking, MMFs were able to market their financial products without jurisdictional restraints. They became popular because they were able to maintain a stable $1 NAV (net asset value) with only rare instances of falling slightly below the $1 value and generally paid more interest than banks. Because of the decline of deposits in the traditional banking sector, they were able later to compete with MMFs as a result of the Depository Institutions

Deregulation and Monetary Control Act of 1980,[35] and the Garn-St. Germain Depository Institutions Act of 1982,[36] which permitted banks to offer their own money market deposit accounts with no limitations on interest payable.

Regulatory Changes

Although MMFs are relatively safe financial vehicles because most of their assets are short term, high quality, and high liquidity, the financial crisis that commenced in 2007 and the bankruptcy of Lehman Brothers in particular brought about changes in the regulatory environment for MMFs. To maintain the $1 NAV, sponsors are often compelled to make investors whole by additional capital injections. The Council, in November 2012, initially proposed three alternatives for reform of MMFs after noting the distress of the industry following the 2007–2009 crisis: (1) requiring MMFs to alter the fixed $1 NAV with a floating NAV; (2) requiring MMFs to have a 1 % capital buffer with a minimum balance at risk; and (3) requiring MMFs to have a 3 % subordinated capital buffer. Some commentators believed that changing the NAV from a fixed 1 % to a floating buffer would accomplish little in the alleviation of possible risk, but suggested that management of the funds should have tools to prevent a sudden run on the funds in times of crisis, to enable them to overcome the immediate need for capital to cover withdrawals on a large scale.[37]

The SEC adopted a final rule under the Investment Company Act of 1940 governing Money Market Fund Reform and Amendments to Form PF on May 1, 2014 (effective October 14, 2014),[38] designed to address the funds' susceptibility to heavy redemptions in times of stress; improve their ability to manage and mitigate potential contagion from such redemptions; and increase the transparency of their risks, while preserving, as much as possible, their benefits. Among the changes is the removal of the valuation exemption that permitted institutional non-government MMFs to maintain a stable NAV and replace it with a floating NAV, with the requirement that these funds sell and redeem shares based on the current market-based value of the securities in their underlying portfolios rounded to the fourth decimal point.[39]

The Final Rule also amends its prior rules to give boards of directors of MMFs new tools to curtail heavy redemptions. They include the discretion to impose a liquidity fee if a fund's weekly liquidity level falls below the required regulatory threshold and discretion to suspend redemptions temporarily (to "gate" funds) under comparable circumstances.

Moreover, the said funds will be required to impose a liquidity fee if the weekly liquidity level falls below a designated threshold unless the board of directors determines that such imposition is not in the best interests of the fund. Other mandates under the rule are to increase the diversification of a MMF portfolio to make the funds more resilient, enhance stress testing, and improve transparency by requiring the MMF to report additional information both to the SEC and to investors. Investment advisers of certain large unregistered liquidity funds that are similar to MMFs will be required to provide information to the SEC concerning the said funds.

6.3.3 Designation of Mutual Funds as SIFIs

Arguments for Inclusion of Mutual Funds as SIFIs

The Office of Financial Research (OFR) issued its report on Asset Management and Financial Stability in September 2013; this discussed the vulnerabilities of asset management activities. The report indicated that the factors that make the industry vulnerable to financial shocks include (1) "reaching for yield" and herding behaviors; (2) redemption risk in collective investment vehicles; (3) leverage, which can amplify asset price movements and increase the potential for fire sales; and (4) firms as sources of risk.[40]

- *"Reaching for yield" and herding behaviors.* In an era of low interest rates, low market volatility, and competitive pressure from the significant increase of hedge funds, there may be a tendency of portfolio managers to "reach for yield" by seeking higher returns by investing in riskier assets or by engaging in "herding" behaviors by investing in assets classes that are popular regardless of their liquidity. Such behavior may contribute to increases in asset prices not justified by their size or liquidity, which may lead to increased market volatility and sudden shock in times of distress.
- *Redemption risk.* Mutual funds offer unrestricted redemption rights, which could face the risk of large redemption requests in a stressed market if investors believe it to be advantageous by being the first to redeem the securities, especially when there is a need for cash to cover redemption requests. Investors with less liquid portfolios after the initial withdrawal by earlier investors may cause a perception that the asset management firm is at risk in the future. The SEC does require mutual funds to hold at least 85 % of their investments

in assets that could be sold within seven days. The problem is that mutual funds have little ability, unlike hedge funds, to impose restrictions to prevent heavy redemptions in times of stress.

- *Leverage*. The OFR noted that during the financial crisis, the use of derivatives to boost leverage resulted in significant losses for some registered funds. Examples included the loss of 80 % and 36 % respectively of its NAV by the Oppenheimer Champion Income Fund and Oppenheimer Core Bond Fund, two fixed-income retail mutual funds. The losses were primarily due to their exposure to *total return swaps*, a type of derivative whereby investors exchange the total gains or losses from a reference asset without owning it – on AAA-rated tranched commercial mortgage-backed securities.
- *Firms as sources of risk*. In the event of the failure of a large asset management firm, the market may undergo significant distress based on its size, complexity, and interaction with other firms.

Arguments Against Designation of Mutual Funds as SIFIs

There are many commentators, both governmental and non-governmental, opposed to the designation of mutual funds as SIFIs. Included are two of five SEC commissioners, Luis A. Aguilar, a Democrat, and Daniel M. Gallagher, a Republican. Aguilar stated that the study by the Office of Financial Research, which suggested to the Council that large asset management companies be designated as SIFIs, was flawed. Gallagher indicated that: "Assets owned on an agency basis do not pose the same threats as we saw in the financial crisis." Both stated at a Mutual Fund Directors Forum on April 2, 2014 that the SEC had no input regarding the SIFI designation and that there was a real danger that omitting its input compromised the validity of the report. The study by the OFR concluded that the asset management industry may pose vulnerabilities to the financial system because of its reaching for yields through alternative investments that are subject to large redemption requests and use of high-risk leverage through derivatives. The SIFI designation would allegedly substantially increase the costs to shareholders in mutual funds through added fees, assessments, and capital requirements.[41]

On the other hand, SEC Commissioner Kara M. Stein appears to agree with the OFR, stating that mutual funds and exchange-traded funds that use complex, risky investment strategies often operate in a gray area of mutual fund regulation. Some investors like alternative mutual funds because they tend to outperform more conservative mutual funds, but they also may pose systemic risks. The alternative find market has risen from $46 billion in 2008 to $311 billion by the end of 2014.[42]

Mutual funds, as might be expected, are vehemently against SIFI designation. Vanguard, in its commentary, *The SIFI search: Some dangerous misconceptions about mutual funds*,[43] noted that the Investment Company Act of 1940 has regulated successfully the mutual fund industry for the past 75 years. The Act severely limits the types of investments that mutual funds and their managers may invest that could cause major investment losses or even bankruptcy. The Act limits *leverage transactions* (short sales, purchase of securities on margin, derivative transactions) that mutual funds may engage in; compels mutual funds to hold a minimum of 85 % of their assets in liquid securities (saleable within seven days) and daily mark-to-market the valuation of fund securities based on market values. Additionally, there is a legal separation between mutual funds and their managers. Mutual funds and the management companies that manage them are separate legal entities so that the bankruptcy of one is not attributable to the other. Transactions between a mutual fund and its management firm are prohibited. The assets of a mutual fund must be maintained with a qualified custodian, ordinarily, a US bank. The fund's assets are to be segregated from other bank assets.[44]

The isolated instances of fraud and mismanagement have resulted in prosecutions but did not affect other funds. Unlike banks that have short-term liabilities and long-term mortgage-type assets that are subject to a "run on funds," a run on mutual funds may be impossible for structural reasons. Banks take deposits which are part of their indebtedness but mutual funds are investments giving the investor equity in the fund which result in gains or losses according to their pro rata participation. A mutual fund satisfies redemptions from the assets of the fund itself. Former Secretary of the Treasury Ben Bernanke has been quoted as stating that equity mutual funds are "not runnable." During the financial crisis in which the S&P Index dropped by 50.9 %, the redemption of mutual funds by investors was only 4.1 %. *Forbes* magazine is in agreement. It noted that unlike BHCs, mutual funds do not go bankrupt. They cannot borrow moneys that they cannot repay. Losses are fully absorbed by the shareholders. The asset management subsidiary of Lehman Brothers survived and continues to operate as a separate company. Moreover, if a mutual company were to fall, the Security Investor Protection Corporation rules would shield investors from its demise. At worst, if large investor redemptions were to cause illiquidity costs, the fund investors would bear the costs.[45]

Additional arguments are also made. The largest US systemically important bank has assets of at least $2.4 trillion while the largest regulated investment fund averaged $159 billion. Banks are interconnected while mutual funds are freestanding in the financial system. The Council differs from the SEC because the latter is expert at regulating capital markets and the risks attendant thereto. The FED, on the other hand, functions as a prudential regulator assuring the safety and soundness of the banking and extended financial system. The FED's focus is on the participants in US capital markets but the SEC is concerned with the liquidity of risk-taking entities rather than capitalization. The SEC's interest in mutual funds is to maintain free and fair capital markets while the FED's concern is to ensure the safety and soundness of the banking system. There is no proof that the FED's application of prudential standards to capital markets would be a benefit.[46] Surprisingly, given the organization's stance in coordination with the FSB, the Chairman of IOSCO, Greg Medcraft, is in agreement that mutual funds do not pose a systemic risk, noting, for example, that when the famed investor Bill Gross departed from the Pacific Management Investment Co. fund, the company was able to withstand a large surge in redemption demand. He indicated that the focus should be on the activities of funds rather than the imposition of bank-like rules upon them.[47]

6.4 International Regulation

6.4.1 European Union's Money Market Proposed Regulations

On April 29, 2015, the EU Parliament adopted a report by the Committee on Economic and Monetary Affairs (ECON) that amended the money market regulations to provide as follows:

Types of MMFs

The Report stated that there are two kinds of MMFs, namely those that offer a constant net asset value (CNAV) per unit or share, for example at $1, €1, or £1, when they distribute income to investors and those that offer a variable net asset value (VNAV). The draft law would limit CNAV MMFs to two types: (1) Retail CNAV, which would be available for subscription only for charities, non-profit organizations, public authorities, and public foundations; and (2) Public Debt CNAV, which would invest 99.5 % of its assets in public debt instruments.

Proposal of New Type of MMF
There would be a new type of MMF: Low Volatility Net Asset Value MMF (LVNAV MMF) that might display a constant net asset value but under strict conditions. Authorizations granted to LVNAVs would lapse after five years; but in undertaking its review, the EU Commission examined the possibility of allowing authorizations for LVNAVs to continue beyond the five year period.

Diversification and Assessment
The draft law should also require MMFs to diversify their asset portfolios, investing in higher quality assets, follow strict liquidity and concentration requirements, and have in place sound stress-testing processes, MMFs would have to have in place a rigorous internal assessment procedure to determine the credit quality of money market instruments. The assets of a MMF would have to be valued at least once a day and the result should be published daily on the website of the MMF. Owing to the discretionary nature of external support, which contributes to uncertainty in times of instability, a MMF should not receive external support from a third party including from its sponsor, if any.

Transparency
Under the draft law, the EU Parliament also tightened the transparency rules. MMFs would have to report weekly all of the following information to their investors: the liquidity profile; the credit profile and portfolio composition; the weighted average maturity (WAM) of the portfolio; the weighted average life (WAL) of the portfolio; and the concentration of the top five investors in the MMF.

Liquidity Fees and Redemption Gates
The Public Debt and Retail CNAVs and LVNAVs should apply "liquidity fees" and "redemption gates" in circumstances to help stem sudden outflows.[48]

6.4.2 IMF Report

The IMF is concerned about the potential risks attendant on the significant growth of the mutual funds industry. In its Global Financial Stability Report of April 2015,[49] it rendered an empirical analysis of the potential risks of the MMF industry flows. With respect to their effect on asset price dynamics, it determined that they affect asset returns in smaller, less liquid markets. Larger MMF holdings and greater concentration adversely affect bond spreads in periods of distress. These effects, however, can be cushioned by liquidity risk management. The IMF found that systemic risk, as noted by US findings above, is contributed by *herding* (following the behavior of other funds) and interconnectedness, particularly by virtue of the ownership of asset management companies by banks and insurance companies.[50]

The IMF found that MMFs' contributions to systemic risk depends less on size than on their investment focus. It called therefore for a revised oversight framework for publicly offered funds whereby investors are given sufficient information to understand the investment products they purchase as well as protection from fraud and other risks. There should be investment restrictions, caps on leverage, liquidity risk management, price and redemption policies, and separation of clients' assets from those of the asset management companies. There should also be greater regulatory oversight of privately offered products to protect against fraud or negligence.[51]

The IMF noted that the limitations of the current oversight include lack of specificity, insufficient supervision of individual, and systemic risks. Suggested improvements included enhanced regulation by providing more specifics for funds' liquidity requirements; strengthening the micro-prudential supervision of risks related to individual institutions; ensuring that funds do not take excessive leverage; adoption of approaches based on products, activities, or both; and raising the quality of supervisory practices across jurisdictions by introducing global standards.[52]

In Chap. 7, we will explore a more controversial non-bank designation as SIFIs, namely that of insurance companies, which allege that their business model is far different from other financial institutions, that they lack a history of failures in times of distress, and that the designation is both inappropriate and likely to create systemic problems.

Notes

1. For a history of hedge funds, see Gregory Connor and Mason Woo, *An Introduction to Hedge Funds* (2004), DISCUSSION PAPER, 477, Financial Markets Group, London School of Economics and Political Science, London, U.K. at Chap. 2 https://www.google.com/search?q=Gregory+Connor+and+Mason+Woo,+An+Introduction+to+Hedge+Funds+at+Ch+2&rls=com.

microsoft:en-US&ie=UTF-8&oe=UTF-8&startIndex=&startPage=1&gws_rd=ssl.

2. SEC Office of Investor Education and Advocacy, *Hedge Funds,* INVESTOR BULLETIN, http://www.sec.gov/investor/alerts/ib_hedgefunds.pdf.
3. Dan Barufaldi, *Hedge Funds: Structures,* INVESTOPEDIA, https://search.yahoo.com/yhs/search?p=Dan+Barufaldi%2C+Hedge+Funds%3A+Structures%2C+Investopedia%2C&ei=UTF-8&hspart=mozilla&hsimp=yhs-002.
4. Hedge Fund fundamentals, *Structuring Offshore Hedge Funds, http://www.hedgefundfundamentals.com/wp-content/uploads/2012/12/HFF_Structuring_Offshore_HedgeFunds_11-2012.pdf.*
5. BNY Mellon, *Hedge Fund Fundamentals: Risk Management* (2012), http://www.hedgefundfundamentals.com/media_posts/hedge-funds-risk-management/.
6. *Id.*
7. Riveles Law Group, *White Paper: Forming a Hedge Fund: An Overview,* http://randwlawfirm.com/white-paper-forming-hedge-fund-overview/.
8. Houman B. Shadab, *Hedge Fund Governance,* 19 STANFORD J. OF LAW BUSINESS & FINANCE, No. 1 (2013) at 169, http://papers.ssrn.com/sol3/papers.cfm?abstract_id=2234482##.
9. Pub. L. 73-22, 48 Stat. 74.
10. Pub. L. 73-291, 48 Stat. 881.
11. 15 U.S.C. 80b-1-21.
12. For a copy of the SEC Regulation exempting certain investment advisers under the Advisers Act, see Securities and Exchange Commission, 17 CFR Part 275 (July 21, 2011), http://www.ecfr.gov/cgi-bin/text-idx?tpl=/ecfrbrowse/Title17/17cfr275_main_02.tpl.
13. Bruce Karpati, *Enforcement Priorities in the Alternative Space* (Dec. 18, 2012), *http://www.sec.gov/News/Speech/Detail/Speech/1365171492012.*
14. H.R. 3606 (Apr. 5, 2012).
15. *Id.* SEC enforcement actions may be found at *http://www.sec.gov/spotlight/insidertrading/cases.shtml.*
16. Regulation: Protecting Investors, Promoting Innovation, www.hedgefundfacts.org/hedge/regulation/.
17. For excellent discussions of hedge funds, see Gregory Connor and Mason Woo, supra at note 13; and EzeCastle Integration, *A Manager's Guide to Establishing a Hedge Fund,* https://www.google.com/search?q=and+EzeCastle+Integration,+A+Manager%E2%80%99s+Guide+to+Establishing+a+Hedge+Fund,&rls=com.microsoft:en-US&ie=UTF-8&oe=UTF-8&startIndex=&startPage=1&gws_rd=ssl.
18. Klara Bakk-Simon, Stefano Borgioli, Celestino Giron, Hannah Hempell, Angela Maddaloni, Fabio Recine, and Simonetta Rosati, *Shadow Banking in the Euro Area: An Overview,* European Central Bank Occasional Paper Series,

No. 133 (April 2012) at 17, https://www.google.com/search?q=Klara+Bakk-Simon,+Stefano+Borgioli,+Celestino+Giron,+Hannah+Hempell,+Angela+Maddaloni,+Fabio+Recine,+and+Simonetta+Rosati,+Shadow+Bankking+in+the+Euro+Area%3A+An+Overview,European+Central+Bank+Occasional+Paper+Series,+No.+133+(April+2012)+at+17,&rls=com.microsoft:en-US&ie=UTF-8&oe=UTF-8&startIndex=&startPage=1&gws_rd=ssl.

19. Alternative Investment Management Association, *The Role of Credit Hedge Funds in the Financial System: Asset Managers, Not Shadow Banks* (March, 2012), file:///C:/Users/Administrator/Downloads/the_role_of_credit_hedge_funds_in_the_financial_system_-_asset_managers_not_shadow_banks_-_an_aima_research_paper_-_march_2012%20(4).pdf.
20. Zoltan Pozsar, Tobias Adrian, Adam Ashcraft, and Hayley Boesky, *Shadow Banking,* FEDERAL RESERVE BOARD STAFF REPORTS, No. 458 (July, 2010 rev. Feb. 2012), http://www.newyorkfed.org/research/staff_reports/sr458.pdf.
21. AIMA, *supra,* note 10.
22. Ben Moshinsky, *Funds With $100 Billion May Be Too Big To Fail, FSB Says,* BLOOMBERGBUSINESS (Jan. 9, 2014), *https://search.yahoo.com/yhs/search?p=Ben+Moshinsky%2C+Funds+With+%24100+Billion+May+Be+Too+Big+To+Fail%2C+FSB+Says%2C+BloombergBusiness+%28Jan.+9%2C+2014&ei=UTF-8&hspart=mozilla&hsimp=yhs-002.*
23. Huw Jones, *Bank-style regulation offered as temporary fix for money market funds* (Jan. 21, 2015), REUTERS, http://www.reuters.com/article/2015/01/21/eu-moneymarket-regulations-idUSL6N0V01UA20150121.
24. Nick Reeve, *Biggest Hedge Funds Pose Worst Systemic Risk, Says Fitch* (March 24, 2015), http://www.ai-cio.com/channel/REGULATION,-LEGAL/Biggest-Hedge-Funds-Pose-Worst-Systemic-Risks,-Says-Fitch/.
25. Financial Stability Board, *Hedge Funds Oversight,* (June 1, 2009), http://www.financialstabilityboard.org/2009/06/cos_090601a/.
26. Securities and Exchange Commission, *Mutual Funds,* www.sec.gov/answers/mutfund.htm.
27. For a simplified comparison of hedge funds vs. mutual funds see Investment Company Institute, ICI, *The Differences Between Mutual Funds and Hedge Funds,* www.ici.org/files/faqs_hedge and WALLSTREETOASIS, *Hedge fundsvs. Mutualfunds,*http://www.wallstreetoasis.com/blog/hedge-funds-vs-mutual-funds.
28. Securities and Exchange Commission, Office of Investor Education and Advocacy, *Mutual Funds: A Guide for Investors, https://www.sec.gov/investor/pubs/sec-guide-to-mutual-funds.pdf.* See, also, GetSmarterAboutMoney, http://www.getsmarteraboutmoney.ca/en/managing-your-money/investing/mutual-funds-and-segregated-funds/Pages/seven-common-types-of-mutual-funds.aspx#.VYlsbkZH6Ws.

29. The statutory authority and regulations are taken from their respective sources, but the order and guidance concerning them may be found a number of sources, including Securities and Exchange Commission, *Valuation of Portfolio Securities and other Assets Held by Registered Investment Companies – Select Bibliography of the Division of Investment Management,* https://www.sec.gov/divisions/investment/icvaluation.htm; Kramer Levin Naftalis & Frankel LLP, *Overview of Key Mutual Fund Regulations,* www.publicalternativefunds.com/.../;; and Investment Company Fact Book, *Comprehensive Regulatory Regime for U.S. Mutual Funds,* www.icifactbook.org.
30. Investopedia, *Derivative, http://www.investopedia.com/terms/d/derivative.asp.*
31. Letter from SEC Chairman Arthur Levitt to Subcommittee on Telecommunications and Finance (Sept. 26, 1994), https://www.sec.gov/news/studies/deriv.txt.
32. Securities and Exchange Commission, *Use of Derivatives Under the Investment Company Act of 1940,* Concept release, request for comments (Aug. 31, 2011), 17 CFR Part 271, [Release No. IC-29776; File No. S7-33-11].
33. *Id.*
34. Terry Tian, *The Use of Derivatives in Mutual Funds* (April 18, 2012), MORNINGSTAR ADVISOR, http://www.morningstar.com/advisor/t/55099923/the-use-of-derivatives-in-mutual-funds.htm.
35. H.R. 4986, Pub.L. 96-221.
36. H.R. 6267, Pub.L. 97-320.
37. For a commentary of the FSOC suggestions , see Samuel G. Hanson, David S. Scharfstein, and Adi Sunderam, *an Evaluation of Money Market Fund Reform Proposals* (May 2014), Harvard University and NBER, *https://www.google.com/search?q=Samuel+G.+Hanson,+David+S.+Scharfstein,+and+Adi+Sunderam,+an+Evaluation+of+Money+Market+Fund+Reform+Proposals&rls=com.microsoft:en-US&ie=UTF-8&oe=UTF-8&startIndex=&startPage=1&gws_rd=ssl.*
38. 17 CFR Parts 230, 239, 270, and 279 (May 1, 2014), RIN 3235-AK61, http://www.sec.gov/rules/final/2014/33-9616.pdf.
39. For an excellent review, which is a source of some of the comments in the text, see David Luttrell, Harvey Rosenblum, and Jackson Thies, *Understanding the Risks Inherent in Shadow Banking* (Nov. 12), Staff Papers No. 18, Federal Reserve Bank of Dallas, http://www.dallasfed.org/assets/documents/research/staff/staff1203.pdf.
40. Office of Financial Research, *Asset Management and Financial Stability* (Sept. 2013), at 9. https://www.google.com/search?q=office+of+financial+research+sept+2013+report&rls=com.microsoft:en-US&ie=UTF-8&oe=UTF-8&startIndex=&startPage=1&gws_rd=ssl.

41. Mark Schoeff Jr., *SEC commissioners push back against systemic designation for mutual funds* (April 3, 2014), https://www.google.com/search?q=Mark+Schoeff+Jr.,+SEC+commissioners+push+back+against+systemic+designation+for,+mutual+funds&rls=com.microsoft:en-US&ie=UTF-8&oe=UTF-8&startIndex=&startPage=1&gws_rd=ssl.
42. Mark Schoeff Jr., *SEC member Stein calls for scrutiny of alternative mutual funds and EFTS* (June 15, 2015), https://www.google.com/search?q=Mark+Schoeff+Jr.,+SEC+member+Stein+calls+for+scrutiny+of+alternative+mutual+funds+and+EFTS,+(June+15,+2015),&rls=com.microsoft:en-US&ie=UTF-8&oe=UTF-8&startIndex=&startPage=1&gws_rd=ssl.
43. (April 2014), https://pressroom.**vanguard**.com/.
44. *Id.*
45. Paul Kupiec, *Our Worst Fears About Dodd-Frank's FSOC Are Being Confirmed* (Nov. 26, 2013), FORBES, http://www.forbes.com/sites/realspin/2013/11/26/our-worst-fears-about-dodd-franks-fsoc-are-being-confirmed/.
46. Paul S. Atkins, *Why FSOC Should Not Designate Mutual Funds as SIFIs* (May, 20 2014), testimony before the Financial Services Committee, U.S. House of Representatives, http://financialservices.house.gov/uploadedfiles/113-79.pdf.
47. David Michaels, *Gross' Pimco Exit Shows Fund Risk Not Systemic, IOSCO Head Says* (June 22, 2015), Bloomberg Business, http://www.bloomberg.com/news/articles/2015-06-22/gross-s-pimco-exit-shows-fund-risk-not-systemic-iosco-head-says.
48. European Parliament, Committee on Economic and Monetary Affairs, *Making money funds more resilient to financial crises* (April 29, 2015), posted by Simon Lovegrove, *European Parliament votes to adopt ECON report on MMF Regulation,* http://www.regulationtomorrow.com/eu/european-parliament-votes-to-adopt-econ-report-on-mmf-regulation/.
49. International Monetary Fund, *Global Financial Stability Report: Navigating Monetary Policy Challenges and Managing Risks* (April, 2015), http://www.imf.org/External/Pubs/FT/GFSR/2015/01/index.htm.
50. *Id.* at 104–106.
51. *Id.* at 114–116.
52. *Id.* at 117–118.

CHAPTER 7

Insurance Companies as SIFIs: The MetLife Inc. Litigation

This chapter discusses whether insurance companies should be regulated as systemically important financial institutions like other non-bank financial entities. A pending lawsuit commenced by MetLife Inc. when it was designated as a systemically important financial institution (SIFI) is an excellent example that highlights the arguments on both sides of the ledger. The litigation also exemplifies how a determination is made by the Council; the issues initiated by the findings; and the consequences of the designation. Both the Final Determination and the Complaint filed by MetLife illuminate the types of questions that have to be addressed by the Council irrespective of the ultimate outcome of the litigation.

7.1 Insurance Companies

7.1.1 US Regulation of Insurance Companies

Within the USA, although almost all insurance policies and other insurance-related activities are interstate by their very nature, nevertheless, they are governed by state law. The reason why insurance is state regulated rather than exclusively federal in nature is due to the passage of the McCarran-Ferguson Act.[1] This, in part, provides that state statutes, regulations, interpretations, orders, and other actions shall not be preempted by the federal government as they relate to the regulation of the business of insurance. The State Insurance Department of each state makes the rules and regulations concerning the registration of insurance companies,

Roy J. Girasa, *Shadow Banking*, DOI 10.1007/978-3-319-33026-6_7

and types of insurance, as well as setting forth the familiar standard forms for such policies. Since 1945, states have had virtually exclusive jurisdiction and governance of insurance.

The pros and cons of state regulation of insurance continue to be debated today. Those favoring state regulation generally believe in greater powers being given to the states vis-à-vis the federal government, and vice versa. Advocates for state control point out that during the financial crisis of 2007–2009 insurance companies under state regulation fared much better than banks. Having the federal government replace or share authority with states over insurance would unnecessarily add another layer of bureaucracy, create high transition costs, and be contrary to the espoused market system. Those favoring federal regulation argue that the multiplicity of states' regulation creates unnecessary confusion concerning the many different forms of regulatory enactments and interpretations, and is more costly to the insurance industry.[2]

7.1.2 AIG Ripple Effect

The American International Group (AIG) debacle, wherein some $140 billion of public funds from the Troubled Assets Relief Program (TARP) was used to rescue the insurance giant, changed the debate. AIG was the world's largest insurance company, with a market value of $239 billion. The problem arose to a great degree when it insured credit-default swaps, which were a form of guarantee to banks and other financial institutions, of over $441 billion, $58 billion of which concerned subprime securities, and $307 billion contracts written on instruments owned by banks in America and Europe. The coverage was used to assure regulators of the banks' asset quality, thereby helping their regulatory capital levels.[3] The collapse of AIG, which would have been forced into bankruptcy with enormous ripple effects upon banks and other financial institutions, was avoided by the TARP rescue, but events illustrated the failure of state regulators to question and prevent the possible collapse of the insurance giant because of over exposure to very questionable assets.

There was also a failure of the Office of Thrift Supervision of the US government to oversee the derivatives operation and the AIG holding company. Federal regulators, especially the FED, stated that a single regulatory authority was needed to perform the task of supervising complex organizations, which move beyond simple issuances of insurance policies to multiple insurance products. Companies of such complexity may be beyond the abilities and authority of individual state regulators. The AIG near-collapse illustrated how such an event may profoundly affect the overall stability of the entire financial system, not only in the USA but also globally. Thus, the passage of the Dodd-Frank Act in part sought to address the problem relating to banking's "too big to fail," which mandated extensive federal governmental financial intervention to prevent a domestic and global financial catastrophe.

Another concern of Congress was that the insurance market has expanded exponentially beyond the borders of individual states to the entire nation and, more importantly, to other nations. The existing legislation of 1945, which allowed states to develop the expertise to serve their constituents, was adequate in that era to serve the needs of the public, but in the new century and for a number of years before, there was an immense growth in globalization, which included the expansion of insurance companies worldwide. This expansion appeared to require national coordination, which was not within the capabilities of individual states.

7.1.3 Financial Stability Oversight Council (Council)

Although the emphasis of the Dodd-Frank Act was on banks and the securities industry, it nevertheless had a number of important provisions which impact the insurance industry. These are scattered throughout the Act, but are mainly set forth in "Title V. *Insurance.*" We previously discussed in Chap. 3 Title I, § 111, of the Dodd-Frank Act that created the Financial Stability Oversight Council in Chap. 3. This is particularly relevant with respect to its application to the insurance industry. Recall that among the voting members of the Council is an independent member with insurance expertise. The non-voting members include a state insurance commissioner to be designated by a selection process determined by the state insurance commissioners. The Council's main authority is to identify risks to the financial stability of the USA that could arise from the material financial distress or failure, or ongoing activities, of large, interconnected bank holding companies or non-bank financial companies, or that could arise outside the financial services marketplace. It also has the duty to respond to emerging threats to the stability of the US financial system.

7.1.4 *Federal Insurance Office*

In addition to Title I that created the Financial Stability Oversight Council, Title V of the Dodd-Frank Act, Subtitle A, entitled "Federal Insurance Office Act of 2010." appears to herald the gradual assumption of federal jurisdiction over the states-dominated insurance industry. Although state insurance departments continue to possess regulatory jurisdiction over the insurance industry, as provided for in the McCarran-Ferguson Act of 1945, nevertheless Congress created federal oversight of the industry which now has national and global implications. The newly created Federal Insurance Office (FIO) is under the jurisdiction and control of the Treasury Department. It is headed by a Director who is appointed by the Secretary of the Treasury.

The Director is granted the authority to:

- Monitor *all* aspects of the insurance industry, including gaps in the regulatory process that could contribute to a systemic crisis in the insurance industry or the US financial system;
- Monitor the extent to which traditionally underserved communities and consumers, minorities and low- and moderate-income persons have access to affordable insurance products regarding all lines of insurance, except health insurance;
- Recommend to the Financial Stability Oversight Council the designation of an insurer to serve as a non-voting member of the Council;
- Assist the Secretary in administering the Terrorism Insurance Program established in the Department;
- Coordinate federal efforts and develop federal policy on international insurance matters, in negotiating covered agreements
- Determine whether state insurance measures are preempted by covered agreements;
- Consult with the states (including state insurance regulators) regarding insurance matters of national importance and prudential insurance matters of international importance; and
- Perform such other related duties and authorities as may be assigned to the Office by the Secretary.

7.1.5 *Preemption of State Laws*

States will continue to be the regulators of insurance companies within their domains, but the Act provides for preemption over state regulation in specifically defined areas. The Director of the FIO has preemptive authority if he or she determines that a state insurance measure results in inconsistent treatment of a non-US insurer domiciled abroad in a country that has a covered agreement with the USA, and that such treatment violates the covered agreement. A *covered agreement* is defined as a written bilateral or multilateral agreement regarding prudential measures with respect to the business of insurance or reinsurance that is entered into between the USA and a foreign government and/or regulatory agencies. The agreement relates to the recognition of measures concerning the business of insurance or reinsurance that achieves a level of protection for insurance or reinsurance consumers that is substantially equivalent to the level of protection achieved under state insurance or reinsurance regulation.

Before making a preemption determination, the Director must notify both the appropriate US state concerning the alleged violation of the international agreement and the US trade representative and publish the inconsistency or preemption in the Federal Register. The state representative has the opportunity to file opposition or suggested comments and seek a determination from the Director.

The preemption authority is limited. It can only apply when the state measure (1) results in less favorable treatment of a non-US insurer compared with a US insurer, and (2) is inconsistent with a written international agreement regarding prudential measures. The agreement must achieve a level of consumer protection that is "substantially equivalent" to the level afforded under state law. The FIO's preemption authority does not apply or extend to state measures governing rates, premiums, underwriting, or sales practices, nor does it apply to state coverage requirements or state antitrust laws. The FIO's preemption decisions are also subject to *de novo* judicial review under the Administrative Procedures Act.

7.2 The Council's Regulation of Insurance Companies as SIFIs

The Council, in each of its final determinations, employs the same format as for other financial companies. It commences with an introduction citing its jurisdiction pursuant to §113 of the Dodd-Frank Act; a summary of its findings; the determination that the company is predominantly engaged in financial activities; the statutory standard and legal framework for the final determination; an analysis of the potential effects of material financial distress at the company by its consideration of the transmission, exposure, asset liquidation, and critical function or service channels; the company's existing supervision; resolvability; the evaluation of statutory considerations; and its conclusions.

7.2.1 *Council's Final Determination Regarding American International Group Inc. (AIG)*

The collapse of AIG, which was viewed as a systemically important financial company, required US government intervention and a bailout of some $140 billion to prevent alleged material financial distress with possible global ramifications to other major financial institutions. Among the obligations that almost brought about its downfall was its credit protection of credit default swaps and collateralized debt obligations. With the overall downturn of the economy reminiscent of the 1930s Depression Era, AIG was not able to meet pending obligations, thereby creating a company downward death spiral which would have led to bankruptcy but for US government intervention. Interestingly, the former CEO of AIG, in what appears to many commentators to be one of the most egregious lawsuits ever commenced, alleged the government exacted excessively punitive measures for its rescue of AIG in violation of the law. The court agreed, but concluded that the plaintiff was not entitled to a damage award.[4]

The Council, with the bailout clearly in mind, determined on June 3, 2013 that AIG could pose a threat to the financial stability of the USA and thus it should be subject to enhanced prudential standards. The determination was not contested. Using its analysis of applicable transmission channels, it opined that a large number of corporate and financial entities had significant exposures to AIG in its capacity as a leading multi-line insurer, including group annuities for private pension funds and stable value wrap products. In the event of financial distress, its 18 million life insurance customers and retirement product customers in the USA could suffer significant losses, leading to large withdrawals of cash surrender value of their policies. Pension plan parties to wrap contracts could be forced to write down their assets from book to market value, resulting in costs for pension plan sponsors.

The Council concluded further that the overall effect of any significant portion of AIG's assets on the financial markets might lead to stress in the entire financial services industry. It was the leading commercial insurance underwriter in the USA and in the event of a withdrawal of its coverages, it would be difficult for competitors to rapidly replace those policies. Operating in 130 countries, its complicated organization structure significantly increased the obstacles of a rapid and orderly resolution should it become necessary. Numerous other factors were considered in the Council's determination, including the extent of AIG's leverage; its transactions and relationships with other significant non-bank financial companies and significant bank holding companies; its off-balance-sheet exposures; its importance as a source of credit for households, businesses, and state and local governments; the extent to which assets are managed rather than owned by AIG and the extent to which ownership of assets under management is diffuse; and the nature, scope, size, concentration, interconnectedness, and mix of activities.[5]

7.2.2 Council's Final Determination Regarding Prudential Financial Inc. (Prudential)

A much more controversial Council determination concerned Prudential Financial Inc. On September 19, 2013, the Council approved by a 7–2 vote (US Securities and Exchange Commission (SEC) Chairperson recused) that Prudential is a non-bank financial company that comes within the jurisdiction of the Council; that material financial distress at Prudential could pose a threat to the financial stability of the USA; and, consequently, it should be supervised by the Federal Reserve and be subject to prudential standards.

The reasons cited for the decision were, in essence, based on Prudential's size and interconnectedness with other financial institutions. It is one of the largest insurance companies in the USA and through its subsidiaries is a market leader in a vast array of financial services including group and individual life insurance, annuities, retirement-related products and services, and asset management. As of the end of 2012, it had \$3.6 billion in total in-force life insurance and \$709 billion in total on-balance-sheet assets. It is interconnected with globally systemically important banks, non-bank financial companies, large insurance companies, and other companies through a broad mix of institutional customers, debtholders, and other counterparties. Corporations, banks, and pension plans have broad exposure to Prudential through retirement and pension products, corporate and bank-owned life insurance, and other group insurance products.

Under the analyses of the Exposure Channel (see Chap. 4 for discussion of applicable channels), it determined that Prudential provided a wide mix of financial services including individual and group life insurance, annuities, asset management, commercial lending, mortgage servicing, trust, and other retirement-related services. As of the end of 2012, it had $424 billion of assets in its general account investment portfolio and $253 billion in separate accounts. Many of its activities had a high degree of interconnectedness, thereby exposing the financial system to Prudential through its capital markets, including derivatives counterparties, creditors, debt, and equity investors, and securities lending and repurchase agreements. It had significant off-balance-sheet exposures owing to derivatives counterparty and credit facilities commitments with large global banks.

With respect to the Asset Liquidation Channel, although Prudential's life insurance and annuity products were long term, nevertheless a substantial portion of them could be subject to immediate withdrawal with little or no penalty. Should a large number of withdrawal and surrender requests take place, the company would have to sell off assets expeditiously to meet its obligations and thus be subject to the company's derivative and short-term funding counterparties, which could require Prudential to post additional collateral or raise cash to close out funding transactions. With respect to its Critical Function or Service Channel, the potential threat of material financial distress could seriously affect the company as a source of credit for households, businesses, and state and local governments.

The Council acknowledged that the company was state regulated as well as in the many countries wherein it conducts business, but nevertheless it concluded that state insurance regulators do not possess the same authority to which non-bank financial companies would be subject if a SIFI determination took place.[6]

Dissenting Views

The resolution was opposed by the Acting Director of the Federal Housing Finance Agency (HFC) and by the Council's independent member with insurance expertise. In addition, there was opposition from the non-voting member, the State Insurance Commissioner Representative. The FHC Director's dissent was based on his opinion that greater weight should have been given to the "mitigants" to the potential threat to the financial stability of the USA; an alternative view of the significance of certain factors; the availability of other tools to address identified risks; and his concerns about the consequences of the designation, including market impacts. He stated that he would have voted to retain the company in Stage 2 and thus be subject to ongoing analysis of the company. Having offered to undertake additional actions to assist the Council in its ongoing analysis, he felt that Prudential should have been given the opportunity to submit a resolution plan.[7]

The Director additionally based his views on the fact that no large financial company had more than a *de minimus* amount of equity capital exposed to Prudential; the company had limited market-based funding; its assets were generally of high-quality government debt and senior corporate securities; and it lacked the intangible assets that had been a key component of past failures of the financial services industry. Further, although the risk to the company's derivatives counterparties could be stronger, the analysis by the majority failed to account for Prudential's unique risks and character of its derivatives activities. Insurance products and liabilities are not the same as bank deposit liabilities- Prudential could delay payment of early withdrawals while still making regularly scheduled distributions. In addition, during the financial crisis of 2007–2009, industry withdrawals were contained.

The Council's dissenting independent member discussed the three transmission channels. The Council had cited two of the three channels that could pose a risk to US financial stability, namely exposure and asset liquidation. With respect to the exposure transmission channel, the dissenting member stated that there was no basis or administrative record to conclude that Prudential's counterparties, creditors, investors, and other market participants were significant enough to pose a threat to US financial stability. It had not been established that an individual counterparty would be materially impaired because of losses to Prudential, nor were any other exposures significant enough to cause instability to the broader financial markets. The asset liquidation transmission channel analysis was also flawed, because it was based on the assumption that variable annuity holders and other contract holders would run *en masse*, causing asset liquidation. This assumed massive liquidation of millions of life insurance policyholders and a significant number of other contract holders, without any basis for the assumption.

Other alleged flawed analyses included the consideration that as a parent holding company Prudential could suffer material distress, but the distress would not include all of its insurance subsidiaries. There was failure to consider mitigants (as stated above by the FHA Director), a lack of precedent for failures of an insurance company such as Prudential, the lack of evidence that state regulators could not resolve insurance issues, and any evidence that the company's material distress would lead to a threat imperiling the broader economy. The non-voting state insurance member also reiterated most of the arguments of the two voting dissenting views.[8]

7.3 METLIFE Litigation

The Council designated MetLife Inc. (MetLife) as a non-bank SIFI. According to the Council, the designation does not imply that the company is experiencing or is likely to experience financial distress but rather is a determination that in the event of material financial distress, if it were to occur, could pose a threat to the financial stability of the USA.[9] MetLife was the fourth non-bank to receive the designation of systemically important on December 18, 2014, and thus became subject to Council overview. The other non-banks to receive the designation, as stated above, were Prudential Financial Inc. (September 19, 2013); General Electric Capital Corporation Inc. (July 8, 2013); and American International Group Inc. (July 8, 2013).[10] Prudential appealed its designation, but lost the appeal and did not litigate the determination. AIG took the approach that such determination was beneficial to the company because it illustrated its financial strength. Thus, MetLife was the first designated SIFI to oppose the designation by commencing litigation.[11] This litigation is discussed here in some detail because it exemplifies the factors that Council considers in determining that a company is a SIFI.

Under §102(a) (6) of the Dodd-Frank Act, a company is predominantly engaged in financial activities if:

> (A) the annual gross revenues derived by the company and all of its subsidiaries from activities that are financial in nature…and, if applicable, from the ownership or control of one or more insured depository institutions, represents 85 percent or more of the consolidated annual gross revenues of the company; or (B) the consolidated assets of the company and all of its subsidiaries related to activities that are financial in nature … and, if applicable, related to the ownership or control of one or more insured depository institutions, represents 85 percent or more of the consolidated assets of the company.

7.3.1 *Background to the Determination*

MetLife was advised on July 16, 2013 that it was under consideration as a SIFI and was requested to furnish specific information for the Council to evaluate. Accordingly, the company submitted some 21,000 pages of data and met the Council representatives on 12 occasions between September 2013 and September 2014. On September 4, 2014, the Council voted affirmatively in a proposed determination to designate MetLife as a SIFI and advised the company of its right to request a hearing before the Council.

Prior to the determination, the CEO of MetLife, accompanied by his attorney, Eugene Scalia, and other persons, appeared at a hearing before the Council on November 3, 2014 to challenge this proposed designation.[12] After the required 60-day period for determination of the proposal, the designation was confirmed. On December 18, 2014, the Council determined that if there was material financial distress at MetLife it could pose a threat to the financial stability of the USA. As a result the company would be subject to the Council's enhanced prudential standards.[13]

7.3.2 *Regulatory Basis for the SIFI Determination*

The Council alleged that it examined information that included the types and amounts of counterparty exposures arising from its issuance of company securities; guaranteed investment contracts and derivatives activities; the size, collateralization, and liquidity of its securities lending program; the impact on capital of the company's use of captive reinsurance; the terms of interaffiliate transactions; and the scale of its insurance liabilities with discretionary withdrawal features. The Council also evaluated the transmission channels for material financial distress. Among the channels are: (1) exposure, that is, whether the non-bank financial company's creditors', counterparties investors', and other market participants' connections to the company are significant enough to impair them and pose a threat to US financial stability; (2) asset liquidation, that is, whether the company holds assets that if liquidated quickly would cause a fall in assets prices and disrupt trading or funding in key markets or cause significant losses; (3) critical function or service, being the potential effects if the company is no longer able or willing to provide critical functions or services relied upon by other market participants; and (4) other threats, such as whether the company's bankruptcy would disrupt key markets or have an adverse impact on other financial firms or markets. In addition, the Dodd-Frank Act states that a company is predominantly engaged in financial activities if at least 85 % of the company and all of its subsidiaries' gross revenues are derived from financial activities.[14]

7.3.3 *Application of Regulatory Factors to MetLife*

The Council decided that MetLife is a global entity that provides insurance and many other insurance-related and financial products to some 100 million customers in over 50 countries. As of 2014, it possessed some $909 billion in total assets and its assets and activities allegedly met the 85 % threshold of Dodd-Frank. The assets consisted of approximately $516 billion of general account invested assets including cash and cash equivalents; $319 billion of separate account assets; and $71 billion of total equity. It provides through subsidiaries a vast array of services, including life insurance, annuity products, and retirement-related products and services. It operates in over 50 countries through 358 subsidiaries. Three-quarters of its revenues are from the USA and Latin America. It is regulated and supervised in the USA by the insurance departments of various states.[15]

The Council placed emphasis on MetLife's issuances of funding agreement-backed notes and securities lending activities, which allegedly expose other market participants to the company and create on- and off-balance-sheet liabilities. By hedging these risks through derivative and other financial activities, they increase the potential for asset liquidations in the event of material financial distress. Its interconnectedness with other financial institutions may therefore jeopardize the US financial system and that of the world. Among the specific findings were:

- MetLife issued approximately % percent of all funding agreement-backed notes for the first six months of 2013 with a total obligation of $52.3 billion;
- MetLife's securities lending program makes it liable for cash collateral under its control of about $30 billion;
- MetLife's guaranteed investment certificates are general account and separate account liabilities of its subsidiaries that are offered to defined contribution plans of $6 billion of traditional outstanding plus $42 billion of separate account liabilities with guarantees;
- MetLife's involvement with *captive reinsurance* (insurance company reinsures a block existing business through the captive, which is subject to lower reserve and capital requirements than the ceding insurance company) and its reliance on internal and external financing arrangements, including internal receivable assets and letters of credit issued by unaffiliated financial institutions to provide equity and capital funding to affiliated reinsurance captives, make it vulnerable to asset liquidation risk;
- MetLife's invested assets are held in two separate accounts: (1) the "general account," in which the assets and liabilities are not allocated to separate accounts but are used to pay claims arising from its insurance policies, annuity contracts, debt, derivatives, and other liabilities; and (2) "separate accounts," where the investment risk is

passed onto the contract holder. The risk is where separate account contracts are supported by the general account through guarantees, thereby exposing holders of these separate accounts to the insurer's credit risk;

- MetLife is the leading variable annuity writer (hybrid insurance and securities contract issued by an insurance company in which the insurer promises to make periodic payments in exchange for the payment of a specified sum of money to the insurance company) and second in overall variable annuity assets in the USA. MetLife reported $100 billion of such annuities as of September 20, 2014 with guaranteed living benefit features and $198 billion with guaranteed death features. Its risk for guaranteed living benefits totaled $1.8 billion, thus making it more vulnerable than term and whole life insurance;
- MetLife's experienced during the financial crisis of 2007 and thereafter exhibited, like other sectors of the economy, significantly decreased total equity. It was compelled to use several emergency federal government-sponsored facilities. Its subsidiary bank had to access the Federal Reserve Term Action facility 19 times for a total of $17.6 billion in 28-day loans and $1.3 billion in 84-day loans. In addition, it had to raise some $397 million through the Temporary Liquidity Guarantee Program run by the Federal Deposit Insurance Corporation and borrowed $1.6 billion through the Federal Reserve's Commercial Paper Funding Facility.[16]

7.3.4 Council's Analysis of Potential Effects in the Event of Material Distress at MetLife

Transmission Channel

The Council considered the three transmission channels stated above that were most likely to pose a threat to US financial stability. Because of MetLife's size, interconnectedness with other large financial firms and markets, and its provision of products that could be surrendered for cash by policyholders and institutional and retail contract holders, it was determined that a significant downturn in the economy could lead to material threat to the entire US financial system. The threat arose primarily from MetLife's exposure and asset liquidation transmission channels.[17]

Exposure Transmission Channel

The Council applied the channel designated as the *exposure transmission channel*, which refers to the direct and indirect exposures of MetLife's creditors, counterparties, investors, policyholders, and other market participants should it incur material financial distress. Among the MetLife exposures to creditors, counterparties, investors, policyholders, and other market participants are *institutional and capital market exposures* to large financial intermediaries, including systemically important banks and global systemically important insurers. Its capital markets activities include securities lending and outstanding indebtedness, and institutional products such as funding agreements and pension closeouts.

For institutional investors, MetLife offers insurance, annuity, and investment products, and funds post-retirement benefits. Although many of the products and services are in separate accounts, the problem arises that it also guarantees these products which are reliant on MetLife's financial strength. As of the close of 2013, the company had $6 billion of guaranteed investment contracts outstanding and $42 billion of separate account liabilities with guarantees. It is also a participant in the pension closeouts and structured settlements markets. Its capital markets exposures include $6 billion of outstanding long-term debt; $3 billion of junior subordinated debt; $30 billion of securities lending agreements; $5 billion of derivatives liabilities; $16 billion of unsecured credit and committed facilities; $52 billion of funding agreements-backed securities and other obligations; and $4 billion of net notional single-name credit default swaps. Its gross notional amount of derivatives was $406 billion including interest rate derivatives, equity derivatives, foreign exchange derivatives, and credit derivatives.[18]

Exposure of US Policyholders and the Guaranty Association. MetLife has over 100 million policyholders worldwide. In the event of a material financial distress it would pose significant risk to policyholders, especially to products with cash values and guaranteed benefits. Retail policies are generally long term and state guaranty and security fund associations may mitigate some of the potential losses. Nevertheless, because of MetLife's size, scope, and withdrawal features, it would take many years for state and guaranty associations to repay losses in the event of the company's liquidation.[19]

Aggregate Exposures and the Risk of Contagion. The risk is that in the event of MetLife's failure, the potential impact thereof could affect the financial health of other firms, their counterparties, or the financial markets in which they are participants.[20]

7.3.5 Asset Liquidation Transmission Channel

The second identifiable channel concerns the potential negative effects that material financial distress could spread to other financial firms or markets, causing significant disruptions with respect to asset values. Material distress could cause policyholders and other parties to liquidate assets to meet obligations to counterparties, contract holders, and policyholders. The two potential liquidity strains could cause forced asset liquidation. There are institutional and capital markets products that can be terminated or not renewed and insurance-related liabilities that can be withdrawn or surrendered by the contract holder or policyholder. MetLife could be compelled to sell assets of some $35–60 billion including securities and other assets. MetLife lends securities to third parties in exchange for cash collateral of 102 % of the fair market value of the securities. The profit is reinvested to purchase securities that may be less liquid than the securities lent to third parties. The mismatch poses a liquidity risk in the event of financial distress.

Another source of potential liquidity strain is the forced asset liquidation of the company's retail insurance and annuity products than can be surrendered for cash. Of the $308 billion in general account liabilities of MetLife's US insurance companies, some $49 billion may be withdrawn with little or no penalty. The disincentives of withdrawal may not be sufficient to prevent withdrawals, thereby posing a threat to the company's ability to meet its obligations. An additional $206 billion of MetLife's separate account liabilities can also be withdrawn or transferred by separate account contract holders, but there are significant disincentives to do so. If the company were to exercise contractual deferral provisions, the impact in so doing would cause uncertainty among its customers, and the contagion would spread throughout the insurance industry. MetLife's liquid assets may be insufficient to meet withdrawal obligations, thereby causing a forced asset liquidation and the accompanying disruption among other insurance companies.[21]

7.3.6 Critical Function or Service Transmission Channel

MetLife has a broad range of services and products in insurance, risk transfer, and capital markets and is a leading company that participates in life insurance, retirement products, and commercial real estate lending. It has a market share of 15 % in the life and health insurance market and is a leader in corporate benefit funding and annuity product markets. It operates lines of business that provide credit to households, businesses, agricultural enterprises, local and state governments, credit to low-income, minority, and underserved communities, and serves as a federal government contractor. If MetLife were to withdraw from the many businesses, there could be significant disruption in the marketplace.

7.3.7 *Existing Supervision, Regulation, and Resolvability*

The Council acknowledged that MetLife is subject to US and international regulators including regulators in all 50 US states, District of Columbia (DC), US territories, and many foreign countries. The Council's perceived difficulty is that none of the authorities has jurisdiction beyond its particular state boundaries. The Council noted that there is no precedent for the resolution of an insurance organization that is the size, scope, and complexity of MetLife. Thus, the Council has taken the position that if there were to be a major financial crisis affecting the company, it would be extremely onerous to coordinate each of the supervisory authorities, home and host jurisdictions, and courts. An orderly resolution of MetLife would require immediate and effective cooperation among all of the governmental entities to avoid disruption to the marketplace, which is highly unlikely to occur. Accordingly, inasmuch as material financial distress at MetLife could pose a threat to the financial stability of the USA, the Council concluded that MetLife should be supervised by the Board of Governors and be subject to enhanced prudential standards.[22]

7.4 METLIFE'S COMPLAINT AGAINST THE COUNCIL

On February 10, 2015, MetLife commenced litigation against the Council in the District of Columbia Federal District Court.[23] The statutory basis for the lawsuit was §113(h) of the Dodd-Frank Act, which states that upon a final determination with respect to a non-bank financial company's designation as a SIFI, it may commence an action in federal district court within 30 days of notice of the determination, for an order requiring that the final determination be rescinded on the grounds that it was arbitrary and capricious. For a court to overturn a decision or regulation of an administrative agency among other grounds, it must find that it was "arbitrary, capricious, an abuse of discretion, or otherwise not in accordance with law."[24] Generally, the court is required to engage in a substantial inquiry, examine relevant data, ascertain whether the action taken was devoid of "reasoned decision-making," and whether there was a clear error of judgment.[25]

The Council requested the Court to grant more time, to May 7, 2015, to respond to the complaint and either to file a motion to dismiss the complaint or motion for summary judgment likely on the grounds of failure to state a cause of action or denial of the claim based on the Council's statutory right to designate MetLife as a non-bank SIFI. In August 2015, the FED and the F.D.I.C. requested dismissal of the MetLife lawsuit but agreed to the request of the presiding federal judge, Rosemary Collyer, to delay compelling the company to file a "living will" until December 31, 2016 pending decision by the court. Judge Collyer ruled on March 30, 2016 in favor of MetLife holding that the Council's action to be "arbitrary and Capricious." The Council has appealed the case to the US Federal Court of Appeals and, likely, thereafter, the case will be decided by the US Supreme Court.

Interestingly, MetLife's 79-page ten-count complaint was signed by Eugene Scalia on behalf of the firm of Gibson, Dunn & Crutcher LLP. He is the son of US Supreme Court Justice, Antonin Scalia, was previously chief solicitor for the US Department of Labor, and has been victorious in litigation that has voided a number of administrative rulings.[26]

In summary, the complaint alleged that the Council's decision to designate MetLife as a non-bank SIFI was arbitrary and capricious as follows:

- The only independent voting member of the Board of Governors with insurance expertise [Roy Woodall, who only voted "Present"] as well as the only nonvoting insurance commissioner on the Council both dissented from the finding;
- MetLife was denied due process by the rules and obligations under Dodd-Frank in the Council making its findings;
- The Council made numerous errors that fatally led to the Council's reasoning in its findings;
- The Council failed to give meaningful weight to the existing comprehensive state insurance regulatory regime;
- MetLife is not predominantly engaged in financial activities as required by the statute's requirement that 85 percent of the Company's revenues and assets relate to financial activities;
- The Council failed to undertake activities-based review for insurance companies;
- The Council failed to assess MetLife's vulnerability to material financial distress;
- The Council's findings were arbitrary and capricious by its reliance on unsubstantiated speculation and irrational economic behavior; and
- The Council failed to examine consequences of its designation decision.

Set forth in detail below is the substance of the complaint, which strongly differs from the findings and recommendations of the Council.

7.4.1 *Parties to the Litigation*

MetLife, Inc. is a life insurance company headquartered in New York and is a holding company incorporated in Delaware. It is predominantly engaged in life insurance products which generates 84 percent of its premiums. Almost all of its assets, liabilities, and revenues are from highly regulated insurance subsidiaries. Approximately 30 percent of its consolidated assets and over 25 percent of its consolidated revenues are derived from outside the U.S. thereby making them less susceptible to "run" risks. It differs from banking firms which borrow short term and lend long term whereas life insurance companies write long-term policies and invest premiums in long term assets. MetLife's subsidiaries are subject to extensive regulatory regimes in all U.S. states including extensive risk-based capital framework developed by states after experiencing a number of insurance failures. There are rigorous state licensing requirements, periodic examination, review of insurance products, and review of material transactions.[27]

The complaint alleges that Congress did not intend to designate insurance companies that engage in traditional insurance company activities as SIFIs. Congress intended the Council to take into account that insurance differs from other financial products including off-balance-sheet and derivative contract exposures. In addition, the Council cannot designate insurance companies engaged in traditional insurance activities as SIFIs without a thorough assessment of the regulatory oversight to which they are subjected by state regulators. Congress intended that insurance be treated separately by its provision for having an independent member with insurance expertise in order to impart understanding to other members of the Council who have limited knowledge of the insurance industry and its operations. Other indications of Congressional intent may be found in the exclusion of oversight of insurance by the Consumer Financial Protection Bureau and the limitations placed upon the jurisdiction of the Federal Insurance Office.[28]

7.4.2 *Statement of Claims by MetLife*

MetLife, through its attorneys, set forth ten counts or objections in its complaint against the Council, all of which state that the Council was arbitrary and capricious. In Count One, it was alleged that the designation of MetLife as a SIFI violated the Dodd-Frank Act and the APA

(Administrative Procedure Act) because MetLife is not a "U.S. nonbank financial company." It alleges that the Council while citing the provisions of §§4(k)(4)(B) and 4(k)(4)(1) of the BHCA (Bank Holding Company Act) concerning the meaning of *financial activities* that MetLife is alleged to be engaged in, which is defined as "insuring, guaranteeing, or indemnifying."

§113 of the Dodd-Frank Act and regulations pursuant thereto also provide that a "U.S. nonbank financial company" is one where more than 85 % of its revenues and assets related to financial activities becomes eligible against loss, harm, damage, illness, disability, or death, or providing or issuing annuities, and acting as principal, agent, or broker for purposes of the foregoing, *in any State*. The Council ignored the last three words. Each of the definitions provided for in the Act emphasizes state law. Inasmuch as more than 30 % of MetLife's consolidated assets and more than 25 % of its consolidated revenues were attributable to insurance activities outside the USA, the company would not be subject to any US state regulation. Thus, it was outside the definitions of the relevant statute and regulations and such designation was arbitrary and capricious. Moreover, while the Council emphasized the possible contagion if MetLife underwent significant financial stress, nevertheless, although AIG faced financial collapse, MetLife fared well during the financial crisis.[29]

In Count Two, it was alleged that the Council violated the Dodd-Frank Act and the APA because its designation was fatally premature. This was premised on the alleged failure to promulgate enhanced prudential standards for a designated insurer, which caused the Council to fail to examine statutory criteria it was required to consider. It thus failed to consider that MetLife was already regulated by other regulatory agencies; the consequences of the designation, such as how added oversight would be superior to state regulation; the inability of MetLife to address and conform to standards for exempting SIFIs, because of the lack of promulgation of enhanced prudential standards; and finally failed to consider an assurance that similar companies receive similar designation determinations.[30]

Count Three alleged that the Council designation as a SIFI violated the Dodd-Frank Act and the APA because it failed to consider alternatives to the designation and to provide a reasoned explanation for rejecting alternatives. Citing statutory authority, MetLife and Congressional correspondence to the Council, and statutory authority, it is alleged that the Council was required to consider alternatives to regulatory action and the reasons for rejection thereof. MetLife requested an activities-based approach to regulating insurers in lieu of company-specific designations but this was rejected without explanation. It allegedly failed to conduct the kind of diligence for the insurance industry that it had undertaken for asset managers. The Council convened a public conference on asset management activities to solicit advice concerning systemic risk, but failed to do so for insurance companies. Other alternatives the Council failed to consider included making recommendations to MetLife's primary state regulator to address any shortcomings, if any.[31]

In Count Four, it was alleged that the Council violated the Dodd-Frank Act and the APA in failing to assess MetLife's vulnerability to material financial distress. The claim was that the APA prevented an agency from imposing onerous burdens on regulated entities merely to stop illusory risks. The Council issued its recommendation for MetLife without addressing the likelihood for and vulnerability to financial distress, including the company's leverage and the degree to which it was already regulated. The Council assumed without basis that MetLife was experiencing financial distress.[32]

MetLife, in Count Five, alleged that the SIFI designation was inconsistent with the statutory criteria set forth in §113(a) (2), stated above. It was alleged that the Council failed to conduct a rigorous examination under the stated criteria by ignoring the statutory factors that favor MetLife, such as leverage and the scope of existing regulatory scrutiny, and focused on its size and interconnectedness with other financial institutions through an invented claim of "transmission channels." It had apparently undertaken a vague and generalized designation inquiry into the "nature" of its various operations, transactions and relationships with other banks, and financial assets. By focusing on its own regulatory criteria, the Council reduced the 11-factor criteria into a generalized analysis that would lead to a SIFI designation for any large financial company. It overemphasized size even though there had been no observed failure of insurance companies that caused contagion to other financial entities.[33]

Count Six alleged a violation of the Dodd-Frank Act and the APA because it depended upon unsubstantiated, indefinite assumptions, and speculation that failed to satisfy the statutory standards for designation and the Council's own interpretive guidance. In 20 pages it is alleged that the Council engaged in sheer speculation rather than logic and evidence. It ignored settled risk analysis principles, resulting in indefinite and unbounded speculation to which MetLife had no meaningful opportunity to respond. Its risk assessment failed to be predicated on scenarios that were carefully described and objectively defined and were reasonably consistent with real-world experience. It is alleged that the Council failed to offer objective definitions of its criteria such as "overall stress" and "weak macroeconomic environment."

The Council failed to delineate or identify scenarios of insolvencies it claimed to have considered in connection with material financial distress. It failed to account for the likely behavioral response of other market participants in the event of market stress in violation of accepted risk analysis principles. Policyholders' responses stated in the Council's scenarios were purely speculative; for example, that they would seek to terminate their insurance coverage early even though penalty provisions and other penalties would make such termination unlikely. It further assumed inadequate and ineffective state regulatory responses or that state regulator responses would reduce confidence and lead to a run across multiple insurance firms. The Council arbitrarily failed to assign values or probabilities in its analysis and arbitrarily failed to examine the likelihood and magnitude of events.

The Council had no reasoned justification for positing material financial distress at MetLife more severe than even the most improbable scenarios examined by Oliver Wyman, who conducted a comprehensive quantitative analysis of MetLife's potential liquidity needs using four scenarios based on assumptions ranging from adverse to wholly implausible. Wyman's asset liquidation study had four increasingly dire scenarios of financial distress at MetLife, which demonstrated that MetLife would not be compelled to engage in asset sales on the scale that it would cause and that MetLife's financial stability would not be threatened. In the scenarios, the Council ignored the efficacy of state regulatory bodies to prevent and mitigate financial distress. It dismissed the ability of state regulators to impose a moratorium on surrenders of policies. Furthermore, it failed to acknowledge that rapid liquidation of policies by policyholders could be prevented by MetLife's invoking of its contractual right to defer payments.

The complaint additionally alleges that the Council grossly exaggerated the economic impact of material financial distress at MetLife, including by sharply exaggerating market participants' purposed exposures to MetLife. The assumptions in the analysis of Oliver Wyman's third scenario was improperly escalated and the fourth scenario was agreed to be too far fetched. Similarly, the Council's "Monte Carl" technique assumed that management would completely abandon its responsibility, and posited a random asset liquidation that underscored its speculative and implausible analysis.

The Council grossly exaggerated the economic impact or material financial distress at MetLife by sharply overstating market participants' purposed "exposures" to MetLife. It unreasonably disregarded the economic effects of established risk reduction measures and the effects of existing state and federal agencies and repeated boilerplate, unsubstantiated assertions that exposures would cause losses to exposed entities. It failed to identify a range estimate or scenario that was being relied on, or reliance on conditions more severe than "material financial distress." The Council analysis suggested an unbounded range of potential losses by MetLife's counterparties. It ignored the accepted effects of widely used risk reduction practices such as the availability of collateral. The regulatory requirements presumed inadequate and ineffective risk-reducing provisions in state and federal regulations, or assumed they did not function in such a capacity. It ignored the SEC's imposition of risk reducing measures on money market mutual funds and withdrew permission for institutional funds to maintain a stable price of $1 per share, thus eliminating the possibility of these funds "breaking the buck." MetLife rebutted the Council's proposed determination calculation of the aggregate capital market exposures of counterparties of MetLife by showing the correct estimate was $90 billion rather than $183 billion.

The Council's systematic risk analysis unreasonably failed to account for existing regulatory scrutiny and erroneously equated MetLife with AIG as a source of contagion. It premised the SIFI designation in substantial part on a contagion theory which was baseless and had never occurred in the insurance industry. It ignored evidence of state regulatory stays and other tools, and stated they would be harmful in the event of financial distress. It failed to address the substance of the submissions of a number of state regulators, who indicated that they closely monitored the largest companies and were most attentive to the earliest signs of trouble. It fundamentally misunderstood the differences between AIG and MetLife. AIG's problems were not insurance related but rather were the result of its capital market financial products, especially credit default swaps. Unlike AIG, MetLife was predominantly engaged in extensively regulated traditional insurance activities and its credit default swaps were substantially different from those of AIG.[34]

Count Seven was the claim that the Council violated the Dodd-Frank Act and the APA because it failed to consider the economic effects of the designation on MetLife. In so doing, the Council failed to appreciate that MetLife was in a highly competitive industry in which it competed with numerous domestic and foreign companies of varying sizes to attract customers and capital. If an insurer was subject to additional regulatory requirements, it would impose materially higher costs than those borne by competition, thereby placing it at a competitive disadvantage. It would have higher capital requirements than its competition, be forced to withdraw from certain markets, increase costs to consumers, and other costs would rise, causing losses of billions of dollars.[35]

Count Eight claimed that the Council violated the due process clause of the Fifth Amendment and the separation of power. It was premised on the Council's ten voting and five non-voting members exercising the three major governmental powers within the agency, namely legislative, executive, and judicial powers. This therefore violated the due process rights of MetLife. Due process was also violated by the lack of adequate notice of what was required and what was prohibited, so that the public could conform to its mandates. It also improperly denied MetLife access to the full record on which the determination was based. Ten requests for records were made to the FIO under the Freedom of Information Act (FOIA) to the Council, the Board, and the Federal Housing Finance Agency (FHFA). The Council and FIO did not respond to the requests. The violation was further enhanced by the Council's reliance on new evidence and analysis not included in its initial proposed determination, all in violation of the due process rights of MetLife.[36]

Count Nine was the claim that the Dodd-Frank Act's provisions concerning the Council's authorities violated the separation of powers by assigning legislative, prosecutorial, and adjudicative functions to the same individuals. The Council identified companies eligible for SIFI designation, issued a proposed determination, and then ratified its determination, which violated the Constitution's separation of powers.[37]

Count Ten was a claim for injunctive relief. Based on the foregoing, the claim was that the Council would irreparably harm MetLife if the SIFI designation was permitted and therefore that injunctive relief against the Council should be granted. It was premised on the grounds that the SIFI designation was made in the absence of enhanced prudential standards for designated insurers; that it was denied due process rights; that the ruling was contrary to the public interest as envisioned by the Dodd-Frank Act; and that the cost to MetLife would be in the hundreds of millions of dollars annually.[38]

7.5 Commentary

7.5.1 Case Law Precedents

Whether or not MetLife will prevail will depend ultimately on the US Supreme Court's interpretation concerning the limits of an administrative agency's regulatory interpretation of the Dodd-Frank Act. The leading case that analyzes the extent of such interpretation and the limits thereof is *Chevron USA., Inc. v. Natural Resources Defense Council, Inc.*[39] In *Chevron*, the issue arose concerning the Environmental Protection

Agency's interpretation of the Clean Air Act of 1977,[40] as the meaning of "stationary source" was not defined in the statute. In doing so, the Supreme Court (opinion by Justice John Paul Stevens) engaged in a two-part analysis (called the "*Chevron* two-step test"), wherein a reviewing court of an agency's construction of a statute determines:

1. "First, always, is the question whether Congress has spoken directly to the precise question at issue. If the intent of Congress is clear, that is the end of the matter; for the court as well as the agency must give effect to the unambiguously expressed intent of Congress."

   "If the court determines Congress has not directly addressed the precise question at issue, the court does not simply impose its own construction of the statute ..."
2. "[I]f the statute is silent or ambiguous with respect to the specific question, the issue for the court is whether the agency's answer is based on a permissible construction of the statute."[41]

The opinion continued that an administrative agency that the Congress created is required to formulate policy and make rules to fill any gaps left, either implicitly or explicitly, by Congress. The court has long recognized in prior precedents that "considerable weight" should be given to an executive department's construction of a statutory scheme that the Congress had entrusted it to administer. Accordingly, the principle of deference to administrative interpretations should be accorded to the agency.[42]

In yet another *Chevron* case,[43] the Supreme Court unanimously upheld a regulation of the Equal Employment Opportunity Commission, which authorized the refusal to hire an individual because his performance on the job would endanger his own health because of a disability. The issue again was whether the interpretation rendered by the Commission permitted the interpretation under the Americans with Disabilities Act of 1990.[44] In upholding the Commission's interpretation, the court (by Justice David Souter) reaffirmed the agency's right to render an interpretation of the statute that was reasonable particularly when Congress left open competing objectives within the statute and had not spoken exhaustively on threats to a worker's own health, while the agency regulation attempted to make sense of the statutory standards.

The US Supreme Court, like the remaining two branches of government, is not immune to ideological interpretations, in which more "liberal" justices tend to favor governmental regulation of business conduct and "conservative" justices tend to be more wary of such intrusion and more ready to strike down statutory and regulatory enactments that they deem either violae the Constitution or, with respect to administrative agencies, are unreasonable and excessive. Thus, with the change in the court's makeup, whereby the more liberal Justices Stevens and Souter had retired, the question that may be raised is whether the present court justices would continue the *Chevron* precedents analyses? The makeup of the Court had been composed of four justices who tended to vote in a "liberal" fashion, while there were four justices of the nine who tended to vote as a conservative bloc. With the death of conservative Justice Antonin Scalia on February 13, 2016 and the apparent refusal of the US Senate to permit President Barack Obama to name a replacement, there may be some confusion concerning the voting behavior of the Court in the near future. The ninth justice is Justice Anthony Kennedy who, though he tends to vote with the conservative faction of the Court in most opinions, is nevertheless often the swing vote in 5–4 split decisions. It appears that the Court has not reversed its prior analyses.

Thus, in *U.S. v. Haggar Apparel Co.*,[45] Justice Kennedy wrote the opinion for a unanimous Court that again upheld the *Chevron* analysis. The case involved regulations issued by the US Customs Service with the approval of the Secretary of the Treasury concerning customs classification of certain imported goods. The Court determined that the interpretation rendered by the Service was a reasonable interpretation and implementation of an ambiguous statutory provision of the Harmonized Tariff Schedule of the United States.[46] As stated by Justice Kennedy, "the statutes authorizing customs classification regulations are consistent with the usual rule that regulations of an administering agency warrant judicial deference." A statute may be ambiguous without being "inartful or deficient." Continuing, he stated that this case exemplified the proposition that Congress need not and likely cannot anticipate all of the possible circumstances that may arise and, thus, the general policy as promulgated in the statute must be given specific effect. Citing *Atlantic Mut. Ins. Co. v. Commissioner*,[47] when a term in a statute is ambiguous (in this case a term in the Internal Revenue Code), the task of the Court was to decide whether the administrative agency's regulation was a reasonable one rather than whether it represented the best interpretation of the statute.

In litigation again concerning customs classification, that of *U.S. v. Mead Corp.*,[48] the problem addressed was whether the *Chevron* doctrine applied to each one of thousands of ruling letters issued by the Customs

Service annually in its 46 port-of-entry offices. Initially, the court opined (by Justice David Souter) that the "*Chevron* deference" applied whenever Congress has delegated administrative authority to the agency to make rules carrying the force of law and that the agency claimed deference in the exercise of its authority. Delegation of such authority may be in the form of adjudication, notice-and-comment rule-making, or some other indication of Congressional intent. The specific Customs ruling in this case failed to qualify under the *Chevron* deference, but could qualify deference under its "power to persuade" under *Skidmore v. Swift*.[49] Although agencies, which are charged with applying a statute, make numerous interpretative choices that are not binding upon judges to follow them, nevertheless, the well-reasoned views of the agencies implementing a statute constituted a body of experience and informed judgment that courts and parties to a litigation may rely on.

While general rule-making authority granted by Congress authorizes the agency to issue regulations having the force of law, a Customs ruling letter in the application of a particular classification does not constitute a classification ruling with the force of law. The 10,000 to 15,000 classifications issued annually by the Customs Service are best treated as interpretations contained in policy statements, agency manuals, and enforcement guidelines. The fact that *Chevron* is inapplicable in the current case does not lead to the conclusion that no deference should be given to a particular action in the form of a letter ruling. An agency's interpretation is to be given deference owing to the specialized experience and broader investigation and information available to the agency. In summary, the *Skidmore* deference should be granted in this particular case.

In a dissenting opinion by Justice Antonin Scalia, he stated that the majority opinion announces a new doctrine by resurrecting the pre-Chevron holding under *Skidmore* that is neither sound in principle nor sustainable in practice. He believed that *Chevron* changed the earlier holding in *Skidmore* and replaced judicial determination with deference to agency holdings in informal rule-making procedures. The consequences were protracted confusion, artificial increase in informal rule-making, and the "ossification" of large portions of statutory law.

The court in *Christensen v. Harris County*,[50] further noted that interpretive guidelines do not receive *Chevron* deference.[51] Opinion letters are entitled to respect but only to the extent that the agency's interpretation has the power to persuade.[52] In this case, Harris County, Texas sheriffs sued, claiming that the County violated the Fair Labor Standards Act of

1938[53] when it adopted a policy requiring its employees to schedule time off in order to reduce the amount of accrued time. In a majority opinion of Justice Clarence Thomas, he stated, in part, that "[W]e confront an interpretation contained in an opinion letter, not one arrived at after, for example, formal adjudication or notice-and-comment rulemaking, interpretations such as those in opinion letters-like interpretations contained in policy statements, agency manuals, and enforcement guidelines, all of which lack the force of law- do not warrant *Chevron* –style deference."

Justice Thomas also opined that the *Skidmore* deference of entitlement of respect may apply to opinion letters but only to the extent of power to persuade. Nevertheless, the Court determined that the opinion letter, whereby the US Department of Labor position that an employer may compel the use of compensatory time but only after the consent by the employees to do so was without merit and not based on the Agency's own regulations. Albeit Justice Scalia concurred in the result of the casel; he disagreed with the *Skidmore* analysis. There was a dissenting opinion mainly on the interpretation of a reading of the pertinent regulation by Justice Stevens, which was concurred in by Justices Ruth Bader Ginsburg and Stephen Breyer.

The *Chevron* analysis was upheld in *Barnhart v. Walton*,[54] when the US Supreme Court, in a 2012 decision, reversed a decision of the US Court of Appeals and upheld the interpretation of the Social Security Administration with respect to the denial of disability benefits to individuals who were unable to engage in any substantial gainful activity unless the impairment had lasted or was expect to last for a continuous period of two months. The Court of Appeals had interpreted the statute so that the 12-month period referred to impairment and not inability to so engage. The *Chevron* analysis appeared to be limited to a formal adjudication or notice-and-comment rule-making. "Interpretations such as those in opinion letters-like interpretations contained in policy statements, agency manuals, and enforcement guidelines, all of which lack the force of law do not warrant *Chevron-style* deference."[55] The reason for the limitation given by the Supreme Court was that internal agency guidelines were not subject to the "rigors" of the Administrative Procedure Act,[56] which includes notice and comment.[57] Justice Stephen Breyer, writing for the Court, recited the *Chevron* doctrine anew that the Agency's interpretation of a statute will be given deference when Congress has unambiguously given the Agency the power to interpret its statutory provisions, but if the statute is silent then the Agency's interpretation will be sustained if it is based on a permissible construction of the Act.

In two more recent cases decided at the end of June 2015, the results were somewhat mixed. In *Michigan v. Environmental Protection Agency*,[58] the US Supreme Court, in a 5–4 decision, determined that the Environmental Protection Agency had interpreted a section of the Clean Water Act unreasonably when it deemed costs as irrelevant in making its decision to regulate emissions of hazardous air pollutants from power plants. Justice Antonin Scalia, in writing for the majority of the Court, noted that courts are to accept an agency's reasonable resolution of an ambiguity in a statute that the agency administers under *Chevron*, but even under these deferential standards, agencies must operate within the bounds of reasonable interpretation.

In *King v. Burwell*,[59] however, in a 6–3 decision concerning the Affordable Care Act, the Court upheld an Internal Revenue Service interpretation that made tax credits available to persons who cannot afford insurance premiums to persons enrolled both under federal and state exchanges, although the statute's wording appears to state that these tax credits are only available to persons enrolled in exchanges established by the states with no mention of federal exchanges. The Chief Justice, John Roberts, in writing for the majority of the Court, noted that in analyzing an agency's interpretation of a statute, the Court often applies the two-step *Chevron* framework in which the Court asks whether the statute is ambiguous and, if so, whether the agency's interpretation is reasonable. The premise for the analysis is that when Congress enacts a statute that is ambiguous, it is an implicit delegation from Congress to the agency to fill in the statutory gaps. In exceptional cases, the implicit delegation may not be applicable. In this action, the court determined that it was unlikely that Congress did delegate the resolution of an ambiguity to the agency, but rather it was the task of the Court to determine the correct reading of the statute. In so doing, the Court found in favor of the interpretation that tax credits were to be made available to persons enrolled both in the state as well as the federal exchanges.

In criminal cases, it is for a court to determine an interpretation of criminal law and, thus, it owes no deference to a prosecution's interpretation. The issue has arisen, yet to be finally decided by the US Supreme Court, whether a court owes deference to an executive agency's interpretation of a law that contemplates both criminal and administrative enforcement. In the denial of a writ of certiorari (permission to appeal to the US Supreme Court) in *Whitman v. U.S.*,[60] Justice Scalia noted that the US Court of Appeals for the Second Circuit had deferred a Securities Exchange Commission's interpretation of §10(b) of the Securities and

Exchange Act of 1934 to the agency,[61] and affirmed the criminal conviction of Whitman. Other US Courts of Appeal have also deferred to executive interpretations of a variety of laws that have both criminal and administrative applications. Inasmuch as the case was denied the writ of certiorari, Justice Scalia stated his opinion that deference in such cases is to be left to the judicial branch and not to the agencies.

7.5.2 Opinions as to the Outcome of the MetLife Litigation

Scholars and financial analysts disagree whether MetLife will succeed in its effort to thwart the efforts of the Council. The company's shares declined slightly the day it instituted the action, dropping 1.2 % to $49.81 per share. A senior analyst with MetLife shareholder Snow Capital Management LP, Anna Wickland, believed that the litigation would go nowhere. Michael Barr, a University of Michigan law professor, who assisted in the creation of the Dodd-Frank Act, indicated that MetLife faced a difficult legal battle to overturn the designation; but Thomas Vartanian, chairman of the law firm of Dechert LLP, which specializes in actions brought before the oversight Council, disagreed with the negative views and stated that MetLife had an excellent chance of prevailing.[62] Possible complications may arise from the fact that the new more onerous capital requirements were formalized by the Treasury Department sometime in 2016.[63] As a result of criticisms from the insurance industry, the financial industry, and members of Congress, the Council indicated it would review the overall process in rendering a decision whether to designate a company as "systematically important."[64]

The Bipartisan Policy Center opined that the FED has become the de facto federal insurance regulator, particularly with the addition of MetLife to its regulation and supervision. It noted that with the transfer of regulatory authority over savings and loan holding companies from the former Office of Thrift Supervision to the FED, which affects many insurance companies that are so organized, such as State Farm and Nationwide, there will be major implications for those companies that were previously state modeled. The Board, with the designation of AIG, Prudential, and MetLife, will conservatively have supervision and regulation over one-fourth and possibly one-third of the insurance industry based on assets. The implication is that the FED is emerging rapidly as the de facto insurance regulator, thus replacing much of the supervision and control formerly exercised by the state insurance departments.[65]

Whether or not the US Supreme Court will take the inevitable appeal against whatever rulings have been made by lower courts in the litigation, it being very likely it will do so, it appears that there will be at least three votes by the current conservative members of the Court in favor of MetLife, to wit those of Chief Justice John Roberts and Justices Samuel Alito and Clarence Thomas; and it is predicted that the "liberal" justices, Ruth Bader Ginsburg, Stephen Breyer, Sonia Sotomayor, and Elena Kagan, will side in favor of the government. Thus, the ultimate decision will be made by the replacement justice and by the views of Justice Kennedy.

According to the American Enterprise Institute (AEI), a conservative think tank, and allegations made in the MetLife complaint, the action by the Council follows the recommendations of the Financial Stability Board (FSB), a mostly European body of bank regulators and central banks of which the US Department of the Treasury and the FED are members. It was created at a meeting of the G20 leaders in 2009. The FSB has published an initial list of nine global systemically important insurance companies that are systemically important financial institutions. Its recommendations have no force under US law and MetLife had no opportunity to challenge the FSB recommendations.[66]

Roy Woodall, the voting member of the Council with insurance expertise, in testimony before the Senate Banking Committee in April 2015, complained that the FSB (discussed in Chap. 8), which makes recommendations to the G20 and has influenced the Council's SIFI recommendations regarding insurance companies, is not representative of US interests inasmuch as US state insurance regulators and other agencies are excluded from its Board. The uniqueness of US federal and state regulation warrants an alternative compliance inasmuch as the federal government is unable to fully comply with FSB mandates.[67]

Insurance Industry Views

A public policy paper sponsored by the National Association of Mutual Insurance Companies concluded, as might be expected, that insurance companies should not be designated SIFIs. Examining the causes of the financial crisis, it stated, with substantial justification, that the causes in order of importance were as follows:

- The federal government's encouragement of Fannie Mae and Freddie Mac to expand rapidly in the early 2000s to support low-income housing, particularly in conjunction with the Community

Reinvestment Act and pressure from the Department of Housing and Urban Development:

- Subprime and Alt-A mortgage lending with low initial interest rates and little down payment requirements with rapid growth of credit default swaps, which spread exposure when housing prices declined and defaults arose;
- BHCs aggressive expansion into mortgage lending and competition with investment banks through off-balance-sheet entities that evaded bank capital requirements and took advantage of the federal deposit insurance umbrella;
- The conversion of leading investment banks from partnerships to limited liability corporate entities and aggressive investing in competition with investment banks, albeit with later supervision under the SEC which permitted relaxed capital requirements for investment banks' broker-dealer subsidiaries;
- Lehman Brothers, AIG, and other major writers of credit default swaps (CDS) instruments which offered low-cost protection to domestic and foreign banks against reduction in values of mortgage related securities;
- Securitization of subprime mortgages and the explosion of CDS and other complex derivatives linked to residential mortgages causing widespread reactions;
- Residential mortgage lending changes to an "originate and distribute" model, whereby the mortgage originators retain little risk that was securitized and distributed broadly; subprime borrowers acquiring property with little or no money down with little loss upon default;
- The FED's role in promoting aggressive borrowing and lending by keeping interest rates at historically low levels.

The author of the opinion piece acknowledged the major role of AIG as a cause of the financial crisis, but stated that apart from this, insurance companies were on the periphery of the crisis, having escaped severe adverse consequences from the subprime meltdown and subsequent events. There were some financial stress and financial rating downgrades. Six insurance companies did apply for and were authorized to receive TARP assistance, but four of them later declined assistance. MetLife was not among them. Leading monoline mortgage and bond insurers experienced major losses but none were impaired by the crisis. Most of the assistance to AIG of

$182.5 billion was paid to bank and investment bank counterparties in credit default swaps and security lending transactions.

The crisis at AIG was precipitated by its financial services division in London, AIG Financial Products (AIGFP), which included consumer finance and aircraft leasing. Its CDS portfolio became seriously affected by the rating downgrades and actual declines in values of senior collateralized debt obligations securities for which the company had written CDSs. According to the author, CDSs are not an insurance which US insurance companies are forbidden to write. The AIG division and that of other investment banks and bank holding companies were primary holders of the CDS market (AIGFP had $533 billion net notional amount outstanding at the end of 2007).

The author's view, agreed with by most insurance observers, is that having insurance companies designated as SIFIs ignores the regulated insurance sector's modest role in the financial crisis. The designation would likely not have been effective because of the imperfect nature of federal regulation of banks and related institutions, and would likely not have avoided the AIG debacle. The crisis does not suggest a need for higher capital requirements for insurance companies, although a federal office that provides insurance information as a liaison with Congress and with international organizations may be suitable for the industry.[68]

In this author's opinion, MetLife's complaint will ultimately be dismissed after a protracted trial in the US District Court, appeal by the party not prevailing to US Court of Appeals, and, ultimately, a trial in the US Supreme Court if it grants the petition for the writ of certiorari (permission to appeal to the court). The complaint exemplifies extraordinary legal competence and persuasiveness in its presentation of MetLife's opposition to its SIFI designation. Nevertheless, in this author's opinion, the complaint will likely fail for the reasons stated below:

- The case law is in favor of the administrative agency's decision to designate MetLife as an SIFI. The *Chevron* two-step process appears to have been satisfied; that is, whether Congress unambiguously expressed its intent concerning the Council's mandates. Congress, in the Dodd-Frank Act, as stated above, did mandate the Council to assess risks to the US financial system; identify potential threats therein; monitor domestic and international financial regulatory proposals and developments, ***including insurance and accounting issues***; and require supervision by the Board of Governors for non-bank financial companies that may pose risks to the financial stability of the USA.

- If a court were to hold that the statute was not unambiguous, the *Chevron* second step is whether the agency's decisions was based on a permissible construction of the statute. It appears from the 31-page Council report of its basis for a final determination regarding Metlife that it was not made haphazardly but based on a thorough examination of MetLife's financial empire.
- It appears that the strongest argument by MetLife is that it is already regulated extensively by the 50 states' insurance departments, territories, and the District of Columbia, and also by global governmental agencies. Although persuasive in theory, nevertheless, it is unlikely that individual state agencies are able to comprehend and regulate an insurance company that has close to \$1 billion in total consolidated assets, \$71 billion of total equity, and a market capitalization of \$61 billion (using the Council's numbers as of September 30, 2014). Coordination among the many regulatory agencies would appear to be almost impossible to achieve.
- Although a persuasive argument is made again by MetLife in that it did not pose a danger to US financial stability during the last crisis, the question does arise of whether a collapse could pose a significant danger to the US and global economies. Its alleged lack of vulnerability to a future financial crisis is somewhat contradicted by the Council's findings that MetLife, during the 2007–2009 crisis experienced significant decreases in the value of its assets; had the second largest unrealized losses among life insurers; and utilized several sources of borrowing from emergency federal government-sponsored facilities for a total of \$17.6 billion in 28-day loans and \$1.3 billion in 84-day loans, as well as other loans or use of access to other capital markets to raise moneys;
- There appears to be little doubt that a collapse, however unlikely, would pose significant risks to trading and funding markets;
- Arguments to be addressed by a trial court include the conflicting opinions of the Council and MetLife as to whether MetLife comes within the purview of §102(a)(6) of the Dodd-Frank Act, which defines a "nonbank financial company" as one which is "predominantly engaged in financial activities" if:
  - (1) the annual gross revenues derived by the company financial in nature (as defined in section 4(k) of the Bank Holding Company Act of 1956) and, if applicable, from the ownership or control of

one or more insured depository institutions, represents 85 % or more of the consolidated annual gross revenues of the company; or

- (2) the consolidated assets of the company and all of its subsidiaries related to activities that are financial in nature (as defined in section 4(k) of the Bank Holding Company Act of 1956) and, if applicable, related to the ownership or control of one or more insured depository institutions, represents 85 % or more of the consolidated assets of the company.

The Council states that the 85 % standard was met by MetLife, while the company denies that the standard has been attained. This is a clear issue of fact that judge and/or jury will have to determine. If, in fact, the standard has not been met, then MetLife's complaint may be upheld and the action taken by the Council would be nullified. It is difficult to believe that the company would alter financial data to satisfy the 85 % rule given the sanctions that would be imposed by a federal court. It remains to be determined how this factor will play out. As indicated previously, the 85 % threshold cannot be modified by the Council and, thus, can be at the heart of MetLife's successful outcome if such were to occur. The outcome of this case may affect significantly the extent of the Council's jurisdiction and power to regulate companies as SIFIs.

7.5.3 Insurance Companies as SIFIs Debate

Commentators who oppose SIFI designation for insurance companies point out that the insurance model is different from the banking model in a number of respects and thus should not be held to the same SIFI standards. As one commentator illustrated, there are four major differences between the two financial sectors of the economy, namely: (1) Insurance companies, unlike banking organizations do not operate within a system and are not institutionally interconnected. Whereas banks are interconnected and exposed to unsecured and secured interbank lending practices, insurance companies are stand-alone concerns and not within an "insurance system"; (2) Banks operate in maturity transformation, transforming short-term risk into longer-term assets, whereas insurance companies are not so engaged and are funded long term, making them less susceptible to the short-term funded banking sector; (3) Insurance companies are substantially less vulnerable to the liquidity risk which underlies banking organizations. Banks have deposits that are short term and may be withdrawn at will, unlike insurance company assets that are long term and much less vulnerable to withdrawals; and (4) Whereas banks are in the business of creating credit and liabilities are money in nature, insurance companies represent an illiquid financial claim and are not part of payment or settlement systems.[69]

As stated previously, voting and non-voting insurance representative members of the Council have dissented from the finding of insurance companies of such SIFIs. The focus by both regulatory agencies on size, global presence, interconnectivity and contagion risk, and ease of substitution may not be the appropriate criteria when applied to reinsurance companies. Although interconnected with other companies, it is alleged that reinsurance is not about short-term funding activity but rather capture transfer and vertical relief, and not horizontal relief as in interbank transfers. With the large number of reinsurers worldwide, its smaller size when compared to other major financial institutions, and past experience, including the 2001 Hurricane Katrina disaster, there is scant evidence that any single reinsurer could pose systemic problems. Unlike other financial entities, contagion is avoided because there is no need for immediate payment of claims, but rather is more of a gradual process thereby permitting affected reinsurers to recover from liabilities' payouts. From past experience of disasters, only about 10 % of payouts occur in the first year and gradually more over the next four years. When reinsurance companies engage in non-traditional non-insurance financial activities then they should abide by rules and regulations for broker-dealers, investments advisers, and the like, rather than receiving SIFI designations.[70]

Even where there are similarities between banks and insurance companies, they differ with respect to possible contagion with important systemic implications. Like banks, insurance companies act as financial intermediaries receiving premiums to insure against individual losses which premiums are reinvested in government and private sector assets. They differ, however, according to experts with respect to leverage, capital, and loss absorption capacity. Banks are the most highly leveraged financial institutions, albeit customers are generally protected by Federal Deposit Insurance Corporation (FDIC) guarantees. After the most recent banking crisis and after major objections, banks have been required to have more capital in relation to assets to cover future adverse conditions. Insurance companies are less vulnerable because they need not incur additional debt to cover liabilities to policyholders; rather the acquired debt is only for the acquisition of fixed assets and for the financing of mergers and acquisitions. There are also major differentials with respect to the role of capital and loss absorption capacity, wherein insurance companies are much less vulnerable than banks in the event of material stress.

There are other significant disadvantages in naming insurance companies as SIFIs. In selecting particular insurance companies, the Council may place the designees at competitive disadvantages vis-à-vis other insurance providers. The costs of added capital requirements will cause affected insurers to lessen consumer benefits by raising the prices of some insurance products and adding other products. Advocates point out that the emphasis on an activities-based approach combined with state regulatory oversight is far better that the singling out of a particular company for heightened prudential standards.[71] There has been some bi-partisan effort in Congress to ease capital requirements imposed on insurance companies under the Dodd-Frank Act, but such efforts have been opposed by lobbyists for the banking sector who demand comparable lessening of such requirements, even though much of the banking crisis of 2007–2009 was attributable to banking malfeasance.[72] It appears, however, that the FED may enact SIFI rules that will differentiate insurance companies from other financial institutions.[73]

Brookings Institution

One of the many publications of the nearly 100-year-old highly respected Brookings Institution gave insightful views into regulating life insurers as SIFIs. As did others, it noted that federal regulators have a different task in determining whether to name life insurance companies as SIFIs because they have a different business model than other non-bank financial institutions. Its business is to take risk by pooling premiums of individuals and other legal persons to pay for the random events that would otherwise leave them destitute. While banks take risks, their primary role is to provide moneys for worthy projects. By offering annuities and other investments to their insured they also act as asset managers. Thus, there is prudential risk from poor performance of variable funds; increased risk when they offer guarantees for investment performance; and they take on much longer maturity obligations than banks but also have more time to respond to problems because of the nature of their long-term liabilities.

Because life insurers have long-term liabilities, they require long-term assets. Thus, if they engage in long-term commitments to pay a certain percentage of interest over, for example, 5 % interest over 30 years, then if their return is half of the said sum in the initial several years, the mismatch could cause systemic problems inasmuch as life insurers would have to reprice their risks and lessen their ability to provide long-term investment funds in US infrastructure. There would be increased volatility and participation in "fire sales" to cover their liabilities. The FED, concerned with variations in market value, may cause it to apply an investment model that is more akin to a bank's.

Although life insurance failures are uncommon, they may err in their assumptions about death rates, health or accidents risk, or bad investments, or simply experience bad luck. Therefore, it is critical for life insurers to maintain appropriate liability reserves for future contingencies. For banks, capital requirements are determined by the FED in conjunction with the rules set forth by the Basel Committee on Banking Supervision. While US insurers are also subject to risk-based capital, the requirements are set forth by the National Association of Insurance Commissioners (NAIC) that become legally applicable in each state. Although similar to that of banks, there are significant differences. The NAIC requires that they take into account not only the asset side but also insurance risk, interest rate risk, and other business risks including litigation. The FED may choose to accept and defer to NAIC capital calculations; use bank calculations; accept the NAIC basic approach but modify it; or use a hybrid approach. In its conclusion, it was suggested that whether or not life insurance companies should be designated as SIFIs, it is important that to note that life insurers "are quite different animals from banks" and regulators should not treat them in the same manner.[74]

7.5.4 Reinsurance as SIFIs

Reinsurance is insurance coverage for insurance companies. Rather than be responsible for all of the risks that may arise, especially in a financial downturn, insurance companies pay premiums to reinsurance companies to assume part or even all of the risks that may occur in the future and to reimburse them for losses that may arise. The fear is akin to individuals who purchase insurance to protect against catastrophic losses that could cause a significant downfall and possibly bankruptcy. Reinsurance may reduce volatility by spreading the risks associated with insurance coverage to the "reinsurer," benefit from the capital reserves of the reinsurer, and possibly increase profitability for the insured company (known as the "ceding company," "cedent," "reassured," or "reinsured"). The ceding company is thus able to obtain capital that is less costly and time consuming than obtaining it from the market and is more flexible by adjusting the amount relied upon annually. Generally, reinsurers are required to be highly solvent to cover the significant losses that may arise and are ceded to it.[75]

The major types of reinsurance policies are:

- *Facultative Reinsurance*—reinsurance applicable to a specific risk or individual. The ceding insurer submits a detailed offer to the reinsurer specifying the risk being undertaken. While offering the advantages of spreading the risks and obtaining the experience of the reinsurer, it also is administratively complex and is highly reliant on the discretion of the reinsurer to accept or reject the proposed contract;
- *Reinsurance Treaty*—The word "treaty" does not refer to an inter-governmental agreement but rather is reinsurance coverage for all risks of a particular portfolio or class as spelled out in the agreement between the ceding company and the reinsurer. Rather than a particular risk, the cedent is covered for all risks within the class and permits the ceding company to free up capital requirements enabling it to expand its liability coverage;
- *Obligatory Treaties*—there are two types of obligatory treaties, proportional and non-proportional treaties:
  - *Proportional Treaty* (Reinsurance)—the reinsurer shares both the premiums received under the insurance policies sold as well as the risks of losses generally in the same percentages or as otherwise agreed;
  - *Non-Proportional Treaty* (Reinsurance)—the cedent is concerned about risk of losses that may arise above a particular amount (priority or retention limit) and, thus, the reinsurer agrees to assume the said risk without having a share of the premiums paid for the particular risk to the cedent. Non-proportional treaties may be calculated or based on a single risk, a specified insurance portfolio, or based on particular events:

- *Excess-of-Loss Treaty (Reinsurance)*—a form of non-proportional reinsurance that protects the cedent against losses above a certain limit generally due and occurring in a catastrophic event, and may include either one claim or more than one claim from the same event as agreed upon in the treaty;

- *Stop Loss (Risk-Attaching Reinsurance)*—the reinsurer agrees to pay a fixed maximum sum for all claims made within a particular time frame for a certain class of business or type of insurance even though the losses occurred outside the effective period of the reinsurance coverage;
- *Loss-Occurring Coverage*—coverage is for all losses that took place within the covered period rather than when the claims are made.[76]

Although reinsurance companies have escaped both the FSB's recommendations to the G20 as globally systemically important insurers (G-SIFIs; see below) and the Council's recommendations as SIFIs, it appears that at least the leading three reinsurance companies may be so designated by either or both of the regulatory agencies. These three companies are Munich Re Group (Munich Re) based in Munich, Germany, Swiss Reinsurance Company (Swiss Re) based in Zurich, Switzerland, and General Re Corporation (Gen Re) through its subsidiary Berkshire Hathaway Reinsurance Group in the USA. Although the earnings of Berkshire Hathaway Reinsurance Group are substantially less than Munich Re and Swiss Re, the Group also owns some 11.8 % of Munich Re as well as substantial interests in other major insurance companies.

Is Warren Buffett's Berkshire Hathaway Inc., which includes the sixth largest reinsurance in the world and interests in other major insurance companies, the next SIFI designation by the Council? Regulators in the United Kingdom (UK) have requested the FSB and US regulators to include the company on its SIFI list that presently contains nine global insurance companies. It appears that Berkshire does meet initial consideration as a SIFI with over $526 billion in assets as of December 31, 2014, including over $4.8 billion of derivatives liability; but the issue arises whether reinsurance or even insurance companies in general should receive FSB and/or Council designations. It is the largest shareholder of Wells Fargo & Co. (483 million shares), American Express Co. (152 million shares), and is a major investor in Bank of America Corp., Goldman Sachs, and other holdings.[77] It clearly meets the threshold, but with over $57 billion in cash reserves and cash equivalents and its wide diversification, its insurance holdings do not appear per se to warrant SIFI designation.

7.6 International Regulation

7.6.1 Financial Stability Board Recommendations

Globally Systemically Important Insurers (GSIIs)

As stated previously, unlike other non-bank financial companies, insurance companies in the USA and in many areas abroad are regulated by a multitude of regulators, including the state insurance commissioners of the 50 US states and insurance regulators of the countries wherein the companies operate. The FSB, in consultation with the International Association of Insurance Commissioners (IAIS) and using the latter's assessment methodology, identified a list of globally systemically important insurers.[78] The FSB has been more aggressive in recommending both insurance companies and reinsurance companies as SIFIs. The list is to be updated annually each November. As of November 3, 2015, the firms on the list were Allianz SE, American International Group Inc.; Aegon N.V.; Aviva plc; Axa SA; MetLife Inc.; Ping An International (Group) Company of China, Ltd; Prudential Financial Inc.;[79] and Prudential plc.[80]

In the FSB's *Key Attributes of Effective Resolution Regimes for Financial Institutions*,[81] as it relates to insurance, it noted that insurance failure may occur in a number of ways, such as through contagion as perceived by policyholders with respect to particular products and by financial links as for example in the derivatives markets. Insurance regimes failure could have an impact on the broader financial market. Tools such as run-off and portfolio transfer procedures may be insufficient to prevent or mitigate the systemic impact of the sudden deterioration of a major insurance institution. Accordingly, the FSB recommends a resolution regime for insurers to resolve a company's crisis with severe disruption to the overall financial system as well as protecting policyholders, shareholders, and taxpayers.

The resolution authority (in the USA it would be the Council and state regulators) should set forth clear standards or indicators to guide insurers that may be incurring financial difficulties. Indicators of financial distress include breach of minimum capital, asset backing technical provisions; strong likelihood on inability to make due payments to policyholders or creditors, and the failure of attempted recovery measures. Resolution authorities should have a broad range or resolution powers which should be exercised, if possible, to permit the affected company to continue operation under existing contracts of insurance, permit the exercise of options under its contracts, and buy reinsurance coverage. The said authority should have the power to restructure, limit, or write down liabilities such as reducing or terminating future benefits and guarantees; reduce the value of contracts upon surrender; terminate or restructure options for policyholders; settle crystallized and contingent insurance obligations; and reduce the value of or restructure reinsurance contracts issued by the company.[82]

The authority should have the power to restructure liabilities with respect to claims that have not yet arisen; claims that have arisen but have not yet been notified; claims that have arisen, been notified, but not yet estimated; or where the identity of the policyholders is not yet known. It should have the power to transfer contracts of insurance and reinsurance and transfer reinsurance associated with transferred policies without consent of the reinsurer. It may also suspend the rights of policyholders by temporarily restricting or suspending rights to withdraw from their contracts with the insurers as well as staying rights of reinsurers to terminate or not reinstate coverage. There should be respect for the hierarchy of claims that should be consistent with policyholder protection. The authority should have the flexibility concerning how to treat creditors or policyholders of the same class or different classes.[83]

Firms that are systemically significant or critical upon failure, including all G-SIFIs, are to be subject to resolvability assessments to include the evaluation of the feasibility and credibility of implementation of the resolution strategy and operational resolution plan. The FSB suggested assessment includes a broad range of 14 areas, such as availability of a transferee or purchaser of some of its business activities; capacity to fund a transfer where there are insufficient assets to resolve all insurance liabilities; the ability of human resources and key personnel; the legal, operational, and financial separation of traditional insurance business from its non-traditional business; the extent of interconnectedness or interdependencies among group entities; and the ability to fund continued operations of critical functions and services.[84]

Consideration is to be given to a material adverse impact on economic activity as a result of the disruption to the continuity of insurance cover and payments; the lack of confidence in other insurers that may trigger a policyholder run; an adverse impact on the resolvability of insurance or other financial operations; large investment losses of other financial institutions that could impact the insurers' capital resources; the termination of securities lending and reverse repo operations that could impact the firm's funding and liquidity; and the impact of financial market disruption owing to the termination of financial guarantees or credit default swaps.[85]

All G-SIFIs and firms that are systemically significant or critical upon failure should be required to undertake an ongoing process of recovery and resolution planning that is tailored to their specific risks and systemic implications. Factors to be taken into account include a firm's derivatives transactions; intercompany guarantees; interaffiliate support arrangements; risk pooling; shared services; risk-management model; and the nature of its assets and liabilities. Recovery plans should be based on severe stress scenarios and the identification of essential and systemically important functions where they are conducted. The firm's recovery plan should be reviewed and, in the case of G-SIFIs, the plan should be carried out. Recovery measures and time are to include actions to strengthen the firm's capital structure; triggering of contingent capital instruments; possible sales of subsidiaries; changes to reinsurance programs; changes to investment strategies and hedging programs; changes to the business mix, sales volume, and product designs; changes to underwriting and claims handling practices; and modifications to contract terms and conditions, the level of fees, and surrender payments, as well as timing of discretionary benefits and incentives.[86]

Resolution strategies and plans, particularly for G-SIFIs, should be developed and should include the identification of policyholders protected by policy protection schemes; actuarial assumptions used for calculating insurance liabilities; review of asset quality and concentration issues; sources of funding; details of transfers of reinsurance; identification of counterparties; and participation in financial market infrastructures. In addition, insurers should be required to maintain information systems and controls that can promptly produce relevant data and information needed to implement resolution measures such as number and types of insurance policies; insurance and financial products; and information of assets and service agreements or outsourcing agreements.[87]

In the near future, in coordination with the IAIS, the FSB intends each November to further develop G-SIFI assessment methodology to address all types of insurance and reinsurance as well as other financial activities of global insurers. The IAIS plans to develop policy measures such as higher loss absorbency requirements by the end of 2015, effective commencing January 2019, with respect to the GIIs identified in November 2017. Its Basic Capital Requirements, published in 2014, will be replaced by a risk-based group-wide global Insurance Capital Standard that will serve as the foundation of higher loss absorbency requirements.[88]

7.6.2 European Union's Views Concerning Insurance Companies as SIFIs

The European Union (EU) noted that risks posed by traditional insurance activities and products were of little concern and were only tangentially relevant to the financial crisis of the last decade. The main focus both in insurance and pension funds has been by their entry into non-traditional business lines. The excessive risks attributable to insurance companies are due to their carrying out of non-traditional/non-insurance activities. The main types of excessive risks under stress conditions are:

- Liquidity risk in funding financial derivatives activities:
  - Sources include downgrade of asset ratings together with regulatory capital requirements causing companies to change the mix of assets held;
  - Collateral calls on derivative positions owing to ratings downgrades of insurance undertakings;
  - National regulations and other restrictions may constrain the cross-border transfer of liquid funds within insurance groups.
- The size of their undertakings; the interconnectedness to banks and other non-bank financial institutions due to their size;
- The threat of asset devaluations in a financial crisis either directly or indirectly or through heightened perceptions of counterparty risk:
  - This arises because of exposures in collateral, securities, and derivatives, and exposure to other banks and non-bank financial institutions especially through over-the-counter markets;
  - Counterparty risk may arise from offering non-traditional credit risk protection through products such as guarantees and credit default swaps;
- Balance-sheet impacts on insurance undertakings:
  - Fire sales of large quantity of assets drive prices down, affecting other financial institutions, which will affect capital or liquidity ratios;
- Impacts on securities markets in general and fixed income markets and securities lending markets:

- Risk to financial stability in the use of assets for the purposes of securities lending which increases the level of interconnectedness to other non-bank financial institutions and to the banking sector;
- The financial crisis of 2008 brought about a significant change in the value of and other equity assets although there has been a substantial rebound thereafter.

Overall, the EU strongly advocates the extensions of substantial regulation over non-bank financial institutions, as more fully described in Chap. 8.

In the final chapter, we will discuss the several international institutions that affect shadow banking, even though they have been discussed in prior chapters where appropriate.

Notes

1. *An Act to express the intent of Congress with reference to the regulation of the business of insurance* (March 9, 1945) [McCarran-Ferguson Act]. 15 USC. 1011 et seq.
2. Joy Schwartzman & Gail Ross, *The Dodd-Frank Act and the insurance industry: Strategic considerations of US financial reform* (27 September 2010), http://insight.milliman.com/article.php?entid=7380.
3. *Size Matters: Why one of the world's biggest Insurers needed a government rescue*, THE ECONOMIST (September 18, 2008), www.economist.com/node/12274070. It should be noted that it now appears that as of May 7, 2012, the US government recouped its losses and made a profit of $15.1 billion from the sale of AIG common stock and other assets. WALL STREET JOURNAL, *US Profit From A.I.G. Rescue: $15.1 Billion*, (May 7, 2012), http://online.wsj.com/article/SB10001424052702304363104577390281150054116.html.
4. *Starr Intn'l Co. Inc. v. U.S.*, (No 11-779C, Ct. Fed; Claims, June 15, 2015).
5. Financial Stability Oversight Council, *Basis of the Financial Stability Oversight's Council's Final Determination Regarding American International Group, Inc.* (July 8, 2013), http://www.treasury.gov/initiatives/fsoc/designations/Documents/Basis%20of%20Final%20Determination%20Regarding%20American%20International%20Group,%20Inc.pdf.
6. Financial Stability Oversight Council, *Basis for the Financial Stability Oversight Council's Final Determination Regarding Prudential Financial, Inc.* (Sept. 19, 2013), http://www.treasury.gov/initiatives/fsoc/designations/Documents/Prudential%20Financial%20Inc.pdf.

7. Edward J. DeMarco, *Views of the Acting Director of the Federal Housing Finance Agency*, (September 18, 2013), Federal Housing Finance Agency, http://www.treasury.gov/initiatives/fsoc/council-meetings/Documents/September%2019%202013%20Notational%20Vote.pdf.
8. *Id.*
9. Financial Stability Oversight Council, *Basis for the Financial Stability Oversight Council's Final Determination Regarding Metlife, Inc.* (Dec. 18, 2014), http://www.treasury.gov/initiatives/Council/designations/Documents/MetLife%20Public%20Basis.pdf.
10. Financial Stability Oversight Council, http://www.treasury.gov/initiatives/Council/designations/Pages/default.aspx#nonbank.
11. Mary Williams Walsh, *US Panel Proposes Subjecting MetLife to Stricter Regulation*, NEW YORK TIMES (Sept. 4, 2014), http://dealbook.nytimes.com/2014/09/04/metlife-is-designated-systemically-important-but-firm-plans-a-fight/?_r=0.
12. DealBook, *MetLife Formally Challenges 'Systemically Important' Designation*, NEW YORK TIMES, (Oct. 3, 2014), http://dealbook.nytimes.com/2014/10/03/metlife-formally-challenges-designation-as-systemically-important/?_r=0 and Ian Katz, *MetLife Executives Appear Before COUNCIL to Challenge Systemic Risk Tag*, INSURANCE JOURNAL (Nov. 4, 2014, http://www.insurancejournal.com/news/national/2014/11/04/345861.htm.
13. *See supra* note 38 at 30.
14. Dodd-Frank Act §102(a)(6).
15. *Id.*at 7–8.
16. *Id.* at 9–14.
17. *Id.*at 15–16.
18. *Id.* at 17–20.
19. *Id.* at 20–21.
20. *Id.* at 21.
21. *Id.* at 21–26.
22. *Id.* at 26–30.
23. *MetLife Inc. v. Financial Stability Oversight Council*, 1:15-CV-00045 (D.C. D.C. Jan.13, 2015).
24. 5 USC. §706 (2)(A).
25. Lawrence D. Rosenberg and Richard M. Re, *Basic Legal Doctrines Frequently Arising in the D.C. Circuit*, citing City of Kansas v. Dep't of Hous. & Urban Dev., 923 F.2d 188, 189 (D.C. Cir. 1991) and Vehicle Mfr. Ass'n v. State Farm Mut. Auto. Ins. Co., 465 US 29, 43 (1983), www.americanbar.org/content/dam/aba/administrative/litigation/materials/sac_2012/34-basic_legal_doctrines.authcheckdam.pdf.

26. For a list of cases in which Eugene Scalia was successful in having administrative regulations overturned, see www.gibsondunn.com/lawyers/escalia.
27. MetLife complaint, pp. 1–9. The complaint may be found at https://www.metlife.com/sifiupdate/index.html.
28. *Id.* at 11–12, citing Congressional statement by Senator Collins and Senator Dodd, one of the co-authors of the Dodd-Frank Act.
29. MetLife complaint, *supra*, note 94 at 40–41.
30. *Id*, at 41–43.
31. *Id.* at 43–47.
32. *Id.*at 47–48.
33. *Id.* at 49–51.
34. *Id.* at 51–71.
35. *Id* at 71–72.
36. *Id.* at 73–75.
37. *Id.* at 76.
38. *Id.* at 77–78.
39. 467 U.S. 837 (1984).
40. Pub.L. 88-206, 77 Stat. 392 (1963).
41. *Chevron USA. v. NRDC*, 467 US 837, 842–843 (1984).
42. *Id.* at 844.
43. *Chevron USA., Inc. v. Echazabal*, 563 US 73 (2002).
44. 104 Stat. 328, 42 U. S. C. § 12101 *et seq.* (1994 ed. and Supp. V).
45. 526 U.S. 380.
46. 19 U.S.C. §1202.
47. 523 U.S. 382 (1998).
48. 533 U.S. 218 (2001).
49. 323 U.S. 134 (1944).
50. *Christensen v. Harris County*, 529 US 576, 587.
51. *Id.*, citing *EEOC* v. *Arabian American Oil Co., 499 U. S. 244*, 256–258 (1991) and *Martin* v. *Occupational Safety and Health Review Comm'n*, 499 U. S. 144, 157 (1991) (interpretative rules and enforcement guidelines are "not entitled to the same deference as norms that derive from the exercise of the Secretary's delegated lawmaking powers").
52. *Id.*, citing *Skidmore v. Swift & Co.*, 323 US 134, 140 (1944).
53. 29 U.S.C. §201(0).
54. 535 U.S. 212 (2012).
55. *Chiristensen v. Harris County*, 529 US 576, 587 (2000).
56. Pub.L.79–404, 60 Stat. 237 (1946).
57. *Id.*, citing *Reno v. Koray*, 515 U.S. 50, 61 (1995).
58. No. 14–46. Argued March 25, 2015- Decided June 29, 2015.
59. No. 14–114. Argued March 4, 2015—Decided June 25, 2015.
60. No. 14–29 (Nov. 10, 2014).

61. 48 Stat. 491, as amended, 15 USC. 78j(b).
62. Victoria McGrane and Leslie Scism, *MetLife Suit Sets Up Battle Over Regulation*, THE WALL STREET JOURNAL, (Jan. 14, 2015), www.wsj.com/articles/metlife-to=challenge-systemically –important-tag-1421152441.
63. Mary Williams Walsh, *US Panel Proposes Subjecting MetLife to Stricter Regulation*, NEW YORK TIMES (Sept. 4, 2014), http://dealbook.nytimes.com/2014/09/04/metlife-is-designated-systemically-important-but-firm-plans-a-fight/?_r=0.
64. Ryan Tracy, *US Regulators to Review 'Systematically Important' Label Process for Financial Firms*, The WALL STREET JOURNAL (Oct. 6, 2014), http://www.wsj.com/articles/u-s-regulators-to-hold-hearing-on-systemically-important-label-for-metlife-1412628515.
65. Bipartisan Policy Center, *How the Federal Reserve Became the De Facto Federal Insurance Regulator* (July 30, 2014), https://www.google.com/search?q=Bipartisan+Policy+Center%2C+How+the+Federal+Reserve+Became+the+De+Facto+Federal+Insurance+Regulator+(July+30%2C+2014&oq=Bipartisan+Policy+Center%2C+How+the+Federal+Reserve+Became+the+De+Facto+Federal+Insurance+Regulator+(July+30%2C+2014&aqs=chrome..69i57.1727j0j7&sourceid=chrome&es_sm=93&ie=UTF-8.
66. Peter J. Wallison, *The regulators' war on shadow banking*, (Jan. 22, 2015), American Enterprise Institute, www.aei.org/+publication/regulators-war-shadow-banking/.
67. Ian Katz, *Global Regulators' Influence Over U.S. Called Inappropriate*, http://washpost.bloomberg.com/Story?docId=1376-NNHP096KLVRO01-1KKAM35EITQ9T3OR87D1N1SFIT.
68. Scott E. Harrington, *The financial Crisis, Systemic Risk, and the Future of Insurance Regulation*, Issue Analysis, National Association of Mutual Insurance Companies (September 2009).
69. Christian Thimann, *How insurers differ from banks: Implications for systemic regulation*, (Oct. 17, 2014), http://www.voxeu.org/article/how-insurers-differ-banks-implications-systemic-regulation.
70. Philip Alexander, *Insurance debate rumbles on as reinsurers face inclusion as SIFIs*, The Geneva Association (Oct. 2014), https://www.genevaassociation.org/media/907272/oct2014_grr_gsifi-designation_brahin-interview.pdf.
71. Dirk A. Kempthorne, *designating Life Insurers as SIFIs Creates Uneven Playing Field*, (Aug. 22, 2014), *http://thehill.com/sponsored/content/218168-designating-life-insurers-as-sifis-creates-uneven-playing-field.*
72. Cheyenne Hopkins, *Banks Balk at Easing Dodd-Frank Capital Requirements for Insurers*, (Dec. 3, 2014), Insurance Journal, http://www.insurancejournal.com/news/national/2014/12/03/348878.htm.

73. Michael Ide, *Yellen Confirms Insurance SIFI Rules Will Differ From Banking Rules*, (Feb. 11, 2014), http://www.valuewalk.com/2014/02/yellen-confirms-insurance-sifi-rules-will-differ-from-banking-rules/.
74. Douglas J. Elliott, *Regulating Systemically Important Financial Institutions That Are Not Banks*, (May 9, 2013), Brookings Report, http://www.brookings.edu/research/papers/2013/05/09-regulating-financial-institutions-elliott.
75. For an extensive analysis of reinsurance including its nature, history, and types, see, Institute of Insurance Sciences, *an Introduction to Reinsurance* (2013), http://www.mapfre.com/documentacion/publico/i18n/catalogo_imagenes/grupo.cmd?path=1074274.
76. Financial Web, *7 Types of Reinsurance*, http://www.finweb.com/insurance/7-types-of-reinsurance.html#axzz3YvDlc3uY.
77. Berkshire Hathaway Inc., *2014 Annual Report*, http://www.berkshirehathaway.com/2014ar/2014ar.pdf.
78. http://www.financialstabilityboard.org/2014/11/fsb-announces-update-of-group-of-global-systemically-important-banks/.
79. Prudential Financial Inc. is listed on the New York Stock Exchange and, according to its website, is a financial services leader with over $1 trillion of assets under management as of December 31, 2014, with operations in the USA, Asia, Europe, and Latin America. It has literally hundreds of subsidiaries worldwide. http://www.investor.prudential.com/phoenix.zhtml?c=129695&p=irol-irhome.
80. Prudential plc is an international financial services group based in the UK with significant operations in Asia, the USA and the UK, with more than 23 million insurance customers and some £457 billion of assets under management. http://www.prudential.co.uk/.
81. Financial Stability Board, *Key Attributes of Effective Resolution Regimes for Financial Institutions*, II-Annex 2: Resolution of Insurers (Oct. 15, 2014), http://www.financialstabilityboard.org/2014/10/r_141015/.
82. *Id.*, II-Annex 2, 3–4 at 76–77.
83. *Id.* at 78–79.
84. *Id.* at 80–81.
85. *Id.* at 81–82.
86. *Id.* at 82–83.
87. *Id.* at 83–34.
88. Financial Stability Board, *2014 update of list of global systemically important insurers (G-SIIs)*, (Nov. 6, 2014), http://www.financialstabilityboard.org/2014/11/2014-update-of-list-of-global-systemically-important-insurers-g-siis/.

CHAPTER 8

International Institutions Affecting Shadow Banking

8.1 International Regimes

Although the financial crisis of 2007 had abated substantially in the USA some three to four years later, global resurgence continues to be either quite modest or non-existent. The European Union (EU) continues to experience tepid growth following the crises, although the crisis in Greece, Spain, and Portugal is now somewhat less severe. The People's Republic of China (China) has experienced growth that is the envy of other nations, but it has also witnessed a slowing of economic activity accompanied by erratic stock market behavior. Africa continues to undergo slow progress, which is complicated by political and religious dissensions in northern states, while sub-Saharan Africa, with exceptions, is dominated by corrupt dictatorial regimes and religious confrontations. Thus, member states of international organizations have come together in an endeavor to transform the continuing economic crises into greater prosperity for the inhabitants of countries in need. The following discussion concerns several of the most important international organizations that are concerned with economic recovery, with a focus on shadow banking.

8.2 G20

The G20 is somewhat of a misnomer. It is comprised of the following nations: Argentina, Australia, Brazil, Canada, China, France, Germany, India, Indonesia, Italy, Japan, Republic of Korea, Mexico, Russia, Saudi

Roy J. Girasa, *Shadow Banking*, DOI 10.1007/978-3-319-33026-6_8

Arabia, South Africa, the United Kingdom (UK), the USA, and also the EU, acting as one member but composed of 28 member states becoming 27 states with the exit of Great Britain. Meeting annually, the nations represent advanced and emerging economies, having two-thirds of the global population and 85 % of the global gross domestic product (GDP). Other nations may be invited as guest members. It is an informal political forum without a secretariat and a binding agenda. Although it lacks obligatory commitments, the annual meetings of world leaders have contributed to substantial reforms and outcomes. For example, a 47-point Action Plan evolved from its 2008 Washington summit, and the 2009 London summit brought about an agreement on $5 trillion of stimulus and a $1.1 trillion package for the International Monetary Fund (IMF) and the World Bank.[1]

A major concern of the G20 is strengthening oversight and regulation of shadow banking. Accordingly, in conjunction with the Financial Stability Board (FSB), which defines "shadow banking" as "credit intermediation involving entities and activities outside the regular banking system,"[2] and the International Organization of Securities Commissions (IOSCO), it has an extensive agenda that includes a policy framework for shadow banking entities; application of numerical haircut floors for non-centrally clearing securities transactions to non-bank-to-non-bank transactions; peer reviews of national and regional approaches for reforms for money market funds; and shadow banking monitoring.[3]

8.2.1 G20 Seoul Summit

At the G20 November 2010 Seoul Summit, among the issues affecting the financial sector that were highlighted was the need to transform the financial system to address the root causes of the financial crisis that had occurred two to three years before the Summit. Accordingly, in its Seoul Summit Document, it endorsed the agreement of the Banking Committee on Banking Supervision (BCBS) concerning the increased requirements of bank capital and liquidity framework; the constraint of the build-up of leverage and maturity mismatches; the "too big or too complicated to fail" restrictions; and, of relevance to this text, the FSB's policy framework, work processes, and timelines to reduce the moral hazard risks posed by systemically important financial institutions (SIFIs).

The Document noted that it will require a multi-pronged framework that combines a resolution framework and other measures to ensure that all financial institutions expeditiously address the destabilizing of the financial system and the exposure of taxpayers to the risk of loss. It further required that SIFIs, especially those which are globally systemic (G-SIFIs), should have higher loss absorbency capacity to reflect the added risk they pose to the global financial system. In addition, there should be more intensive supervisory oversight, robust core financial market infrastructure to reduce contagion risk from individual failures, and other supplementary prudential measures as determined by national authorities. These other prudential measures may include liquidity surcharges, tighter large exposures restrictions, levies, and structural measures. It determined further that G-SIFIs should be subject to a sustained process of mandatory international recovery and resolution planning and regular peer reviews by the FSB.

The G20 noted that also to be addressed are: macro-prudential policy frameworks; regulatory reforms issues pertaining specifically to emerging market and developing economies; strengthening regulation and supervision of shadow banking; regulation and supervision of commodity derivative markets; improving market integrity and efficiency; and enhancing consumer protection.[4]

8.3 Financial Stability Board

The FSB is an international organization established by the G20 to promote financial stability. Established in April 2009, it is the successor of the Financial Stability Forum that had been created a decade earlier by the G7, which consisted of ministers of finance, central bank governors, and supervisory and regulatory authorities from France, Germany, Italy, Japan, the USA and the UK, and four major financial centers, namely Hong Kong, Singapore, Spain, and Switzerland. Its mandate is to make non-binding recommendations that rely on moral persuasion and peer pressure rather than compulsion and punitive measures. Through its six regional consultative groups, it interacts with some 70 additional countries to effect financial policies therein.

Its organizational structural setup consists of:

- The *Plenary*: decision-making body. It adopts reports, principles, standards, recommendations, and guidance developed by the FSB; establishes standing committees and working groups; decides on membership of the FSB; seat assignments to members in the Plenary; composition of the steering committee and the standing committees; approves the work program and the budget of the FSB; and appoints the chairs of the standing committees, the Secretary General, and the external auditor of the FSB.

- *Steering Committee*: coordinates operational work between the Plenary and the steering committees. It also has responsibility for monitoring and guiding the progress of ongoing work; promoting coordination across the standing committees and working groups and commissioning work from them; ensuring effective information flow to the full membership; and coordinating and conducting reviews of the policy development work of the international standards setting bodies.
- Three steering committees: (1) the *Steering Committee on Assessment of Vulnerabilities*, whose mission is to identify and assess risks; (2) the *Standing Committee on Supervisory and Regulatory Cooperation*, whose mission is undertake supervisory analysis or framing a regulatory or supervisory policy response to an identified vulnerability; and (3) the *Standing Committee on Standards Implementation*, which monitors the implementation of agreed upon policy initiatives and international standards.[5]

8.3.1 Mission of the FSB

Specifically, the FSB mission is to:

- Assess vulnerabilities affecting the global financial system as well as to identify and review, on a timely and ongoing basis within a macroprudential perspective, the regulatory, supervisory and related actions needed to address these vulnerabilities, and their outcomes;
- Promote coordination and information exchange among authorities responsible for financial stability;
- Monitor and advise on market developments and their implications for regulatory policy;
- Monitor and advise with regard to best practice in meeting regulatory standards;
- Undertake joint strategic reviews of the international standard setting bodies and coordinate their respective policy development work to ensure this work is timely, coordinated, focused on priorities and addresses gaps;
- Set guidelines for establishing and supporting supervisory colleges;
- Support contingency planning for cross-border crisis management, particularly with regard to systemically important firms;

- Collaborate with the International Monetary Fund (IMF) to conduct Early Warning Exercises; and
- Promote member jurisdictions' implementation of agreed commitments, standards and policy recommendations, through monitoring of implementation, peer review and disclosure.[6]

8.3.2 FSB and Shadow Banking

A major concern of the G20 is strengthening oversight and regulation of shadow banking. Thus, it requested the FSB to develop recommendations with other international setting bodies to address the problem. Accordingly, the FSB set forth an agenda to comply with the G20 request.

It acknowledged that there are beneficial aspects to shadow banking; namely, by providing market participants and corporations with an alternative source of funding and liquidity as well as offering more cost-effective credit intermediation with its specialized expertise. Nevertheless, the financial crisis in the latter part of the first decade of the new century illustrated its actual and potential risks both directly and through its interconnectedness with other segments of the financial community, including the regular banking system, inasmuch as shadow banking occurred often within the banks' subsidiaries. Initially, the FSB set out to clarify the meaning of shadow banking and its role and risks in the financial system; approaches for effective monitoring of the shadow banking system; and the preparation of regulatory measures to address the systemic risk and regulatory arbitrage concerns that were posed by the shadow banking system.[7]

In conjunction with IOSCO, the FSB has an extensive agenda that includes a policy framework for shadow banking entities; application of numerical haircut floors for non-centrally clearing securities transactions to non-bank-to-non-bank transactions; peer reviews of national and regional approaches for reforms for money market funds; and shadow banking monitoring.[8]

The FSB response to the G20 concerns about the risks and the global need for monitoring and regulating shadow banking is evidenced by two reports, namely, "Strengthening Oversight and Regulation of Shadow Banking" (2013),[9] and "Global Shadow Banking Report 2014."[10] In the 2013 report, the focus was on five areas:

- To mitigate the spill-over effect between the regular banking system and the shadow banking system;

- To reduce the susceptibility of money market funds (MMFs) to "runs";
- To assess and align the incentives associated with securitization;
- To dampen risks and procyclical incentives associated with securities financing transactions, such as repos and securities lending, that may exacerbate funding strains in times of market stress; and
- To assess and mitigate systemic risks posed by other shadow banking entities and activities.

The shadow bank entities that were enumerated and examined are: (1) credit investment funds; (2) exchange-traded funds; (3) credit hedge funds; (4) private equity funds; (5) securities broker-dealers; (6) securitization entities; (7) credit insurance providers/financial guarantors; (8) finance companies; and (9) trust companies. The difficulty, as noted both in the report and in many other reports in addressing issues of shadow banking, is that there are numerous, highly diverse business models and risk profiles, and that these models are dynamic and can rapidly expand.

The Report made its assessment on five economic functions of the shadow banking entities, followed by overarching principles and tools to address them. The five economic functions assessed are:

Economic Function 1. Management of collective investment vehicles (CIVs) with features that make them susceptible to runs;

Economic Function 2. Loan provision that is dependent on short-term funding;

Economic Function 3. Intermediation of market activities that is dependent on short-term funding or on secured funding of client assets;

Economic Function 4. Facilitation of credit creation; and

Economic Function 5. Securitization-based credit intermediation and funding of financial entities.[11]

The Report then addresses the governmental oversight needed with respect to non-bank financial entities that are identified as posing risks through their involvement with the stated economic functions. Thus, the authorities should refer to four basic principles:

- Principle 1: Authorities should define, and keep up to date, the regulatory perimeter to ensure financial stability (to ensure financial stability).
- Principle 2. Authorities should collect information needed to assess the extent of risks posed by shadow banking. They should assess the

degree of maturity/liquidity transformation and use of leverage by other shadow banking entities in determining measures to be taken with respect to the risks posed by them.

- Principle 3. Authorities should enhance disclosure by other shadow banking entities as necessary so as to help market participants understand the extent of shadow banking risks posed by such entities.
- Principle 4. Authorities should assess their non-bank financial entities based on the economic functions and take necessary actions drawing on tools from the policy toolkit.[12]

8.3.3 FSB Policy Toolkit for Economic Functions

Management of CIVs:

- Redemption gates: Limit redemption amounts to specific proportion on any given redemption day to prevent a run or other herding liabilities;
- Suspension of redemptions: Exceptional measure to allow assessment, remedies, and determining when to permit redemption;
- Imposition of redemption fees or other redemptions restrictions in times of stress to manage redemption pressures;
- Side pockets: Legally separating impaired from illiquid portions of an investment to prevent impacting CIVs returns used when portion of portfolio cannot be properly valued under adverse market circumstances.[13]

Manage Liquidity Risk:

- Place limits on investments in illiquid assets: Lessen risk of "fire sales";
- Liquidity buffers: Comprising highly liquid cash or near-cash instruments to lessen need for "fire sales." Size is based on nature of CIV, its high-risk profile, and types of stresses that it may confront;
- Limits on asset concentration: Quantitative limit on proportion of portfolio assets that may be invested in any one sector or issuer to manage risk;
- Limits on leverage: Governments to either limit leverage that enhances returns for CIVs but may create risk because of interconnectedness with banks;

- Restrictions on maturity of portfolio assets: May assist in preventing or mitigating risks from maturity and liquidity transformation, for example, limit duration or weighted average of fund's portfolio and limits on maturity of portfolio securities.[14]

Loan provision dependent on short-term funding:

- Improve bank prudential regulatory authority regimes on deposit-taking nonbank loan providers: Have similar regulations for non-banks engaged in maturity/liquidity transformation and leverage;
- Capital requirements: Impose appropriate level of capital for entities providing loans to prevent excessive leverage in the financial system. Entities should design and calibrate capital level/ratios for both pro-cyclical and countercyclical events;
- Liquidity buffers: Authorities should impose liquidity regulations to address risks arising from maturity/liquidity transformation, especially where there is high interconnectedness to other entities;
- Leverage limits: Authorities should impose limits to mitigate potential risks from entities' use of leverage, especially when it becomes a possible threat to the financial system;
- Limits on large exposures: Authorities should impose limits on claims of particular obligors with excessive risk concentrations;
- Restrictions on types of liabilities: Example includes use of funding instruments when the entities do not have appropriate securitization and risk-management processes in place.[15]

Intermediation of market activities that is dependent on short-term funding or on secured funding of client assets:

- Impose prudential regulatory authority regimes equivalent to those of banks: Non-bank market intermediaries lead to the same profile as banks and susceptibility to runs by lenders and other counterparties in wholesale funding markets;
- Liquidity requirements: Authorities could impose liquidity requirements based on Basel III for non-bank intermediaries to mitigate risks associated with liquidity transformation;
- Capital requirements: Authorities may impose capital requirements to mitigate excessive use of leverage and procyclicality associated with their funding structure, such as a minimum capital ratio or minimum levels of liquid net capital;

- Restrictions on use of client assets: Non-bank entities hold client assets as, for example, prime brokers may experience difficulties if used to fund longer term assets. There should be limitations on such use to avoid run risks arising from maturity/liquidity transformation.[16]

Facilitation of credit creation:

- Capital requirements: Authorities should require entities to hold capital sufficient to cover potential losses from risks such as those arising from financial guarantees and credit insurance. They should be designed and calibrated to meet capital requirements in counter-cyclical times as well as procyclical periods;
- Restrictions on scale and scope of business: Authorities should impose restrictions on the scale and scope on entities that facilitate credit creation through providing financial guarantees and credit insurance products where it appears they are unable to price and manage their products to avoid inappropriate risks;
- Liquidity buffers: Entities funded with short-term insurance may be vulnerable to creditor runs and, therefore, may require sufficient to satisfy potential insurance/guarantee liabilities;
- Enhanced risk-management practices to capture tail events: Firms should introduce enhanced risk-management practices such as loss modeling, including stress testing for entities providing financial guarantees and credit insurance;
- Mandatory risk: Sharing between the insurer-guarantor and insured/guaranteed (i.e., deductible, co-insurance). Risk-sharing between the two entities by use of a deductible or a co-payment will cause a sharing of losses and encourage a more careful scrutiny of the risk profile underlying the borrower.[17]

Securitization-based credit intermediation and funding of financial entities:

- Restrictions on maturity/liquidity transformation: There should be restrictions to mitigate risk arising from the maturity/liquidity transformation through securitization where securitization vehicles are used as funding channels, as through the issuance of short-term liabilities;
- Restrictions on eligible collateral: Authorities may impose restrictions on the quality of collateral that may be accepted or swapped, such as highly liquid collateral and trades on a regulated and transparent

market. This is aimed at situations where banks use non-bank financial entities to fund an illiquid portfolio on their balance sheet that cannot be financed in the wholesale market such as through repos;
- Restrictions on exposures to, or funding from, banks/other financial entities: Authorities may impose restrictions on the exposures of banks or other financial entities to alternative sources of funding such as securitization, which may lead to excessive creation of credit and regulatory arbitrage opportunities.[18]

8.3.4 *FSB Methodologies for Identifying G-SIFIs*

At the G20 Cannes Summit that took place in November 2011, the FSB was requested to prepare methodologies to identify SIFIs. Accordingly, after an initial earlier proposal a year earlier, the FSB, in March 2015, prepared and issued in consultation with IOSCO and other standard setting bodies its *Consultative Document*, setting forth a high-level framework and an operational framework for identifying G-SIFIs that would apply to all systemically important non-bank non-insurer financial entities (NBNIs) as well as sector-specific methodologies for finance companies, market intermediaries (broker-dealers), and investment funds including hedge funds. A summary of its findings and proposed methodologies follows, but should be familiar to the reader as they were discussed in Chap. 2 and were applied specifically to insurance companies in Chap. 7.[19]

Channels. Under systemic risk and transmission mechanisms, the likely channels whereby financial distress is likely to be transmitted to other financial entities and markets are: (1) *exposures/counterparty channel*, which affects creditors, counterparties, investors, or other market participants; (2) *asset/liquidation/market channel*, where the failure of a NBNI financial entity could affect other market participants such as by quickly liquidating assets; and (3) the *critical function or service/substitutability channel*, whereby the NBNI is no longer willing or able to provide a critical function or service to other market participants or clients.

8.3.5 *High-Level Framework for Identifying NBNI G-SIFIs*

The basic factors that the FSB set forth are necessarily broad because of the wide range of NBNI financial entities, unlike the methodologies of the BCBS, whose methodologies are specific to banking or that of the International Association of Insurance Supervisors (IAIS) that are devoted to the insurance industry. The basic set of factors the FSB identified that may have substantial financial impact are: (1) size (the larger the scale of financial activity, the greater the impact); (2) interconnectedness (systemic risk resulting from interlinkages with other financial entities); (3) substitutability (risk increases when other financial entities cannot provide the same or similar services of the firm); (4) complexity (the more complex the financial entity, the more difficult and time-consuming to resolve its distress); and (5) global activities and cross-jurisdictional activities (extent of global impact from a financial firm's distress or failure).[20]

8.3.6 NBNI Financial Sector-Specific Methodologies

The four sectors designated in conjunction with IOSCO for the application of specific methodologies are finance companies, market intermediaries (broker-dealers), investment funds, and asset managers. They were chosen because of their large size and their historical impact in the global financial system when undergoing financial distress or failures.

8.3.7 Finance Companies

The FSB identified finance companies into four types: (1) subsidiaries or affiliates of banks; (2) captive finance companies owned by manufacturers or distributors that finance sales of their parents' products only (e.g., finance companies owned by large auto companies); (3) specialist providers (or monolines) that finance only one particular type of asset such as railroad or aircraft leasing companies; and (4) independents and captives operating in multiple financing markets (large finance companies whose business is in multiple, diverse products and often are international in scope). Regulation of finance companies vary among the many global jurisdictions from high prudential standards comparable to banks, while other jurisdictions treat finance companies like other corporate entities. Some jurisdictions do not collect the data necessary for assessing systemic importance, while others may not share data because of privacy regulations and concerns.

The systemic importance of finance companies arises because they provide credit to businesses, such as invoice finance and equipment leasing, and to consumers through store credit or for auto purchases. Because some companies specialize in concentrated markets, a sudden withdrawal of funding for these markets could lead to serious market disruption.

Captives are vulnerable to financial distress, which in turn may transmit such stress to its industrial parent and the company's liability holders. Finance companies rely on wholesale funding sources such as bank loans, unsecured debt, commercial paper, asset-backed commercial paper, and other securitized products and this reliance makes them particularly susceptible to financial crises, such as the one experienced in 2007–2009. Their interconnections with other financial institutions could potentially pose a serious risk to the entire financial system.

The indicators for assessing systemic importance are;

Size: the indicators are the total globally consolidated balance-sheet assets and the total globally consolidated off-balance-sheet exposures;

Interconnectedness. Indicators are:

1. The *intra-financial system assets* calculated as the sum of lending to financial institutions; holdings of securities issued by other financial institutions; net mark-to-market reverse repurchase agreements with other financial institutions; net mark-to-market securities lending to financial institutions; and net mark-to-market over-the-counter (OTC) derivatives with financial institutions;
2. The *intra-financial system liabilities* calculated as the sum of borrowings from financial institutions; all marketable securities issued by the finance company; net mark-to-market repurchase agreements with other financial institutions; net mark-to-market securities borrowing from financial institutions; and net mark-to-market OTC derivatives with financial institutions;
3. Borrowings split by type. A company's borrowings may have a significant effect on other financial institutions. For example, if a company has a large amount of holdings such as commercial paper (CP), including asset-backed commercial paper (ABCP), unsecured debt, securitizations, or other indebtedness, a failure of the company may cause significant distress upon other firms with whom it possesses such holdings;
4. Leverage ratio calculated as the total shareholder equity divided by the sum of on-balance-sheet assets and off-balance-sheet exposures. Leverage may cause distress upon other financial companies with increased exposure and increased size of and asset liquidation the company may be forced to undertake.

Substitutability. The key indicator is a qualitative assessment that examines the firm's market share in various financing markets and ease of substitutability by other providers of funding. The assessment is to take into account the firm's market share in the various financing markets broken down in types such as auto financing, mortgages, and the like. Regulators are to take into account barriers to entry, substitutability in benign and stress credit environments, and ease of transferability of loans to other competing institutions.

Complexity. Indicators are:

1. *OTC derivatives notional amount.* The concern is the amount of OTC derivatives not cleared through a central counterparty: the greater the number of non-centrally cleared OTC derivatives that a finance company enters into, the more complex its activities. Notional values of all types of derivatives should be captured (sum of foreign exchange, interest rate, equity, commodities, credit derivatives) where the breakdown of OTC derivative contracts and centrally cleared derivative contracts are not available to authorities. *Notional amount* generally refers to the nominal or face amount on a financial instrument in which the instrument does not change hands;
2. *Difficulty in resolving a firm.* Authorities are to examine the firm's operational and legal complexity; the degree of internal interconnectedness; and its membership in financial market infrastructures and quality of management information systems;
3. *Amount of less liquid assets.* A finance company poses a risk to the extent that its assets are illiquid and complex to evaluate. There is a risk of contagion to other similar classes of assets throughout the financial system.

Global activities—cross-jurisdictional activities. A firm that is experiencing distress may affect other firms across jurisdictions. Indicators are:

1. *Size of cross-jurisdictional claims*;
2. *Size of cross-jurisdictional liabilities*;
3. *Number of jurisdictions in which the finance company conducts operations*; and
4. *Assets or revenues in foreign jurisdictions.*[21]

8.3.8 Market Intermediaries (Securities Broker-Dealers)

Definition. Market intermediaries are NBNI financial entities engaged in the business of managing individual portfolios, executing order, and dealing in or distributing securities, which may include receiving and transmitting orders; proprietary trading/dealing on his or her own account; securities underwriting; providing funding to clients such as margin loans and reverse repos; and placing of financial instruments without a firm commitment basis.

Systemic importance. IOSCO's Objectives and Principles of Securities Regulation,[22] with respect to market intermediaries, states as follows:

29. Regulation should provide for minimum entry standards for market intermediaries.

30. There should be initial and ongoing capital and other prudential requirements for market intermediaries that reflect the risks that the intermediaries undertake.

31. Market intermediaries should be required to establish an internal function that delivers compliance with standards for internal organization and operational conduct, with the aim of protecting the interests of clients and their assets and ensuring proper management of risk, through which management of the intermediary accepts primary responsibility for these matters.

32. There should be procedures for dealing with the failure of a market intermediary in order to minimize damage and loss to investors and to contain systemic risk.[23]

Regulation is to be directed at identifying and mitigating risks to capital, client assets, and public confidence. Particular attention is to be paid to Principle 30, which requires an intermediary to have sufficient liquid assets to be able to wind down its operations in an orderly fashion and be able to transfer the client's assets to a solvent market intermediary. Intermediaries having extensive exposures and liabilities are a serious risk to the financial system through their interconnectedness and the potential they have for disrupting certain funding and/or derivatives markets. The indicators for assessing systemic importance are similar to those of size as stated above.[24]

8.3.9 Investment Funds

Definition. Investment funds are collective investment schemes that include authorized/registered open-end funds as well as closed ones. There are many categories from public funds to exchange-traded funds and to private funds. Public funds include mutual funds and money market funds, while private funds include hedge funds, private equity funds, and venture capital funds.

IOSCO's Objectives and Principles affecting investment funds are as follows:

24. The regulatory system should set standards for the eligibility, governance, organization and operational conduct of those who wish to market or operate a collective investment scheme.

25. The regulatory system should provide for rules governing the legal form and structure of collective investment schemes and the segregation and protection of client assets.

26. Regulation should require disclosure, as set forth under the principles for issuers, which is necessary to evaluate the suitability of a collective investment scheme for a particular investor and the value of the investor's interest in the scheme.

27. Regulation should ensure that there is a proper and disclosed basis for asset valuation and the pricing and the redemption of units in a collective investment scheme.

28. Regulation should ensure that hedge funds and/or hedge funds managers/advisers are subject to appropriate oversight.[25]

Channels. Investment funds, by their size, transfer of moneys to securities markets, and offering to investors of alternative investment opportunities are very important to the overall economy and thus are of systemic importance. In the event of stress leading to forced liquidation, they may have a destabilizing impact on other market participants. The FSB, utilizing the channels format, concluded with respect to the Exposures/Counterparty channel that investment funds have a substantial impact on other market participants which are exposed to a distressed fund. Investment funds seeking to increase returns enter into agreements with counterparties by borrowing of money or assets from other market participants such as banks or broker-dealers or acquire leverage through financial instruments such as options, futures, forwards, swaps, and other types of derivatives. Private funds, in particular, which have little regulatory leverage limits, have the potential to become heavily leveraged or concentrated, giving rise to systemic risk.

Asset liquidation/Market channel comes into play if there is a forced liquidation. An investment manager may be compelled to sell assets of the investment fund to meet redemptions or liabilities. Circumstances that may arise include the loss of investor confidence; the distress of a highly leveraged fund to meet margin requirements; the sudden, large termination of securities loans; and reputational risks caused by a firm's distress or liquidation. Investment funds that operate in less liquid markets can lead to market contagion in the event of distress. With respect to the critical function or services/Substitutability channel, the FSB and IOSCO are unclear and are seeking advice from market participants concerning investment funds that are unique and may have few substitutes. Under such circumstances, there may be systemic risk implications.

Thresholds for investment funds. The FSB and IOSCO have decided that the following materiality thresholds should be observed:

- Investment funds: $100 billion *AUM* (the amount that investors' capital is at risk);
- Hedge funds: Between $400 and 600 billion in Gross Notional Exposure (GNE—calculated as the absolute sum of all long and short positions, considering notional values for derivatives);
- Private funds (including hedge funds, private equity): $400 billion GNE;
- Traditional investment funds:
  - Option 1: $30 billion in net asset value (NAV) and balance-sheet financial leverage of three times NAV, with a size-only backstop of $100 billion net assets under management (AUM);
  - Option 2: $200 billion in gross assets under management unless it can be shown that the investment fund is not a dominant player in its markets.

Assessment of Systemic Importance of investment funds:
Size. The indicators are:

1. The net assets under management for the fund;
2. For hedge funds and where available, the GNE as an alternative indicator

Interconnectedness. The indicators are:

1. Balance-sheet financial leverage of the investment fund: can take several forms depending on metrics used;
2. Leverage ratio of the investment fund alternative way to measure financial leverage of an investment fund;
3. Ratio of GNE to the NAV for the investment fund;

4. The ratio of collateral posted by the investment fund to its NAV;
5. Counterparty credit exposure to the investment fund: how much would be lost by the financial system if the fund were to be liquidated immediately or face significant distress;
6. Intra-financial system liabilities to G-SIFIs: net credit exposure of G-SIFIs to the investment fund;
7. Nature of investors of the funds: systemic implications if problems with an investment fund to large institutional investors such as banks, insurance companies, or major corporate entities.

Substitutability. Indicators are:

1. Daily trading volume of certain asset classes of the fund compared to the overall daily trading of the same market segment if very active; could have systemic problems if fund becomes distressed;
2. Fund holdings per certain asset classes compared to the overall daily trading volume of the same asset class. Potential impact of fire sales and ability of the market to absorb the sales;
3. NAV of the fund compared to the size of the underlying market: the higher the market share, the higher the potential risk.

Complexity. Indicators are:

1. Non-centrally cleared derivatives trade volumes of the fund (total trade volumes of the fund): a significant volume in these trades that tend to be more complex and exposed to higher counterparty risk may pose systemic risk;
2. Ratio of collateral posted by counterparties that has been reused by the Fund: the larger the reuse proportion, the greater the potential risk in the event of material distress;
3. Proportion of an investment fund's portfolio using High Frequency Trading strategies: these trades may pose system risk owing to their complexity and risk of operational errors;
4. Investment fund liquidity profile: if the fund cannot meet its obligations because of inability to liquidate its portfolio in a timely manner, then it may pose systemic risk under certain market conditions;
5. For leveraged funds, ratio of unencumbered cash to GNE: if the fund has little unencumbered cash, then it may not be able to meet margin calls or be able to post collateral under adverse market conditions;

6. The ratio of unencumbered cash to the NAV of the investment fund: use of a large derivatives portfolio or investments in illiquid cash may create liquidity risk;
7. Amount of less liquid assets: assets that cannot be sold promptly in adverse market conditions could lead to contagion and systemic risk.

Cross-jurisdictional activities (global activity). The indicators are:

1. Number of jurisdictions in which a fund invests: the more global, the more impact;
2. Number of jurisdictions in which the fund is sold/listed: if in many jurisdictions, impact will be greater;
3. Number of jurisdictions where the fund has counterparties: the more jurisdictions through its counterparties with varying laws and regulations, the more complex the situation becomes if necessary to liquidate.[26]

8.3.10 Asset Managers

Definition

The FSB defines *asset managers* (investment advisers) as financial entities that generally manage client assets through individual accounts and/or investment funds. They manage assets as agents on behalf of others in accordance with a specified investment strategy or mandate as stated in the prospectus given to the investor-clients. They operate in accordance with statutory and regulatory provisions as well as being subject in certain jurisdictions to self-regulatory organizations such as the Financial Industry Regulatory Authority (FINRA) in the USA.[27] Asset managers may also use their own money together with that of their clients in the various investment funds, and may also engage in securities lending agent, provision of risk-management platforms or pricing services to clients, and consulting/advisory services that rely on their expertise.

Systemic Importance of Asset Managers

Asset managers facing distress could potentially cause risk to the overall financial system under certain circumstances. Again utilizing the various channels, with respect to the exposures/counterparty channel, the FSB indicated that systemic risk may arise when the asset manager acts not only as an agent but also as a counterparty. They may invest their equity in new funds and provide securities lending agent services including indemnification against losses if the borrower fails to return the borrowed securities. The asset liquidation/market channel may be implicated through the asset manager's off-balance-sheet activities or through its reputational/ operational risks. Although the critical function or services/substitutability channel usually is not implicated, it may arise when an asset manager engages in specific activities for which he or she has a specific skill not easily transferable to other asset managers.

Materiality Thresholds for Asset Managers
FSB and IOSCO considered two types of materiality thresholds for managers that may generate risks. They are:

- Balance-sheet total assets: most investment managers have low balance sheets owing to their primary responsibility of acting as agents for investors, but a large balance sheet may indicate significant non-asset management activities and possible added risks. The suggested monetary threshold is $100 billion;
- Assets under management: asset managers having higher amounts of such assets have a greater potential systemic impact on the global markets where the risks are transferred through the assets they manage.

Indicators for Assessing Systemic Importance of Asset Managers:
Size. The indicators are:

1. Net AUM: asset managers with higher amounts of AUM may have a greater potential impact on the global financial system, especially interconnectedness with other financial entities;
2. Balance-sheet assets: an asset manager's off balance sheets may be difficult to ascertain and may pose risks.

Interconnectedness. The indicators are:

1. Leverage ratio: the greater the manager's leverage, the greater the potential impact in the event of distress;
2. Guarantees and other off-balance-sheet exposures: the risks posed concern off-balance-sheet exposures particularly when the manager guar-

antees the performance of investment funds that it manages or provides guarantees to other market participants to facilitate certain market activities.

Substitutability. Specialized services by an asset manager may not be readily transferred to another asset manager. Thus, the indicators are:

1. Substitutability, measured by a percentage of the asset manager's revenues as compared to the total revenues attributable to the relevant business: when an asset manager engages in non-traditional activities, he or she may not be readily transferable to other assets managers;
2. Market share, measured by a percentage of the asset manager's AUM in a particular strategy as compared to the total AUM invested in the same strategy for all managers: the more the asset manager provides services in a global market, the greater the systemic risk on a global scale.

Complexity. The indicators are:

1. Impact of the organizational structure: the business models and organizational structures are relevant, and may include models such as broker-dealer, pool operator or trading advisor, futures commission merchant, bank, trust company, municipal advisor, securities-based swap dealer, and major securities-based swap dealer. The use of these models may have spill-over effects to other activities performed by its subsidiaries and/or affiliates;
2. Difficulty in resolving a firm: dependent on how easily an asset manager's contracts may be transferred to other asset managers, its interconnectedness, and quality of its management information systems.

Cross-jurisdictional activities (global activity). Its indicator is the number of jurisdictions in which the asset manager has a presence: the more cross-border activities, the greater the likelihood of global impact.[28]

8.3.11 FSB 2014 Report

Using data compiled in 2013 from 25 countries and the euro area (80 % of global GDP and 90 % of global financial system assets), the FSB report on its monitoring of shadow banks found that non-bank financial intermediation globally had grown conservatively by 7 %, $5 trillion in 2013, to reach $75 trillion mainly by advanced economies constituting 25 % of total financial assets, half of banking system assets, and 120 % of GDP. Investment Funds grew about 10.3 % albeit with widely differing percentages from country to country. Other Financial Intermediaries (OFIs) showed the greatest increase in emerging market jurisdictions with growth above 10 %. Other sub-sectors of financial intermediation included a 42 % growth by Trust Companies and Other Investment Funds by 28 %. The Report cautions that the Hedge Fund subsector is significantly underestimated because of off-shore financial centers, and the total growth percentage may be narrowed down by assets not directly involved in credit intermediation.[29]

8.3.12 Other NBNI Financial Entities

The FSB noted that sector-specific methodologies may be developed as the need arises. These entities include any corporation or other legal form primarily engaged in financial intermediation or in related auxiliary financial activities and not otherwise assessed in the stated four sector-specific methodologies. *Financial intermediation* is defined by the FSB as "an activity in which an institution raises funds by incurring liabilities on its own account for the purpose of channeling these funds to other entities by lending or otherwise acquiring financial assets." They include non-bank deposit-taking institutions, finance companies, investment funds, and specialized vehicle companies. Systemic risks may arise by reliance on short-term wholesale funding markets, size; exposures to lending and derivative transactions; when they play a critical function; and when there is a risk of the need for a fire sale of assets in times of distress.[30]

8.4 International Organization of Securities Commissions (IOSCO)

IOSCO is an international organization established in 1983 and located in Madrid, Spain, which, according to its website, "develops, implements, and promotes adherence to internationally recognized standards for securities regulation." It coordinates its activities with both the G20 and the FSB. Its membership comprises some 110 countries constituting over 95 % of the global securities markets and is divided into ordinary, associate, and affiliate members. The 124 ordinary members represent the national securities commissions in their jurisdictions; the 15 associate members are agencies or branches of governments that are concerned with securities markets but also include the IMF and the World Bank; and the 62 affiliate members are self-regulatory organizations, stock exchanges, financial market infrastructures, investor protection funds, and compensation funds. In the Preamble to the Bylaws, the members of the representative countries agree to the following:

- To cooperate in developing, implementing and promoting adherence to internationally recognized and consistent standards of regulation, oversight and enforcement in order to protect investors, maintain fair, efficient and transparent markets, and seek to address systemic risks;
- To enhance investor protection and promote investor confidence in the integrity of securities markets, through strengthened information exchange and cooperation in enforcement against misconduct and in supervision of markets and market intermediaries; and
- To exchange information at both global and regional levels on their respective experiences in order to assist the development of markets, strengthen market infrastructure and implement appropriate regulation.[31]

The mission of IOSCO is to develop securities markets and improve their efficiency; coordinate the enforcement of securities regulation, and implement common standards. The work of the organization is accomplished through numerous committees including the Presidents Committees (presidents or chairs of ordinary and associate members); the IOSCO Board of 34 securities regulators whose policy work is conducted through eight committees; the Growth and Emerging Markets Committee; four regional committees; the Affiliate Members Consultative Committee; the Committee on Emerging Risks; the Assessment Committee; task forces; and the Joint Forum that coordinates with the BCBS and the IAIS.

The work of IOSCO, particularly with respect to shadow banking, is accomplished in conjunction with the FSB and the G20. Thus, the documents and reports stated above issued by the FSB were prepared with its assistance and need not be repeated here. In a 2014 survey of respondents globally that included all regions of the world from developed and emerging nation of varied organizations and groups from academia, regulators, financial firms, global and regional organizations, and others, the results in summary were:

- The five areas most important to maintaining financial stability with respect to areas of risk and concern in order of importance were: regulatory uncertainty; capital flows; banking vulnerabilities; corporate governance; financial risks disclosure; shadow banking; and some 19 other categories;
- When risk categories were coupled with subsectors within the categories, shadow banking coupled with repo-securities lending collateral ranked highest;
- Securities' regulators believed that the risks within their domain that posed a systemic risk concern included, in descending order of importance, the international regulatory framework, corporate governance, disclosure of financial risks, shadow banking, and high frequency trading.[32]

8.4.1 Possible Conflict of FSB and IOSCO Regarding Regulation of Asset Managers

It was anticipated that the FED was likely to raise interest rates commencing in late 2015 from a near zero rate and did so in mid-December 2015 from 0 to 0.25 % to a range of 0.25 to 0.5 %. The policy, as expressed by the FSB Chairman Mark Carney, is in accord with central bankers, which allegedly have great influence on the FSB, and which have called for bank-like rules for asset managers and specialist funds including capital requirements to meet the possible extreme volatility in bond prices should the US FED raise borrowing rates. IOSCO, which is a member of the FSB and with which it has to coordinate polices as described in this text, opposes the regulation of the global largest asset managers which traditionally have been regulated by market supervisors. The fear, as voiced by its chairman, Greg Medcraft, is that the additional requirements upon them would lead to higher trading costs, reduced liquidity, and possibly increased volatility. He was quoted as stating: "We don't regulate markets like we regulate banks," ...."It is like creating a square peg for a round hole".... "Wherever we land after this work and whatever guidance we develop, we need to be sure we don't unduly stifle risk taking."[33]

8.5 European Union (EU)

8.5.1 Historical Evolution

The EU arose from the ashes of World War II as the vision of European leaders, mainly Jean Monnet and Robert Schuman of France, as well as Winston Churchill who envisioned a "United States of Europe" modeled after Great Britain's former colony in North America, as well as others. Its primary aim was to put to an end to the ceaseless wars among Western European countries initially by dealing with a major area of disagreement, the coal and steel emanating particularly from the Ruhr Valley. The European Coal and Steel Community (ECSC) was created under the Treaty of Paris in 1951 to establish a common market for coal and steel among six nations, namely Belgium, France, West Germany, Italy, the Netherlands, and Luxembourg.

On March 22, 1957 the Treaty of Rome (Treaty Establishing the European Economic Community) was signed by these six nations to create the European Economic Community (EEC), better known as the "Common Market." Also signed was the agreement that established the European Atomic Energy Community (EURATOM) for the development of atomic energy. Thus, there were three communities, the ECSC, EURATOM, and the EEC. On January 1, 1973, three additional member states, Denmark, Ireland, and the UK, were added to the six nations followed by a tenth nation, Greece, in 1981 and two more, Spain and Portugal, in 1986. The Single European Act was signed in 1986, seeking to create a fully integrated single market of the member states. The Maastricht Treaty (Treaty on the European Union) of February 7, 1992 eventually led to the creation of the European Union, which is presently the governing body of 28 nations, the last being Croatia which joined in 2013.[34] Founders of the EU had wished for a total political and economic union of the member states but had to settle for an economic union which, at times, appears to be in jeopardy.

8.5.2 EU Institutions

The EU is composed of the following main bodies:

- The *European Council*, composed of the President of the European Commission and heads of government of the 28 member states becoming 27 states with the exit of Great Britain, which sets the overall political direction of the EU but has no legislative powers;

- *Legislative Bodies*:
  - The *European Parliament*, whose members are elected representing their constituents within the respective member states and share legislative powers with the Council of the European Union (not to be confused with the European Council) as well as supervising the work of the Commission and adopting the EU budget;
  - The *Council of the European Union*, which shares legislative powers with the Parliament but represents the individual governments of the member states by espousing their economic, fiscal, and social policies within the legislative process; and
  - The *European Commission*, representing the EU as a whole, prepares and implements EU legislation, regulations, directives, and decisions;
- *Judiciary*:
  - The *European Court of Justice*, consisting of one Justice from each member state, is the ultimate judicial body that determines and upholds EU laws and regulations, determines requests for preliminary rulings from the national courts of the individual member states and some actions for annulment, as well as appeals;
  - The *General Court*, which determines actions for annulment instituted by individuals, companies, and governments mainly concerning competition law, trade, agriculture, intellectual property rights, and state aid; and
  - The *Civil Service Tribunal*, which decides on disputes between the EU and its staff. An additional important body is the Court of Auditors that concerns the finances of the EU.[35]
- The *Court of Auditors* which is responsible for examining and checking the financing of the EU.
- Miscellaneous specialized institutions such as the *European Central Bank*, the *European Investment Bank*, the *European Economic and Social Committee*, and other organizations under EU supervision.[36]

8.5.3 Shadow Banking

Roadmap. The EU has closely followed the shadow banking developments globally, particularly following the crisis commencing in 2007. It has sought to implement the G20 commitments in instituting financial reforms that at times appeared to threaten its unified existence. The reforms were initially outlined by the European Commission in its 2010 "Roadmap for Financial Reform,"[37] in which it outlined initiatives taken and to be undertaken in the near future. The roadmap consisted of four areas: transparency, responsibility, supervision, and crisis prevention and management.

Transparency

A major theme emanating from the financial crisis of 2007–2009 was the alleged lack of transparency owing to the complexity of financial instruments that had evolved over the prior several decades. These financial instruments escaped regulation, oversight, and supervision by regulators. Accordingly, the roadmap for reform would include the appropriate tools for regulators particularly as proposed in the Alternative Investment Fund Managers (AIFM) Directive proposal and the Markets in Financial Instruments Directive (MiFID). Under AIFM, the Commission is to establish common rules to monitor the potential risks for investors, counterparties, and other market participants with respect to hedge funds or private equity firms that finance operating companies by use of risky or high-yield strategies. Alternative fund managers would not be able to operate in the EU with compliance with the said rules and regulations.

With respect to derivatives including *credit default swaps* (financial contracts linking two parties to the future value or status of the underlying asset to which it refers) and *short-selling* (lender sells assets borrowed from a third party that will later be repurchased; investor makes a profit if the assets falls in value), the Commission is proposing that the standard derivative contracts be cleared through central clearing parties to reduce the risk should a default occur. Moreover, all such transactions within the EU are to be reported to trade repositories and be accessible to supervisory authorities.

The Commission intends to expand the 2004 MiFID by ensuring transparency in the trading of financial instruments in order to permit regulators and market participants to have greater understanding of the trade in the said instruments.

Responsibility

The roadmap calls for stiffer penalties for errant behavior by market participants that engage in "short-termism" and excessive risk-taking. The reforms contemplated concern two key areas, prevention of market abuse and corporate governance. The Market Abuse Directive is to be revised to deter insider trading and market manipulation by use of the treat of effective enforcement and significant penalties encompassing twice the amount of illegal gains. The Directive would be extended to OTC derivatives and financial instruments admitted to trading on Multilateral Trading Facilities,

Corporate governance is to be improved by better supervision of senior management by boards of directors; limiting the number of mandates board members may hold; and providing tests for assuring expertise especially in risk management and independence. Greater authority and independence is to be given to chief risk officers of a firm in conjunction with a risk committee established at the board level to monitor and assess implementation of risk strategies. Greater shareholder involvement is contemplated by disclosure of voting policies and practices of institutional investors and of external auditors and financial supervisors. Remuneration for sound risk management and avoidance of excessive risk undertaking should be enacted.

Supervision

Greater supervision is necessary at the EU particularly since many of the financial firms are outside its orbit. In 2011, the European Systemic Risk Board was established to monitor early macro-economic risks together with the three sectoral European supervisor authorities, namely, the European Banking Authority, the European Securities and Markets Authority (ESMA), and the European Insurance and Occupational Pensions Authority. The said authorities have established a Single Rule Book.

Since 2009, credit rating agencies have had to register and comply with rigorous oversight and regulatory standards. The roadmap envisions increased EU supervision by requiring the agencies to register with ESMA, which shall have supervisory authority including investigations, on-site inspections, and request information.

Crisis Prevention and Management

In order to prevent future crises, the Commission proposes initiatives governing the Capital Requirements Directive to introduce capital buffers that may be utilized in times of stress; accounting standards that better reflect a company's finances; pre-financed resolution funds for the orderly wind-up of troubled banks; and consumer confidence by ensuring, under the Deposit Guarantee Schemes Directive, that every EU bank guarantees deposits up to €100,000 to all depositors. Furthermore, the Investor Compensation Scheme Directive is to be amended to provide up to €50,000 for investors against any fraudulent misappropriation.[38]

8.5.4 European Commission Green Paper

Based on the FSB analysis, the EU Commission, albeit cautioning that shadow banking is continually evolving, is concerned with the "two intertwined pillars" of the shadow banking system, namely:

First Pillar: Entities operating outside the regular banking system engaged in one of the following: (1) accepting funding with deposit-like characteristics; (2) performing maturity and/or liquidity transformation; (3) undergoing credit risk transfer; and (4) using direct or indirect financial leverage.

Second Pillar: Activities acting as a source of funding for non-bank entities including securitization and securities lending and repurchase transactions (repos).

The EU Commission has become focused on five major entities and two activities of the shadow banking system. The entities are:

- Special purpose entities which perform liquidity and/or maturity transformation as, for example, securitization vehicles such as ABCP conduits, Special Investment Vehicles (SIV), and other Special Purpose Vehicles (SPV);
- MMFs and other types of investment funds or products with deposit-like characteristics, which make them vulnerable to massive redemptions (runs);
- Investment funds, including Exchange Traded Funds (EFTs) that provide credit or are leveraged;
- Finance companies and securities entities providing credit or credit guarantees, or performing liquidity and/or maturity transformation without being regulated like a bank; and
- Insurance and reinsurance undertakings which issue or guarantee credit products.

The activities are securitization and securities lending and repo.[39]

According to the EU Green Paper, shadow banking activities are a useful part of the financial system in that it performs four basic functions well: (1) they provide alternatives for investors to bank deposits; (2) they channel resources towards specific needs more efficiently through increased specialization; (3) they are an alternative source of funding especially when traditional banking and market channels become temporarily impaired; and (4) they are a possible source of risk diversification away from the banking system.

The major risks are also four in nature, namely: (1) deposit-like funding structures may lead to "runs" owing to a lack of restraints imposed by banking regulation and supervision; (2) build-up of high, hidden leverage, with shadow banking activities highly leveraged with collateral funding; (3) circumvention of rules, regulatory arbitrage, regulatory fragmentation, and "race to the bottom" as banks and other financial intermediaries mimic shadow banking by circumventing rules and transferring risk outside the scope of banking supervision; and (4) disorderly failures affecting the banking system, with risks of shadow banking transferred to banking system through direct borrowing and massive sales of assets with repercussions on prices of financial and real assets.[40]

There are three challenges which the Commission envisions for supervisory and regulatory authorities: (1) identify and monitor the relevant entities and their activities, filling the current gap in the interconnectedness between banks and shadow banks globally; (2) determine which approach is to be taken in the supervision of shadow banking, national and/or European; be proportionate; take into account existing supervision and expertise; and be integrated with macro-prudential framework; and (3) make the appropriate responses needed such as extending the scope and nature of prudential regulation as shadow banking issues arise. The EU is already addressing some of the concerns in its Capital Requirements Directive of 2009, which requires originators and sponsors of securitized assets to retain a substantial share of their underwritten risks; the 2010 amendments strengthening capital requirements; introduction of explicit liquidity requirements as of 2015; and an amendment to the International Financial Reporting standards to improve disclosure requirements relating to financial assets.[41]

In addition to capital requirements, the EU has extended the scope of prudential regulation to cover shadow banking activities. It is directly regulating shadow banking with respect to investment funds in its Alternative Investment Fund Managers Directive, requiring asset managers to monitor liquidity risks and employ a liquidity management system. Other actions taken include stringent regulation on credit rating agencies, which have a major role in the credit intermediation chain and greater emphasis on insurance regulation centered on a risk-based and economic approach. Nevertheless, issues to be resolved, according to the Green Paper, include bank exposure to shadow banking entities; asset movement regulation issues; securities lending and repurchase agreements; securitization; decisions concerning which entities are to be regulated; data collection; and gaps in regulatory regimes.[42]

8.5.5 EU Commission Communication

In a Communication to organs of the EU, the Commission rendered a detailed economic review of financial regulations after the EU financial crisis of 2008–2012. There were two related documents, the *Commission Staff Working Document: Economic Review of the Financial Regulation Agenda* and the *Communication from the Commission to the European Parliament, the Council, the European Economic and Social Committee and the Committee of the Regions: A Reformed Financial Sector for Europe.*[43] In the economic review, the Commission noted that the crisis required €1.5 trillion of state aid (over 12 % of 2012 EU GDP) to prevent the collapse of the financial system, resulting in a deep depression, unemployment, and significant losses in income, wealth, and opportunities for EU households. It was estimated that output declined during this period by 50–100 % of pre-2008 crisis (about €6–12.5 trillion); financial wealth by 14 %; job losses rose to 10.8 % from pre-crisis 7.2 %, and far higher in certain countries such as Greece and Spain; and household trust in the financial sector declined to 60 %.[44] Thus, the EU has taken measures to create "a safer, more transparent, and more responsible financial system" to accomplish particular objectives, namely:

- Restoring and deepening the EU single market in financial services by establishing a single rulebook with a single regulatory framework and uniform application in place of allowing member states to individually monitor their financial services sector. The EU thus created the European System of Financial Supervisors (ESFS) which includes ESMA and the European Insurance and Occupational Pensions Authority (EIOPA) to assure consistent supervision and coordination among the national supervisory authorities, and the European Systemic Risk Board (ESRB) to monitor macro-prudential risks across the EU;
- Establishing a Banking Union that is mandatory for member states with the euro as its currency and also all other EU member states. The Banking Union consists of: (1) the Single Supervisory Mechanism (SSM), which transfers major supervisory tasks in participating states to the European Central Bank that will engage in conducting asset quality reviews and stress tests among the member states, to restore confidence in the European banking system; and (2) the Single Resolution Mechanism (SRM), which is to apply an

integrated and effective resolution process for all banks in the member states. The Banking Union is expected to ensure high common standards for prudential supervision and resolution for all EU banks;
- Building a more resilient and stable financial system by enactment of a series of reform measures across all segments of the EU financial system. Among the measures taken and being implemented are:

- Deposit guarantee schemes for bank deposits with a harmonized coverage of €100,000 (effective since 2010);
- The EU's Capital Requirements Regulation and Directive (CRD IV), which requires banks to increase the level and quality of bank capital and minimum liquidity standards as well as additional capital buffers in the event of future stress;
- EU Directive for Bank Recovery and Resolution (BRRD), which provides procedures in the event of bank failures to avoid costs to taxpayers and allow for the resolution to be accomplished in an orderly fashion;
- Revised Markets in Financial Instruments Directive (MiFID II), which seeks to strengthen organizational requirements and safety standards for financial markets and their infrastructures;
- The European Market Infrastructure Regulation (EMIR) and MiFID II impose common, prudential, organizational, and business conduct standards to improve the transparency of derivatives traded over the counter and reduce their counterparty risk;
- The Regulation on Central Securities Depositories (CSDR) increases resilience of EU central securities depositories and enhance the safety of the settlement process;
- Other key measures taken to reduce systemic risk include the Alternative Investment Fund Managers Directive, the proposed Regulation on Money Market Funds, and a risk-based regulatory framework for the insurance sector (Solvency II).

- Enhancing transparency, responsibility, and consumer protection to secure market integrity and restore consumer confidence by a series of measures that include the following:

- The revised Market Abuse Regulation and Directive on Criminal Sanctions for Market Abuse (MAR/CSMAD), which regulates and punishes market abuse, and the proposed Regulation on financial

benchmarks that seeks to enhance the robustness and reliability of benchmarks and prevent abuses thereof. Among the failures was the manipulation of interest rate benchmarks (London Interbank Offered Rate (LIBOR)) and the European Interbank Offered Rate (EURIBOR)) and the manipulations of benchmarks in foreign exchange and commodity markets;
- Regulation on Credit Rating Agencies (CRAs), which seeks to assure the independence and integrity of the ratings system;
- Audit reforms to improve the quality of statutory audits in the EU;
- Reforms in the international accounting standards to be applied throughout the EU to restore investor confidence in the financial system.

- Improving the efficiency of the EU financial system by the following efforts:

- Improved disclosure and reporting requirements to increase transparency and reduce information asymmetries for all market participants;
- Establishment of the Banking Union and single rulebook to bring about greater efficiency by leveling the playing field, facilitate cross-border financial activities, reduce competitive distortions, correct mispricing of risk, and improve the functioning of financial markets;
- Access provisions of MiFID II, European Market Infrastructure Directive (EMIR), and CSDR will reduce access barriers to financial market infrastructures; promote competition in the financial markets; and the revised CRA Regulation and audit reforms will facilitate market entry and increase the visibility of new entrants; and
- Reform measures to enhance small and medium-sized enterprises in aiding them to secure external finance that will lead to the creation of employment and foster sustainable growth;
- Reducing the implicit subsidy, estimated at €72–95 billion in 2011 and €59–82 billion in 2012 or 0.5–0.8 % of the annual EU GDP, whereby SIFI banks benefited from a credit uplift owing to the expectation that there would be an implicit bail-out guarantee by the EU;
- Ensuring that risks are properly reflected in prices by the improved prudential framework for banks and the new risk-based capital requirements for insurers under the provisions of Solvency II.

8.6 China

The halcyon days of China's financial expansion have witnessed something of a downturn. As a consequence of the US Federal Register's publication of US regulatory enactments concerning shadow banking, there was a comparable result in part in China. China has become concerned with the alleged undisciplined activities of its shadow banks that are composed of trust companies, insurance firms, leasing companies, pawnbrokers, and other non-traditional bank lenders. As in the USA and other nations, it had until this time avoided significant oversight. The government noted that the rapid expansion of credit could lead to a debt crisis. In early June 2013 the People's Bank of China began lessening the available funds for China's interbank-lending market by significantly raising the cost of funds that banks lend to each other and to shadow banks. The fear was that unregulated lending practices could lead to risks such as had occurred in the US subprime mortgage expansion and ultimate collapse.

China's traditional banks had begun to lend moneys to non-bank financial entities thus leading to the expansion of shadow banks. During the period of 2010–2012, shadow bank lenders doubled their lending to ¥36 trillion ($5.8 trillion) which constituted some 69 % of China's GDP.[45] The China Banking Regulatory Commission (CBRC) has somewhat different numbers and percentages, which stated that the shadow banking sector was some ¥33 trillion ($5.29 trillion) in 2013, equivalent to 80 % of China's GDP.[46] The expansion of shadow banking in China commencing in 2009 might have been a symptom of the nation's fear that the global financial crisis would have serious effects. As a result, the government encouraged the increase in credit to finance real estate construction and infrastructure.[47]

Part of the difficulty in analyzing China's shadow banking is that its governance is quite different from other national entities. It may be viewed in a narrow or a broader sense, which will lead observers to estimate its financing anywhere from ¥6 trillion to ¥27 trillion by the end of the third quarter of 2013. Its total assets are about 20 % of total banking assets. Its risks are mainly from an incomplete infrastructure and a lack of understanding of risks that may result from the system's lending through banks, trusts, securities firms, insurance companies, and other financial entities. According to one scholar who has analyzed China's system in depth, the regulatory authorities, including the People's Bank of China, the CBRC, the China Securities Regulatory Commission (CSRC), the China

Insurance Regulatory Commission CIRC), and the State Administration Foreign Exchange, have developed a framework for regulating interbank financing, including that of shadow banks. It is an active member of the FSB and has been attentive to the FSB's toolkit discussed above, but making it applicable to China's one-party political system and its unique financial regulatory setup.[48]

It is problematic to ascertain whether shadow banking may be an Achilles heel for China. The chairman of the China Investment Corporation (CIC), which manages the currency reserves of China, Ding Xuedong, stated to the cable news network CNBC that the issue of shadow banking is exaggerated and that the overall financial system is sound. On the other hand, the director of floor operations at UBS, Art Cashing, stated to CNBC that shadow banking in China could potentially be 2007 all over again.[49] Other commentators question whether shadow banking may lead to a Lehman-type crisis in the future. The government has allegedly indicated that it will not bail out non-bank financing instruments. Banks that have extended credit to non-bank entities are able to withstand large losses because of current sizeable profit margins. Another basis for absorbing non-bank financing losses is the very high national savings, almost half of China's GDP.[50] Some commentators fear that the biggest threat to China's financial system is that the government will curtail shadow bank lending too forcefully, which could precipitate a run on these entities and lead to a drying up of moneys available while the domestic market regroups and reassesses the risks arising therefrom.[51]

8.7 Other National Entities

The FSB, in its 2013 report, noted that banks in Brazil, Indonesia, India, and Saudi Arabia have a decided increase in credit risk because of their exposure to shadow banking entities. They face funding risks because of their reliance on funding from banks that adds to the risks associated with interconnectedness.[52] In Canada, the FSB noted that government-insured mortgages have grown substantially since 2007. By issuing debt securities backed by insured mortgages, shadow banking has overtaken the role of mortgage issuance by traditional banks. By so doing, there is increased risk to the financial system, albeit the risk is relatively low. Macro-economic risk arises from the growth in the stock of insured mortgages coupled with securitized instruments linking the government and financial institutions; the prevalence of mortgage securitization increases the complexity and interconnectedness in the Canadian financial system; and low funding costs may encourage growth in leverage at lightly regulated financial institutions which can underpin stronger mortgage credit growth.[53]

In South Africa, the FSB noted that the banking sector and the insurance and pension fund sector represent 34 and 38 % of the total financial assets of financial intermediaries. Banks still provide 92 % of the credit. Finance companies consist mainly of vehicle finance companies, consumer finance companies, and retail finance companies. These companies are regulated by the National Credit Regulator in South Africa. Most OFIs are not linked to banks. Owing to its small size, shadow banking does not pose systemic problems for the nation.[54]

In the UK, there is strong interconnectedness between banks and other financial companies which, while facilitating effective collateral management, support market liquidity, and aiding price discovery, nevertheless does pose a potential threat of systemic risk. Repo markets constitute a significant component of the UK financial system, which facilitates credit intermediation within and without the regular banking system.[55]

8.8 Conclusion

The shadow banking system, little known to the general public, is a major component of the overall financial system. The banking crisis of 2007–2009 revealed the inherent risks that banks have experienced. The exposure of inordinate lending practices, lack of knowledge of financial basics, and outright fraud by some actors in the financial sector led to the passage of the Dodd-Frank Act, which sought to curb some of the excesses of the banking system. By the passage of statutory and regulatory constraints which inhibited extension of credit to less than stellar companies, new sources of credit intermediation were sought which lacked such constraints. The shadow banking system thus arose to meet credit demands, which system arguably is more important than the traditional banking system. The goal of the Dodd-Frank Act, in part, was to prevent credit lending excesses that posed substantial risk to the overall financial system of the USA. The relatively unregulated shadow banking system potentially does pose a systemic threat to the financial sector. As a result, it is incumbent upon Congressional and other political actors to examine the complexity of the shadow banking system and initiate legislative and other actions to avoid yet another crisis like the one experienced less than a decade ago.

Notes

1. https://g.20.org/about-G-20/past/summits/.
2. Financial Stability Board, *Shadow Banking: Strengthening Oversight and Regulation: Recommendations of the Financial Stability Board* (Oct. 27, 2011) at 1, http://www.financialstabilityboard.org/wp-.
3. G-20, *Updated G-20 Roadmap towards Strengthened Oversight and Regulation of Shadow Banking in 2015, 1* https://G-20.org/wp-content/uploads/2014/12/updated_G-20_roadmap_strengthened_oversight_regulation_2015.pdf.
4. G-20 Seoul Summit, *The Seoul Summit Document*, (Nov. 12, 2010), at 7–8, http://www.G-20.utoronto.ca/2010/G-20seoul-doc.html.
5. Financial Stability Board, *Organizational Structure and Governance*, http://www.financialstabilityboard.org/about/organisation-and-governance/.
6. Financial Stability Board, *About the FSB*, http://www.financialstabilityboard.org/about/.
7. *Id.*, at 2.
8. G-20, *Updated G-20 Roadmap towards Strengthened Oversight and Regulation of Shadow Banking in 2015, 1* https://G-20.org/wp-content/uploads/2014/12/updated_G-20_roadmap_strengthened_oversight_regulation_2015.pdf.
9. Financial Stability Board, *Strengthening Oversight and Regulation of Shadow Banking: Policy Framework for Strengthening Oversight and Regulation of Shadow Banking Entities*, (Aug. 29, 2013), http://www.financialstability-board.org/wp-content/uploads/r_130829c.pdf?page_moved=1.
10. Financial Stability Board, *Global Shadow Banking Monitoring Report 2014*, (Oct. 30, 2014), *http://www.financialstabilityboard.org/2014/11/global-shadow-banking-monitoring-report-2014/*.
11. *Id.*, at 6–11.
12. *Id.*, at 13–14.
13. *Id.* at 14–15.
14. *Id.*, at 15–17.
15. *Id.* at 17–18.
16. *Id.*, at 18–19.
17. *Id.*, at 19–21.
18. *Id.*, at 21–22.
19. Financial Stability Board, *Consultative Document (2nd): Assessment Methodologies for Identifying Non-Bank Non-Insurer Global systemically Important Financial Institutions- Proposed High-Level Framework and Specific Methodologies* (March 4 2015), http://www.financialstabilityboard.org/wp-content/uploads/2nd-Con-Doc-on-NBNI-G-SIFI-methodologies.pdf.
20. *Id.* at 5–7.
21. *Id.* at 16–23.

22. OICU-IOSCO, *Objectives and Principles of Securities Regulation* (June 2010), https://www.iosco.org/library/pubdocs/pdf/IOSCOPD323.pdf.
23. *Id.* at 11.
24. *Supra*, note 23 at 24–29.
25. *Supra*, note 23 at 10.
26. *Supra*, note 23 at 30–46.
27. For a detailed discussion of the rules and regulations applicable to investment advisers, see Roy J. Girasa, *Laws and Regulations in Global Financial Markets*, (2013), Palgrave Macmillan, Ch. 1.
28. *Supra*, note 23 at 47–55.
29. Financial Stability Board, *Global Shadow Banking Monitoring Report 2014* (Oct. 30, 2014), http://www.financialstabilityboard.org/wp-content/uploads/r_141030.pdf.
30. *Id.* at 56–57.
31. OICU-IOSCO, *Fact Sheet* (April 2015), https://www.iosco.org/about/?subsection=about_iosco.
32. Shane Worner, *A Survey of Securities Market Risk Trends 2014: Methodology and Detailed Results*, STAFF WORKING PAPER, OICU-IOSCO (June, 2014), http://www.iosco.org/research/pdf/swp/SWP5.pdf.
33. Huw Jones, *Market watchdogs fight back against central banks* (June 22, 2015), REUTERS, http://www.rE.U.ters.com/article/2015/06/22/us-markets-global-regulations-insight-idUSKBN0P21OC20150622.
34. European Union, *The history of the European Union*, http://Europa.E.U./about-E.U./E.U.-history/index_en.htm.
35. European Union, *E.U. Institutions and other bodies*, http://Europa.E.U./about-E.U./institutions-bodies/index_en.htm.
36. European Union, *E.U. institutions and other bodies*, http://Europa.E.U./about-E.U./institutions-bodies/.
37. European Commission, *the European Union's roadmap for Financial Reform* (2010), http://ec.E.U.ropa.E.U./internal_market/finances/docs/road-map/finanial_reform_en.pdf.
38. *Id.*
39. *Id.*, at 3–4.
40. *Id.*, at 5–6.
41. *Id.* at 7–8.
42. *Id.*, at 10–13.
43. European Commission, *Commission Staff Working Document: Economic Review of the Financial Regulation Agenda* (May 15, 2014, SED(2014) 158 final, http://ec.E.U.ropa.E.U./internal_market/finances/docs/general/20140515-erfra-working-document_en.pdf, which accompanies the Commission's Communication from the Commission to the European

Parliament, the Council, the European Economic and Social Committee and the Committee of the Regions: A Reformed Financial Sector for Europe May 15, 2014), COM(2014) 279 final.

44. *Id.*, E.U. Commission Communication at 7–8.
45. Lingling Wei and Bob Davis, *China's 'Shadow Banks' Fan Debt-Bubble Fears*, THE WALL STREET JOURNAL (June 25, 2013), http://www.wsj.com/articles/SB10001424127887324637504578563570021019506.
46. Yue Wang, China's Shadow Banking Sector Valued at 80 % of GDP, FORBES (May 21, 2014), http://www.forbes.com/sites/ywang/2014/05/21/chinas-shadow-banking-valued-at-80-of-gdp/.
47. Peter Boone and Simon Johnson, China's Shadow Banking Malaise, NEW YORK TIMES (March 27, 2014), http://economix.blogs.nytimes.com/2014/03/27/chinas-shadow-banking-malaise/?_r=0. The difficulty of ascertaining the true financial status of non-bank financial institutions is illustrated by another commentary which stated that they only account for 2.4 % of the total financial assets in 2012. Nicholas Borst, *Flying Blind*, (Winter, 2014), THE INTERNATIONAL ECONOMY, 12–13, 71, https://search.yahoo.com/yhs/search?p=Nicholas+Borst%2C+Flying+Blind-%2C+%28Winter%2C+2014%29%2C+The+International+Economy%2C+12-13%2C+71%2C&ei=UTF-8&hspart=mozilla&hsimp=yhs-002.
48. Zheng Liansheng, *The Shadow Banking System of China and International Regulatory Cooperation*, Center for International Governance, Paper No. 6 (March 2015).
49. Geoff Culmore and Dhara Ranasinghe, *China shadow banking fears: Overstated or justified*, CNBC (May 22, 2014), www.cnbc.com/id/101699368.
50. *See supra* note 26.
51. Jingjiang, *Shadow banking in China: Battling the Darkness*, (May 10, 2014), THE ECONOMIST, http://www.economist.com/news/finance-and-economics/21601872-every-time-regulators-curb-one-form-non-bank-lending-another-begins.
52. *Id.* at 21–23.
53. *Id.* at *26–29.*
54. *Id.* at. 30–31.
55. *Id.* a*t 32*–35.

Index

Roy J. Girasa, *Shadow Banking*, DOI 10.1007/978-3-319-33026-6

Printed by Printforce, the Netherlands